Heidelberger Schriften
zum Wirtschaftsrecht und Europarecht

Herausgegeben von
Prof. Dr. Dr. h.c. mult. Peter Hommelhoff
Prof. Dr. Dr. h.c. mult. Peter-Christian Müller-Graff

Band 64

Prof. Dr. Roman Petrov

Exporting the Acquis Communautaire through European Union External Agreements

Nomos

Die Deutsche Nationalbibliothek verzeichnet diese Publikation in
der Deutschen Nationalbibliografie; detaillierte bibliografische
Daten sind im Internet über http://dnb.d-nb.de abrufbar.

ISBN 978-3-8329-6434-4

1. Auflage 2011
© Nomos Verlagsgesellschaft, Baden-Baden 2011. Printed in Germany. Alle Rechte, auch die des Nachdrucks von Auszügen, der fotomechanischen Wiedergabe und der Übersetzung, vorbehalten. Gedruckt auf alterungsbeständigem Papier.

Special thanks to the Alexander von Humboldt-Stiftung and Jean Monnet Programme which provided support for developing and printing this work

Besonderer Dank gilt der Alexander von Humboldt-Stiftung und dem Jean Monnet Programm, welche die Entwicklung und den Druck dieses Werkes unterstützten.

Preface

I express my gratitude to many people and friends who have helped me with completing this research project. Their contributions have been invaluable in many respects. Special thanks to my academic supervisors Professor Marise Cremona, Professor Loukas Mistelis and Professor Peter-Christian Müller-Graff for their never-ending patience and inspiration. I express everlasting gratitude to my family who have stood behind me and supported me throughout all this time. This book is devoted to the memory of my first academic supervisor Professor Alexander Chuvpilo.

Roman Petrov
January 2011

Prof. Dr. Roman Petrov – Jurist (Donetsk State University (Ukraine), 1996); LLM (University of Durham (UK), 1998); PhD (National Academy of Science of Ukraine, 2000); PhD (Queen Mary, University of London (UK), 2005); Max Weber postdoctoral research fellow (European University Institute (Italy), 2006 - 2008); visiting research fellow at University of Oxford (UK), 2009; Alexander von Humboldt research fellow at University of Heidelberg (Germany) (2010 - 2012); President of the Ukrainian European Studies Association since 2006; Jean Monnet Chair in EU Law at National University "Kyiv-Mohyla Academy" (Ukraine) since 2010.

Table of Contents

Table of Abbreviations — 15

Abstract — 19

Introduction — 21

Chapter 1. Internal and External Dimensions of the Acquis Communautaire — 26
1.1. Introduction — 26
1.2. Evolution of the concept "acquis communautaire" — 29
    1.2.1. Historical background of the acquis communautaire — 29
    1.2.2. External dimension of the acquis communautaire — 33
    1.2.3. Concluding remarks — 34
1.3. Conceptualising the acquis communautaire — 35
    1.3.1. Academic discussion about the context and meaning of the acquis communautaire — 35
    1.3.2. Concluding remarks — 40
1.4. The internal dimension of the acquis communautaire — 42
    1.4.1. Introduction — 42
    1.4.2. The nature and scope of the "fundamental acquis" — 42
        1.4.2.1. Core of the "fundamental acquis" — 42
        1.4.2.2. EU founding Treaties' objectives and the "fundamental acquis" — 46
        1.4.2.3. General principles of EU law and the "fundamental acquis" — 47
        1.4.2.4. Doctrines and concepts of EU law and the "fundamental acquis" — 60
        1.4.2.5. "Institutional acquis" and the "fundamental acquis" — 62
        1.4.2.6. Concluding remarks — 63
    1.4.3. International law and the acquis communautaire — 65
        1.4.3.1. International peremptory norms jus cogens, general principles of international public law and the acquis communautaire — 65
        1.4.3.2. International agreements and the acquis communautaire — 66
        1.4.3.3. Concluding remarks — 69
    1.4.4. The scope of the "Union acquis" — 69
        1.4.4.1. Elements of the "Union acquis" — 69
        1.4.4.2. Concluding remarks — 71
    1.4.5. EU "soft law" as a part of the acquis communautaire — 71

1.4.5.1. Elements of EU "soft law"	71
1.4.5.2. Concluding remarks	72
1.5. The external dimension of the acquis communautaire	73
1.5.1. Introduction	73
1.5.2. The "accession acquis"	73
1.5.3. Further implications of the acquis communautaire in its external dimensions	86
1.5.3.1. The acquis communautaire in EU external agreements	86
1.5.3.2. The scope of the acquis communautaire and "approximation clauses" in EU external agreements	87
1.5.3.3. Sectoral acquis communautaire	88
1.6. Conclusion	90

Chapter 2. The Scope of the Acquis Communautaire in EU External Agreements	93
2.1. Introduction	93
2.2. The scope of the acquis communautaire in EU external agreements. Comparative study	93
2.2.1. European Economic Area Agreement (EEA)	94
2.2.1.1. Objectives of the EEA Agreement	94
2.2.1.2. The scope of the relevant acquis communautaire in the EEA Agreement	96
2.2.1.3. Concluding remarks	103
2.2.2. EC–Switzerland sectoral agreements (SAs)	105
2.2.2.1. Objectives of the EC–Switzerland SAs	105
2.2.2.2. The scope of the relevant acquis communautaire in the EC–Swiss SAs	110
2.2.2.3. Concluding remarks	114
2.2.3. Europe Agreements (EAs)	115
2.2.3.1. Objectives of the EAs	115
2.2.3.2. The scope of the relevant acquis communautaire in the EAs	117
2.2.3.3. Concluding remarks	124
2.2.4. Stabilisation and Association Agreements (SAAs)	125
2.2.4.1. SAAs objectives	125
2.2.4.2. The scope of the acquis communautaire in the SAAs	126
2.2.4.3. Concluding remarks	134
2.2.5. EUROMED Association Agreements (EMAAs)	136
2.2.5.1. Introduction	136
2.2.5.2. EC-Turkey Association Agreement	139
2.2.5.2.1. Objectives of the Agreement	139

2.2.5.2.2. The scope of the acquis communautaire to be implemented by Turkey	139
2.2.5.2.3. Concluding remarks	142
2.2.5.3. EC-Israel EMAA	143
2.2.5.3.1. Objectives of the Agreement	143
2.2.5.3.2. The scope of the acquis communautaire in the EC-Israel Agreement	144
2.2.5.3.3. Concluding remarks	146
2.2.5.4. EC-Tunisia EMAA	147
2.2.5.4.1. Objectives of the EC-Tunisia EMAA	147
2.2.5.4.2. The scope of the acquis communautaire in the EC-Tunisia EMAA	148
2.2.5.4.3. Concluding remarks	149
2.2.5.5. Conclusion	149
2.2.6. Partnership and Cooperation Agreements (PCAs)	151
2.2.6.1. Objectives of the PCAs	151
2.2.6.2. The scope of the acquis communautaire in the PCAs	154
2.2.6.3. Concluding remarks	158
2.2.7. Cotonou Agreement	162
2.2.7.1. Objectives of the Cotonou Agreement	162
2.2.7.2. The scope of the acquis communautaire in the Cotonou Agreement	163
2.2.7.3. Concluding remarks	167
2.2.8. Trade development and cooperation agreements (TDCAs)	168
2.2.8.1. Introduction	168
2.2.8.2. EC- South Africa TDCA	168
2.2.8.2.1. Objectives of the EC-South Africa TDCA	168
2.2.8.2.2. The scope of the acquis communautaire within the EC-South Africa TDCA	170
2.2.8.2.3. Concluding remarks	171
2.2.8.3. The EC - Korea Framework Agreement for Trade and Cooperation	172
2.2.8.3.1. Objectives of the EC-Korea Framework Agreement for Trade and Cooperation	172
2.2.8.3.2. The scope of the acquis communautaire in the EC-Korea TDCA	173
2.2.8.3.3. Concluding remarks	174
2.2.8.4. EC - Mexico Framework Agreement for Trade and Cooperation	175
2.2.8.4.1. Objectives of the EC-Mexico Framework Agreement for Trade and Cooperation	175
2.2.8.4.2. The scope of the acquis communautaire in the EC-Mexico Framework Agreement for Trade and Cooperation	176
2.2.8.4.3. Concluding remarks	178

2.2.8.5. EC-MERCOSUR Interregional Framework Cooperation Agreement (IFA)	178
2.2.8.5.1. Objectives of the EC-MERCOSUR Interregional Framework Cooperation Agreement	178
2.2.8.5.2. The scope of the acquis communautaire in the EC-MERCOSUR IFA	180
2.2.8.5.3. Concluding remarks	182
2.3. Conclusion	183

Chapter 3. Substantive and Procedural Means of Exporting the Acquis Communautaire into the Legal Systems of Third Countries — 187

3.1. Introduction	187
3.2. Substantive means of exporting the acquis communautaire into the legal systems of third countries	188
3.2.1. Export of the fixed acquis into the legal systems of third countries	188
3.2.2. Exporting the dynamic acquis communautaire into the legal systems of third countries	190
3.2.2.1. Introduction	190
3.2.2.2. Homogeneity	190
3.2.2.3. Binding and soft-harmonisation commitments	196
3.2.2.4. Approximation clauses	201
3.2.2.5. Mutual recognition agreements	206
3.2.2.6. Regional integration initiatives	209
3.2.2.7. Concluding remarks	212
3.3. Procedural means of exporting the acquis communautaire into the legal systems of third countries	214
3.3.1. Formal/informal involvement of third countries in the EU decision-making process	214
3.3.2. Exchange of information	220
3.3.3. Technical, administrative, and financial assistance on behalf of the EU to third countries	224
3.3.3.1. Introduction	224
3.3.3.2. Reforms of the EU technical, administrative and financial assistance to third countries (ENPI and DCECI)	225
3.3.3.3. Technical, administrative and financial assistance within EU sectoral agreements	228
3.3.3.4. Concluding remarks	229
3.4. Institutions set up within EU external agreements	230
3.4.1. Introduction	230

3.4.2. The impact of common institutions set up under EU external agreements on the export of the acquis into the legal orders of third countries	230
3.4.3. Concluding remarks	236
3.5. Adoption of the acquis communautaire by judiciary in Ukraine. Case study	238
3.5.1. The European Neighbourhood Policy and its impact on the adoption of the acquis communautaire by the judiciary in Ukraine	239
3.5.2. Adoption of the acquis communautaire by the Ukrainian judiciary	241
3.5.3. Concluding remarks	247
3.6. Conclusion	249
3.7. Overall conclusion	252
Bibliography	255
Table of Cases	263
Table of Laws	269
Annex I	277
Annex II	293

Table of Abbreviations

AA	Association Agenda
ACP	Africa, the Caribbean, and the Pacific
ALA	Programme of financial assistance and technical assistance to, and economic cooperation with, the developing countries in Asia and Latin America
AP	Action Plan
CARDS	Community Assistance for Reconstruction, Development and Stability in the Balkans
CBD	Convention on Biological Diversity
CCP	Common Commercial Policy
CEE	Central and Eastern Europe
CFI	Court of First Instance
CFSP	Common Foreign and Security Policy
CIS	Commonwealth of Independent States
CJEL	Columbia Journal of European Law
CML Rev.	Common Market Law Review
CMLR	Common Market Law Reports
CS	Common Strategy
CSCE	Commission on Security and Cooperation in Europe
DCECI	"Development Cooperation & Economic Cooperation" Instrument
EA	Europe Agreement
EC	European Community
	When following a Treaty Article, Treaty establishing the European Community
EEC	European Economic Community
ECAA	European Common Aviation Area
EC Bull.	Bulletin of the European Communities
ECJ	European Court of Justice
ECLR	European Competition Law Review
ECR	European Court Reports
ECSC	European Coal and Steel Community
EEA	European Economic Area
EFA Rev.	European Foreign Affairs Review
EFTA	European Free Trade Area
ECHR	European Convention on Human Rights
ECtHR	European Court of Human Rights
EIDHR	European Initiative for Democracy and Human Rights

ELJ	European Law Journal
EL Rev.	European Law Review
EMAA	Euro-Mediterranean Association Agreement
EMP	Euro-Mediterranean Partnership
EMU	European Monetary Union
ENA	European Neighbourhood Agreement
ENP	European Neighbourhood Policy
ENPI	European Neighbourhood and Partnership Instrument
EP	European Parliament
EPL	European Public Law
EU	European Union
FATF	Financial Action Task Force on Money Laundering
FRONTEX	European Border Exchange Agency
FYROM	Former Yugoslav Republic Of Macedonia
GATS	General Agreement on Trade in Services
GATT	General Agreement on Trade and Tariffs
GSP	Generalised System of Preferences
ICJ	International Court of Justice
ICLQ	International and Comparative Law Quarterly
ICTY	International Criminal Tribunal for the former Yugoslavia
IEC	International Electrotechnical Commission
IFA	Inter-Regional Framework Agreement for Cooperation
IGC	Intergovernmental Conference
ILO	International Labour Organisation
IMF	International Monetary Fund
INTERREG	Financial instrument within the framework of the European Union"s Structural Funds which supports cross-border and international cooperation among the EU Member States and neighbouring countries
IPA	Pre-Accession Instrument
IP	Intellectual Property
ISO	International Organisation for Standartisation
ISPA	Instrument for Structural Policies for Pre-Accession
JCMS	Journal of Common Market Studies
JHA	Justice and Home Affairs
LIEI	Legal Issues of Economic Integration
MEDA	Principal financial instrument of the European Union for the implementation of the Euro-Mediterranean Partnership.
MERCOSUR	Regional integration agreement between Argentina, Brasil, Paraguay, and Uruguay
MFN	Most Favoured Nations regime

MJICL	Maastricht Journal of International and Comparative Law
MRA	Mutual Recognition Agreement
NAFTA	North American Free Trade Agreement
NATO	North Atlantic Treaty Organisation
NIS	Newly Independent States
NPAA	National Programme for the Adoption of the Acquis
OECD	Organisation for Economic Cooperation and Development
O.J.	Official Journal of the European Union
PCA	Partnership and Cooperation Agreement
PHARE	Pre-accession instrument financed by the European Union to assist the applicant countries of Central and Eastern Europe in their preparations for joining the European Union
RSC	Robert Shuman Center
RTDE	Revue Trimestrielle de Droit Européen
SA	Sectoral Agreement
SAA	Stabilisation and Association Agreement
SAP	Stabilisation and Association Process
SAPARD	Special Accession Programme for Agriculture and Rural Development
SEA	Single European Act
SME	Small and Medium Enterprises
TACIS	Technical Assistance for the Commonwealth of Independent States
TDCA	Trade Development and Cooperation Agreement
TEU	Treaty on European Union
TFEU	Treaty on the Functioning of the European Union
ToA	Treaty of Amsterdam
ToL	Treaty of Lisbon
TRIPS	Agreement on Trade-Related Aspects of Intellectual Property Rights
UEPLAC	Ukrainian-European Legal Advice Center
UK	United Kingdom
UN	United Nations
USA	United States of America
USSR	Union of Soviet Socialist Republics
WTO	World Trade Organisation

Abstract

This book is a study of the legal dimensions of the concept of "acquis communautaire". Using primary sources, it identifies and delimits the scope of the term in different contexts within EU legal discourse.

The book starts by tracing the internal and external dimensions of acquis communautaire. These dimensions are distinguished by different objectives. The major objective of acquis communautaire in its internal dimension is to enable the consistent development of European Union (EU) law while preserving EU patrimony by Member States. The objective of the acquis communautaire application in its external dimension is twofold. First, it is to export the acquis communautaire overseas in order to push third countries at the forefront of the acquired level of economic, political and legal cooperation achieved by the EU. Second, it is to stimulate third countries to share European and international common democratic values and thereby to preserve integrity of the acquis communautaire in relations with third countries. It is argued that the acquis communautaire in its external dimension is not coherent, but mirrors the specific objectives of relation between the EU and third countries.

In order to investigate the rationale behind this research hypothesis this work examines in detail the terms of a variety of EU external agreements from association to trade, development and co-operation. The book provides the reader with a more detailed insight into the linkage between the political environment, and the obligations undertaken in relation to the acquis communautaire by a third country in agreements with the EU.

It is concluded that the acquis communautaire is a complex legal category of a dynamic nature. One must take into consideration the general objectives of EU external agreements, and the status of bilateral relations between the EU and third countries, in order to comprehend the fullest scope of the applicable acquis communautaire. Therefore, it could be argued that the acquis communautaire within EU external agreements as a dynamic category that directly depends not only on the explicit objectives of these agreements but also on the wider framework of relations between the parties and the general political climate of bilateral relations.

Introduction

Recent years have seen profound and wide-ranging changes to the nature and structure of the EU. The adoption of the Lisbon Treaty has paved the way for European nations to realise the ambitious aim of the Maastricht Treaty, that is to create an "ever closer union among the peoples of Europe", based on the values and principles shared by all Member States. This has been achieved through the identification of the Union as the incarnation of democratic values and principles which are respected worldwide. The Lisbon Treaty "depicts" the future EU from a twofold perspective: internal and external. In the former instance it entrusts the EU with the role of guardian of common values, principles, and objectives. In the latter case it recognises the EU as the "exporter" of a political, economic and legal heritage to the wider world.[1] In both cases, the "acquis communautaire" plays the pivotal role. Throughout the history of European integration, this notion has remained one of the least-well defined, and one of the most-frequently applied. Having been conceived as a notion linked to the EU legal order, the "acquis communautaire" has quickly become associated with the wider domains of EU policies. In particular, the EU has actively used the acquis communautaire to serve its far-reaching external policy ambitions.

From the outset, the acquis communautaire has emphasised the dynamic, or *sui generis*, nature of the EU legal order. In this respect, the dynamism of the EU legal order entails its never-ending evolution, under the pressure of various internal and external factors, such as the need for closer economic development inside the EU, and the enhancement of security and political stability along EU borders. The dynamism of the EU legal order is based on acquired common rules, practices and values, which are embraced by the complex notion "acquis communautaire". In other words, the acquis communautaire ensures the continuity of the EU legal order through the fact that it encompasses everything that has been achieved within the EU, even beyond legal practices. In general, the acquis communautaire may be seen as the result of the application of various tools/instruments/powers which the EU possesses both internally and externally. Commentators have correctly compared the dynamic nature of the EU legal order to a living organism.[2] In our opinion, the acquis communautaire may be associated with the memory, education and genes of this living organism. If, in a

---

[1] Article 2 and Article 3(5) TEU (O.J. C 83/13 2010)
[2] L. Auzolai, "The *Acquis* of the European Union and International Organisations", 11(2) ELJ 196-231 (2005), at 196.

similar vein to Kipling's Mowgli, the EU were to lose its heritage – the acquis communautaire – one could hardly predict how it would survive the pressures of the jungle of the international community.

The "acquis communautaire" has proved to be a particularly useful concept in the course of EU external action. The notion "acquis communautaire" has gradually become one of the most significant tools underpinning EU's tailor-made actions towards third countries, ranging from accession to partnership and cooperation initiatives. At the same time, the ambiguity of this notion has resulted in its gradual transformation into a universal category, which has no fixed context and scope, but which must be comprehended exclusively within the particular circumstances of EU external action towards third countries. For example, in the context of accession, the adoption of the acquis communautaire by candidate countries has meant the implementation of the whole EU legal heritage. In the context of the EU policy of partnership and cooperation with third countries, the acquis communautaire has a narrower scope, and embraces mainly sectoral EU legislation within priority areas of cooperation. Hitherto, the acquis communautaire has remained at the top of the EU agenda for external action. The European Neighborhood Policy encourages neighbouring states to adhere to the EU "common values", and to adopt the vast scope of the acquis communautaire in order to achieve mutual access to markets of goods, services and capital.[3]

Gradually, the acquis communautaire has stretched the boundaries of a mere legal concept, and has been used in other contexts, including the political, social, and historical. This view has been shared by many experts in European studies. Gialdino,[4] Weatherill,[5] Delcourt[6] and Azoulai[7] have emphasised the dynamic nature of the acquis communautaire within its legal context. Krenzler and Everson[8] have argued for an even broader understanding of the acquis communautaire as a

---

[3] Communication from the Commission "Wider Europe-Neighbourhood: A New Framework for Relations with our Eastern and Southern Neighbours" (COM (2003) 104 final). Communication from the European Commission "European Neighbourhood Policy Strategy Paper" COM (2004) 373 final.

[4] C. Gialdino, "Some reflections on the acquis communautaire", 32 CMLRev. 1089-1121 (1995).

[5] S. Weatherill, "Safequarding the *Acquis Communautaire*", in T. Heukels / N. Blokker/M. Brus (eds), *The European Union after Amsterdam,* (The Hague/London/Boston, Kluwer Law International 1998) 153-178, 161-162.

[6] C. Delcourt, "The *Acquis Communautaire:* Has the Concept Had Its Day?", 38 CMLRev. 829-870 (2001).

[7] L. Auzolai, "The *Acquis* of the European Union and International Organisations", 11(2) ELJ 196-231 (2005).

[8] H. G. Krenzler/M. Everson, *Preparing for the acquis communautaire. Report of the Working Group on the Eastward Enlargement of the European Union,* October 1998 (European University Institute, RSC Policy Paper № 98/6). <http://www.iue.it/RSCAS/WP-Texts/98_06p.htm>, last visited 18 January 2011.

legal framework, embracing real and potential rights within the EU system. Wiener[9] has gone further and advocated the theory of the "embedded acquis" which covers practices, policy objectives and informal ideas and values. The Dutch legal scholar Mortelmans[10] has depicted the acquis communautaire as "a political or policy concept", and has clearly distinguished it from the basic tenets of EU law. In our view, hitherto, scholars have dealt with general issues related to the acquis communautaire such as its scope and relations with other domains of social studies apart from the legal. No contemporary studies has explicitly studied the acquis within specific EU policies, *inter alia* EU external action.

The purpose of this study is to fill this gap and to focus on the acquis' role within the domain of EU external policy. We do not see the legal context of the acquis communautaire as a "snapshot" at the moment of signing of the Lisbon Treaty. Instead, we endeavour to comprehend its scope within the relevant time and context. In other words, our major concern is not to depict the "true" scope of the acquis communautaire, but to learn the logic and methodology behind its application within EU external policy towards third countries.

In general, this book pursues two major objectives. The first is to shed some light on the legal context of the acquis communautaire. For this purpose we have speculated extensively on the elements which may characterise the acquis communautaire. The second is to study the phenomenon of the acquis communautaire as an instrument of the EU external policy. This approach should prove a valuable tool for anyone seeking a better legal understanding of overall EU external policy. Indeed, we believe that the acquis communautaire has become one of the most effective means to "export" the EU's fundamental values and principles into the political and legal systems of third countries. Since the unprecedented EU enlargement at the end of the 20th and early 21st centuries, the need to adopt the acquis communautaire is being considered as an essential pre-requisite for maintaining and enhancing good political and economic relations between the EU and third countries.

The structure of this book works according to a simple methodology, which aims to give the reader a broad legal overview and analysis of our research subject matter. It comprises four chapters. Chapter I addresses the legal, political and historical background of the acquis communautaire. We put forward the theory that the acquis communautaire should be perceived in both its internal and external dimensions. Consequently, we argue that the scope of the acquis communautaire is not identical in both these dimensions owing to the different objec-

---

9   A. Wiener, "The Embedded Acquis Communautaire: Transmission Belt and Prism of New Governance", 3 ELJ 294-315 (1998).
10 K. Mortelmans, "Community Law: More than a Functional Area of Law, Less than a Legal System", 1 LIEI 23-48 (1996).

tives of their application. The major objective of the acquis communautaire in its internal dimension is to enable the consistent development of the EU while preserving EU patrimony. Thus, the acquis communautaire in its internal dimension is characterised by its coherence and consistency. This embraces core elements which are intrinsic to the unique EU legal order: the fundamental acquis, international law commitments, and the "soft" acquis. Conversely, the objective of the acquis communautaire application in its external dimension is to push candidate countries to the forefront of the acquired level of economic, political and legal cooperation achieved by the EU. We argue that the acquis communautaire in its external dimension is not coherent, but mirrors the specific objectives of relations between the EU and third countries. For instance, candidate countries have been urged to implement the whole acquis communautaire, which exceeds what is adopted by the Member States. Conversely, third countries which do not want to join the EU have more flexibility in selecting elements of the acquis in line with objectives of agreements with the EU.

In Chapter II we endeavour to test our hypothesis with regard to the specific scope of the acquis communautaire in its external dimension. Therein, we attempt to identify the acquis communautaire in EU external agreements. For this purpose, it was decided to focus on the particular elements of the acquis communautaire which EU external agreements undertake to export into the legal systems of third countries. In particular, we cast our attention on association, development, partnership and cooperation, trade and cooperation, as well as framework agreements concluded by the EU with third countries. We believe that such an extensive analysis provides us with the necessary data to demonstrate the findings of our research. Rather than simply giving an outline of all elements of the acquis communautaire in its external dimension, this work attempts to provide the reader with a more detailed insight into the linkage between the political environment, and the obligations undertaken in relation to the acquis communautaire by a third country in agreements with the EU.

In Chapter III we examine the dynamism of the acquis communautaire in its external dimension. Therefore, this chapter is dedicated to the analysis of the substantive and procedural means by which the acquis communautaire in EU external agreements is exported into the legal orders of third countries. The Chapter III is supplemented by case study on the adoption of the acquis communautaire by judiciary in Ukraine. The objective of this case study is illustrate what substantive and procedural means to export the acquis communautaire have been employed by the EU and what results have been achieved with regard to export the acquis communautaire into a third country covered by a specific EU external policy (European Neighbourhood Policy). We conclude with the preposition that the acquis communautaire is a complex legal category of a dynamic nature. One must take into consideration the general objectives of EU external agreements, and the status of bilateral relations between the EU and third countries, in order to comprehend the fullest scope of the applicable acquis communautaire.

The ancillary idea of this research is to give the reader a rather more comprehensive view of the way in which the logic behind the acquis communautaire operates. Our methods and research findings are not exclusive to the acquis communautaire. We believe that the same approaches may be applied to other dynamic notions, such as "values of the Union" and "EU general principles". The contemporary scholar would find it difficult to operate with the "acquis communautaire" without possessing a comprehensive knowledge of all the potential dimensions of this notion. Thus, it is hoped that, in many respects, this study can be used as a self-contained guide for determining the likely scope of the acquis communautaire in the course of the negotiations of future EU external agreements by third countries.

Furthermore, our study has highlighted other problems which warrant investigation in the near future. The first problem is that third countries may experience difficulties in accepting legal norms developed elsewhere. Phrases from EU legal acts may be incorporated into the legal systems of third countries. However, ideas and objectives of these norms cannot be replicated without exporting entire regulatory and institutional mechanisms accumulated within the EU throughout the history of European integration. The second problem relates to the impact of political agenda in relations between the EU and third countries in the process of harmonisation/approximation of laws. The third problem involves the implications of the ac-quis as an international law obligation for a third country. The export of the acquis communautaire implies a drastic change of third countries' constitutional foundations. In most cases, third countries must revise their constitutions in order to enable the legal effect of the acquis, and in particular, of EU general principles and common values. However, the modest level of cooperation provided in most EU external agreements and non-binding harmonisation/approximation commitments provide very little incentive for comprehensive constitutional reform in third countries. We have endeavoured to express our view on these issues. However, they require deeper study and a more comprehensive research analysis. Therefore, we hope that this book will complement prolonged discussion on the external dimension of the acquis communautaire, and will provide lavish food for further explorations of this subject.

Chapter 1. Internal and External Dimensions of the Acquis Communautaire

1.1. Introduction

Sooner or later, every novice in the field of European integration encounters the puzzle that is the "acquis communautaire". Indeed, this elegant-sounding French phrase has become common parlance, without anyone appearing to know its precise meaning.

Unquestionably, "acquis communautaire" has become a seminal concept in the process of European integration, especially during EU constitutional reforms and the accelerating enlargement towards the east. The success of these processes requires a homogeneous understanding of the "acquis communautaire". For instance, the Laeken Declaration on the Future of the European Union acknowledged the importance of the acquis communautaire in revising the delimitation of competencies between the EU and the Member States.[11] The Lisbon Treaty acknowledges the existence of "the acquis which has to be accepted by candidate countries for the accession to the Union".[12] Furthermore, a uniform understanding of the acquis communautaire is imperative for the further simplification and codification of EU legislation.[13]

Nevertheless, these tasks are not easy to achieve, since the nature and scope of the acquis communautaire is not yet fixed. One can easily question the uniformity of the manner in which the acquis communautaire is applied throughout the EU and abroad. This dilemma is aggravated by the fact that the scope of the acquis communautaire is not identical for EU Member States and third countries. In the former case, the acquis communautaire appears to be an *ex post* label which mirrors EU achievements. Consequently, the EU Member States are bound to follow and accept such legal heritage to fulfil their membership commitments. In the latter case, the acquis communautaire has more of a constitutive/dynamic nature. Candidate countries could be expected to adhere to the acquis communautaire which is not yet binding for the present EU Member States. Besides, the scope of the acquis communautaire within an EU external agreement could be revisited by either of the parties at any time to reflect a change in

---

11 Laeken Declaration, SN 273/01 (15 December 2001).
12 Article 20(4) TEU.
13 Commission Communication "Updating and simplifying the Community acquis" (COM (2003) 71 final).

bilateral relations. Subsequently, one may argue that the acquis communautaire within the EU external agreements is a dynamic category that directly depends not only on the objectives of these agreements, but on the general political climate between the parties as well.

Therefore, the Member States and certain third countries face the reality of being bound by a category without precise nature or scope. Undeniably, third country negotiators ought to possess negotiating skills when discussing the acquis communautaire with the EU on various occasions. For instance, in order to maintain an effective bargaining power in talks with the EU on objective and scope of new non-accession (partnership/association) agreements or on the format of participation in the EU's external policies third country negotiators must possess a clear idea about the nature and scope of the acquis communautaire. Such skills could be of primer importance for determining limits of the "voluntary harmonisation" of their national legislation to EU law standards, and other means of enhancement of their level of co-operation with the EU.

That is why our conceptual focus in this chapter is placed upon the consideration of the nature and analysis of basic elements of the scope of the acquis communautaire. In the first case, one must ascertain whether the "acquis communautaire" is a legal or political, static or dynamic, normative or descriptive category. In the second case, one has to be able to distinguish the basic elements of the "acquis communautaire" for the purpose of correct application.

In this book we put forward the proposition that the "acquis communautaire" is a concept of variable nature. It is argued that the nature and scope of the acquis communautaire varies depending on the objective of its application. In this regard, we suggest that two dimensions in the application of the acquis communautaire can be identified. The first dimension is the internal application of the acquis communautaire by the present Member States. The second dimension is the external application of the acquis communautaire in agreements with the candidate countries or other third countries. As further study shows, the scope of the acquis communautaire in internal and external dimensions is not identical.

Therefore, we attach significance to internal and external applications of the acquis communautaire and suggest that the scope of the acquis communautaire varies depending on the objective of application. That is to say, the objective of the acquis communautaire in its internal dimension is to enable the consistent development of the EU while preserving EU political and legal patrimony. Conversely, the objective of the acquis communautaire application in its external dimension is to push candidate countries at the forefront of the economic, political and legal development closer to the EU.

It is worth noting that, despite the different objectives of internal and external application, the acquis communautaire might contain certain similarities. Hence, we search for the elements of the acquis communautaire that constitute its hard core. For this purpose, study of the European Court of Justice (ECJ) and General Court (formerly Court of First Instance (CFI)) practice is essential, because of its responsibility in ensuring the uniform application of EU law throughout the EU.

The first part of the chapter deals with the evolution of the acquis communautaire. It depicts how the acquis communautaire acquired its current seminal standing through the various stages of enlargement. The second part reviews academic discussions on the nature and scope of the acquis communautaire that have emerged in literature over the last three decades. Then the internal dimension of acquis communautaire application is analysed. In this part of the chapter we focus on the major elements of the acquis communautaire, *inter alia* the "fundamental acquis". This provides an analysis of the external dimension of acquis communautaire application. Its main concern is the dynamic nature of the scope of the acquis communautaire in the process of enlargement. The final part of the chapter briefly examines how the external dimension of acquis communautaire application has had further implications, in particular "approximation clauses" in EU external agreements and "sectoral acquis".

The entrance into force of the Lisbon Treaty on 1st December 2009 played a significant role for the reconsideration of the whole EU legal order, and the notion of "acquis communautaire" in particular. On the one hand, formal abolition of the "pre-Lisbon" three pillars European Community and its succession by the single pillar EU implied the usage of the notion "acquis" without outdated "communautaire". One could argue that it would be more reasonable to apply new and more relevant label - "Union acquis". However, for the sake of coherence and clarity in this book and frequent references to the "pre-Lisbon" EU laws and EU external agreements we shall further apply these definitions interchangeably to avoid any possible confusion. On the other hand, the Lisbon Treaty by amending two major EU founding treaties captured the scope of the acquis communautaire at a specific time thereby providing useful guidelines for the comprehension of this notion for readers. In general, the purpose of this chapter is not to resolve the long-lasting debate on the nature and scope of the acquis communautaire, but to highlight certain significant factors related to acquis communautaire application by the Member States and third countries. Herein, we focus on indicating the basic elements of the acquis communautaire, and on establishing a framework or analytical method of the application of the acquis which can be employed in the subsequent chapters of this book.

1.2. Evolution of the concept "acquis communautaire"

1.2.1. Historical background of the acquis communautaire

The process of European Economic Community (EEC) enlargement has engendered the concept of acquis communautaire. Therefore, the acquis communautaire has been intrinsically linked with the accession of new Member States from the very beginnings of European integration. Firstly, the existence of a common legal patrimony for all Member States was acknowledged at the second meeting of the Heads of State and Government at Bad Godesberg on 18 July 1961 where the early foundations of political cooperation were laid down. Participants of the meeting agreed that the applicant Member States should "assume in every respect the same obligations and responsibilities" as the present Member States.[14] Shortly after, the Report by the foreign ministers of the Member States "on the best way of achieving progress in the matter of political unification, within the context of enlargement"[15] (known as the "Davignon Report") provided that applicant countries must adhere to all activities and policies before joining the EEC:

"The Ministers stress the correlation between membership of the European Communities and participation in activities making for progress towards political unification" (Part Four, point 1); "The applicant States must be kept informed of the progress of the work of the Six, since they will have to be consulted on the objectives and machinery described in the present report and will have to adhere to them when they join the Communities" (Part Four, point 2)".

Thus, many years prior to the first phase of EEC enlargement, it was explicitly emphasised that applicant states must not simply adopt and accept EEC "patrimony" in its entirety, but must consent to participation in future initiatives which will inevitably lead towards further political unification.

The first reference to the acquis communautaire in English can be found in the Draft European Union Treaty by the European Parliament on 14 February 1984, known as the "Spinelli Draft", wherein it was referred to as the "Community patrimony".[16] It has always been difficult to translate the precise meaning of the acquis communautaire into the various Member States' languages without undermining its uniform application. The literal translation from the French means "acquired" or "achieved", whereas subsequent translations into other EU lan-

---

14 EC Bull, 1961, 7-8, 41.
15 Approved by the foreign ministers of the Member States on 20 July 1970 and adopted on 27th October 1970 in Luxembourg, EC Bull 1970, 11, 13.
16 Article 7 draft EU Treaty states: "The Union shall take over the *Community patrimony*".

guages embrace a variety of meanings, from "a complex of rules" in Finnish and "Community law in force" in Danish, to "normative accomplishment" in Swedish and "accumulation" in Portuguese.[17] Such a kaleidoscope of potential meanings justified the later preference for the French term, especially as the exact meaning of this term has not yet been fixed. Additionally, an English-friendly version, "Community acquis" ("Union acquis" after the adoption of the Lisbon Treaty), has been applied more and more frequently in recent English versions of EU official documents, and especially in those concerning accession.[18]

The term "acquis communautaire" became part of the EEC official language when the UK, Ireland and Denmark started EEC accession proceedings in 1969. However, it was used rather sporadically in selected official documents, for example in the Advisory Opinion of the Commission to the Council of 1 October 1969 concerning the accession requests of the UK, Denmark, Ireland and Norway.[19] Nevertheless, neither the founding Treaties nor the articles of the Acts of Accession directly referred to the acquis communautaire. Some years later, the ECJ acknowledged the existence of the rules that encompass "what the Community has achieved in relation to the unity of the market".[20] Thereafter, the notion of the acquis communautaire took an explicit dual meaning by its application in relation not only to the external "Community", but also to internal "Community" as well. Soon after, the idea of internal "Community patrimony" was fixed in the Single European Act (SEA). For instance, Article 1(3) of the SEA refers to "the procedures agreed in the reports of Luxembourg (1970), Copenhagen (1973), London (1981), the Solemn Declaration on European Union (1983) and the practices gradually established among the Member States".[21] Consequently, the "internal Community patrimony" was recognised in Article 2(4) Treaty on European Union (TEU) (repealed by the Lisbon Treaty) as one of the objectives of the newly-founded EU:

"*to maintain in full the acquis communautaire and build on it* [emphasis added] with a view to considering to what extent the policies and forms of cooperation introduced by this Treaty may need to be revised with the aim of ensuring the effectiveness of the mechanisms and institutions of the Community".[22]

17 For a comprehensive overview of various translations of the acquis communautaire into EU languages see *supra note* 4.
18 For example, see "Towards the Enlarged Union" Strategy Paper and Report of the European Commission on the progress towards accession by each of the candidate countries (COM (2002) 700 final).
19 Bull EC, Suppl. 9/10-1969.
20 Joint Cases 80 and 81/77, *Commissionnaires Rèunis et Ramel,* [1978] ECR 927, at 36.
21 *Supra note* 4, at 1095. In opinion of C. Gialdino this provision forms the "historic frozen acquis".
22 Treaty on European Union (O.J. 2006 C 321/1).

Article 3(1) TEU (repealed by the Lisbon Treaty) endorsed the importance of the acquis communautaire as a foundation of the EU and of the whole institutional system.

"The Union shall be served by a single institutional framework which shall ensure the consistency and the continuity of the activities carried out in order to attain its objectives while respecting and building on the *acquis communautaire* [emphasis added]".

Provisions of the TEU, as amended by the Treaty of Nice, on the enhanced cooperation between the Member States, (Article 44 TEU (now Article 20 TEU)) provided that acts and decisions resulted from the enhanced cooperation "shall not form part of Union acquis".

Further references to the acquis communautaire are found in Protocol № 7 of the application of the principles of subsidiarity and proportionality annexed to the Treaty establishing the European Community (EC Treaty) by the Treaty of Amsterdam (ToA),[23] and in Declaration № 51 concerning Article 10 TEU (repealed by the Lisbon Treaty) accompanying the ToA.[24] Moreover, the acquis communautaire is mentioned in the Preambles to the "Protocol of the Twelve" and "the Agreement of the Eleven" which form the integral part of the EC Treaty.

"without prejudice to the provisions of the Treaty, particularly those relating to social policy which constitute an integral part of the acquis communautaire …[the High Contracting Parties] state their wish …to implement the 1989 Social Charter on the basis of the acquis communautaire".[25]

At the same time, Protocol № 2 ToA refers to all agreements and related provisions listed in the Annex to this Protocol as the "Schengen acquis", thereby locating the acquis communautaire within a specific area/sector of EU legislation.

The Draft EU Constitutional Treaty, which was signed by heads of governments of all EU Member States on 29 October 2004 in Rome but failed to enter into force due to the negative vote by the French and Dutch referendums, endeavoured to provide more or less coherent clarification of the scope of the acquis communautaire. The Draft EU Constitutional Treaty's provisions on succes-

---

23 Provision 2 related to the acquis communautaire reads: "The application of the principles of subsidiarity and proportionality shall respect the general provisions and the objectives of the Treaty, particularly as regards the maintaining in full of the acquis communautaire and the institutional balance…".
24 Provision related to the acquis communautaire reads as follows: "The Treaty of Amsterdam repeals and deletes lapsed provisions of the Treaty establishing the European Community……as they were in force before the entry into force of the Treaty of Amsterdam and adapts certain of their provisions……Those operations do not affect the "acquis communautaire".
25 Treaty establishing the European Community (O.J. 2006 C 321/1).

sion and legal continuity specified elements of the acquis communautaire to be transposed into one pillar of EU legal order. These elements encompassed the following: EU founding treaties; acts of institutions, bodies, offices and agencies; interinstitutional agreements, decisions and agreements arrived at by the Representatives of the Governments of the Member States; the agreements concluded by the Member States on the functioning of the EC/EU or linked to action by the EC/EU: the declarations, including those made in the context of intergovernmental conferences, as well as the resolutions or other positions adopted by the European Council or the Council and those relating to the EC/EU adopted by common accord by the Member States.[26] The ECJ/CFI case law remained the source of interpretation of EU law and of the comparable provisions of the Draft EU Constitutional Treaty. There was no reference to other elements of the acquis communautaire apart from EC/EU legal acts. Therefore, the Draft EU Constitutional Treaty regarded the acquis communautaire as a normative concept that encompasses binding and non-binding EU legal acts.

The Lisbon Treaty does not replicate the Draft EU Constitutional Treaty's provisions on the legal continuity of the acquis communautaire. In fact, it mentions the acquis communautaire only in the context of the enhanced cooperation and the Schengen acquis. After the Lisbon Treaty entered into force references to the acquis communautaire in Articles 2(4) and 3(1) TEU were substituted with other wording without any reference to the acquis communautaire. In particular, the new version of Articles 3 and 4 TEU amended by ToL does not list the EU's objective to "maintain in full the acquis communautaire and build on it". It could be explained by several reasons. The first reason could be based on the fact that while not denying the existence of the acquis communautaire the drafters of the Lisbon Treaty decided not to associate it with the legal system of the EU thereby recognising its dynamic nature which could evolve reflecting further constitutional reforms in the EU. The second reason could be more pragmatic. The exclusion of any references to the acquis communautaire in the context of the EU objectives was intended to avoid any impression of the existence of a concept of either political or legal nature which might remind the Member States about the supranational legal system of the EU, which is often associated with the acquis communautaire. In this case, the exclusion of explicit references to the acquis communautaire contributed to the smooth ratification process in the Member States.

---

26 Articles IV-437 and IV-438(3,4) Draft EU Constitutional Treaty (O.J. 2004 C 310).

1.2.2. External dimension of the acquis communautaire

The concept of the "acquis communautaire" has acquired a clear external dimension through its extensive application in EU external policy. In this regard, the acquis communautaire is used both in terms of EU accession and in building up closer economic and political cooperation between the EU and third countries.

In the first instance, the full acceptance without reservation of the entire acquis communautaire has become a major pre-requisite of a candidate country's EU membership. For example, Agenda 2000 has underlined the seminal importance of the candidate states' ability to adhere to the acquis communautaire in order to join the EU as a compulsory condition for EU accession.[27] The Strategy of the Accession urges new Member States to conform to the so called "acquis criterion", and, consequently, to ensure the successful implementation of the acquis communautaire and its effective enforcement within their territory.[28] For instance, the Commission calls on the acceding Central and Eastern European countries (CEEs) to pursue vigorously the improvements still required in the context of the political and economic criteria for membership and in relationship to the adoption, implementation and enforcement of the acquis communautaire.[29]

In the second instance, third countries that enter into association and partnership agreements with the EU and the Member States are encouraged to adapt their national laws to the acquis communautaire in accordance with "approximation clauses" in respective agreements. For instance, "approximation clauses" in the Stabilisation and Association Agreements (SAAs) with South-European

---

27 Agenda 2000 (EU Bull. Suppl. 5/97 at 45) states, "The progressive adoption of the *acquis* in these different areas in this three stage framework is a task which the applicant countries need to complete as far as possible before accession".

28 "Towards the Enlarged Union" Strategy Paper and Report of the European Commission on the progress towards accession by each of the candidate countries (COM (2002) 700 final, at 1.4). The notion "acquis communautaire" is frequently applied in the Final Act to the Treaty of Accession to the EU by the Czech Republic, the Republic of Estonia, the Republic of Cyprus, the Republic of Latvia, the Republic of Lithuania, the Republic of Hungary, the Republic of Malta, the Republic of Poland, the Republic of Slovenia and the Slovak Republic and other related documents (O.J. 2003 L 236). There are no references to the notion "acquis" in the Treaty of Accession to the EU by the Republic of Bulgaria and Romania but there are references in Protocol concerning the conditions and arrangements for admission of the Republic of Bulgaria and Romania to the EU as well as other annexes to the Treaty of Accession (O.J. 2005 L 157).

29 European Commission Opinion of 19 February 2003 on the applications for accession to the EU by the Czech Republic, the Republic of Estonia, the Republic of Cyprus, the Republic of Latvia, the Republic of Lithuania, the Republic of Hungary, the Republic of Malta, the Republic of Poland, the Republic of Slovenia and the Slovak Republic (O.J. 2003 L 236). See also European Commission Opinion of 22 February 2005 on the applications for accession to the EU by the Republic of Bulgaria and Romania (O.J. 2005 L 157).

countries envisage a two-stage approximation process.[30] The first stage is aimed at bringing national laws into conformity with "certain fundamental elements of the Internal Market acquis as well as other trade-related areas". The second stage of approximation will cover other elements of the acquis communautaire.[31] In this case, the consistent "voluntary" adoption of the acquis communautaire by the SAAs countries proves to be the essential condition of the liberalised market access for associated countries' goods and services to the EU.[32]

1.2.3. Concluding remarks

As shown, two dimensions of the acquis communautaire application can be seen from the early years of EEC/EU evolution. First, it is exercised in the internal context, where the acquis communautaire serves as the foundation of the EU legal and political order, which must be "maintained" at all costs and built upon. Second, the acquis communautaire is employed in EU external policy as an ultimate condition of new Member States' accession into the EU. Intrinsically, as analysis in this work proves, the scope of the acquis communautaire is not identical in internal and external dimensions. Still, owing to a paradox or some hidden logic, neither the EU primary treaties nor secondary legislation defines the precise scope and nature of the acquis communautaire. Instead, the EU institutions refer to various self-developed definitions ("Schengen acquis", "Community acquis" or simply "acquis"[33]), quite often without defining their meaning and scope.[34] Unfortunately, the Lisbon Treaty does not rectify this dilemma. It

---

30   The Stabilisation and Association Agreements were signed with Bosnia and Herzegovina, Croatia, Former Yugoslav Republic of Macedonia (FYROM), Montenegro, Serbia and Albania. The SAAs countries only "endeavour to ensure the gradual compatibility of their laws to the EC". Therein, the approximation of national legislation is mentioned as a core element of developing economic and international cooperation of the SAA countries. The Preambles of the SAAs contain references to status of the parties to these agreements as a "potential candidate for the EU membership" and a possibility of establishing a free trade area with the EU. For example see the Preamble and Article 1(2) EU-FYROM SAA (O.J. 2000 C 339/266).
31   Article 68 EU-FYROM SAA.
32   M. Cremona, "The European Union as an International Actor: Issues of Flexibility and Linkage" 3 EFARev. 67-94 (1998) at 86.
33   Protocols to the Lisbon Treaty provide that "the words *acquis communautaire*" shall be replaced by "Community or Union *acquis*" (See Protocol on the position of the United Kingdom and Ireland in respect of the area of freedom, security and justice (O.J. 2007 C 306/50)).
34   For instance, see "Towards the Enlarged Union" Strategy Paper and Report of the European Commission on the progress towards accession by each of the candidate countries (COM (2002) 700 final), and Communication from the Commission "Enlargement Strategy and Main Challenges 2008-2009" (COM (2008) 674 final). In these documents there

refers to various types of the acquis communautaire being engulfed by the newly-born single pillar EU legal order without clarifying the meaning and scope of its successor. This juncture requires EU decision makers, national authorities and academic community to deliberate over the precise and accurate application of this definition. Perhaps the EU does not want to fix the scope of the acquis communautaire in the EU legal system, but wishes to apply it as a "moving concept". However, this approach does not contribute to the legal certainty of the EU legal system, but merely provides the EU institutions with a *carte blanche* to keep the notion "acquis communautaire" in a state of flux. Thus, endeavours to clarify the scope of the acquis communautaire must be undertaken to achieve legal certainty within the EU legal system, and to ease the candidate countries' efforts to join the EU.

1.3. Conceptualising the acquis communautaire

1.3.1. Academic discussion about the context and meaning of the acquis communautaire

When discussing internal and external dimensions of the acquis communautaire, one must be certain about the nature and scope of these categories. Unfortunately, EU official sources have never endeavoured to clarify whether the internal and external application of the acquis communautaire presumes any difference in their scope. Moreover, the EU institutions are inclined to emphasise the legal nature of the acquis communautaire. For instance, the EU's Glossary plainly considers the acquis communautaire (Community acquis) "the body of common rights and obligations which bind all the Member States together within the European Union".[35] The 2009-2010 Enlargement Paper from the Commis-

---

is no single reference to the "acquis communautaire" but only to the "acquis". Presidency Conclusions of the latest European Councils do omit the reference to the "acquis communautaire" as well, but apply solely the "acquis". The Laeken Declaration refers to the "acquis communautaire" solely in the meaning of Articles 2(4) and 3(1) EC Treaty.

35 As the EU's Glossary of definitions provides: "The Community *acquis* is the body of common rights and obligations which bind all the Member States together within the European Union. It is constantly evolving and comprises: the content, principles and political objectives of the Treaties; the legislation adopted in application of the treaties and the case law of the Court of Justice; the declarations and resolutions adopted by the Union; measures relating to the common foreign and security policy; measures relating to justice and home affairs; international agreements concluded by the Community and those concluded by the Member States between themselves in the field of the Union's activities. Thus the Community *acquis* comprises not only Community law in the strict sense, but also all acts adopted under the second and third pillars of the European Union and the

sion equates the acquis communautaire with EU legal order.[36] The same approach was undertaken in the Draft EU Constitutional Treaty, which indirectly associated the acquis communautaire with the EU legal order.[37] However, the narrow understanding of the acquis communautaire as a mere legal concept has been repeatedly challenged by academics and commentators. It is almost universally agreed that the acquis communautaire is not equivalent to the EU legal order, but constitutes a much broader concept with clear political emphasis.

Some commentators are convinced that the concept of the acquis communautaire exceeds the boundaries of the EU law, but encompasses all "achievements reached under founding Treaties including legislation and case law".[38] Therefore the acquis communautaire is regarded as a category of "variable" nature: "The acquis is not some privileged category of the Community legal order rather, it is an ambiguous concept amendable by the Member States".[39] Professor Stephen Weatherill argues in favour of the variable nature of the acquis communautaire by insisting that "the function of the *acquis communautaire* varies according to the context". He notes that the acquis communautaire can be used as a badge designed to pin credibility to any alteration in the Community's constitutional and institutional framework. As a result, Weatherill calls for a precise definition of the acquis communautaire. Otherwise, "there is a danger that assertions at times of Treaty revision of maintenance of the acquis communautaire may conceal some attacks upon important aspects of the Community legal order".[40] Thus,

    common objectives laid down in the Treaties. The Union has committed itself to maintaining the Community *acquis* in its entirety and developing it further. Applicant countries have to accept the Community *acquis* before they can join the Union. Derogations from the *acquis* are granted only in exceptional circumstances and are limited in scope. To integrate into the European Union, applicant countries will have to transpose the *acquis* into their national legislation and implement it from the moment of their accession". EU Glossary <http://europa.eu/scadplus/glossary/community_acquis_en.htm>, last visited 18 January 2011.
36   Communication from the European Commission "Enlargement Strategy and Main Challenges 2009-2010" (COM (2009) 533).
37   Article IV-438 (3-4) Draft EU Constitutional Treaty.
38   K. Lasok, *Law & Institutions of the European Union* (7th Ed. London, Butterworths 2001), at 32. A. Toth describes the acquis communautaire as "the Community patrimony: the whole body of rules, principles, agreements, declarations, resolutions, positions, opinions, objectives, and practices concerning the EC, *whether or not binding in law*, which has been accepted by the EC institutions and the Member States as governing their activities". A. G. Toth, *Oxford Encyclopedia of European Community Law*, vol. 1, (Oxford, Clarendon Press 1990), at 9.
39   *Supra note* 10, at 27. H. Lyndahl, "Acquiring a Community: The *Acquis* and the Institution of European Legal Order", 9 ELJ (2003), at 434.
40   *Supra note 5,* at 153-178, 161-162. See also V. Muraviov, "The Acquis Communautaire as a Basis for the Community Legal Order" 4(2) Miskolc Journal of International Law 38-45 (2007).

Weatherill favours a fixed normative perception of the acquis communautaire. Otherwise, the application of the acquis communautaire should rather be abandoned in EU and Member States' courts. Weatherill's approach towards the fixed normative perception of the acquis communautaire is echoed by scholars who apply the notion "acquis communautaire" to describe EU sectoral legislation (e.g. "consumer acquis", "contract law acquis"). However, even in these cases, academics tend to consider EU sectoral acquis as wide as possible including not only relevant EU primary and secondary legislation but also "soft law", best practices and even "desirable rules based on political decisions which may entail a regulatory framework".[41]

Carlo Gialdino has made a respectful effort to systematise the different categories of the acquis communautaire. He recognises the existence of the "fundamental acquis" as a privileged category of the acquis communautaire which is made up of the fundamental principles concerning the structure of the EU legal order and ECJ case law. The "fundamental acquis" guards the essence of the EU, and, consequently, constitutes an untouchable hard core of EU law and prevailing even over EU primary rules.[42] Along with the "fundamental acquis", Gialdino distinguishes the "institutional acquis", "Union acquis", "accession acquis" and acquis for every particular agreement of the EU with a third country. They are aimed at acquiring different objectives, and therefore, their scope and binding force vary.

French academic Christine Delcourt shares Gialdino's view on the existence of the "fundamental acquis" which is "situated at the apex of the hierarchy of sources of Community law".[43] The author notes the ambiguity in the application of the concept of the acquis communautaire. Delcourt's description of the acquis communautaire proves that the "fundamental" and "Union" acquis differ in their internal dimension from the "accession" acquis which is the compulsory reference framework for third countries wishing to gain accession to the EU. Delcourt therefore characterises the acquis communautaire as "a single term superseded by a notion with variable content".[44] In response to this ambiguity, Delcourt proposes regarding the acquis communautaire both in its narrow sense and the broad

---

41 For instance, N. Jansen and R. Zimmerman, "Restating the *Acquis Communautaire*? A Critical Examination of the 'Principles of the Existing EC Contract Law'", 71(4) MLRev. 505-534 (2008). S. Grundmann, "The Optional European Code on the Basis of the *Acquis Communautaire*-Starting Point and Trends", 10(6) ELJ 698-711 (2004).
42 *Supra note 4*, at 1108.
43 *Supra note 6*, at 842.
44 *Ibid*, at 848. In Delcourt's words the notion of the "acquis communautaire" covers "a plurality of elements, of varying nature and origin, which are assembled and combined to form a number of "acquis", which are more or less "communautaires", more or less encompassing, or more or less specific; a number of "acquis" which are also more or less essential".

sense. In the former case, the acquis communautaire includes only the founding treaties and acts adopted on the basis of those treaties. Here it encompasses all the provisions which provide the foundations of the EU system, as well as all the provisions adopted in the framework of this system. In the end, Delcourt urges that one must specify the specific acquis communautaire to which one is referring. The author proposes the use of "acquis communautaire" whenever it refers to the whole Union acquis, or to some of its elements.[45]

Furthermore there is a trend to consider the acquis communautaire a notion which, apart from existing political and constitutional EU values, embraces also potential policy-objectives, as well as the institutional means for the establishment of future EU policy-objectives and their implementation. Therefore, it is argued that the acquis communautaire is a complicated amalgamation of constitutional, political and legal matrixes. For instance, Krenzler and Everson[46] consider the acquis communautaire not as a mere legal concept but rather as the "unitary legal framework in which shared policies/values are established and through which they are implemented".[47] They are "all the *real* and *potential rights* [emphasis added] of the EU system and its institutional framework". In this case, EU legal order plays the role solely of guarantor regarding the acquis communautaire and provides the means by which sovereign Member States' pure political commitments can be translated into legally binding supranational principles. Then these practices "may themselves be further elaborated into substantive EU policies with the aid of the common institutions of supranational political decision-making".[48]

The idea that the acquis communautaire includes potential policy-objectives was laid down into the foundation of Wiener's concept of the "embedded acquis". In the opinion of the author the acquis communautaire mirrors the result of legislative, policy and political practices over time and represents the continuously changing concept which results from the constructive progress of "integration through law".[49] It is suggested that the legal body of the acquis communautaire is linked to social practices. Thus, acquis communautaire is understood not as a fixed but as a flexible institutional framework whose meaning is socialy-

---

45 *Ibid,* at 869.
46 *Supra note* 8.
47 *Ibid.* The authors argue that the acquis communautaire "goes far beyond the internal market and including areas, such as, agriculture, the environment, energy and transport. In addition to existing and settled policies which have been concretised as legal obligations in the EU, the acquis also entails the long term principles – that are currently in development (CFSP, EMU and JHA)".
48 *Ibid.*
49 A. Wiener, "The Embedded Acquis Communautaire: Transmission Belt and Prism of New Governance", 3 ELJ 294-315 (1998).

constructed. Wiener puts forward the argument that the acquis communautaire has been applied in either a descriptive or a normative fashion. The descriptive use of acquis communautaire is commonly applied in the course of enlargement, and more recently in the course of "opting-out" of the acquis communautaire at IGCs. The normative application of the acquis communautaire has been identified as a constructive "push factor", similar to the concept of "integration through law" employed by the ECJ. Thus, Wiener suggests that the "embedded acquis" encompasses informal resources such as shared values, ideas and world views on the one hand, and the routinisation of practices which lead to agreement on policy objectives on the other. To express it in more straightforward way, Wiener distinguishes three levels of the "embedded acquis":

- formal binding and non-binding sources; rules, procedures, regulations;
- routinisation; practices, policy objectives;
- informal sources; ideas, values (they do not necessarily need to become formal sources but may be routinised as a policy objective by lobbying interest groups).

Therefore, a change in the embedded acquis potentially involves two processes. One includes the expansion of formal resources (changes in the treaty, directives, and regulations). The other covers a formalisation based on routinised practice or the constitutionalisation of informal resources (ideas, shared principles, practices as suggested by European Parliament resolutions and Commission proposals or other documents). For instance, the author's study of the citizenship acquis[50] suggests that shared values, normative ideals and functional perspectives, were all crucial factors affecting the shape of the acquis in that field.

To conclude, Wiener articulates that the "fundamental acquis", which is formed by formal resources such as legal procedures, treaty provisions and directives, is not independent from previously established informal resources like shared values and norms on the one hand and routinised practices and policy objectives on the other. Experience of European integration shows that informal resources (shared values and norms) were mobilised by interest groups to enforce their demands to create new forms of the "embedded acquis".[51]

Accepting Weiner's concept of the normative and descriptive fashions of the acquis, one always should not overestimate the weight of "informal sources". We must distinguish the political, sociological and legal perceptions of the acquis

---

50 A. Wiener, *European Citizenship Practice: Building Institutions of a Non-State* (Westview Press 1998) at 312.
51 J. Shaw, "Constitutional Settlements and the Citizen After Amsterdam," in K. Neunreither / A. Wiener (eds), *Institutional Dynamics and Prospects for Democracy* (1999, OUP).

communautaire, since the subject matter of our study is the legal nature of the acquis communautaire and its further implications for the approximation of laws in third countries. It is presumed that the nature and scope of the acquis communautaire in its internal dimension is shaped by EU institutions, especially by the ECJ. One can scarcely deny that the ECJ is not always keen in taking into account merely informal sources, but considers all possible factors including preserving its own autonomous judicial discretion. However, the external dimension of the acquis communautaire is more likely to be influenced by other "informal sources", which are underpinned by external political and economic factors. For instance, it could be either the progress in bilateral relations or hampering of economic relations between the EU and a third country. Nonetheless, it is emphasised that the acquis communautaire in the context of accession loses its sensitivity to "informal sources" after the formalisation in the Acts of Accession. At this stage, the acquis communautaire represents the pure political consensus formalised in the Treaty on the scope of competencies transferred by new Member States to the EU. To support this view, Dutch legal scholar Mortelmans also perceives the acquis communautaire as "a political or policy concept" and clearly distinguishes it from the basic tenets of EU law. However, the author rejects the view that the acquis communautaire encompasses potential policy objectives and rights. Mortelmans argues that "the acquis refers to all those matters which have been brought within Community powers and cannot therefore return to the sphere of national law".[52] Weiler echoes this view by regarding the acquis communautaire as the "holiest cow [of] the constitutional framework of the Community".[53]

1.3.2. Concluding remarks

To summarise, academic discussion on the nature of the concept of the acquis communautaire displays an almost unilateral acknowledgement that the acquis communautaire is a much broader category than a mere legal concept and therefore embraces all the achievements reached under the founding Treaties, including non-binding rules and so-called "informal sources". Commentators emphasise the variable nature of the acquis communautaire. This is why one should always specify which particular element of the acquis communautaire is being referring to. Subsequently, it is acknowledged that the acquis communautaire may

---

52 *Supra note* 10, at 23-48. See also P. Pescatore, "Aspects judiciaries de l'acquis communautaire", RTDE 617-651 (1981).
53 J.H.H. Weiler, *"The Constitution of Europe "Do the new clothes have an emperor?" and other essays on European integration"* (Cambridge University Press 1999), at 222.

be perceived in either a normative or descriptive fashion in accordance with the various dimensions of application. For instance, the normative fashion of the "pre-accession" acquis embraces the Copenhagen criteria, while the descriptive fashion reflects actual progress in the adoption of the acquis by a candidate country. Finally, the manifest expansion of the acquis communautaire into political and social domains of the EU framework is apparent. Yet there are several issues which still demand thorough scrutiny. One of these is the determination of the elements of this broad and vaguely applied definition which may be binding, or potentially binding, and on whom. Another is to clarify which elements of the acquis communautaire must be associated solely with political, sociological and other values. Therefore, the call for legal certainty entails the thorough scrutiny of all elements of the "acquis communautaire" for the purpose of correct application by the Member States and third countries.

1.4. The internal dimension of the acquis communautaire

1.4.1. Introduction

The objective *"to maintain in full the acquis communautaire and build on it"* was principal in grasping the evolutionary character of the newly-born EU.[54] Furthermore, this objective led to "communitarisation" of the two "pre-Lisbon" intergovernmental EU pillars and the subsequent creation of a single, hierarchically coherent EU legal order after the Lisbon Treaty came into force.

Therefore, we accept that the acquis communautaire in its internal dimension is applicable within the EU structure among the present Member States. It is argued that the acquis communautaire must be seen in its widest scope as a patrimony of binding and non-binding rules, principles and practices that distinguish the EU supranational legal order from other creations of international and national legal systems.

We consider that elements of the acquis communautaire in its internal dimension produce, or intend to produce a legal effect. Firstly, the acquis communautaire is based on the "fundamental acquis", i.e. the sum of objectives, policies, general principles and rules, which constitute the core of the supranational EU legal order. These elements comprise the skeleton of the whole acquis communautaire, and therefore cannot be altered or repealed without destroying the unique nature of the EU. Secondly, the acquis communautaire embraces various international law provisions that bind the EU and the Member States. Thirdly, the acquis communautaire covers a quite distinctive patrimony of what had been acquired within the EU intergovernmental areas of cooperation. Fourthly, EU "soft law" provisions must be respected by the present Member States and therefore belong to the acquis communautaire.

1.4.2. The nature and scope of the "fundamental acquis"

1.4.2.1. Core of the "fundamental acquis"

Several decades ago Pescatore gave the original definition of the "fundamental acquis" as "definitive achievements, which would not be open to challenge and must be safeguarded and maintained at all costs".[55] These achievements have shaped the unique framework of the Community legal order which cannot be

---

54 Articles 2(4) TEU and 3(1) TEU (repealed after adoption of the Lisbon Treaty).
55 P. Pescatore, "Aspects judiciaries de l'acquis communautaire", RTDE 617-651 (1981), at 618.

changed or reconsidered without altering the unique supranational nature of the EEC (now EU).

We propose associating the "fundamental acquis" with the supranational EU legal order. In the *Van Gend en Loos* case the ECJ recognised that the EEC (now EU) is governed by a new legal order of international law for the benefit of which Member States have limited their sovereign rights, albeit within limited fields,[56] and "have thus created a body of law which binds both their nationals and themselves".[57] Hence, the ECJ explicitly acknowledged that the EU "new legal order" is based on the articles of the EU founding Treaties, which lay out the objectives of the EU, and the means by which they are to be achieved. In spite of its conclusion in the form of an international agreement, the EU founding Treaties constitute the EU's constitutional charter based on the rule of law.[58] Therefore, we suggest consorting the "fundamental acquis" with the EU legal order, which is a body of laws comprising the transferred sovereign rights of the Member States. The rights which form the EU supranational competence are accumulated in the EU founding Treaties.[59] Thus, the "fundamental acquis" enshrines the achievements of the EU legal order that constitute its unique framework, and, which must be preserved at all costs, and which consequently distinguish the supranational EU legal order from a legal order of other international organisations. Otherwise the supranational nature of the EU legal order might vanish.[60] Rules that regulate the issues of inter-governmental cooperation within

---

56   Case 26/62 *Van Gend en Loos v. Nederlandse Administratie der Belastingen* [1963], CMLR 105.

57   In Case 6/64, *Costa v. ENEL* [1964] ECR 585 the concept of the EEC legal order was further elaborated as "real powers stemming from a limitation of sovereignty or transfer of powers from the State to the Community, the Member States have limited their sovereign rights, albeit within limited fields, and have thus created a body of law which binds both their nationals and themselves".

58   Opinion 1/91 on the EEA [1991] ECR I-6079.

59   EU founding Treaties comprise: 1) the Treaties establishing the EU (TEU, TFEU); 2) of the Treaties that amend and supplement them (Convention on Certain Institutions Common to the European Communities, Merger Treaty, First Budgetary Treaty, Second Budgetary Treaty, Single European Act, Maastricht Treaty, ToA, Nice Treaty, Lisbon Treaty); 3) Acts of Accession of the new Member States. Annexes and Protocols form an integral part of the founding Treaties. The status of joint declarations is not yet clear since some of them bear a purely political significance, whereas others have a legal effect. T. Hartley refers to them as "constitutive treaties" and considers the EEA Agreement as part of the founding Treaties. T. C. Hartley, *The Foundations of European Community Law* (6th Ed. Oxford University Press 2007), at 91.

60   In the opinion of Wyatt, the following facts underline the unique nature of the EC/EU legal order: 1) the EC Treaty modified the legal position of individuals in their national legal systems, 2) EC law is supreme over Member States laws, 3) Member States courts are under a duty to give direct effect to clearly defined and unconditional obligations in the EC Treaty, 4) techniques of interpretation by the ECJ differ from the current international

the EU (for instance, Common Foreign and Security Policy (CFSP)) belong to the acquis communautaire, but owing to their inter-governmental nature cannot be regarded as part of the "fundamental acquis". The concept of the "fundamental acquis" is inherent to the EU legal order in the Lisbon Treaty. Though the Lisbon Treaty does not contain any explicit references to the need to ensure the continuity of the acquis communautaire as it was done in the Draft EU Constitutional Treaty.[61] Nevertheless, it follows from the Lisbon Treaty that the "post-Lisbon acquis" will be built on the "fundamental acquis" of the European Community (EC) supranational pillar by erecting a coherent edifice of common principles, objectives, and values on which the EU is based.[62]

The existence of the "fundamental acquis" within the EU legal order had been endorsed by the ECJ which acknowledged the existence of "the internal constitution of the Community", "very foundations of the Community" and even the "Constitutional Charter of the Community".[63] Thereby the certain scope of EU law was envisaged as being of higher value and hierarchy,[64] and certain provisions of EU law were regarded as fundamental, and consequently unamendable.[65]

Indeed, despite the fact that there is no ban on the revision of provisions of the EU legal order,[66] specific values and principles of EU law must be considered as unamendable and static in their meaning, even in the case of revision or simplification of the entire EU legal order.[67] Consequently, those aspects of EU law are

    practice, *inter alia* the ECJ is inclined to apply the teleological interpretation of EC laws. D. Wyatt, "New Legal Order or Old?" 7 ELRev 147-148 (1982).

61   The Preamble of the Draft EU Constitutional Treaty stated that the new EU is "determined to continue the work accomplished within the framework of the Treaties establishing the European Communities and the Treaty on the European Union, by ensuring the continuity of the Community *acquis*".

62   Articles 2 and 3 TEU.

63   Opinion 1/76 [1977] ECR 741, para 12, Opinion 1/91 [1991] ECR 6079, para 21. Joint Cases C-402/05 and C-415/05 *Ahmed Ali Yusuf and Al Barakaat International Foundation v. Council and Commission; Yassin Abdullah Kadi v. Council and Commission.* [2008] ECR I-6351.

64   C. Gialdino suggests that, in this case, the ECJ has adopted the theory of a constitutional hard core "high values" (*Verfassungskern*) elaborated by Carl Schmidt and already accepted by a number of the Member States Constitutional Courts. See *supra note* 4, at 1110.

65   Opinion 1/91 on the EEA [1991] ECR I-6079, at 71.

66   For instance, the European Commission has explicitly stated that "any amendment of the fundamental principles of the Treaties may be carried out only through the revision procedures laid down in the Treaties themselves". See "General considerations on the enlargement of the Community" of the Council on 20 April 1978, EC Bull., 1-78, 15, para 49.

67   C. Gialdino argues that "certain principles are considered unamendable insofar as they qualify the entire system; interpreted in this sense, they are not simply higher rules but

bound to prevail even over primary rules, including the rule governing the revision itself.[68] The following rules correspond to these criteria and, therefore, can be regarded as part of the "fundamental acquis":

- The EU shall act within the limits of the powers conferred by the EU founding Treaties and of the objectives assigned (Article 5(2) TEU – principle of conferral);
- The EU Courts (ECJ, General Court and specialised courts) shall ensure that in the interpretation and application of the EU founding Treaties the law is observed (Article 19 TEU (as provided in the *Kadi* case);
- Member States shall take all appropriate measures to ensure the fulfilment of the obligations arising from the EU founding Treaties and resulting from action taken by the institutions of the EU (Article 4(3) TEU – principle of sincere cooperation);
- all discrimination on grounds of nationality, sex, racial or ethnic origin, religion or belief, disability, age or sexual orientation is prohibited in the EU (Article 10 Treaty on the Functioning of the European Union (TFEU) – principle of non-discrimination);
- a guarantee of the rights of citizenship that provides the right to move and reside freely within the EU (Article 8 TEU);
- the abolition of customs duties and all charges of equivalent effect on exports and imports between Member States, and the functioning of the custom union by adopting a common customs tariff in relations with third countries, abolition of all measures which could lead to quantitative restrictions on imports and exports to and from Member States (Articles 28-36 TFEU);
- no restrictions/discrimination by monopolies of a commercial character regarding conditions under which goods are procured and marketed in the Member States (Article 37 TFEU);
- free movement of workers and self-employed that entail the abolition of any discrimination based on the nationality of workers and self-employed from the Member States as regards employment, remuneration and other conditions of work and employment (Article 45-48 TFEU);
- the right of establishment of companies and firms formed in accordance with the law of a Member State and operating there (Article 49 TFEU);
- the freedom to provide services envisages the abolition of any discrimination in respect of nationals of the Member States who are already established (Article 49-55 TFEU);
- the free movement of capital (Article 63 TFEU);

rather "different entities irreducible to the normative" in their "pure essence of values". *Supra note* 4, at 1114.
68   *Ibid*, at 1090.

- no measures that distort competition (Article 106 TFEU);
- no aid incompatible with the common market (Article 107-109 TFEU);
- no discriminatory taxes (Article 110 TFEU);
- environmental protection (Article 191 TFEU);
- consumer protection (Article 169 TFEU)
- no excessive government deficits (Article 126 TFEU).

1.4.2.2. EU founding Treaties' objectives and the "fundamental acquis"

The "fundamental acquis" is inextricably linked to the EU founding Treaties' objectives. This is because the ECJ extensively refers to the EU founding Treaties' objectives in the course of the teleological interpretation of EU rules. For these purposes the ECJ endeavour to resolve any ambiguity in the application and interpretation of EU laws. Besides, compliance with the EU founding Treaties' objectives tests the legitimacy of new EU legislation. In accordance with the principle of effectiveness the Member States must facilitate the achievement of the EU tasks and abstain from any measure which could jeopardise their attainment.[69] Hence, actions of the EU institutions and the Member States should contribute to acquiring the following objectives of the EU:
- the establishment of an economic and monetary union;
- the implementation of common policies and activities;
- the promotion of measures aimed at the harmonious, balanced and sustainable development of economic activities;
- ensuring a high level of employment and of social protection;
- the provision of equality between men and women;
- the acquisition of sustainable and non inflationary growth;
- the preservation of a high degree of competitiveness and convergence of economic performance;
- the provision of a high level of protection and improvement of the quality of the environment;
- the improvement in the standard of living and in economic and social cohesion and solidarity among Member States.

The Lisbon Treaty had significantly extended the list of objectives by adding political, cultural, security and justice dimensions to the conventional economic dimension:
- the EU's aim is to promote peace, its values and the well-being of its peoples (Article 3(1) TEU);

---

69 Article 4(3) TEU.

- the EU shall offer its citizens an area of freedom, security and justice without internal frontiers, in which the free movement of persons is ensured in conjunction with appropriate measures with respect to external border controls, asylum, immigration and the prevention and combating of crime (Article 3(2) TEU);
- the EU shall establish an internal market (Article 3(3) TEU);
- the EU shall work for the sustainable development of Europe based on balanced economic growth and price stability, a highly competitive social market economy, aiming at full employment and social progress, and a high level of protection and improvement of the quality of the environment (Article 3(3) TEU);
- the EU shall promote scientific and technological advance (Article 3(3) TEU);
- the EU shall combat social exclusion and discrimination, and shall promote social justice and protection, equality between women and men, solidarity between generations and protection of the rights of the child (Article 3(3) TEU);
- the EU shall promote economic, social and territorial cohesion and solidarity among Member States (Article 3(3) TEU);
- the EU shall respect its rich cultural and linguistic diversity, and shall ensure that Europe's cultural heritage is safeguarded and enhanced (Article 3(3) TEU).

The "fundamental acquis" embraces secondary legislation (regulations, directives, and decisions) issued within exclusive competencies that have been transferred by the Member States to the EU. Listed in Article 3 TFEU these competencies are of profound importance for the maintenance of the "untouchable" core of the "fundamental acquis", since they cannot be reclaimed without risking the loss of EU membership. Exercising these competencies, EU institutions issue binding legislation that takes precedence over conflicting Member States' legislation. In cases of infringement of EU legislation, the Member States bear material liability. Interpretation of EU legislation adopted within these competencies by the ECJ constitutes the integral part of the "fundamental acquis".

1.4.2.3. General principles of EU law and the "fundamental acquis"

General principles of EU law form the essential component of the "fundamental acquis". EU general principles have emerged from the ECJ's practice aimed at ensuring that "law is observed" in the interpretation and application of the EU founding Treaties.[70] Furthermore, Article 263 TFEU empowers the ECJ to annul any EU act for "infringement of an essential procedural requirement, infringement of the Treaties or of any rule of law relating to their application, or misuse of powers". These provisions awarded the ECJ with a competence unprecedented for an international court which enables it to elaborate on the means and approaches of the interpretation and application of EU law. As a result, the ECJ has engendered a set of general principles that are based on the principles of national constitutional law and international agreements with which Member States are associated. The Lisbon Treaty formalised many of the newly-elaborated EC/EU general principles into the EU legal order. In general, in contrast to the Draft EU Constitutional Treaty[71] the Lisbon Treaty does not consolidate many of the newly formalised through the ECJ case law EU general principles, along with "classical" EC general principles (principle of sincere cooperation, principle of non-discrimination), into the "fundamental acquis" of the EU. However, we argue that EU general principles left behind by the Lisbon Treaty (principle of legal certainty, principle of Member States' liability in damage for breach of EU law, principle of environmental damage – the polluter should pay, doctrines of supremacy and direct effect) still maintain utmost importance for the whole EU legal order due to their prominence established by the ECJ in its case law.

Principles of law constitute a very important part of any legal system or legal order. It may be argued that any principle is a general proposition of law of some importance from which concrete rules derive.[72] Principles do not constitute any binding rules that follow automatically from them, but stipulate certain way of reasoning in the courts' application of these rules.[73] In our case, the ECJ has developed a set of principles which have occupied the apex of the EU legal order and which are bound to be observed by Member States' courts throughout the EU. As Charlesworth and Cullen rightly argue,[74] EU general principles emerged on two levels. Firstly, they serve as guidance for the effective functioning of the EU legal order. Secondly, they provide the justification for judicial creativity as a result of the many gaps in EU primary laws. It follows that the ECJ will maintain its significant influence over the preservation of the established EU general

---

70   Article 19 TEU.
71   The Draft EU Constitutional Treaty indented to formalise principles of: legal certainty, supremacy, direct effect, environmental damage.
72   T. Tridimas, *General Principles of EU Law,* (2d ed. Oxford University Press 2007), at 1.
73   A rule answers the question "what", whereas a principle answers the question "why". See Sir Gerald Fitzmaurice, "The General Principles of International Law" 92 Collected Courses of the Hague Academy of International Law 7 (1957).
74   A. Charlesworth / H. Cullen, *European Community Law*, (London, Pitman Publishing 1994), at 97.

principles and development of new EU general principles in the "post-Lisbon" era.

As a reflection of the *sui generis* EU legal order, EU general principles may be organised into three categories. The first category comprises the general principles derived from the national laws of the Member States. Article 340(2) TFEU provides that the EU may incur non-contractual liability "in accordance with the general principles common to the laws of the Member States". Account must be taken of the laws of different Member States when interpreting EU law.[75] Indeed, issues of property rights,[76] application of preliminary ruling procedure[77] and estoppel[78] were exported from the Member States' laws. However, the ECJ always tends to preserve sufficient discretion in picking principles of national legal systems to be transferred into the EU legal order. Judicial review is at the heart of the EU legal order, as stated in the *Les Verts* case.[79] It is believed that, owing to the use of these principles, the ECJ has been able to fashion EU legislation into a coherent legal order. These principles have been derived from the legal orders of the Member States.[80] As a consequence, the ECJ may potentially recognise any general principle of a particular Member State as part of the EU legal order, although they are not recognised in the laws of all Member States. Furthermore, the scope of a principle as applied by the ECJ may differ from that which it has in the law of an original Member State.[81] Till now, the ECJ has incorporated a few principles and concepts from the Member States which have become fundamental principles of the EU legal order (for instance, principles of equal treatment and non-discrimination, proportionality, legal certainty, protection of legitimate expectations, fundamental rights, and the rule of law principle). Being cautious to protect its own judicial autonomy, the ECJ has explicitly stated that the nature of a "general principle common to the laws of the Member States is a matter of Community law determined by the ECJ, whatever the national origins of that principle."[82] Therefore, the "fundamental acquis" does not automatically

---

75   In Opinion by the AG Roemer in Case 6/54 *Netherlands v. High Authority* [1954-6] ECR 103.
76   Case 44/79 *Hauer v. Land RheinlandPfalz* [1979] ECR 3727.
77   Case 13/61 *De Geus v Bosch* [1962] ECR 45.
78   Case 108/63 *Merlini v High Authority* [1965] ECR 1.
79   Case 294/83 *"les Verts" v European Parliament*, [1986] ECR 1339.
80   F. Jacobs, "The Evolution of the European Legal Order" 41 CML Rev. 303-316 (2004), at 312 and 316.
81   Takis Tridimas provides an excellent passage describing the place of Member States' principles in the EC legal order "the general principles of law are children of national law, as brought up by the Court, they become *enfants terribles*: they are extended, narrowed, restated, transformed by a creative and eclectic judicial process". *Supra note 74*, at 6.
82   Case 63 to 69/72 *Werhahn and others v. Council and Commission* [1973] ECR 1229.

cover all principles that might be recognised as common to all Member States, but embraces those that were explicitly acknowledged by the ECJ as fundamental for the correct functioning of the EU legal order and best suited to the correct observation of EU law.

The second category covers principles derived from international law. The ECJ takes into account principles of international law in so far as they are binding upon the Member States.[83] Moreover, it is for the ECJ to determine the nature and scope of international public law principles to be transferred into the EU legal order. The Lisbon Treaty confirms the power of the ECJ to distinguish which fundamental rights guaranteed by the ECHR result from the constitutional traditions common to the Member States and therefore constitute EU law general principles despite the fact that after the Lisbon Treaty enters into force the EU is bound to become a party to the European Convention on Human Rights (ECHR).[84] Most interestingly, after the Lisbon Treaty came into force both the EU Charter of Fundamental Rights and the ECHR belong to EU primary law thereby potentially may conflict with each other.[85] It goes without saying that the ECJ will play a decisive role in compiling elements of the EU human rights acquis. Furthermore, the Lisbon Treaty elevates the status of international law in the EU legal order by stating that the EU in its external relations ensures "the strict observance and the development of international law, including respect for the principles of the United Nations Charter".[86]

Lately, the EU has distinguished the fundamental character of the common values of the international community for the EU legal order. For example, the EU Charter of Fundamental Rights sets out that the "Union is founded on the indivisible, universal values of human dignity, freedom, equality and solidarity".[87] Article 2 TEU unequivocally states that

"The Union is founded on the values of respect for human dignity, freedom, democracy, equality, the rule of law and respect for human rights, including the rights of persons belonging to minorities. These values are common to the Mem-

---

83 In the words of the ECJ "international treaties for the protection of human rights on which the Member States have collaborated or of which they are signatories, can supply guidelines which should be followed within the framework of Community law". See Case 4/73 *Nold v. Commission* [1974] ECR 491 at 507.
84 Article 6(3) TEU amended by ToL.
85 On the "Pre-Lisbon" close interrelations of case law of the ECJ and ECtHR and emergence of common European Human Rights acquis see S. Douglas-Scott, "a Tale of Two Courts: Luxembourg, Strasbourg and the Growing European Human Rights *Acquis*" 43 CML Rev. 629-665 (2006) and F. van den Berghe, "The EU and Issues of Human Rights Protection: Same Solutions to More Acute Problems?" 16 ELJ 112-157 (2010).
86 Article 3(5) TEU.
87 Charter of Fundamental Rights of the EU, (O.J. 2000, C 364/1).

ber States in a society in which pluralism, non-discrimination, tolerance, justice, solidarity and equality between women and men prevail."

Interestingly, the Lisbon Treaty does not specify whether the EU common values are universal or strictly European. The Preamble to the TEU states that *"drawing inspiration from the cultural, religious and humanist inheritance of Europe, from which have developed the universal values* [emphasis added] of the unavoidable and inalienable rights of the human person, freedom, democracy, equality and the rule of law". In our view this statement endorses universal values as values of European origin and therefore giving although indirectly a right to the EU to influence a scope of these values.[88]

EU common values may be regarded as belonging to the "fundamental acquis" in so far as its elements are specified and correspond to the objectives of the EU. In general, we suggest setting the boundaries of the "fundamental acquis" solely within the provisions of the international treaties binding on the EU and the Member States that have been explicitly recognised by the ECJ as fundamental principles of EU legal order.

The third category encompasses principles derived from the express provisions of the EU founding Treaties (the concept of Union preference, the principle of subsidiarity, proportionality, non-discrimination).[89] Undeniably, these principles constitute the core of the "fundamental acquis" and must be preserved and built upon.

The acceptance of EU general principles as part of the "fundamental acquis" is founded on their seminal standing within the EU legal order. It is acknowledged that EU general principles are equivalent to EU primary law and are superior to EU secondary legislation. This is because acts adopted by EU institutions are subject to review on grounds of compatibility with EU general principles which derives from their character as constitutional principles emanating from the rule of law (respect to fundamental rights, equality, proportionality, and legal certainty). An international agreement which infringes on a general principle of EU law may not enter into force unless the procedure for the amendment of the founding Treaties provided in Article 48 TEU has been followed.

To be considered a part of the "fundamental acquis", EU general principles must be either formalised in the founding Treaties or/and regarded by the ECJ as "fundamental principles" of the EU legal order. EU general principles that fall within this category may be named principles of "unamendable character", and

---

88 P. Leino, R. Petrov, "Between 'Common Values' and Competing Universals: The Promotion of the EU's Common Values through the European Neighbourhood Policy", 15(5) ELJ, 654-671 (2009).

89 This relates to different provisions in different parts of the TEU. Case 5/67 *Beus v. Hauptzollamt München* [1968] ECR 83.

may consequently form the "internal constitution" of the EU legal framework. As a result, the "unamendable principles" may not be repealed in full or in part without altering the system enshrined in the founding treaties "in such a way that the legal order would lose its basic characteristic of a "Community based on the rule of law"".[90] The principles of "unamendable character" could be considered as "supra-constitutional" in their nature and, therefore, should be considered beyond any further revision.[91] The latest snapshot of the fundamental EU general principles is enshrined in the Treaty of Lisbon which adds very little to the list of the fundamental EU general principles already formalised in the EU founding treaties. By the way, the failed Draft EU Constitutional Treaty contained formal references to the principles of supremacy of EU law and doctrines of direct effect. None of these provisions which directly or indirectly elevate the supranational standing of the EU could be found in the Lisbon Treaty. However, the ECJ may develop new fundamental EU general principles based on the new objectives of the EU specified in Articles 3 and 4 TEU. In any case, the Lisbon Treaty as well as the other EU founding Treaties do not consider the fundamental EU general principles a formal category.

We propose that the following provisions and practices which characterise and distinguish the supranational EU legal order should are considered principles of "unamendable" character":

The principle of sincere cooperation/effectiveness is based on Article 4(3) TEU and is recognised by the ECJ as a general principle of the EU legal order.[92] This principle has been regarded by Pescatore as the "very soul of legal rules".[93] The principle of sincere cooperation/effectiveness obliges Member States to undertake all appropriate measures, whether general or particular, to ensure the fulfilment of obligations arising from the EU founding Treaties or actions of the EU institutions and to assist each other in carrying out tasks which flow from the EU founding Treaties. Hence, this principle facilitates the achievement of EU objectives. It imposes on EU institutions reciprocal duties of sincere cooperation with Member States (disclosure of documents to Member States national courts, quick

90   *Supra note* 4, at 1113.
91   Opinion 1/91 on the EEA [1991] ECR I-6079, at 71. In Case 43/75 *Defrenne v. Sabena* [1976] ECR 455, at 58 the ECJ stated that, apart from exceptions expressly recognised in the Treaty itself, the EC Treaty "can only be modified by means of the amendment procedure carried out in accordance with Article 236".
92   Jointed Cases C-36-37/97 *Hilmar Kellinghusen v. Amt für Land-und Wasserwirtschaft Kiel and Ernst-Detlef Ketelsen v. Amt für Land-und Wasserwirtschaft Husum* [1998] ECR I-6337.
93   P. Pescatore, "The Doctrine of "Direct Effect": An Infant Disease of Community Law" 8 ELRev 135-155 (1983). Also see fundamental contribution by J. Temple Lang, "The duties of cooperation of national authorities and courts under Article 10 EC: Two more reflections", 26 ELR 84-93 (2001).

response to formal requests from a Member State). The ECJ has frequently applied the principle of sincere cooperation/effectiveness to justify the application of new principles and concepts (direct effect, the duty of interpretation and the Member States liability for failure to implement EU laws into national legal systems).[94]

The principle of non-discrimination has repeatedly been considered by the ECJ as one of the fundamental principles of EU law.[95] According to Article 3(3) TEU and Article 10 TFEU the principle of non-discrimination prohibits "any discrimination on the grounds of nationality". Firstly, this principle bans any form of discriminative treatment of EU nationals in the free movement of workers, the freedom of enterprise and the freedom to provide services.[96] However, the principle of non-discrimination is not breached by differences existing between the laws of the Member States "as long as they affect all persons subject to them in accordance with objective criteria and without regard to their nationality".[97] Secondly, Article 10 TFEU provides that the Council may take appropriate action to combat discrimination based on sex, racial or ethnic origin, religion or belief, disability, age or sexual orientation. Thirdly, in accordance with Article 110 TFEU the principle of non-discrimination prohibits any discrimination in the context of the taxation of goods.[98] Thus, it prevents the discriminative taxation of similar or competing products where the category of goods carrying the higher rate is composed largely or exclusively of imported goods. Fourthly, Article 157

---

[94] Supra note 80, at 308. Also see E. Neframi, "The Duty of Loyalty: Rethinking its Scope through its Application in the Field of EU External Relations", 47 CML Rev. 323–359 (2010).
[95] See Case 117/76 and 16/77 *Ruckdeschel v HZA Hamburg-St Annen* [1977] ECR 1753, at 1769, Case C-13/94 *P v S and Cornwall County Council* [1996] ECR I-2143. Besides, the ECJ referred to the principle of equality of treatment that is not limited to nationality, which is binding on the EC institutions (Case C-37/89 *Weiser v Caisse Nationale des Barreaux Français* [1990] ECR I-2395) and described it as a "fundamental right". For comprehensive academic overview see M. Bell, *Anti-discrimination law and the European Union* (Oxford University Press, 2002).
[96] Case 186/87 *Cowan v Trésor public* [1989] ECR 195, Cases 286/82 and 26/83 *Luisi and Carbone* [1984] ECR 377, Case 293/83 *Cravier v City of Liège* [1985] ECR 593, Case C-47/93 *Commission v Belgium* [1994] I-ECR 1593.
[97] J. Usher, *General Principles of EC Law* (London and New York, Longman 1998) at 20.
[98] The first paragraph of Article 110 TFEU states that "no Member State shall impose, directly or indirectly, on the products of other Member States any internal taxation of any kind in excess of that imposed directly or indirectly on similar domestic products". The second paragraph of this Article states that "no Member State shall impose on the products of other Member States any internal taxation of such a nature as to afford indirect protection to other products". For the differences on consequences on applying these TFEU provisions see Case 27/67 *Fink-Frucht v HZA München-Landsbergerstrasse* [1968] ECR 223. Article 110 TFEU prohibits discrimination against imported and exported goods (Case 142/77 *Statenskontrol v Larsen* [1978] ECR 1543).

TFEU provides for the abolition of gender discrimination by establishing the principle of equal pay for male and female workers for equal work or work of equal value. Besides, Article 157(3) TFEU means the European Parliament and the Council ensures "the application of the principle of equal opportunities and equal treatment of men and women in matters of employment and occupation".[99] Fifthly, Article 40(2) TFEU prohibits any discrimination between producers or consumers within the EU in the common organisation of agricultural markets.[100] In general, the ECJ has considered the principle of non-discrimination to be of a general nature and extended its application to other categories of economic operators which are subject to the common organisation of the EU Internal Market.[101]

The principle of protection of fundamental rights and democracy[102] was acknowledged by the ECJ as the "integral part of the general principles of law protected by the Court of Justice".[103] According Article 6 TEU the EU Charter of Fundamental Rights acquires the same legal value as the EU founding Treaties. It implies the extension of the ECJ competence to rule on human rights issues. Apart from human rights provisions in international treaties to which the EU and the Member States are signatories, this principle provides the application of international conventions and treaties not signed by the EU. For example, the ECJ unequivocally endorsed the ECHR as part of the EU legal order.[104] Besides, Article 6(3) TEU manifestly commits the EU to respect fundamental rights guaranteed by the ECHR as general principles of EU law, as they result from constitutional traditions common to the Member States. In case of a serious and persistent breach of principles mentioned in Article 6(3) TEU, a Member State may be suspended of certain rights, including the voting rights of a representative of this Member State in the Council (Article 7(2) TEU). The Lisbon Treaty promulgates the need for the reformed EU to accede to the ECHR in as far as it does not hin-

---

99 Case 32/71 *Sabbatini v European Parliament* [1972] ECR 345, Case C-409/95 *Marshall v Land Nordrhein Westfalen* [1997] ECR *I-6363,* Case C-13/94 *P v S and Cornwall County Council* [1996] ECR I-2143.
100 It targets the regulation of prices, aids the production and marketing of various products, storage and carryover arrangements and common machinery for stabilising imports and exports. For an example of discrimination see Case 309/89 *Codorniu v Council* [1994] ECR I-1853.
101 Case C-280/93 *Germany v Council* [1994] ECR I-4973.
102 The Commission considers that "the principles of liberty, democracy, respect for human rights and fundamental freedoms and of the rule of law form part of the common heritage of the peoples of the States brought together in the European Union and constitute therefore essential elements of membership of the said Union" (O.J. 1994, C241/3).
103 Case 11/70 *Internationale Handelsgesellschaft v. Einfuhr-und Vorratsstelle Getreide* [1970] ECR 1125 at 4. The first acceptance of fundamental rights as part of EC law by the ECJ was in Case 29/69 *Stauder v Ulm* [1969] ECR 419.
104 For example see Case 136/79 *National Panasonic v. Commission* [1980] ECR 2033.

der EU competencies.[105] Furthermore, the Lisbon Treaty strengthens the status of fundamental rights guaranteed by the ECHR and formally recognises them as general principles of EU law but only in case if they result from the constitutional traditions common to the Member States. The legality of EU acts[106] and implementing measures by the Member States[107] may be questioned if they conflict with the need to protect fundamental human rights in the EU. The principle of protection of fundamental rights has engendered other principles that have been considered as general principles in EU legal order. Among them are the principles of fair *legal process*[108] and of *national identity*.[109]

The principle of rule of law[110] is regarded by the EU alongside human rights, democracy, good governance and transparency as one of the "core values embraced by the EU and its Member States".[111] Article 6(1) TEU explicitly designates the rule of law into the foundation of the whole EU. Furthermore, the ECJ has already acknowledged the whole "Community based on the rule of law".[112] The EU institutions are explicit in regarding the rule of law as a "fundamental principle of any democratic system seeking to foster and promote rights, whether civil and political or economic, social and cultural. This entails means of recourse enabling individual citizens to defend their rights. The principle of placing limitations on the power of the State is best served by a representative government drawing its authority from the sovereignty of the people".[113] The Treaty

---

105 Article 6(2) TEU.
106 Opinion 2/94 [1994] ECR I-1759, at 34.
107 Case 5/88 *Hubert Wachauf v. Federal Republic of Germany* [1989] ECR 2609, at 19.
108 Case C-185/95P *Baustahlgewebe GmbH v Commission* [1998] ECR I-8417.
109 See the Declaration on European Identity adopted by the Heads of State and Government at the Summit in Copenhagen on 14 15 December 1973 (EC Bull. 1973 12, 130). The Commission tends to refer to the principle of European identity in almost all its Opinions on the applications for accession to the EU.
110 For more on this principle see the report by Prof. Marise Cremona "Regional Integration and the Rule of Law: Some Issues and Options" at the Conference on Regional Integration and Trade in the Development Agenda on 31 May – 1 June 2001, the Brookings Institution, Washington D.C. Also see K. Lenaerts, "The Rule of Law and the Coherence of the Judicial System of the European Union", 44 CML Rev. 1625-1659 (2007).
111 Common Strategy of the EU on the Mediterranean Region on 19-20 June 2000 (O.J. L 183).
112 Case 294/83 *"les Verts" v European Parliament*, [1986] ECR 1339.
113 As clarified by the Commission this principle implies: "a) a legislature respecting and giving full effect to human rights and fundamental freedoms; b) an independent judiciary; c) effective and accessible means of legal recourse; d) a legal system guaranteeing equality before the law; e) a prison system respecting the human person; f) a police force at the service of the law; g) an effective executive enforcing the law and capable of establishing the social and economic conditions necessary for life in society". See the Commission Communication of 12 March 1998 on Democratisation, the rule of law, respect for human rights and good governance: the challenges of the partnership between the European Union and the ACP (COM (1998) 146, at 4).

of Nice elevates the principle of the rule of law to one of the EU external objectives.[114] The Lisbon Treaty and the EU Charter on Fundamental Rights list the rule of law as one of the fundamental EU values, but fail to provide an explicit explanation of its meaning and scope.[115]

The principles of transparency and accountability of EU institutions have occupied a very important place in the EU legal order following their insertion into Article 15 TFEU, and following the elaboration of these principles by the ECJ.[116] These principles bestow an explicit right on any natural or legal person residing or having their registered office in a Member State to access European Parliament, Council or Commission documents. All limits on the access to information must be legitimised in due procedure. Furthermore, Article 1 TEU enshrines the seminal importance of transparency and accountability in the EU system by requiring decisions to be taken "as openly as possible and closely as possibly to the citizen". The European Ombudsman clarifies that "transparency requires not only that documents should be publicly available to the maximum extent possible, but also that any denial of access to documents should be justified by rules laid down in advance".[117] The Lisbon Treaty enshrines the principles of transparency and accountability of EU institutions before EU citizens and representatives of civil society. It considers accountability a part of the principle of representative democracy.[118] Unfortunately, the ECJ does not recognise this principle as applicable to Member States to the same extent as to EU institutions.[119] Otherwise, it could complement the list of elements of the acquis communautaire to be adopted in the course of accession.

The principle of legal certainty guarantees that every subject of EU law should be aware of the precise scope of imposed rights and obligations under EU law.[120] Otherwise, a respective EU measure may not be exercised.[121] The principle of legal certainty must be applied in the process of implementation of EU

---

114 Article 212 TFEU provides that economic, financial and technical cooperation measures, including assistance, in particular financial assistance, with third countries other than developing countries. Such measures shall be consistent with the development policy of the Union and shall be carried out within the framework of the principles and objectives of its external action.
115 Article 2 TEU.
116 Prof. Lenaerts calls this principles "trust-enhancing principles of EU law". See K. Lenaerts, "In the Union We Trust": Trust-Enhancing Principles of Community Law", 41 CMLRev, 317-343 (2004).
117 Declaration of the European Ombudsman in its own initiative inquiry into public access to documents (O.J. C44/9, 1998).
118 Article 15 TFEU.
119 Case C-70/95 *Sodemare v Regione Lombardia*, [1997] ECR I-3395.
120 Case C-233/96 *Kingdom v Denmark v Commission* [1998] ECR I-5769.
121 Case C-143/93 *Gebroeders van Es Douane Agenten BV v Inspecteur der Invoerrechten en Accijnzen* [1996] ECR I-431.

acts by the Member States which are under obligation to align their own laws to EU standards. Mere administrative practices may be regarded as inadequate for this purpose.[122] The *principle of legitimate expectations* and the *principle of non-retroactivity* have been considered complementary to the principle of legal certainty.[123] The principle of legitimate expectations provides that subjects of EU law should not be frustrated in their expectations by the application of EU rules.[124] This principle may be invoked against EU rules only where an EU rule has previously given rise to a legitimate reasonable expectation.[125] In particular, it operates to protect individuals where their rights provided by EU or Member States measures have been aggravated.[126] There are certain limits to the principle of legitimate expectations. It was stated by the ECJ that traders may not rely on this principle to protect them from changes in EU legal regimes.[127] Furthermore, the principle of legitimate expectations may not be relied upon to protect against a precise or unambiguous provision of EU law,[128] by undertaking that it has committed a manifest infringement of the rules in force.[129] The principle of non-retroactivity precludes a secondary legislation measure from taking effect before its publication.[130] However, the ECJ stated that in exceptional cases a secondary legislation measure could take effect before its publication "where the purpose to be achieved so demands and where the legitimate expectations of those concerned are duly respected".[131]

The principles governing Member States' *liability in damages* for breach of EU law,[132] and the principle of *EU's liability for any damage* caused by its institutions or by its servants in the performance of their duties in accordance with

---

122 Case 102/79 *Commission v Belgium* [1980] ECR 1473.
123 Case C-63/93 *Duff and Others v Minister for Agriculture and Food, Ireland, and the Attorney-General* [1996] ECR I-569.
124 A. Arnull / A. Dashwood / M. Ross / D. Wyatt, *European Union Law* (4th Ed. London: Sweet & Maxwell 2000) at 137.
125 Case C-375/96 *Galileo Zaninotto v Ispettorato Centrale* [1998] ECR I-6629. The principle of legitimate expectations does not cover speculative profit. Case 2/75 *EVGF v Mackprang* [1975] ECR 607.
126 Case C-174/89 *Hoche v. Bundesanstalt für landwirtschaftliche Marktordnung* [1990] ECR I-2681.
127 Case 230/78 *Eridania v. Minister for Agriculture and Foresty* [1979] ECR 2749.
128 Case 316/86 *Firma P. Krücken* [1988] ECR 2213 and Jointed Cases C-31-44/91 *SpA Alois Lageder and others* [1993] ECR I-1761.
129 Case 67/84 *Sideradria v Commission* [1985] ECR 3983.
130 Case 63/83 *R v Kirk* [1984] ECR 2689.
131 Case 99/78 *Weingut Gustav Decker KG v. Hauptozollamt Landau* [1979] ECR 101, at 111.
132 Jointed Cases C-6 and C-9/90 *Francovich* [1991] ECR I-5357. Jointed Cases C-43 and C-48/93 *Brasserie du Pècheur v. Germany and the Queen v. Secretary of State for Transport, ex parte Factortame Ltd.*[1996] ECR I-1029.

Article 340 TFEU, are intrinsic to the EU legal order. In this instance the EU suffers liability for any damage caused by EU administrative action or a legislative measure in the occurrence of a "sufficiently flagrant violation of a superior rule of law for the protection of the individual".[133] In the former case a Member State is liable for damages caused to an individual for failure to transpose an EU act into national law,[134] or for a breach of EU law as a result of action by the national legislature.[135]

Principles that protect the *procedural rights and privacy* of subjects of EU legal order have been successfully imported by the ECJ from the Member States' legal systems. Based on constitutional traditions common to the Member States, *the principle of effective judicial protection* deprives a Member State or competent authority of any chance to undermine rights conferred on any individual by EU acts.[136] The second major procedural principle is *the right of defence*. Under the ambit of this principle, the ECJ recognised that it is necessary not only to protect the right of defence in administrative procedures which might lead to the imposition of penalties, but also to prevent the impairment of those rights during preliminary inquiry procedures.[137] The right of defence encompasses a range of other procedural principles which were formulated by the ECJ and regarded as general principles of EU law. One of them is the *principle of natural justice* which guarantees an individual's right to make known his views if his interests are affected by EU law.[138] *The duty to give reasons* envisages that a person whose rights under EU law are adversely affected by a decision must be informed of the reasons of such decision.[139] *The right to due process* enables such decisions and reasons to be challenged.[140] No penalty, even one of a non-criminal nature, unless it has a clear and unambiguous legal basis, may be imposed on a subject of EU law.[141] A subject of EU law may not be tried more than once for the same crime.[142] *The right to be heard*[143] means that public servants

---

133 Case C-146/91 *Zuckerfabrik Schöppenstedt* [1994] ECR I-4199, at 58.
134 Jointed Cases C-178, C-179, C-188 to C-190/94 *Dillenkofer and Others v. Federal Republic of Germany* [1996] ECR I-4845.
135 Joint Cases C-46/93 and C-48/93, *Brasserie du Pecheur v. Germany and The Queen v. Secretary of State for Transport, ex-p Factorame* [1996] ECR I-1029.
136 Case 222/84 *Johnston v Chief Constable of the RUC* [1986] ECR 1651.
137 For example, the right of undertaking to avoid the provision of answers which might involve an admission of an infringement and consequent penalties. Case C-374/87 *Orkem v Commission* [1989] ECR 3283, at 34-35.
138 Case 17/74 *Transocean Marine Paint Association* (1974) ECR 1064.
139 Case 222/86 *UNECTEF v Heylens* [1987] ECR 4097.
140 Case 222/84 *Johnson v Chief Costable of the Royal Ulster Constabulary* [1986] ECR 1651.
141 Case 117/83 *Karl Könecke GmbH v Bundesanstalt für landwirtschaftliche Marktordung* [1984] ECR 3291.
142 Cases 18 and 35 /65 *Gutmann v EAEC Commission* [1966] ECR 103.

and individuals must have the opportunity to reply to allegations before any disciplinary decision is made on them. The ECJ has treated the right to be heard as a fundamental principle which must be guaranteed even in the absence of specific rights.[144] *The right of legal professional privilege* is inherent to the right of defence and must be respected by the EU institutions and the Member States.[145] Another fundamental EU principle is the protection of *the right of privacy*.[146] However, this right relates only to an individual and not to a business undertaking. Any intervention into the right of privacy should not be arbitrary or disproportionate.

The ECJ referred to the *principle of property rights protection* as a general principle of EU law.[147] Article 345 TFEU provides "this Treaty shall in no way prejudice the rules for Member States governing the system of property ownership". The ECJ confirmed that property rights within the EU are subject to inherent obligations, to social requirements, and the requirements for the common good. Hence, property rights and the freedom to carry out business activities may be subjected to restrictive measures taken by relevant authorities in the general interest of the EU. This means that such restrictive measures must comply with the objectives of the EU policies, and that they must to be proportionate to the result they seek to achieve.[148] Thus, an appropriate balance must always be main-

---

143 Case 32/62 *Alvis v. Council* [1963] ECR 49, at 55.
144 Case C-85/87 *Dow Benelux v Commission* [1989] ECR 3137. The ECJ stated that the right to be heard applies in all proceedings initiated against a person which are liable to culminate in a measure adversely affecting that person. Otherwise, the EU measure may be annulled (Case C-135/92 *Fiscano v Commission* [1994] ECR I-2885).
145 The ECJ has considered that the right of protection of written communication between a lawyer and his client is subject to two conditions: the communications must be made "for the purpose and in the interest of the client's rights of defence" and "they must emanate from independent lawyers, that is to say, lawyers who are not bound to the client by a relationship of employment" (Case 155/79 *AM & S Europe v Commission* [1982] ECR 1575).
146 For instance, the inviolability of the home was considered as breach of fundamental rights and a principle common to all the Member States (Cases 46/87 and 227/88 *Hoechst v Commission* [1989] ECR 2859).
147 Case 44/79 *Hauer v Land Rheinland – Pfalz* [1979] ECR 3727. See also Case C-265/87 *Schräder v. Hauptzollamt Gronau* [1989] ECR 2237. Therein the ECJ recognised the right of property and the freedom to pursue a trade or profession as a general principle of EC law, though they must be viewed in light of the social function of the activities protected thereunder. Therefore, these rights may be restricted in the context of the common organisation of the market. Usher believes that the concept of the "very substance" of a property right corresponds to the "specific subject-matter" of a property right in intellectual property law.
148 For instance, the ECJ can order the payment of compensation to protect the right of property. See Case C-38/94 *The Queen v. Minister of Agriculture, Fisheries and Food, ex parte Country Land-owners Association* [1995] ECR I-3875.

tained between the protection of the general interests of the EU and the requirements of the protection for the individual's property rights.[149]

The principles of the EU Internal Market were acknowledged by the ECJ as fundamental for the functioning of the EU Internal Market. Firstly, this includes the principle of free market which envisages the proper functioning of the four fundamental freedoms within the EU Internal Market (free movement of goods, free movement of workers, services, and capital). Secondly, this also includes the principles developed by the ECJ and enshrined in EU legislation, in particular: the principle of "home country control" (insurance, investment, banking, and deposit guarantee), as well as the principle of mutual recognition (free movement of goods, services, persons, freedom of establishment). Thirdly, the principle of "Union preference" which justifies the more favourable treatment of EU products in comparison to those from third countries, depending on the Member State into which products are imported.[150]

1.4.2.4. Doctrines and concepts of EU law and the "fundamental acquis"

The "fundamental acquis" embraces a set of doctrines and concepts developed by the ECJ to expand the scope of application of the EU founding Treaties. These concepts and doctrines have steadily penetrated into the legal systems of the Member States and must consequently be applied by national courts. Firstly, these are the concepts of the *supremacy* and *direct effect* of EU law, which form the "essential characteristics of the Community legal order".[151] The concept of direct effect enables an individual to rely on specific provisions of either EU primary or secondary legislation before his domestic courts. The general test for considering which provision of EU legislation may have direct effect has been

---

149 Case C-84/95 *Bosphorus Hava Yollari Tourism ve Ticaret AS v. Minister for Transport and the Attorney General* [1996] ECR I-3953. The right of property protection does not cover the right to dispose, for profit, of an advantage such as reference quantities allocated in the context of the common organisation of a market which does not derive from the assets or occupational activity of the person concerned (Case C-44/89 *Gorg von Deetzen v. Hauptzollamt Oldenburg (II)* [1991] ECR I-5119, at 27).
150 The principle of "Union preference" the ECJ regarded this principle as one of the underlying principles of the EU in Case 5/67 *Beus v. HZA München* [1968] ECR 83, Case 55/75 *Balkan v. HZA Berlin-Packhof* [1976] ECR 11, Case 236/84 *Malt v HZA Düsseldorf* [1986] ECR 1923, Case C-353/92 *Creece v Council* [1994] ECR I-3411. For academic overview see P. Oliver, W.-H. Roth, "The Internal Market and the Four Freedoms" 41 CML Rev. 407-441 (2004).
151 Opinion 1/91 on the EEA [1991] ECR I-6079, at 21.

developed by the ECJ in a set of seminal cases.[152] Again, the concept of supremacy of EU law over conflicting laws of the Member States, as specified by the ECJ in the cases *Costa v. ENEL*[153] and *Simmental,*[154] constitutes the integral part of the EU legal system. According to the concept of supremacy, Member States' laws that conflict with supreme EU provisions must not be applied or even repealed.[155] Furthermore, certain provisions of EU law prevail even over the Member States constitutions. Otherwise, if national laws were to override conflicting EU laws, this would deprive the whole EU legal order of its supranational character. In contrast to the Draft EU Constitutional Treaty the Lisbon Treaty did not endorse the principle of supremacy of EU law as part of the EU legal order.[156] The second concept is *the duty of interpretation* of Member States laws in accordance with obligations arising under EU law and in conformity with the fundamental provisions and principles of EU law (known as the "indirect effect" of EU law). The duty of interpretation commits the Member States to apply and to interpret their national laws in the light of the wording and purpose of an EU measure, in order to achieve the result referred to in the EU founding Treaties.[157] The third doctrine is the *Member States' liability for the improper implementation or breach of EU acts.*[158] This doctrine protects individuals' rights bestowed upon them by EU law, though these rights may not satisfy the requirements of the direct effect test. The ECJ recognised the concept of Member States' liability as inherent to the objectives of the EU founding Treaties, as it follows from the principle of effectiveness of EU law in Article 4(3) TEU.[159] After the Lisbon Treaty entered into force the principle of supremacy of EU law as

---

152 For the direct effect of EU primary law see Case *Van Gend en Loos v. Nederlandse Administratie der Belastingen* [1963], CMLR 105. For the direct effect of EU secondary legislation see Case 9/70 *Grad v. Finganzamt Traunstein* [1970] ECR 825 and Case C-152/84 *Marshall v. Sauthampton and South West Hampshire Area Health Authority* [1986] ECR 723.
153 Case 6/64 [1964] ECR 585.
154 Case 106/77, *Amministrazione delle Finanze dello Stato v. Simmental* [1978] ECR 629.
155 Jointed Cases C-43 and C-48/93 *Brasserie du Pècheur v. Germany and the Queen v. Secretary of State for Transport, ex parte Factortame Ltd.*[1996] ECR I-1029 and Case 167/73, *Commission v. France* [1974] ECR 359.
156 Article I-6 Draft EU Constitutional Treaty stated that "[t]he Constitution and law adopted by the institutions of the Union in exercising competences conferred on it shall have primacy over the law of the Member States".
157 Case 14/83 *Von Colson v. Land Nordrhein – Westfalen* [1984] ECR 1891. Also see Case C-106/89, *Mareleasing SA v. La Comercial Internacional de Alimentacion SA* [1992] 1CMLR 305.
158 Jointed Cases C-6 and C-9/90 *Francovich v. Italy* [1991] ECR I-5357.
159 Case C-213/89, *R v. Secretary of State for Transport, ex parte Factortame* [1990] ECR I-2433.

well as other doctrines and concepts of EU law developed by the ECJ continue to depend upon the ECJ and follow from the ECJ case law.

1.4.2.5. "Institutional acquis" and the "fundamental acquis"

We argue that EU institutional and procedural rules which are referred to as the "institutional acquis" also belong to the ambit of "fundamental acquis". Of course, "institutional acquis" rules are subject to revision and possible modification by the Member States, and therefore may not be regarded as principles of "unamendable character". However, the "institutional acquis" articulates the edifice of the EU institutional framework which distinguishes the EU from other international organisations (for instance, the outstanding competence of the ECJ). Therefore, the "institutional acquis" represents a "snapshot" of the EU institutional balance, which must be preserved in case of the revision of the entire EU legal order.

There are some examples of the rules and principles that belong to the "institutional acquis":

Principles of *proportionality* and *subsidiarity* govern the relations between EU institutions and Member States' authorities. In accordance with Articles 5(1) and 5(4) TEU, the principle of proportionality ensures that "the content and form of Union action shall not exceed what is necessary to achieve the objectives of the Treaties". This means that the legitimacy of any measure taken at EU or national level may be questioned pursuant to EU rules.[160] The proportionality principle may be applied to actions of Member States in the context of Articles 36, 45 (3) and (4) TFEU. The principle of subsidiarity is enshrined in Article 5 5(1) TEU and applied in areas which do not fall within the EU exclusive competence. This principle may be applied "only if and insofar as the objectives of the proposed action cannot be sufficiently achieved by the Member States and can therefore, by reason of the scale or effects of the proposed action, be better achieved by the Community". According to the Protocol on Subsidiarity and Proportionality the

---

160 The ECJ stated that "[t]he principle of proportionality...requires that measures adopted by Community institutions do not exceed the limits of what is appropriate and necessary in order to attain the objectives legitimately pursued by the legislation in question; when there is a choice between several appropriate measures recourse must be had to the least onerous, and the disadvantages caused are not to be disproportionate to the aims pursued". See Case C-331/88 *R v Minister of Agriculture, Fisheries and Food and the Secretary of State for Health, ex p. Fedesa* [1990] ECR I-4023. For academic overview of the principle see N. Emiliou, *The Principle of Proportionality in European Law* (Kluwer, 1996). S. Prechal, "Free Movement and Procedural Requirements: Proportionality Reconsidered" 35(3) LIEI 201-216 (2008).

principle of subsidiarity does not question the powers conferred on the EU, but provides a guide as to how those powers must be exercised. As a dynamic concept, subsidiarity should be applied in the light of the objectives set out in the EU founding Treaties.[161] The principle of subsidiarity is essential for the interpretation of EU acts, since the EU institutions have taken it into account in the process of drafting EU legislation. The ECJ may intervene and annul any EU act issued by an EU institution beyond its discretion of competence.[162]

Rules which govern relations between the EU institutions in the framework of the decision-making process, in particular when the Member States have lost their absolute powers, belong to the "institutional acquis". For instance, when the Council wishes to alter a Commission proposal, this should be on the basis of unanimity, and that is of equal importance as the principle that a qualified majority vote is required in order to adopt such a proposal.[163]

The rule of specific representation of the Union interest by the Commissioners as it enshrined in Article 245 TFEU.

The duty of loyal or sincere cooperation binds all EU institutions to assist the EU in achieving its objectives.[164]

The principle of "compromise" in conciliation committee meetings between the Council and the European Parliament, which is necessary for the good functioning of the Communities and the EU.

1.4.2.6. Concluding remarks

To conclude, we consider that the "fundamental acquis" is a pure legal category that contains elements which have a normative character and which consequently have a binding effect upon all subjects of EU law. In general, the "fundamental acquis" must be perceived as an unwritten EU Constitution[165] which consists of binding rules of a superior rank applicable to the Member States. As we have

---

161 EC Bull 12, 1992, p. 9.
162 On critics of the principle of subsidiarity see G. Davies, "Subsidiarity: the Wrong Idea, In the Wrong Place, at the Wrong Time" 43 CML Rev. 63-84 (2006).
163 For example, C. Delcourt argues that once the Commission looses its exclusive power of legislative initiative in accordance with Article 250(1) EC it the role of the Commission would be reduced to that of a secretariat and, subsequently, the EU would become a model classic international organisation. *Supra note* 6, at 842-845.
164 Case 2/88, *J.J. Zwartveld and Others*, [1990] ECR 3365. See also Case C-65/93 *Parliament v Council* [1995] ECR I-643.
165 Commentators describe the "fundamental acquis" as "intangible constitutional principles of substantive law", "Witschafftsverfassung", or "Economic constitution". For instance see M. P. Maduro, "Reforming The Market or the State? Article 30 and the European Constitution: Economic Freedom and Political Rights" 3(1) ELJ 55-82 (1997).

seen, the "fundamental acquis" did not get any significant enhancement in the Lisbon Treaty, and, therefore, does not formally occupy the apex of the hierarchy of sources of EU law. In general, the "fundamental acquis" could be distinguished by several characteristics. First, it is unequivocally associated with the EU legal order, which is the body of laws encompassing the transferred sovereign rights of the Member States. Second, the "fundamental acquis" is based exclusively on the binding "supranational" provisions of the EU founding Treaties which form "the internal constitution of the Community" and concern "the very foundations of the Community" (for instance Articles 2 and 4 TEU, Articles 18, 34, 106 TFEU). Third, we suggest that the "fundamental acquis" is inextricably linked to the EU founding treaties' objectives, since they test the legitimacy of EU primary and secondary legislation and of the Member States' laws. Fourth, the "fundamental acquis" embraces EU secondary legislation (regulations, directives, and decisions) issued within competencies that have been transferred by the Member States to the supranational EU. Fifth, EU general principles form the entire framework of the "fundamental acquis". Those principles must be formalised in the EU founding Treaties or/and be regarded by the ECJ as "fundamental principles" of the EU legal order. The "fundamental acquis" comprises the EU general principles, doctrines and concepts developed by the ECJ, as well as and institutional and procedural rules applied within the EU legal order which are referred to as the "institutional acquis". This represents the "snapshot" of the achieved EU institutional balance that likely to be preserved in case of the revision of the entire EU legal order. Last but not least, the "fundamental acquis" covers seminal judgments of the ECJ (*Van Gend en Loos, Cassis,* and others) that provide the interpretation of the EU founding Treaties provisions, and which thereby fill in considerable lacunas in its application. The significance of such rulings justifies their later incorporation into the EU founding Treaties.

Finally, we argue that the "fundamental acquis" contains general, institutional and procedural provisions which are liable to become supreme provisions reflecting the goals of the EU and the content of the EU policies. Consequently, they better to be preserved during potential future constitutional revision of the EU legal order and must be maintained in full and respected throughout the further EU progress.[166]

---

166 C. Gialdino emphasises that "there is a prior need to limit and define as precisely as possible the scope of the "fundamental acquis" in order to be able to use the notion as a limit to the power to revise the treaties. TEU has sanctioned the acquis at a constitutional level but the technique of annexing protocols has laid bare its inherent weakness; the ECJ is weak in defending the acquis and did not identified the correct hierarchy of values and "EC constitutional charter". *Supra note* 4, at 1121.

1.4.3. International law and the acquis communautaire

The notion "acquis communautaire" covers various international law sources that fall within the realm of EU law. British academic Trevor Hartley regards international law as an "anomalous source of Community law" owing to its origin outside the EU legal order.[167] Nevertheless, the ECJ has explicitly accepted that certain provisions and rules of international law comprise the "integral part of Community law".[168] The Lisbon Treaty confirms the EU's strong commitment to contribute to "the strict observance and the development of international law, including respect for the principles of the United Nations Charter".[169]

1.4.3.1. International peremptory norms jus cogens, general principles of international public law and the acquis communautaire

International peremptory norms *jus cogens* and general principles of international public law have been always respected in EU external policy and in the Member States' foreign affairs. However, the acceptance of international peremptory norms and general principles of international law as part of the acquis communautaire has neither been enunciated nor rejected by the EU institutions. For instance, the TEU as amended by the Lisbon Treaty implicitly prioritises certain principles of international law and consider them binding on the Member States.[170] Furthermore, the Preamble of the EU Charter of Fundamental Rights reaffirms these rights, as they result from "international obligations common to the Member States". However, in the *Kadi* case the ECJ has ruled out the primacy of the UN Charter and the UN Security Council's binding resolutions over the EU "fundamental acquis" and one more time confirmed the autonomous character of the EU legal order.[171] To avoid any explicit admittance of the bind-

---

167 *Supra note* 59, at 155.
168 Case 181/73 *Haegeman v. Belgium* [1974] ECR 449, at 5.
169 Articles 3(5) TEU.
170 These are: principles of the UN Charter (Article 3(5) TEU; Article 21(1) TEU, Article 21(2) TEU); principles of the Helsinki Final Act and the objective of the Paris Charter (Article 21(2) TEU); principles of international cooperation, democracy, rule of law, respect for human rights and fundamental freedoms (Articles 2, 3(5), 21(1), 21(2) TEU); fundamental rights, as guaranteed by the ECHR as they result from the constitutional traditions common to the Member States, as general principles of EC law (Article 6(2) TEU; Article 6(3) TEU).
171 Joint Cases C-402/05 and C-415/05 *Ahmed Ali Yusuf and Al Barakaat International Foundation v. Council and Commission; Yassin Abdullah Kadi v. Council and Commission.* [2008] ECR I-6351. For detailed analysis see N. Lavranos, *Joint Cases C-402/05P, Ahmed Ali Yusuf and Al Barakaat International Foundation v. Council and Commission;*

ing standing of general principles of international law in the EU legal order, the EU seems to employ the notion "common values", thereby leaving significant discretion to its institutions to decide on their scope.[172] Nevertheless, one can barely question the prominent – though not formalised – standing of general principles of international law in the EU legal order.

EU acts could potentially be considered invalid if they are contrary to "a rule of international law".[173] In accordance with Article 38 of the International Court of Justice (ICJ) Statute, this notion covers international agreements, international customary law and general principles of international law. Yet the ECJ has never considered an EU measure invalid on the grounds that it is contrary to "a rule of international law". Furthermore, the ECJ is consistent in recognising international customary law and general principles of international law as part of the EU legal order though without recognising these rules as directly effective.[174] Eventually, the ECJ might do so, especially in light of recent extensive expansion of the EU's external competence and the subsequent elevation of the EU role as an international actor on the acquisition of a single legal personality after the Lisbon Treaty came into force.

1.4.3.2. International agreements and the acquis communautaire

The Member States are bound by the commitments in the EU exclusive and mixed agreements with third countries.[175] In accordance with Article 216(2) TFEU "agreements concluded by the Union are binding upon the institutions of

---

Case C-415/05, *Yassin Abdullah Kadi v. Council and Commission*, 36(2) LIEI 157-183 (2009).

172 For example, the EU Charter of Fundamental Rights sets out that the "Union is founded on the indivisible, universal values of human dignity, freedom, equality and solidarity". Furthermore, the Lisbon Treaty amends TEU with Article 2, listing among the EU's values: respect of human dignity; freedom; democracy; equality; the rule of law and respect of human rights, including the rights of persons belonging to minorities.

173 For more deliberations on this issue see I. Macleod / I. Hendry / S. Hyett, *The External Relations of the European Communities* (Oxford: Clarendon Press 1996) at 135. Also see Case C-162/96 *Racke* [1998] ECR I-3641, Case C-84/95 *Bosphorus Hava Yollari Tourism ve Ticaret AS v. Minister for Transport and the Attorney General* [1996] ECR I-3953.

174 Case C-286/90 *Anklegemindigheden v. Poulsen and Diva Navigation* [1992] ECR I-6019, Case T-115/94, *Opel Austria GmbH v. Council*, [1997] ECR II-39, Case C-162/96 *Racken v Hauptzollampt Mainz* [1998] ECR I-3641. More on this issue see Koutrakos P., *EU International Relations Law* (Oxford, Hart Publishing 2006), 244-249.

175 As for the mixed agreements the ECJ ruled out in the Case 12/86 *Demirel v. Stadt Schwäbisch Güdn* [1987] ECR 3719 that Article 310 EC (now Article 217 TFEU) empowered the EU to guarantee commitments towards third countries in all fields covered by the EU founding Treaties.

the Union and on its Member States". Thus, an international treaty, duly concluded by one of the EU, becomes "an integral part of Union law" and "Union legal system" from the date of its entry into force. Consequently, directly effective provisions of those agreements override any conflicting EU measure.[176] Mixed agreements constitute part of the EU legal order only in respect of those provisions of agreements which are within the competence of the EU. The ECJ bears the jurisdiction for the uniform interpretation of both exclusive and mixed agreements, since the effects of agreements concluded by the EU may not vary according to whether their implementation is the responsibility of the EU or of the Member States.[177] The Lisbon Treaty clarified the boundaries of the EU exclusive competence to conclude agreements with third countries in line with the existing ECJ case law[178] and considerably extended the scope of the EU mixed competence to conclude international agreements.[179]

The ECJ treats EU succession agreements that were originally concluded by the Member States but then substituted by the EU as part of the EU legal order.[180] Therefore, they could be treated as part of the acquis communautaire as well. In accordance with Article 351 TFEU, international agreements that do not

---

176 Case 21-4/72 *International Fruit Co NV v Produktaschap voor Groenten en Fruit (№ 3)* [1972] ECR 1219. Case C-280/93, *Germany v. Council (Banana Case)* [1994] ECR I-4973. This rule is applied except if the EU act was intended to give effect to an obligation under the international agreement (Case C-69/89 *Nakajima v Council* [1991] ECR I-2069) and where the EU act already expressly refer to the international agreement (Case 70/87, *Fediol v. Commission* [1989] ECR 1781).
177 Case C-188/91 *Deutsche Shell v. Hauptzollamt Hamburg-Hamburg* [1993] ECR I-363. at para 14. Case 104/81 *Hauptzollamt Mainz v C.A. Kupferberg* [1982] ECR 3641. Case C-61/94 *Commission v. Germany* [1996] ECR I-3969. Case C-13/00 *Commission v. Ireland* [2002] ECR *I-2943*, Case C-239/03 *Commission v France* [2004] ECR I-9325.
178 In accordance with Article 3 TFEU the EU exclusive competence covers: a) customs union; (b) the establishing of the competition rules necessary for the functioning of the internal market; (c) monetary policy for the Member States whose currency is the euro; (d) the conservation of marine biological resources under the common fisheries policy; (e) common commercial policy. Furthermore, the EU has exclusive competence to conclude an international agreement "when its conclusion is provided for in a legislative act of the Union or is necessary to enable the Union to exercise its internal competence".
179 Articles 4-6 TFEU. Also other fields, like readmission of third country nationals (Article 83(3) TFEU).
180 Case 266/81, *SIOT v Ministero delle Finanze* [1983] ECR 731. See also Case 21-4/72 *International Fruit Co NV v Produktaschap voor Groenten en Fruit (№ 3)* [1972] ECR 1219, at para 18. Therein, the ECJ stated that "the Community has assumed the powers previously exercised by Member States in the area governed by the General Agreement, the provisions of that agreement have the effect of binding the Community". See also Case 38/75, *Douaneagent der NV Nederlandse Spoorwegen v Inspecteur der Invoerrechten en Accijzen* [1975] ECR 1439 with regard to the Convention on the Nomenclature for the Classification of Goods in Custom Tariffs and the Convention Establishing the Customs Cooperation.

fall within the EU competence but were concluded by a Member State prior to the EC Treaty (1 January 1958) are not binding either on the EU or on the remaining Member States. However, the EU should not impede Member State's fulfilment of its obligations under these agreements.[181]

Judgments made by a judicial organ competent to settle disputes between the EU and other parties are binding on the ECJ.[182] Decisions of bodies created by the EU external agreements (various "councils" and "committees") constitute part of the acquis communautaire too where they are empowered by the respective agreement to issue binding decisions and provisions of which have clear wording and confer in clear, precise and unconditional terms rights on individuals.[183] Non-binding decisions may have some legal effect as far as they are taken into account in determining the commitments of the parties under the agreement.[184]

ECJ rulings on international agreements are intrinsic to the EU legal order and therefore belong to the acquis communautaire. First, these rulings consider the legality of acts adopted by EU institutions in the process concluding external agreements.[185] Second, these rulings clarify the validity of the acts of EU institutions regarding their compatibility with provisions of international agreements binding on the EU.[186] Third, these rulings ensure the uniform interpretation of the agreement throughout the EU. The ECJ tends to interpret the provisions of international treaties against their object and purpose. Identical wording to the founding treaties does not entail the same interpretation of international agreements.[187]

Acts of Member States' representatives (when those representatives are acting as members of the Council) may be regarded as part of the acquis communautaire if they relate to the functioning of the EU. Some of them are regarded as international agreements and have the same status as subsidiary conventions concluded between the Member States. Others do not have any bearing apart from a political compromise (the "Luxembourg Accords"). Therefore, they may not be considered part of the EU legal system, but may belong to the acquis communautaire as EU "soft law". Finally, acts exercised by the representatives upon a competence conferred jointly on Member States (for example Article 17(1) TEU) and adopted unanimously also belong to the acquis communautaire.

---

181 Case 812/79, *Attorney-General v. Burgoa* [1980] ECR 2961.
182 Opinion 1/91 on the EEA [1991] ECR I-6079, at 39-40.
183 Case C-192/89 *Sevince v. Staatssecretaris van Justitie* [1990] ECR 3461/3501.
184 *Supra note* 59 (Hartley), at 176-181.
185 Case C-268/94 *Portugal v Council* [1996] ECR
186 Case C-280/93 *Germany v. Council* [1994] ECR I-4973.
187 Case 270/80 *Polydor Ltd. V. Harlequin Record Shops* [1982] ECR 329.

1.4.3.3. Concluding remarks

Two points are relevant here. First, the ECJ enjoys considerable power in filtering the sources of international law which may be brought within the domain of the EU legal order, and to the acquis communautaire. The major criterion seemingly employed by the ECJ is the conformance of international law provisions to the EU objectives, while respecting the autonomy of the EU legal order. Therefore, it is quite probable that any provision of international public law more or less compatible with EU objectives may sooner or later be considered part of the "acquis communautaire". The newly refined and extended list of EU objectives in the Lisbon Treaty unequivocally contributes to the adoption of such practice by the ECJ. Second, the acquisition of a single legal personality by the EU brings new challenges to the ECJ's influence over the uniform interpretation of international law sources within the EU. As a result of this, the ECJ already faces certain difficulties in keeping the exclusive nature of the "new legal order" intact from the penetrating influence of international law (for example the influence of the European Court of Human Rights in Strasburg case law on the EU legal system after the projected by the Lisbon Treaty EU's accession to the ECHR).[188]

1.4.4. The scope of the "Union acquis"

1.4.4.1. Elements of the "Union acquis"

The application of the acquis communautaire appears to be inconsistent throughout the EU legal sources. EU documents alternate between the "acquis communautaire" and the "Union acquis".[189] Furthermore, in some cases EU institutions do not clarify to which particular acquis they are referring. Instead, the neutral

---

[188] More on this see Lavranos N., "Protecting European Law from International Law" 15 EFA Rev. 265–282 (2010), Isiksel N., "Fundamental rights in the EU after *Kadi and Al Barakaat*" 16 ELJ 551-577 (2010), Dawes A., and Kunoy B., "Plate tectonics in Luxembourg: The *ménage à trois* between EC law, international law and the European Convention on Human Rights following the UN sanctions cases" 46 CML Rev. 73–104 (2009).

[189] Delcourt has vigilantly traced the inconsistency in application of these terms by the EU institutions. For example, the French version of the Opinions concerning Slovakia (COM (97) 2004 final of 15 July 1997) and Estonia (COM (97) 2006 final of 15 July 1997) at pages 82 and 86 respectively refer to the "acquis de l'Union" while the English version specify the same as "the justice and home affairs (JHA) acquis" (*supra note 6*, at 833). See also the Presidency Conclusions of the European Council of Luxembourg, December 1997 (EU Bull., 12-1997, at.9) where it was referred to the "Union acquis" and the Presidency Conclusions of the European Council of Madrid of December 1995 (EU Bull., 12-1995, at.19) where it was referred to the "acquis communautaire".

term "acquis" is used.[190] Most frequently, the term "Union acquis" can be found in advisory opinions concerning the various accession requests formulated by candidate countries, as well as in regular reports on the accession progress made by these countries. Nevertheless, even in these cases the application of "Union acquis" does not exclude the eventual reference to "acquis communautaire". The Lisbon Treaty provides that the notion "acquis communautaire" should be replaced by "Community or Union acquis" thereby acknowledging the difference between these two notions.[191] Yet there is no definite consensus yet on whether the "Union acquis" scope is broader than, or identical to, the "acquis communautaire".

However, it should be recognised that after the Lisbon Treaty formally came into force the notion "acquis communautaire" should be labelled the "Union acquis" owing to the dismantling of the three-pillar EU structure. Consequently, the "post-Lisbon acquis" carries "communautaire" characteristics to reflect the single-pillar EU structure. In this book, we suggest regarding the "Union acquis" as an overarching category encompassing what has been acquired not only under supranational cooperation but also within intergovernmental cooperation of the Member States. The core part of the "Union acquis" comprises the EU objectives enshrined in Article 3 TEU. These objectives, omitting those implemented at supranational level, determine the legality and boundaries of the EU acts, and the Member States actions within the areas of the intergovernmental cooperation in the TEU concern mainly the need to assert EU identity on the international scene, in particular through the implementation of a common foreign and security policy.

In addition to the sources of the acquis communautaire the Union acquis encompasses decisions adopted under Title V of the TEU "The Union's External Action and Specific Provisions on a Common Foreign and Security Policy". The European Council unanimously adopts these binding decisions to implement its "general guidelines for the common foreign and security policy, including for matters with defence implications".[192]

The Union acquis also covers other instruments of non-legislative nature: guidelines, codes of conduct and or statements by the Council and the Presidency of the EU. However, for the sake of clarity and consistency the notions "acquis

---

190 Conclusions of the European Council of Helsinki of December 1999 (EU Bull. 12-1999, at.8).
191 Protocol on the position of the United Kingdom and Ireland in respect of the area of freedom, security and justice amended by ToL (20(d)) and Article 2 of the Protocol on the position of Denmark amended by ToL.
192 Article 26(1) TEU.

communautaire" and "Union acquis" will be applied interchangeably throughout this book.

1.4.4.2. Concluding remarks

It is suggested that the notions "acquis communautaire", "Community acquis" and "Union acquis" may be applied interchangeably if one refers to what has been achieved under the whole EU structure. Nonetheless, we suggest that the distinctive feature of the "Union acquis" is what has been achieved under intergovernmental cooperation between the Member States of the EU. We suggest that the "Union acquis" is characterised by the set of distinctive features to be taken into account. Among them are the requirement of unanimity vote, the possibility of abstention and the absence of direct effect within the Member States' legal systems. Therefore, in contrast to the supranational "fundamental acquis", the "Union acquis" is too dependant on the political will of the Member States which can either partition its scope by abstention or impede its implementation into national legal systems. The division of the acquis communautaire into "Community acquis" and "Union acquis" became irrelevant at the moment that the Lisbon Treaty came into force. This is because the Lisbon Treaty abolished the three-pillar EU structure in favour of a more coherent single EU pillar.

1.4.5. EU "soft law" as a part of the acquis communautaire

1.4.5.1. Elements of EU "soft law"

The acquis communautaire includes EU "soft law" provisions which concern all those non-binding rules of conduct and which, according to the intention of their drafters, are entitled to a legal effect.[193] The legal effect of EU soft-law provi-

---

[193] K. C. Wellens and G. M. Borchardt, "Soft Law in European Community Law" 14 ELRev 267-321 (1989) at 285. Authors highlight the following sources of EC/EU soft law: 1) interinstitutional agreements that display a practical manifestation of sincere cooperation between the EU institutions; 2) non-binding recommendations and opinions as provided in Article 288 TFEU; 3) conclusions and resolutions of the EU institutions or the Member States or the two of them together; 4) published or unpublished declarations of EU institutions or the Member States or the two of them together; 4) programmes that indicate a future policy to be pursued by EU institutions or the Member States; 5) communiqués (press releases, declarations, conclusions and resolutions-non binding acts with further impulses for further development) and conclusions of the institutions or of the Member States in which the result of the meeting is laid down. See also L. Senden, *Soft Law in European Community Law* (Oxford, Hart Publishing 2004) and B. Van Vooren, "A case-

sions is considered on a case-by-case basis in accordance with the ECJ's interpretation. To decide if non-binding EU "soft-law" sources may be regarded as having a certain legal effect, the ECJ usually analyses their contents and the intention of the drafters.[194] Indeed, the ECJ has already ruled on the legal effect on certain "soft-law" sources.[195] EU soft laws that are entitled to a legal effect can serve as the legal basis for the enactment of Member States' legislation to implement rules of conduct; they provide the legal framework for future discussions and negotiations between Member States, third states and international organisations. Furthermore, EU soft law can also be used as a means for interpretation with respect to hard-law provisions with either a treaty or a customary law nature.[196] Intrinsically, EU soft law creates an expectation (not a commitment) that the conduct of the Member States, as well as legal and physical persons, will be in conformity with EU non-binding rules of conduct.

1.4.5.2. Concluding remarks

EU "soft law" provisions can be regarded as part of the acquis communautaire on case by case basis upon the ECJ's scrutiny of their real and potential legal effect. When the intention for legal commitment is demonstrated by the ECJ, then it is possible to consider a "soft-law" provision as having a certain legal effect. However, where this intention cannot be demonstrated, or where the drafters were explicit on avoiding any commitments, we must deal with purely political commitments.

---

study of "soft law" in EU external relations: the European Neighbourhood Policy" 34 ELRev 696-719 (2009).

194 *Ibid (*Wellens and Borchardt), at 285.
195 For example, see Case 44/84, *Hurd v. Jones* [1986] 46 CMLR 2, 42 where the ECJ stated that Article 3 of the Act of Accession of the UK, Denmark and Ireland (on observation of the principles and guidelines deriving from declarations, resolutions and other positions) "does not attach any additional legal effect" to these acts. Further, The ECJ stated that certain resolutions of the Member States merely express the political desirability without any legal effect (Cases 90 and 91/63, *Commission v. Luxemburg and Belgium* [1964] ECR 625, Case 10/73, *Rewe Central v. Hauptozollant Kehl* [1973] ECR 1175; Case 59/75, *Pubblico Ministero v Flavia Manghera and others* [1976] 17 CMLR 557) but certain resolutions of the EP have legal consequences and possible treaty violations could flow from them (Case 230/81, *Luxemburg v. Parliament* [1983] ECR 255, Case 294/83 *"les Verts" v European Parliament* [1986] ECR 1339; Case 34/86, *Council v. European Parliament* [1986] ECR 2155).
196 With regard to application of the Joint Declaration on Human Rights within the EU legal order see Case 44/79, *Hauer v. Land Rheihland-Pfalz* [1979] ECR 3727.

1.5. The external dimension of the acquis communautaire

1.5.1. Introduction

The notion "acquis communautaire" appears to be frequently applied in EU external policy, though the latest EU official documents tend to substitute it with the simple notion "acquis". For instance, the Commission Strategy Paper "Towards the Enlarged Union" 2002 refers to the "acquis communautaire" only once, but applies the terms "Community acquis" and "acquis" interchangeably throughout the text.[197] In the latest version of this document the Commission does not use either the notion "acquis communautaire" or "Union acquis" at all but, instead, apply more neutral "acquis" in different contexts and meanings.[198]

Generally, EU external policy employs the acquis communautaire in a twofold manner. In the first case, EU institutions refer to the "acquis criterion" in the context of the accession of new Member States.[199] Academics consider this the same as the "accession acquis".[200] In the second case, many EU association/partnership agreements contain provisions explicitly referring to either the "acquis communautaire" or "acquis". Henceforth, for the purpose of legal clarity, this book will refer to the acquis communautaire in the context of accession as the "accession acquis", thereby distinguishing it from the acquis applied in the EU agreements with third countries.

1.5.2. The "accession acquis"

The notion "accession acquis" is a legal and political category of a distinctive nature and scope. The "accession acquis" or, in the Commission words, the "acquis criterion",[201] is one of the intrinsic elements of the Copenhagen Criteria, *inter alia* the "ability to take on the obligations of membership, including adherence to the aims of political, economic and monetary union".[202] The Copenhagen Crite-

197 "Towards the Enlarged Union" Strategy Paper and Report of the European Commission on the progress towards accession by each of the candidate countries (COM (2002) 700 final).
198 Communication from the Commission "Enlargement Strategy and Main Challenges 2008-2009" (COM (2008) 674 final).
199 Curti Gialdino regarded this phenomenon as the "criterion of global integration" (*supra note* 4, at 1091).
200 *Supra note* 6, at 837, 869.
201 *Supra note* 197, at 1.4.
202 Conclusions of the Copenhagen European Council in 1993, available at <http://ue.eu.int/ueDocs/cms_Data/docs/pressdata/en/ec/72921.pdf>, last visited 18 January 2011.

73

ria is supplemented by the Madrid Criteria in 1995 which provides that candidate countries are expected to ensure the effective application of the "accession acquis" through their appropriate administrative and judicial structures.[203]

The scope of the "accession acquis" corresponds to Wiener's idea of the "descriptive" acquis, since it embraces not just the whole acquis communautaire/"Union acquis",[204] but all that has been accumulated under the EU framework, including "the real and potential rights" and "political objectives of the treaties".[205] In short, the "accession acquis" is a "snapshot" of the situation existing at the moment of accession of the new Member States[206] which comprises the entirety of rules, judicial decisions, present and in some cases it may contain future political arrangements to be accepted by new Member States. Therefore, the "accession acquis" appears to exceed the scope of the "acquis communautaire" in its internal dimension, because the fulfilment of the "acquis criterion" is not only limited by the implementation of the former, but envisages the candidate countries' adherence to EU political principles and even possibly future political arrangements (for instance, may cover new integration initiatives, participation in EU policies in which not all Member States participate at the moment of the accession).[207] In addition, the accomplishment of the "acquis criterion" requires candidate countries to pursue various legal and political reforms as to ensure not only the implementation, but also the effective application of the acquis communautaire, through appropriately functioning national administrative and

---

203 Conclusions of the Madrid European Council in 1995, available at <http://www.europarl.europa.eu/summits/mad1_en.htm>, last visited 18 January 2011.
204 Regular report of the Commission on progress towards accession by Poland (COM (1998) 712 final of 17 Dec 1998). Some of the latest EU accession documents (The Communication from the Commission "Enlargement Strategy and Main Challenges 2006-2007" (COM (2006) 649 final and 2004 Regular Report on Bulgaria's progress towards accession (COM (2004) 1199) define the acquis as the EU legal order and policies. However some of the Commission's official documents circumscribe the acquis communautaire in the context of accession by solely EC primary and secondary legislation (COM (1998) 745 final of 11 Dec 1998. See also 2005 Enlargement Strategy by the Commission (COM (2005) 561 final).
205 Bull EC, suppl 3/92, at 12.
206 Articles 32, 69, 84 and 112 of the Act concerning the conditions of accession of Austria, Finland, and Sweden (O.J. 1994, C 241/22). See also the Resolution on the environmental aspects of the enlargement of the Community to include Sweden, Austria, Finland and Norway, adopted by the European Parliament on 18 January 1994 (O.J. 1994. C 44, 49). Also see Article 39 of the Act concerning the conditions of accession of the Republic of Bulgaria and Romania and the adjustments to the treaties on which the European Union is founded (O.J. 2005, L 157/203).
207 In the context of accession the EU defines the notion "acquis" as "capacity to assume the obligations of membership, that is, the *acquis* expressed in the Treaties, the secondary legislation, and the policies of the Union" (See the Commission's Regular Report 2008 on Turkey's progress towards accession (COM(2008) 674).

judicial structures which in many cases imply revision of national constitutional law.[208] On the whole, the objective of the "accession acquis" adoption is to fulfil the Copenhagen and Madrid Criteria and subsequently to qualify for EU membership.

The "accession acquis" does not replicate the structure and hierarchy of sources inherent to the acquis communautaire in its internal dimension. The formal minimum requirement for membership is enshrined in Article 49 TEU which does not require candidate countries to accept the whole of the acquis communautaire, but solely to comply with the "political" conditions for accession. The "after-Lisbon" version of Article 49 TEU considerably widens the scope of the "accession acquis". First, the Lisbon Treaty made the EU membership conditional on candidate countries' commitment to "respect" common European values listed in Article 2 TEU [human dignity, equality and respect for human rights, including the rights of persons belonging to minorities]. Second, the Lisbon Treaty requires candidate countries not only respect these values and are committed to "promote" them. From practical point of view it could mean that candidate countries should be able to show through their internal and external policies that they pursue policies in line with the EU internal (promotion of market economy, liberalization of markets) and external (promotion of human rights, fight with terrorism and international crime, etc). Third, the Lisbon Treaty de facto legalises Copenhagen and Madrid Criteria for the EU membership and any additional criteria to be adopted by the European Council in the future. The Lisbon Treaty entrusts considerable power to the European Council to revisit the scope of the "accession acquis" at any time in light of specific political, economic and legal circumstances in the EU and thereby either to ease or to hinder the accession path of candidate countries into the EU.

A more explicit scope of the "accession acquis" may be drawn from the Acts of Accession which represent a final result of the negotiation saga. Acts of Accession and respective annexes that formulate in detail what is to be adopted by a new Member State in the course of accession.[209] It should be noted that in opin-

---

208 *Supra note* 197, at 1.4. Also see A. Lazowski, "And then They were Twenty-Seven...a Legal Appraisal of the Sixth Accession Treaty", 44 CML Rev. 401-430 (2007), at 420.
209 For example, see the Joint Declaration on Common Foreign and Security Policy (O.J. 1994, C 241/381), annexed to the Act on the conditions of accession of Austria, Sweden, Finland and Norway. It states that the Parties agreed to the "full acceptance of the rights and obligations attaching to the Union and its institutional framework, known at the acquis communautaire, as it applies to present Member States. This includes in particular the content, principles and political objectives of the Treaties, including those of the TEU". See also the Act on the conditions of accession of the Czech Republic, the Republic of Estonia, the Republic of Cyprus, the Republic of Latvia, the Republic of Lithuania, the Republic of Hungary, the Republic of Malta, the Republic of Poland, the Republic of Slovenia and the Slovak Republic to the European Union (O.J. 2003, L 236) and the Act

ion of the ECJ no provision of an Act of Accession could be interpreted as validating measures in contradiction with the EU founding treaties.[210] Therefore no revision of the "fundamental acquis" in the Acts of Accession is possible. The "accession acquis" appears to be not a static but a dynamic concept, since it displays a comprehensive picture of the "snapshot", that is to say, what has been achieved in the EU framework at the moment of the accession.[211] Consequently, during the pre-accession process candidate countries pursue a challenging task to approximate national legislation to a "moving target" of dynamic, constantly developing acquis.[212]

The objective of the pre-accession stage is to prepare a candidate country for eventual EU membership. For this purpose the EU assist candidate countries in the gradual accomplishment of the Copenhagen Criteria whose priorities, intermediate objectives and conditions are enshrined in the individual candidate country Accession Partnerships (issued by the Council through qualified majority vote following a proposal from the Commission).[213] Thereupon, based on the Accession Partnership and annual Commission Regular Reports on the progress towards accession, every candidate country issues a National Programme for Adoption of the Acquis (NPAA) which sets up a detailed adaptation action plan in accordance with national specifics. In some cases the Commission may assist candidate countries in emphasising what elements of the acquis communautaire should be prioritised in the course of the approximation process.[214] For instance, the White Paper entitled "Preparation of the associated countries of Central and Eastern Europe for integration into the internal market of the Union" (Approximation White Paper) highlighted specific areas of EC (now EU) Internal Market

on the conditions of accession of the Republic of Bulgaria and Romania to the European Union (O.J. 2005, L 157).
210 Case 185/73, *Hauptzollamt Bielefeld v. König*, [1974] ECR 607.
211 For instance, in contrast to the enlargement in 1995 the newest Member States Bulgaria and Romania had to implement the not only the whole first pillar acquis, which has considerably grown since that time, but also the third pillar acquis, like the European Arrest Warrant (*supra note* 208 (Lazowski), at 421).
212 K. Inglis, "Case C–413/04, *European Parliament v. Council*, Judgment of the Court of Justice (Grand Chamber) of 28 November 2006; Case C–414/04, *European Parliament v. Council*, Judgment of the Court of Justice (Grand Chamber) of 28 November 2006. Case C–273/04, *Republic of Poland v. Council*, Judgment of the Court of Justice (Grand Chamber) of 23 October 2007" 46 CML Rev. 641-663 (2009).
213 Council Regulation 622/98 on assistance to the applicant States in the framework of the pre-accession strategy, and in particular on the establishment of Accession Partnerships (O.J. 1998 L 85).
214 For more detailed account see H. Xanthaki, "Trasposition of EC Law for EU Approximation and Accession: The Task of National Authorities", VII European Journal of Law Reform 89-110 (2005).

legislation to be considered as priorities of the acquis' adoption.[215] Such priorities usually reflect every candidate country's level of economic, political and legal readiness to absorb the acquis communautaire. For example, in the case of Latvia one of key concerns of the "pre-accession" stage was the issue of minority rights and protection of minorities.[216] In the case of Bulgaria, it was the reform of the judiciary and the development of anti-corruption measures.[217]

Eventually, the adoption of the "pre-accession acquis" is pushed towards full compliance with the acquis communautaire. This means that in order to fulfil the "acquis criterion", a candidate country is expected to implement the whole scope of the acquis communautaire within the single package of all negotiation chapters".[218] However the example of the Bulgarian and Romanian accession in 2007 shows that the EU is not always strict with this rule. Due to various political and legal reasons Bulgaria and Romania were admitted into the EU without fulfilling all necessary membership criteria, in particular in areas of democracy and fight with corruption. The EU hoped to improve the situation with democratic reforms in Bulgaria and Romania with help of safeguard clauses in the Acts of Accession which envisage up to 3 years economic, internal market and Justice and Home Affairs (JHA) safeguards. However Bulgaria and Romania preferred to go through "cosmetic" reforms avoiding real changes of their political and legal systems. The EU's reluctance to enforce rigid requirements of the Act of Accession of Bulgaria and Romania shows visible shortages of the EU's policy of conditionality with regard to the new Member States.[219]

---

215 White Paper "Preparation of the associated countries of Central and Eastern Europe for integration into the internal market of the Union" (COM (95) 163).
216 2001 Regular Report on Latvia's Progress towards Accession, SEC(2001) 1749.
217 2001 Regular Report on Bulgaria's Progress towards Accession, SEC(2001) 1744.
218 For example the Commission's Regular Report 2008 on Turkey's progress towards accession (COM(2008) 674) refers to the following "accession acquis" chapters: 1) free movement of goods; 2) free movement of persons; 3) free movement of services; 4) free movement of capital; 5) right of establishment and freedom to provide services; 6) public procurement; 7) company law; 8) competition policy; 9) intellectual property law; 10) agriculture and rural development; 11) food safety, veterinary and phytosanitary policy; fisheries; 12) transport policy; 13) taxation; 14) economic and monetary policy; 15) statistics; 16) social policy and employment; 17) energy; 18) enterprise and industrial policy; 19) trans-European networks; 20) judiciary and fundamental rights; 21) justice freedom and security; 22) science and research; 23) education and culture; 24) information society and media; 25) regional policy and co-ordination of structural instruments; 26) environment; 27) consumers and health protection; 28) customs union; 29) foreign, security and defence policy; 30) financial services; 31) financial control; 32) financial and budgetary provisions; 33) external relations.
219 *Supra note* 209. Also see V. Pop, "MEPs turn screw on Romanian and Bulgaria corruption", EU Observer, 24.04.2009, available at <http://euobserver.com/22/27999>, last visited 18 January 2011 and E. Vucheva, "Bulgaria criticised for cosmetic changes to judici-

The subsequent results of the negotiations are fixed in the Acts of Accession - constitutional treaties of equal status to the founding Treaties ratified by all Member States. As mentioned above, the scope of the "accession acquis" is not static and tends to expand with every subsequent enlargement to cover the whole of what has been acquired by the EU at the moment of accession. In general, the following elements belong to the "accession acquis":[220]

New Member States must adhere to the "fundamental acquis" including the founding treaties, amendments, annexes and protocols as a whole which came into force before the accession.[221] Acts enacted by the EU institutions (regulations, directives, decisions, recommendations, opinions) are binding on new Member States and apply under the conditions laid down in the founding Treaties and a respective Act of Accession. Unequivocally, the "judicial acquis" must be accepted by candidate countries in the course of accession since this constitutes the core of the "fundamental acquis" and consequently enshrines the fundamental tenets and general principles of the EU legal order.[222] Acceptance of the principles laid down in ECJ case law derives automatically from the EU membership. Therefore, candidate countries are expected to adopt not only general principles set up by the ECJ but whole "judicial acquis" binding on the existing Member States, because a refusal to acknowledge it would undermine the unity and identity of the EU legal order.

The "Union acquis" must be accepted by new Member States in its entirety as it is described in section 1.4.4. of this chapter. This includes in particular the content, principles and political objectives of the EU founding Treaties. Therefore, new Member States are expected to participate fully and actively in the Common Foreign and Security Policy (CFSP) from the time of their accession into the EU, as well as to support the specific policies of the EU in force at the time of accession. In the field of JHA, new Member States must accede to those

---

ary" EU Observer, 08.04.2009, available at <http://euobserver.com/22/27930>, last visited 18 January 2011.

220 For example, the Commission's Regular Report 2004 on Bulgaria's progress towards accession (COM(2004) 657 final) contains 29 chapters of the "accession acquis" but the Commission's Regular Report 2005 on Turkey's progress towards accession (COM(2005) 561 final) refers to 33 chapters of the "accession acquis".

221 For critical analysis of the adoption of the "fundamental acquis" by candidate countries see D. Kochenov, *EU Enlargement and the Failure of Conditionality: Pre-Accession Conditionality in the Fields of Democracy and the Rule of Law* (The Hague, Kluwer Law International 2008).

222 The Approximation of Laws White Paper refers to ECJ case law as part of the acquis to be adopted by the candidate countries. Furthermore, it is stated in the Joint Declaration on the ownership of fishing vessels (concerning Norway) that "the Contracting Parties take note of the rulings of the Court of Justice of the European Communities" (O.J. 1994, C 241/387).

conventions and instruments which are inseparable from the attainment of the objectives of the TEU. By the date of accession those acts must be signed by the present and new Member States. Besides, new Member States must implement even non-adopted acts which have been drawn up by the Council and recommended to the Member States. Furthermore, new Member States must introduce administrative and other arrangements already adopted by the date of accession by the present Member States or the Council, as to facilitate practical cooperation between the Member States in the field of the JHA.[223]

New Member States must accede to EU external agreements (concluded within the EU-Member States mixed competence) with third states, international organisations or with a national of a third state,[224] including measures adopted by organs of these agreements. EU exclusive agreements are binding on new Member States from the date of accession. In the case of EU mixed agreements and other related agreements, new Member States "undertake to accede" to them in due course in accordance with conditions in the respective Act of Accession and national constitutional procedures.[225] New Member States must take appropriate measures where necessary to adjust their position in international organisations that have agreements with the EU or the present Member States in accordance with their new EU Member State rights and obligations.[226] Moreover, new Member States shall "undertake all necessary steps" to eliminate incompatibilities of their international agreements concluded before accession into the EU.[227] The Acts of Accession urge new Member States to "undertake to accede" to all other agreements concluded by the present Member States and related to the functioning of the EU.[228] Furthermore, the Commission frequently emphasises the necessity for the candidate countries to ratify international and regional conventions which explicitly refer to the functioning of the EU Internal Market or the whole EU, and/or they should be aimed at the establishment of uniform rules throughout the EU. For instance, 2002 Regular Reports on the candidate countries' Progress towards accession consider it necessary for new Member States to accede to the Convention on the Customs Treatment of Pool Containers, the Convention on Mutual Assistance and Co-operation between Customs Administrations, the Convention on Civil Aspects of International Child Abduction and

---

223 See the Joint Declaration on Common Foreign and Security Policy annexed to the Final Act of the Meeting at Corfu on 24 June 1994 (O.J. 1994, C 241/381). See also the Declaration by the new Member States on Articles 3 and 4 of the Act of Accession (O.J. 1994, C 241/398).
224 *Ibid*, Article 5(1).
225 *Ibid*, Article 5(2).
226 *Ibid*, Article 5(4).
227 *Ibid*, Article 6. This should be done in accordance with procedure in Article 351 TFEU.
228 *Ibid*, Article 4(1).

the Rome Convention on the law applicable to contractual obligations.[229] Since the European Convention on Human Rights is already considered as part of the acquis communautaire, candidate countries are expected to accede to variety of other Council of Europe conventions which more or less fall within EU objectives.[230] Besides, the EU may expect a candidate country either to accede to an international organisation (World Trade Organisation (WTO)), or to enhance co-operation with international (North Atlantic Treaty Organisation (NATO)) or regional (Council of Europe, European Patent Office) organisations, and even with some international agencies (the International Organisation of Supreme Audit Institutions, the Lisbon European Monitoring Agency on Drugs and Drug Addiction).

Candidate countries are expected to adhere to the EU "political acquis". The objective of "an ever closer union among the peoples of Europe"[231] entails that new Member States "assume in every respect the same obligations and responsibilities"[232] as had been undertaken by the present Member States in the course of further political integration. Firstly, new Member States must accede to decisions and agreements adopted by the Representatives of the Governments of the Member States meetings within the Council. It is presumed that these sources cover non-binding decisions and agreements taken by Member States' representatives.[233] Second, new Member States are regarded in the same situation as the present Member States in respect to "declarations or resolutions or other positions taken up by the European Council or the Council" or the positions adopted "by common agreement of the Member States".[234] Subsequently, new Member States observe and ensure implementation of the principles and guidelines deriving from those declarations, resolutions or other positions.[235]

The "accession acquis" covers EU "soft law" provisions[236] that concern all those non-binding and/or non-adopted rules of conduct which, according to the

---

229 For example, see 2002 Regular Report on Bulgaria's Porgress towards accession (COM (2002) 700 final).
230 For instance, the Council of Europe Civil Law Convention on Corruption, Council of Europe Criminal Law Convention, the Council of Europe Convention on the Protection of Individuals with regard to Automatic Processing of Personal Data, the Council of Europe Convention on Cybercrime, the Convention against Torture, the Convention on Elimination of all forms of Racial Discrimination.
231 Article 1 TEU.
232 EC Bull, 1961, 7-8, 41.
233 For a detailed account of the EU "soft acquis" see title 1.4.5. of this chapter.
234 Article 4(3) of the Act of Accession of Austria, Finland and Sweden (O.J. 1994, C241/22), Article 3 of the Republic of Bulgaria and Romania (O.J. 2005, L157/48).
235 *Ibid.*
236 *Supra note* 193 (Wellens and Borchardt), at 285.

intention of their drafters, are entitled or not entitled to produce legal effect.[237] However, those provisions should be aimed at supporting either existing objectives of the founding Treaties or at justifying recent/future political arrangements between the present Member States that have not yet been formalised.

The scope of the "accession acquis" reflects not only the consistent expansion of the EU patrimony but also indicates the candidate country capacity to meet and apply specific elements of the acquis and (at a lesser scale) the state of a candidate country's bargaining power at the time of accession negotiations. Formally, every new Member State must accept the whole acquis communautaire without any exemptions and derogations.[238] As a rule, the EU may consider granting derogation from the acquis to a new Member State in strictly exceptional circumstances.[239] However, as the accession practice shows, the EU may potentially grant derogations from the "accession acquis" to a new Member State in two cases. First case, it is when a new Member State is not ready and, consequently excluded, from full participation in certain EU policies (EMU, Schengen acquis). Second case, it is upon mutual consensus of the parties resulted from accession negotiations[240] and only if these derogations do not undermine the fundamental principles of the founding Treaties. There are two types of derogations which could be granted to a new Member State. The first type is "transitional arrangements" which result from the negotiation process and imply a temporary exclusion of a new Member State from specified elements of the acquis communautaire. In case of Bulgarian and Romanian Acts of Accession transitional arrangements concern certain aspects of free movement of people, services and capital; agriculture, transport, taxation, social policy, energy, telecommunication, competition policy, environment. These transitional arrangements may be justified by the necessity of protecting a candidate country's essential characteristics or preferences (agriculture, environment), or to safeguard seminal national eco-

---

237 "The fact that the Community adopted these measures or will only adopt them at a relatively late stage in the internal market's evolution does not necessarily reduce their importance for the CEECs. Measures in the process of being adopted are likely to form part of the "acquis" to be accepted by future Member States". (O.J. 1994, C 241/387, at 3.19).
238 As the EU puts it "Adoption of only part of the *acquis communautaire* might seem an attractive solution. In practice, this option could, without settling the basic problem, the solution of which would merely be deferred, give rise to even greater new difficulties" (EC Bull. EC Suppl. 8/82, p.7). On the confirmation of this approach in the course of the latest wave of enlargement see K. Inglis, "The Union's Fifth Accession Treaty: New Means to make Enlargement Possible", 41 CML Rev. 937-973 (2004), at p.947.
239 For instance, see list of requests for derogations in Agenda 2000 ((EU Bull. Suppl. 5/97).
240 Article 2 of the Act of Accession of Austria, Finland and Sweden (O.J. 1994, C 241/22). "Towards the Enlarged Union" Strategy Paper and Report of the European Commission on the progress towards accession by each of the candidate countries (COM (2002) 700 final).

nomic or social interests (e.g. tax benefits, preservation of sensitive national industries, fishing rights, access to oil reserves, alcohol monopoly).[241]

There is a clear tendency on behalf of the EU to decrease the amount and scope of transitional arrangements in every succeeding wave of accession. For example, Austria, Sweden and Finland have negotiated upon their accession in 1995 more than 209 transitional arrangements lasting from one to ten years in duration. Areas of agriculture and taxation have proved to contain most of them. Candidate countries of the subsequent wave of accession negotiated much fewer transitional arrangements. For example, Poland obtained more than 40 transitional arrangements lasting from 1 to 12 years versus the Czech Republic which was granted fewer than 20 transitional arrangements related to the "accession acquis". Subsequently, the number of transitional arrangements related to the "accession acquis" for Romania almost doubles the number of transitional arrangements for Bulgaria. Agriculture and taxation have proved to be the areas which attracted most transitional arrangements from the "accession acquis" in two latest waves of enlargement. The Member States and EU institutions must interpret transitional arrangements with "regard to the foundations and the system of the Community as established by the Treaty",[242] and "in such a way as to facilitate the achievement of the objectives of the Treaty and the application of all its rules".[243]

The second type of derogations is called "temporary derogations". They are granted in regarding the new acquis communautaire adopted between the signature of the Act of Accession and its entry into force.[244] Temporary derogations can be granted by unanimity vote of the Council on "duly substantiated request" of a new Member State regarding applicability of new acquis adopted between the end of negotiations and the signature of the Act of Accession.[245] However "temporary derogations" can not be granted in respect of a new EU law adopted between the date of signature of the Act of Accession and its entry into force.[246]

---

241 On detailed account of derogations obtained by new Member States after 5th and 6th waves of enlargement see *supra note* 238 (Inglis) and *supra note* 221(Kochenov). P. Nicolaides, "Preparing for Accession to the European Union: How to Establish Capacity for Effective and Credible Application of EU Rules" in M. Cremona, ed., *The Enlargement of the European Union*, (Oxford University Press 2003), 43-78.
242 Case 231/78, *Commission v. United Kingdom*, [1979] ECR 1447.
243 Joined Cases 194 and 241/85, *Commission v. Greece* [988] ECR 1037.
244 For instance Czech Republic, Slovakia, Hungary, Latvia and Lithuania, Slovenia have requested temporary derogations from the EC Directive on waste electrical and electronic equipment. Poland requested temporary derogation (15 years) from the EC acquis on pharmaceuticals. For more detail see *supra note* 238 (Inglis), at 963.
245 Article 55 of the Act of Accession of Poland (O.J. 1994, C 241/398).
246 K. Inglis, "Case C–413/04, *European Parliament v. Council*, Judgment of the Court of Justice (Grand Chamber) of 28 November 2006; Case C–414/04, *European Parliament v.*

There are other accustomed ways of limiting the application of the acquis communautaire in the course of accession.[247] Thus, candidate countries may be allowed to preserve national higher standards, for example in areas of safety and health control. These standards may be preserved for a fixed period of time, thereby allowing the EU to review its own standards in accordance with higher standards in individual Member States. Furthermore, the EU may allow flexible discretion to a particular candidate country in the interpretation of certain provisions of EU legislation. For instance, Austria was permitted to apply its own interpretation of Article 28(2) of Sixth Council Directive 77/388 on value added tax until final interpretation by the ECJ. Besides, the correct interpretation of the acquis may be postponed until the completion of approved scientific studies (sustainability of fishing stock in Norway and the degree of environmental pollution caused by the transit of heavy vehicles through Austria).

The application of the acquis communautaire may be limited to geographically selected areas within new Member States and associate countries through granting permanent derogations from the acquis communautaire. The EU founding Treaties define two kinds of such territories: 1) outermost territories (Article 349 TFEU); 2) associated overseas countries or territories (Article 355 TFEU). The acquis communautaire does not apply to the full extent to these territories either due to special arrangements in international treaties (the Svalbard area) or due to specific national particularities (climate, geographical position, historical or political reasons, (for example, Aland Islands and Channel Islands).[248]

The current trend of decreasing derogations from the acquis communautaire for new Member States meets quite opposite trend of extending so called "economic safeguard clauses".[249] "Economic safeguard clauses" in the Acts of Accession enable the Commission and the present Member States to apply "neces-

---

Council, Judgment of the Court of Justice (Grand Chamber) of 28 November 2006. Case C–273/04, *Republic of Poland v. Council*, Judgment of the Court of Justice (Grand Chamber) of 23 October 2007" 46 CML Rev. 641-663 (2009).

247 For very good historical account on practices limiting application of the acquis communautaire see P. Nicolaides. "Negotiating Effectively for Accession to the European Union: Realistic Expectations, Feasible Targets, Credible Arguments", EIPA, available at < http://www.eipa.eu/files/repository/eipascope/scop98_1_2.pdf>, last visited 18 January 2011. P. Nicolaides / S. R. Boean / F. Bellon / P. Pezaros, *A Guide to the Enlargement of the European Union (ii). A Review of the Process, Negotiations, Policy Reforms and Enforcement Capacity*, (Maastricht, European Institute of Public Administration 1999) at 39.

248 D. Kochenov, "Substantive and Procedural Issues in the Application of European Law in the Overseas Possessions of European Union Member States", 17(2) Michigan State Journal of International Law 195-288 (2008-2009).

249 K. Inglis, "The Accession Treaty and its Transitional Arrangements: A Twilight Zone for the New Member States", in C. Hillion (Ed.), *EU Enlargement: a legal appraisal* (Hart Publishing, 2004), 77-109.

sary protective measures" in situations where "difficulties arise which are serious and liable to persist in any sector of the economy or which could bring about serious deterioration in the economic situation of a given area".[250] If only a one-year safeguard clause has been applied in the Acts of Accession of Austria, Sweden and Finland[251] in the latest accession of twelve Central and Eastern European (CEE) countries the duration of application of the economic safeguard clause has been extended to three years with the possibility of a further extension. These most recent Acts of Accession go beyond safeguard measures applied in previous waves of enlargement and impose so called "specific safeguard clauses", which concern potential violations by new Member States of policies within the EU Internal Market, and "justice and home affairs safeguard clauses". For example, the Acts of Accession with Central and Eastern European countries envisage temporary suspension of the judicial cooperation between the EU Member States and new Member States in case of serious shortcoming in transposition, the state of implementation and application of the framework decisions and other legal instruments under Title V of the TEU. The gradual extension of safeguard measures meets justified critique from academics who argue that these safeguard clauses establish a system of monitoring imported from the EU pre-accession strategy, which undermine the internal EU compliance principles applicable to the "old" Member States.[252]

The fulfilment of the "acquis criterion" envisages not only the implementation of the acquis communautaire but also the effective capacity to enforce it within a candidate country's domestic legal system. The significance of this element of the "acquis criterion" has repeatedly been highlighted by the European Councils. For instance, the Madrid European Council of 1995 emphasised the importance of adjusting candidate countries' administrative structures for the purpose of integration. The Fiera European Council of 2000 stressed that "progress in the negotiations depends on the incorporation by the candidate countries of the acquis in their national legislation and especially on their capacity to effectively implement and enforce it", by strengthening their administrative and judicial structures. Furthermore, the Göteborg European Council of 2001 reiterated the need for candidate countries to pay particular attention to the establishment of adequate administrative structures, and to the reform of their judicial systems and civil service. The Approximation of Laws White Paper stresses that approxima-

---

250 Article 3.4 of the "Towards the Enlarged Union" Strategy Paper and Report of the European Commission on the progress towards accession by each of the candidate countries (COM (2002) 700 final).
251 Article 152 of the Act of Accession of Austria, Finland and Sweden (O.J. 1994, C 241/22).
252 C. Hillion, "The European Union is Dead. Long Live the European Union...A Commentary on the Treaty of Accession 2003", 29(5) ELRev. 583-612 (2004).

tion of CEECs national laws to EC (now EU) law requires not only the implementation of EC "right" legislation, but also "the full framework of technical and other structures necessary to ensure the effective implementation of such legislation".[253]

Until recently, there was no explicit list of measures to guarantee effective implementation of the "accession acquis". In 2005, the Commission issued an informal but comprehensive "Guide to the main administrative structures required for implementation of the acquis", which provides "a set of standards, on the basis of which an assessment can be made of the administrative capacity of each country for each chapter of the acquis, including the performance of the relevant administrative structures".[254] As well as providing an overview of EU official documents on accession, this document also draws our attention to the variety of actions that need to be taken by candidate countries. In general, candidate countries are expected to pursue radical domestic institutional reforms to ensure the sustainable functioning of their own administrative and judicial structures in accordance with the principles of rule of law and justice. For this purpose, appropriate educational and training programmes for public servants must be undertaken and efficiently working infrastructure management and regulatory bodies must be set up. The independence of certain public institutions (Central Bank, Supreme Court, and Audit Office) must be ensured, and suitable regulatory frameworks to enable the proper functioning of the EU Internal Market freedoms should be established. Candidate countries must pursue effective anti-corruption policies. Public offices, especially police and custom services, are expected to be provided with modern facilities, equipment and access to sustainable information technology. Subsequently, computerisation must take place at all levels of the public service, including connections to major EU computer databases. The process of due enforcement of the acquis goes beyond actions of the government and administration, but envisages the active involvement of the whole of civil society, in particular local government, business structures and professional organisations.[255]

---

253 White Paper "Preparation of the associated countries of Central and Eastern Europe for integration into the internal market of the Union"(COM (95) 163, Article 2.20).
254 The text of the "Guide to the main administrative structures required for implementation of the acquis" can be found at <http://ec.europa.eu/enlargement/pdf/enlargement_process/accession_process/how_does_a_country_join_the_eu/negotiations_croatia_turkey/admin structures_version_may05_35_ch_public_en.pdf>, last visited 18 January 2011.
255 For a more comprehensive picture of what has to be done in the course of effective implementation of the acquis communautaire see "Making a success of enlargement", Strategy Paper and Report of the Commission on the progress towards accession by each of the candidate countries (COM (2001) 700 final at 3(a)) and the regular Commission's accession reports for each candidate country.

On the whole the "accession acquis"/"acquis criterion" is a dynamic category which clearly exceeds the scope of the "acquis communautaire" in its internal dimension.[256] In general, the "accession acquis" consists of the whole "fundamental acquis" and the "normative" "acquis communautaire", and which are consequently fixed in the Acts of Accession. Besides, the "accession acquis" encompasses various non-binding political measures within the scope of the EU actual and potential objectives and priorities. New Member States must adhere to them before acquiring EU membership so as to avoid undermining the pace of integration and political unification within the EU. Consequently, the adoption of the "accession acquis" neither can be fulfilled neither without its due implementation into the legal systems of the candidate countries, nor without the effective functioning of their administrative and judicial structures. Therefore, the "accession acquis" does not cover mere legal rules and practices, but requires that candidate countries ensure the proper functioning of their national economic, political and judicial systems as envisaged by the Copenhagen and Madrid Criteria. On the whole, the "accession acquis" provides a "snapshot" of the EU economic, political and legal achievements that have been acquired at the moment of accession. Therefore, each new Member State is characterised by a distinctive individual "accession acquis" that is balanced by acquired transitional arrangements and temporary derogations, as well as by safeguard clauses to be applied by the EU to restore any potential damage to present Member States' interests. This does not mean that such balance exists in reality. In practice, one can see that every wave of enlargement makes the accession requirements towards candidate countries more stringent.

1.5.3. Further implications of the acquis communautaire in its external dimensions

1.5.3.1. The acquis communautaire in EU external agreements

Clearly, not all third countries aim to accede to the EU or, conversely, not all EU external agreements contain as an objective of the eventual membership of the third country Party. However, many EU association or partnership agreements contain so-called "approximation clauses" which refer to the "acquis" within the specific context of such an agreement. This means that the scope of the acquis communautaire cannot always be consistent, but varies from one EU external agreement to another. That is to say that the acquis communautaire in the Lomè

---

256 C. Delcourt argues that the scope of the "accession acquis" is understood in an "excessive" manner (*supra note* 6, at 861).

and Cotonou Agreements differs from the acquis communautaire in the European Economic Area (EEA) Agreement, which in turn differs from the Partnership and Cooperation Agreements (PCAs). In other words, the scope of the acquis communautaire in association and the PCAs does not replicate the scope of the EU acquis communautaire, but must be carefully weighted against the objectives of each particular agreement. We argue that the "external" acquis communautaire within the specific EU external agreement embraces the totality of legal acts issued by common institutions (Association Councils, Joint Committees, and Courts – such as the European Free Trade Area (EFTA) Court). In addition, it encompasses the relevant acquis in its internal dimension which is in line with the specific objectives of an EU external agreement (customs union, sectoral cooperation, association), and the international law acquis (conventions, treaties, decisions of international organisations) circumscribed in an EU external agreement (not always applicable to the present EU Member States). Further chapters of this paper concentrate on the scope of the acquis communautaire within specific EU external agreements.

1.5.3.2. The scope of the acquis communautaire and "approximation clauses" in EU external agreements

Some EU external agreements envisage commitments of third countries to adhere to the acquis communautaire through the exercise of a so-called "approximation clause". This imposes a soft-law obligation to "endeavor to ensure" the compatibility of its legislation within specified "priority areas" of EU legislation. As a result, third countries willing to enhance their level of partnership with the EU pursue "voluntary harmonisation" of their national laws to EU legal rules which have no binding force in relation to them, and in the framing of which those third countries have no real participation.[257] In this case, a third country

---

[257] This process was defined by Andrew Evans as "voluntary harmonisation" in A. Evans, "Voluntary Harmonization in Integration between the European Community and Eastern Europe" 22 ELRev 201-220 (1997). On link between voluntary harmonisation and conditionality criteria see K. Inglis, 'EU Enlargement: Membership Conditions applied to Future and Potential Member States', in S. Blockmans and A. Lazowski, eds., *The European Union and its Neighbours: a Legal Appraisal of the EU's Policies of Stabilisation, Partnership and Integration* (The Hague, T.M.C. Asser Press 2006) p. 61. Other authors define it as "autonomous adaptation". For example see M. Maresceau (ed.), *Enlarging the European Union: Relations Between the EU and Eastern Europe* (London, Longman 1997) and P.-C. Müller-Graff, "The Legal Framework for the Enlargement of the Internal Market to Central and Eastern Europe" 6 MJICL 2 (1999) at 196. On relations between approximation and legislation transplants see H. Xanthaki, "Legislation transplants in legislation: defusing the trap", 57 ICLQ (2008) p. 659. A. Lazowski, "Enhanced Multi-

can legitimately avoid the "blind" reception of the whole "Union acquis", but may align national legislation within specified priority areas of the acquis communautaire in accordance with the objectives and aims of an association or partnership agreement. That is to say that there is no need for the PCA country to approximate its legislation to the EU "company law acquis". Instead, a PCA country is expected to concentrate upon the elimination of any obstacles and discriminative measures that impede the national treatment of the Member States' companies, branches and subsidiaries within its territory. This approach to approximation corresponds precisely to the PCAs objectives of mere "economic cooperation" between the Parties.

To summarise, the scope of acquis communautaire within various EU external agreements varies in accordance with the agreement's aims or objectives, and extends the scope of the acquis communautaire in its internal dimension. A more precise description of the "acquis" within the EU external agreements will be provided in the following chapter of this paper.

1.5.3.3. Sectoral acquis communautaire

The notion "acquis communautaire" has been segregated into other much smaller meanings, since even the founding treaties refer to the acquis in specific sectors or policies, such as the "Schengen acquis", the "social acquis" or the "acquis of the Union in the area of freedom, security and justice".[258]

The EU internal and external documents as well as academic literature tend to consider that each area of the acquis communautaire has its own acquis, such as the "transport acquis" or the "environmental acquis", thereby promulgating the new category of so called "sectoral acquis".[259] This encompasses a whole range of legal rules, principles and other values within a certain EU policy or the EU activity as a whole, which has been achieved in the process of the European integration within this specific field. Hitherto, the notion of the "sectoral acquis" has not been well defined or classified. In its internal dimension the notion "sectoral acquis" is widely applied by the EU institutions to describe the acquis commun-

---

lateralism and Enhanced Integration without Membership in the European Union", 45 CML Rev. 1433-1458 (2008).
258 Article 10 of the Lisbon Treaty Protocol 10 on Transitional Provisions. See also the Lisbon Treaty Protocol on the position of Denmark (O.J. 2007 C 306/50).
259 For academic analysis of sectoral acquis see *supra note* 41 (Jansen and Zimmerman), (Grundmann).

autaire within a specific area of EU legislation.[260] In its external dimension the application of the notion "sectoral acquis" appears to be more complicated. In the course of enlargement the "sectoral acquis" has been referred as one of the objectives of the approximation of laws process when candidate countries acquire to fulfil the Copenhagen Criteria. However after the adoption of the Agenda 2000 the EU institutions have been always clear on the fact that the adoption of the "sectoral acquis" should not led to partitioning of the whole acquis communautaire for sake of the EU's political objectives.[261] Therefore, in context of the accession any references to "sectoral acquis" should be considered as indivisible part of the "accession acquis". On the contrary, different political objectives of EU external policies (European Neighbourhood Policy, Euro-Mediterranean Union, and Eastern Partnership) imply more flexibility for concerned third countries in adopting relevant "sectoral acquis". In other words, "sectoral acquis" therein can be applied in line with the level of relations of a third country with the EU. In other words third countries pursue the "voluntary harmonisation" of their national legislation with "sectoral acquis". It means that in one case "sectoral acquis" may be applied interchangeably to the acquis communautaire within a specific area of EU legislation.[262] In other case concerned third countries may pick up certain elements of the EU "sectoral acquis" in order to fulfil short-term objectives of a relevant EU external agreement.

In conclusion it is argued that the "sectoral acquis" is a broad category that exceeds the scope of EU sectoral legislation. The "sectoral acquis" comprises binding and non-binding rules, rules still pending its adoption, political principles and judicial decisions that regulate EU competence within a specific policy or activity in the process of accession. Furthermore, it covers actual and potential rights that flow from the founding objectives and further constitutional developments within the EU. Adoption of "sectoral acquis" implies the fulfilment of technical and other measures necessary to ensure the effective implementation of such rules. A more precise analysis of the "sectoral acquis" will be provided in the following chapters.

---

260 For instance see "Green Paper on Review of the Consumer Acquis" (COM (2006) 744 final). Also relevant is European Research Group on Existing EC Private Law "Acquis Group", <http://www.acquis-group.org,>, last visited 18 January 2011.
261 *Supra note* 238 (Inglis), at 947, 954-955.
262 Communication from the Commission and the European Parliament to the Council "Eastern Partnership" (COM (2008) 823 final). See also "European Neighbourhood and Partnership Instrument. Ukraine. Country Strategy Paper 2007-2013", available at <http://ec.europa.eu/world/enp/pdf/country/enpi_csp_ukraine_en.pdf>, last visited 18 January 2011.

1.6. Conclusion

In the introduction of this chapter it was argued that the "acquis communautaire" as a notion of variable nature. Subsequently, we put forward the view that the nature and scope of the "acquis communautaire" varies in accordance with the objective of its application. In order to clarify this, it was proposed to examine the nature and the scope of the internal and external dimensions of the acquis communautaire.

In the first half of this chapter the historical evolution of the acquis communautaire and the state of long-going academic debate on the issue were reviewed and analysed. In the second half of this chapter major elements and characteristics of the internal and external dimensions of the acquis communautaire were scrutinized.

Several relevant points emerge from our study as having relevance. First, the nature and scope of the acquis communautaire are not identical in their internal and external dimensions. The major factor that justifies differentiation is an objective of the acquis communautaire's application. That is to say, the objective of the acquis communautaire in its internal dimension is to ensure the consistent development of the EU while preserving EU patrimony. Conversely, the objective of the acquis communautaire in its external dimension is to push candidate countries to the forefront of the acquired level of economic, political and legal cooperation within the EU and to stimulate third countries to share European and international common democratic values. Furthermore, other types of the acquis communautaire with opposing scopes might emerge within one dimension of their application. For instance, the external application of the acquis communautaire engenders the "accession acquis" and the relevant acquis within a specific EU external agreement. The former is aimed at preparing a candidate country for membership in the EU, while the latter is targeted merely at maintaining partnership relations between the parties. However, in both these cases the objective of the acquis' export is to encourage third countries to share European and international democratic values.

The second issue that merits our consideration is the matter of conceptualising the acquis communautaire. In other words, neither EU institutions nor EU legislation clearly specifies what the notion "acquis communautaire" is, or how it should be applied. Therefore, it is inevitable that one encounters problems in defining the scope of the acquis communautaire in each particular case of application.

It must be emphasised once more that the goal of this chapter is not to answer all the questions related to the nature and scope of the acquis communautaire, but merely to trace the major patterns in its application. Thus, it is better to conclude with a suggestion that the term "acquis communautaire" represents a notion of interdisciplinary nature that can be applied with regard to many aspects of European studies. In other words the acquis communautaire should be perceived as a broad concept encompassing not only legal, but political, social, and historical contexts. Within its legal context the acquis communautaire covers everything that has been achieved throughout continuing EU evolution, including the objectives of the founding treaties, principles, primary and secondary legislation, and soft non-binding legislation.

Chapter 2. The Scope of the Acquis Communautaire in EU External Agreements

2.1. Introduction

In this chapter the external dimension of the acquis communautaire shall be scrutinized in more detail. This chapter examines the scope of the acquis communautaire in EU external agreements which themselves display different approaches and objectives of EU foreign policy towards third countries: the EEA Agreement; association and other agreements with the objective of full EU membership (SAAs, EAs); association and sectoral agreements aimed at the liberalisation of mutual trade (EMAAs, EC-Swiss SAs); and partnership agreements (PCAs, TDCAs). Towards the end our study brings us to the conclusion that the internal and external dimensions of the acquis communautaire are not identical. On the one hand, the scope of the acquis communautaire within EU external agreements embraces elements identical to those within the internal dimension of the acquis communautaire: binding and non-binding EU legislation and rules; EU general principles and doctrines; rulings by the ECJ's and the General Court; international law acquis; and EU soft law. On the other hand, the scope of the acquis communautaire varies from one agreement to another, reflecting specific objectives of these agreements and the priorities of changeable EU external policy towards third countries.

2.2. The scope of the acquis communautaire in EU external agreements. Comparative study

The preposition that the concept of "acquis communautaire" in the EU external agreements is not uniform and varies from one agreement to another implies serious consequences for third countries. For instance, national governments of third countries – parties to EU external agreements – may face difficulties in picking up elements of the acquis communautaire which are applicable to them. For example, third countries, which pursue the voluntary approximation of their national legislation to that of the EU, face uncertainty with regard to the precise scope of the sectoral acquis to be implemented into their national legal systems.[1]

---

[1] R. Petrov, "Recent developments in the adaptation of Ukrainian legislation to EU law" 8(5) EFARev. 125-141 (2003).

This is because the relevant EU external agreements (PCAs, EMAAs) neither envisage the objective of full EU membership for these countries, nor clarify how the approximation of laws might contribute to achieving this objective. That is why EU external agreements carefully tailor the acquis communautaire to the specific objective of maintaining relations between the EU and the parties with which it enters into agreements. In order to follow the logic of such tailoring one must be able to overview the scope of the acquis communautaire in all groups of EU external agreements. Unfortunately, recent studies in EU external relations law do not offer a comprehensive analysis of this subject.[2] This chapter fills this gap by studying the scope of the acquis communautaire in the major groups of EU external agreements (association, partnership and cooperation, trade and co-operation, and development) through the application of comparative law methodology. On the one hand, comparative methodology serves as a tool to achieve the ambitious aims of our research. It helps compile a coherent picture of elements that constitute the external dimension of the acquis communautaire as reflected in EU external agreements. On the other hand, it allows us to prove that the objectives of EU external agreements determine the scope of the acquis communautaire applicable towards third countries. As a result, readers of this title can examine the separate elements of the acquis communautaire through the prism of the objectives of EU external agreements.

2.2.1. European Economic Area Agreement (EEA)

2.2.1.1. Objectives of the EEA Agreement

The EEA Agreement[3] is an association agreement based on 310 EC (now Article 217 TFEU), which aims at "a high degree of integration with hopes for a "fundamentally improved free trade area",[4] or even exceeding a mere free trade area".[5] However, the EEA Agreement goes beyond that. In opinion of the EFTA Court it is "an international agreement *sui generis* that have created a legal order

---

2   With the exemption of works by A. Evans which are not so recent (A. Evans, *The Integration of the European Community and Third States in Europe: a Legal Analysis*, (Oxford, Clarendon Press 1996), at 412. A. Evans, "Voluntary harmonisation in integration between the European Community and Eastern Europe", 22(3) ELRev. 201-220 (1997)).
3   O.J. 1994, L 1/3.
4   EFTA Court Case E-2/97, *Mag Instrument Inc. v. California Trading Company (Maglite)*, 1997 EFTA Court Report.
5   Case T-115/94, *Opel Austria*, [1997] ECR II-39.

of its own".[6] The EEA Agreement enables the EFTA Member States that signed the EEA Agreement (Iceland, Norway, and Liechtenstein)[7] to join the EU Internal Market (with the exemption of some important aspects of internal markets, for example agriculture, fisheries and tax) without acquiring formal EU membership or setting up a customs union.

The expansion of the EU Internal Market to EFTA Member States entails the formation of a harmonised legal environment. Therefore, the creation of EU-EEA common rules and their effective enforcement are prime objectives of the EEA Agreement. The Preamble of the EEA Agreement explicitly states that "a dynamic and homogeneous EEA" shall be based on "common rules and equal conditions of competition" supplemented with "the adequate means of enforcement including at the judicial level". The key method of ensuring the correct functioning of common rules is the maintenance of "a uniform interpretation and application of this Agreement and those provisions of Community legislation which are substantially reproduced in this Agreement". In other words, it implies that the EFTA Member States are expected to adhere to the relevant acquis communautaire at the moment of signing the agreement, and to ensure its homogeneity henceforth.

The homogeneity of EU-EEA rules is the distinctive feature of the EEA Agreement and its major objective, which "consistently guided the jurisprudence of the [EFTA Court] as well as [the ECJ]".[8] The following chapter deals with the procedural mechanism of homogeneity in detail. In short, homogeneity presupposes the existence of EU-EAA common rules or the common acquis communautaire which is supported by uniform interpretation. As a result, EEA institutions are responsible for the timely review and subsequent adoption of the dynamic acquis communautaire into the EEA legal order. Although the EEA Agreement does not bind the EFTA Member States to the new developments in the acquis communautaire, homogeneity remains the pivotal tool in maintaining the proper functioning of the EEA.

---

6 Case E-9/97, *Erla Maria Sveinbjörnsdottir v. the Government of Iceland*, 1998 EFTA Court Report, 95. In particular it states "The depth of integration of the EEA Agreement is less far-reaching then under the EC Treaty, but the scope and the objective of the EEA Agreement goes beyond what is usual for an agreement under public international law".
7 Switzerland does not participate in the EEA Agreement due to the negative result of the 1992 national referendum. Hereafter under "EFTA Member States" we refer to the recent Parties to the EEA Agreement.
8 Case E-1/104, *Fokus Bank*, 2004 EFTA Court Report, 11, at 22.

2.2.1.2. The scope of the relevant acquis communautaire in the EEA Agreement

We argue that the EEA Agreement provides for two types of the relevant acquis communautaire to be implemented by the EFTA Member States: the "pre-signature" relevant acquis communautaire; and the "post-signature" relevant acquis communautaire. The "pre-signature" relevant acquis communautaire encompasses the whole body of the acquis communautaire through the EEA's 49 Protocols and 22 Annexes. The "post-signature" relevant acquis covers the new acquis communautaire to be implemented by EFTA Member States through the homogeneity procedure. The EFTA Member States have assumed all the acquis communautaire, which is "relevant" to them. The notion of the "relevant acquis" is not expressly defined in the EEA Agreement. Nevertheless, we shall argue that the "relevant acquis" mirrors the EEA Agreement's objectives which target the extension of the EU Internal Market freedoms to the EEA. In general, the EEA Agreement arrays the "pre-signature" relevant acquis communautaire into three categories pursuant to the degree of their binding force and the EU competence within specific subject areas: 1) the EU Internal Market acquis; 2) EEA horizontal provisions relevant to EU Internal Market freedoms; 3) the EEA flanking policies acquis.

The EU Internal Market acquis is binding for all EFTA Member States. It covers rules that are essential for the functioning of the EU Internal Market: the free movement of goods, services, people and capital; competition and state aids; procurement; product liability; energy; social security; transport. However, it omits certain important elements of the EU Internal Market acquis: agriculture; fisheries; and tax. The precise scope of the relevant EU Internal Market acquis is clarified in the EEA Agreement annexes which refer to specific EU acts and identify their scope relevant to the EEA Agreement (i.e. object, subject, definition of terms, provisions that do not apply to the EFTA Member States). Furthermore, the EEA Agreement Annexes indicate the hierarchy of the EU relevant acquis, thereby clarifying its binding force for the EFTA Member States. The first group of EU acts in the annexes is labelled "acts referred to" which refer to the relevant EU secondary legislation. The second group is called "acts of which the Contracting Parties shall take note". This embraces the relevant soft acquis communautaire (Commission Communications and Recommendations, Council Resolutions and Recommendations).

The EEA Agreement Annexes amend EU legislation with the purpose of extending the applicability of the latter to the EEA legal order.[9] This means that in

---

9   For instance, Article 1 of the EEA Agreement Annex XVIII on the equal treatment for men and women states that "Article 119 of the Treaty shall be read as "Article 69 of the EEA Agreement".

the context of the EEA Agreement, provisions of the relevant EU legislation must be interpreted as applicable in the EEA.[10] However, the relevant EU act must be applied in accordance with the EEA Agreement objectives, since the mere fact of reference to an EU act does not imply identical application within the EEA legal order.[11]

The EEA Agreement Annexes do not specify the acquis communautaire with regard to horizontal provisions relevant to the four freedoms of the EU Internal Market. Instead, the Annexes either envisage the application of minimum requirements having regard to the conditions and technical rules in each of the EFTA Member States[12], or merely call for the "good functioning" of the EEA horizontal provisions relevant to the four freedoms of the EU Internal Market.[13] For instance, in the field of statistics, the adoption of the acquis communautaire is limited by the application of harmonised methods, definitions and classifications without clarifying their substance.[14] The EEA Agreement horizontal provisions relevant to the four freedoms of the EU Internal Market cover the areas of: social security (including health and safety at work, labour law and the equal treatment of men and women); consumer protection; environment; statistics, and company law.

The EU flanking policies acquis covers issues of shared competence outside the EU Internal Market acquis: research and technological development; education; social policy; training, and youth; Small and Medium Enterprises (SME); tourism; audio visual services and access to justice. Within these areas, the EU - EEA cooperation has to be strengthened and broadened as far as possible. The EU flanking policies acquis is not based on the acquis communautaire *stricto sensu*, as no reference is made to the relevant legally binding EU acts in the EEA Agreement.[15] Nonetheless, the recent record of implementing the relevant EU flanking policies acquis (legislation and policies) into the legal order of the EEA Agreement, and, consequently, to the legal orders of the EFTA Member States,

---

10 The EEA Agreement Protocol 1 "On horizontal adaptations" of the EEA Agreement.
11 Introduction to Annex XIV of the EEA Agreement warns that "preambles, the addresses of the EC acts; references to territories or languages of the EC; references to rights and obligations of EC Member States, their public entities, undertakings and individuals in relation to each other; and references to information and notification procedures are specific to the EC legal order" and therefore can not be identically applied to the EFTA Member States.
12 Article 67(1) EEA Agreement.
13 Articles 67(2) and 68 EEA Agreement.
14 Article 76(2) EEA Agreement.
15 In accordance with the EAA Agreement Protocol 31 "on co-operation in specific fields outside the four freedoms the EFTA Member States adhered to relevant soft Acquis communautaire (Decisions of the EP and the Council, Resolutions of the Council and the Representatives of the Governments of the Member States).

is consistently positive.[16] Furthermore, the EFTA Member States pursue active means of cooperation by accessing the EU flanking framework programmes, albeit in return for a substantive financial contribution.[17] Cooperation within EU flanking policies is exercised through the participation of EFTA Member States in meetings (without the right to vote) of EU agencies such as the European Environmental Agency, as well as through: cooperation on certain topics of particular interest; the creation of common networks; the exchange of information; cooperation between competent EU/EEA Member States' organisations; and seminars and conferences and other types of cooperation.

The Parties to the EEA Agreement are bound by the ECJ case law acquis adopted prior the signature of the EEA Agreement.

"Without prejudice to future developments of case law, the provisions of this Agreement, in so far as they are identical in substance to corresponding rules of the [EC and ECSC founding treaties] and acts adopted in application of these two treaties, shall in their implementation and application be interpreted in conformity with the relevant rulings of the ECJ given prior to the date of signature of this Agreement".[18]

Article 6 of the EEA Agreement, even given its widest interpretation, only refers to cases decided prior to the signature of the EEA Agreement. Future case law of the ECJ is to be "received" through an act of political will by the EEA Joint Committee.[19] The EFTA Member States are not, unlike the EU Member States, under an unconditional obligation to follow wherever the ECJ leads, although it is unlikely that they would enforce a contrary view due to the risk of damaging the EEA structure.[20] On the contrary, the EFTA Court – from the outset – made full use of, and very much based itself on ECJ jurisprudence without making any particular distinction between the "pre- and post-signature" rulings,

---

16 For instance, in accordance with the EEA Joint Committee Annual Report 2002 the EEA Joint Committee implemented 64 EC legal acts and pursued active cooperation in other flanking policies (participation in 34 EC funded programmes and activities to which they contribute financially), in 2005 the EEA Joint Committee implemented 314 EC legal acts, in 2006 349 EC legal acts, in 2007-2008 469 EU acts, in 2009 283 EU legal acts <http://secretariat.efta.int/eea/eea-institutions/eea-joint-committee.aspx>, last visited 18 January 2011.

17 Article 82(1)(a) EEA Agreement. The EFTA Member States contributed 218.89 millions EURO to the EU budget in 2009 for their participation in various EU programmes (the largest and most expensive among all is the Seventh Framewok Programme on Research) and agencies. See the EEA Joint Committee Annual Report 2009, available at <http://secretariat.efta.int/eea/eea-institutions/eea-joint-committee.aspx>, last visited 18 January 2011.

18 Article 6 EEA Agreement.

19 Article 105 EEA Agreement.

20 M. Cremona, "The 'Dynamic and Homogeneous EEA': Byzantine Structures and Variable Geometry" 19 ELRev. 508-526 (1994), at 523.

and, consequently, "there is not a single judgment rendered by the EFTA Court without reference to decisions by the Court of Justice".[21] The EFTA Surveillance Authority also cooperates with the EU Commission in a "spirit of partnership", and is guided by ECJ jurisprudence in "good will".[22]

Some founding doctrines of ECJ case law have been employed by the EFTA Court. For instance, the EFTA Court has held that the "Contracting Parties to the EEA Agreement are obliged to provide compensation for loss and damage caused to an individual by the incorrect implementation of a directive incorporated into the EEA Agreement". In other words, it applied the *"Francovich"* doctrine in an EEA context, albeit without having passed through the stages of direct effect and primacy of the acquis communautaire in the EFTA Member States' legal orders.[23] In the *Sveinbjörnsdottir* case the EFTA Court justified the application of the *"Francovich"* doctrine on the objectives of the EEA Agreement.

"The Court finds that the homogeneity objective and the objective of establishing the right of individuals and economic operators to equal treatment and equal opportunities are so strongly expressed in the EEA Agreement that the EFTA States must be obliged to provide for compensation for loss and damage caused to an individual by incorrect implementation of a directive".[24]

Thus, the EFTA Court considered the principle of state liability an integral part of the EEA Agreement and national legislation in implementing the Agreement.[25] There are some limits to the application of ECJ case law within Article 6 of the EEA Agreement. This provision must, like all other provisions of the EEA Agreement, be interpreted in light of the "aims and context" and "characteristics" of the EEA Agreement.[26] Therefore, Article 6 of the EEA Agreement on its own cannot achieve the objective of homogeneity of the EEA countries' legisla-

---

21 See "EFTA Court legal framework and case law 2008", available at <http://www.eftacourt.int/images/uploads/Legal_Framework_Finalweb.pdf>, last visited 18 January 2011. Also see C. Baudenbacher, P. Tresselt, T. Orlygsson, eds., *The EFTA Court. Ten Years on* (Oxford, Hart Publishing, 2005). For the most recent analysis of the EFTA Court case law see H. Fredriksen, "The EFTA Court 15 Years On" 59 ICLQ 731-760 (2010).
22 See The EFTA Surveillance Authority Annual Report 2008, available at <http://www.eftasurv.int/information/annualreports/dbaFile16167.pdf>, last visited 18 January 2011. Also see N. Levrat, R. Schwok, "Switzerland's Relations with the EU after the Adoption of the Seven Bilateral Agreements" 6 EFARev. 335-354 (2001), at 346.
23 Case E-9/97, *Erla Maria Sveinbjörnsdottir v. the Government of Iceland*, 1997 EFTA Court Report, 95, at 97. Case note by M. Eyjolfsson, 37 CMLRev. 191-211 (2000).
24 *Ibid*, at 60.
25 Further, the principle of state liability was confirmed by the EFTA Court in case E-4/01 *Karl K. Karlsson v. The Icelandic State*, 2002 EFTA Court Report, 240. Therein the EFTA Court decided that the principle of state liability is not contingent upon recognition of a principle of direct effect of EEA rules.
26 Opinion 1/91 [1991] ECR 6079.

tion to the pre-and post-EEA Agreement signature acquis, since it pursues different objectives to the EC Treaty (no internal market, no EMU).[27] Thus, the EFTA Court and other common EU-EEA institutions possess full discretion in circumscribing the precise scope and context of ECJ rulings to be implemented by the EFTA Member States. In practice the EFTA Court acknowledged that the fundamental goal of creating a dynamic and homogeneous EEA may make a dynamic interpretation of EEA provisions and principles necessary.[28] The EFTA Court has been searching for a fair balance between the imperative of homogeneity and the different aims and lack of legislative powers of the EEA. For this purpose the EFTA Court case law went as far as recognizing the EEA Agreement as a new legal system, albeit placed about halfway between the EU legal system and public international law.

"The EEA Agreement is an international treaty *sui generis* which contains a distinct legal order of its own. The depth of integration of the EEA Agreement is less far-reaching than under the EC Treaty, but the scope and objective of the EEA Agreement goes beyond what is usual for an agreement under public international law".[29]

The "pre-signature" acquis communautaire encompasses EU general principles. For example, the EEA Agreement and the EFTA Court case law frequently refer to the principle of non-discrimination.[30] Parties to the EEA Agreement should prohibit any form of discrimination on the grounds of nationality and gender;[31] in trade in goods;[32] in conditions of marketing and procuring goods;[33]

---

27 M. Cremona emphasises that "divergences between the aims and context of the EEA and of Community law stood in the way of the objective of homogeneity". *Supra note 20*.
28 Case E-4/04 *Pedicel A/S v. Sosial- og helsedirektoratet*, 2005 EFTA Court Report, 1, at 28.
29 Case E-9/97, *Erla Maria Sveinbjörnsdottir v. the Government of Iceland*, 1997 EFTA Court Report, 95. See also Case E-2/03 *Ákæruvaldið (The Public Prosecutor) v. Ásgeir Logi Ásgeirsson, Axel Pétur Ásgeirsson and Helgi Már Reynisson* [2003] EFTA Court Rep. 185.
30 For example, Case E-1/94 *Ravintoloitsijain Liiton Kustannus Oy Restamark*, 1994-1995 EFTA Court Report, 15; Case E-6/96 *Tore Wilhelmsen AS v Oslo kommune*, 1997 EFTA Court Report, 53; Case E-1/01 *Hörður Einarsson v The Icelandic State*, 2002 EFTA Court Report, 1.
31 Articles 4 and 28 (2) EEA Agreement. Case E-5/98 *Fagtún ehf v Byggingarnefnd Borgarholtsskóla, íslenska ríkinu, Reykjavíkur og Mosfellsbær*, 1999 EFTA Court Report, 51, at 42, Case E-1/00 *State Debt Management Agency v Íslandsbanki-FBA*, 2000-2001 EFTA Court Report, 8, at 35 and 36, Case E-1/02 EFTA *Surveillance Authority v Kingdom of Norway*, 2003 EFTA Court Report, 1, at 7 and 40.
32 Article 13 EEA Agreement. Case E-1/94 *Ravintoloitsijain Liiton Kustannus Oy Restamark*, 1994-1995 EFTA Court Report, 15, Case E-1/01 *Hörður Einarsson v The Icelandic State*, 2002 EFTA Court Report, 1, Case E-6/96 *Tore Wilhelmsen AS v Oslo kommune*, 1997 EFTA Court Report, 53.
33 Article 16 EEA Agreement.

in the right of establishment;[34] in the free movement of workers;[35] in the free movement of services and capital;[36] in transport charges;[37] in state aid;[38] and in equal pay for men and women.[39] The EFTA Court developed considerable case law on protection of fundamental rights of people through frequent references to the ECHR and judgments of the European Court of Human Rights.[40] Beyond that, the EFTA Court strongly advocates the extension of the whole scope of EU general principles to the EEA legal order, similar to what has happened in the *Sveinbjörnsdottir* case. Therein, the EFTA Court extended the application of the principle of state liability as applied in the EC to the EEA legal order, despite no mention in the EEA Agreement. As commentators believe, in the *Sveinbjörnsdottir* case the EFTA Court opened the door for EFTA institutions to deduce unwritten principles of the acquis communautaire, and to apply them within the EEA legal order.[41] Indeed, the EFTA Court justified the application of the principle of state liability by specific objectives of the EEA Agreement, *inter alia* by the reference to the above-mentioned Article 6 of the EEA Agreement – to acquire the identical interpretation of the EFTA Member States laws with the "pre-signature" ECJ case law acquis.[42]

With regard to the "post-signature" acquis communautaire, Parties to the EEA Agreement combine their efforts to form an identical interpretation of their respective laws, which are as "as uniform as possible", with the relevant acquis communautaire. For this purpose, the EEA Joint Committee keeps the development of the acquis communautaire under constant review in accordance with the homogeneity procedure, which comprises two elements: 1) the timely implemen-

---

34 Case E-3/98 *Herbert Rainford-Towning*, 1998 EFTA Court Report, 205, Case E-8/04 *EFTA Surveillance Authority v the Principality of Liechtenstein*, 2005 EFTA Court Report, 46, Case E-1/04 *Fokus Bank ASA*, 2004 EFTA Court Report, 11.
35 Case E-3/05 *EFTA Surveillance Authority v The Kingdom of Norway*, judgment of 3 May 2006, nyr
36 Articles 40 and 42 EEA Agreement. Case E-1/03 *EFTA Surveillance Authority v Iceland*, 2003 EFTA Court Report, 143.
37 Article 50 EEA Agreement.
38 Article 61 EEA Agreement.
39 Article 69 EEA Agreement.
40 For example, Case E-8/97 *TV 1000 Sverige AB v The Norwegian Government*, 1998 EFTA Court Report, 68, Case E-2/02 *Technologien Bau- und Wirtschaftsberatung GmbH and Bellona Foundation v EFTA Surveillance Authority*, 2003 EFTA Court Report, 52, Case E-2/03 *Ákæruvaldið (The Public Prosecutor) v Ásgeir Logi Ásgeirsson, Axel Pétur Ásgeirsson and Helgi Már Reynisson*, 2003 EFTA Court Report, 185.
41 H. P. Graver, "Mission Impossible: Supranationality and National Legal Autonomy in the EEA Agreement" 7 EFARev. 73-90 (2002), at 81. J. Forman, "The EEA Agreement five years on: Dynamic homogeneity in practice and its implementation by the two EEA courts" 36 CMLRev. 751-781 (1999), at 756.
42 For more precise account of the principle of homogeneity see section 3.2.2.2. in Chapter 3.

tation of EU legislation into the EEA Agreement;[43] 2) the uniform interpretation of the adopted acquis communautaire and the EFTA rules. In practice, the principle of homogeneity means that as soon as a relevant EU rule has been formally adopted by the Council or the EU Commission, the EEA Joint Committee must take a decision concerning the appropriate amendment of the EEA Agreement "with a view to permitting a simultaneous application" of legislation in the EU and the EEA countries.[44] The incorporation of the relevant acquis communautaire cannot take place at all in the absence of an agreement between the EU on the one hand and the EEA countries "speaking with one voice" on the other.[45] Therefore, once a political decision has been taken on the level of the EEA Joint Committee, the new acquis communautaire becomes part of the EEA legal order, and, subsequently, should be implemented by the EFTA Member States. The acquis communautaire adopted within the homogeneity procedure does not differ from the "pre-signature" acquis communautaire. The EFTA Court has been consistent in favouring the export of EU general principles and doctrines into EFTA Member States, such as: protection of fundamental rights;[46] non-discrimination;[47] duty of loyal cooperation;[48] primacy and direct effect,[49] proportionality,[50] good administration,[51] legal certainty and protection of legitimate expectations.[52]

43 Article 102(1) EEA Agreement.
44 Article 102(1) EEA Agreement.
45 Article 93(2) EEA Agreement.
46 Case E-2/03 *Ákæruvaldið (The Public Prosecutor) v. Ásgeir Logi Ásgeirsson, Axel Pétur Ásgeirsson and Helgi Már Reynisson* [2003] EFTA Court Rep. 185.
47 Case E-1/94, *Ravintoloitsijain Liiton Kustannus Oy Restamark v. Helsingin piiritullikamari*, 1994-1995 EFTA Court Report, 15.
48 Case E-1/04 *Fokus Bank ASA*, 2004 EFTA Court Report, 11. Also Cases E-7/97 *EFTA Surveillance Authority v Norway*, 1998 EFTA Court Report, 62; E-10/97 *EFTA Surveillance Authority v Norway*, 1998 EFTA Court Report, 134; E–2/99 *EFTA Surveillance Authority v Norway*, 2000-2001 EFTA Court Report, 1.
49 The EFTA Court recognised quasi direct effect to the EEA Agreement in the EFTA Member States legal orders (Case E-1/94 *Ravintoloitsijain Liiton Kustannus Oy Restamark*, 1994/1995 EFTA Court Report, 15, at 94). The issue of direct effect of the EEA Agreement within the EC legal order was affirmed in *Opel Austria* case (Case T-115/94, *Opel Austria GmbH v. Council*, [1997] ECR II-39). Case note by P. Fischer, 35 CMLREV. 765-781 (1998).
50 For example: Case E-1/03 *EFTA Surveillance Authority v Iceland*, 2003 EFTA Court Report, 143, at 35; Case E-8/04 *EFTA Surveillance Authority v the Principality of Liechtenstein*, 2005 EFTA Court Report 46, at 23.
51 Case E-2/05 *EFTA Surveillance Authority v Iceland*, 2005 EFTA Court Report, 202, at 22.
52 For example, Joined Cases E-5/04, E-6/04 and E-7/04 *Fesil and Finnfjord and Others v EFTA Surveillance Authority*, 2005 EFTA Court Report, 117, at 163.

Being influenced by the EFTA Court's pro-EU interpretation of the EU dynamic acquis the EFTA Member States' national courts also aspire to ensure harmonious application of the ECJ's "pre- and post-signature" rulings in own judgments even in cases when it does not fully comply with their national constitutional law. It happens even in cases when the EEA Agreement influences legal orders of the EFTA Member States even in areas that fall outside the scope of this Agreement. This situation puts national legislature and judiciary to revise their traditional methods of application of international law within their national legal orders. Dynamic nature of the "post-signature" acquis in the EEA Agreement implies "dynamic" interpretation of the relevant EU acquis by the EFTA Member States' legislature and judiciary.[53]

Overall, the application of homogeneity has proved to be a well-functioning means of aligning legal systems of the EEA countries with those of the EU.[54]

2.2.1.3. Concluding remarks

To conclude, the EEA Agreement ensures the implementation by the EFTA Member States of the extensive acquis communautaire that is relevant to the objectives of the Agreement. The body of the relevant acquis communautaire comprises: selected provisions of the EU founding Treaties; vast EU secondary legislation exported into its sophisticated annexes and protocols; ECJ case law adopted before the signing of the EEA Agreement; principles and doctrines developed by the EU institutions. As opposed to other EU external agreements, the EEA Agreement envisages the homogeneity procedure for the timely implementation of the dynamic "post-signature" acquis communautaire into the EFTA Member States' legal orders. The EFTA institutions, in particular the EFTA Court, are dedicated thoroughly to ensuring homogeneity and to enforcing EEA law. Furthermore, they have displayed an impressive judicial activism in transposing unwritten EU law principles into the legal orders of EFTA Member States.

53 K. Bruzelius, "The Impact of EU Values on Third Countries' National Legal Orders: EU Law as a Point of Reference in the Norwegian Legal System" and T.I. Harbo. "The EEA and Norway: A Case of Constitutional Pluralism", in (F. Maiani, R. Petrov, E. Mouliarova) (eds.) *European Integration without EU Membership: Models, Experiences, Perspectives*, European University Institute (Max Weber Programme) Working Papers, 2009/10. In this regards see Case E-1/99, *Storebrand Skadeforsikring AS v. Veronika Finanger,* 1999 EFTA Court Report, 119.
54 The EEA Joint Committee Annual Reports affirm the positive functioning of the EEA Agreement,
http://secretariat.efta.int/Web/EuropeanEconomicArea/institutions/EEAJointCommittee last visited 18 January 2011.

The example of the EEA Agreement represents a successful endeavour on behalf of the EU to export a significant scope of the acquis communautaire within the framework of an association agreement which does not explicitly envisage full EU membership for its signatures. We believe that this success is based on two factors. First, the EEA Agreement provides a convenient framework for EFTA Member States to share all the benefits of the EU Internal Market in return for adopting the relevant acquis communautaire. Second, the EFTA/EEA institutions have successfully extended the EEA Agreement beyond the scope of an international public law treaty towards some degree of supranationality as "a distinct legal order which went beyond what was usual under public international law".[55] For instance, the EFTA Court steadily promotes the direct effect of the EEA Agreement within the EFTA Member States' legal orders, regardless of their national constitutional arrangements, and consistently replicates "pre and post-signature" ECJ rulings into the EEA legal order, such as in the *Sveinbjörnsdottir* case. Despite its complexity, the homogeneity procedure entailed the productive implementation of the dynamic "post-signature" acquis into the EFTA Member States' legal orders. As a result, some EFTA Member States possess a better record in the implementation of the acquis communautaire than some EU Member States.[56]

---

55   Case E-9/97, *Erla Maria Sveinbjörnsdottir v. the Government of Iceland*, 1998 EFTA Court Report, 95, at 56(b).
56   For instance, since the entry into force in 1994 about 6,000 new legal acts were incorporated into the EEA Agreement's annexes. See "Internal Market beyond the EU: EEA and Switzerland", Briefing paper requested by the European Parliament's Committee on Internal Market and Consumer Protection, (European Parliament, 2010).

2.2.2. EC–Switzerland sectoral agreements (SAs)

2.2.2.1. Objectives of the EC–Switzerland SAs

Since 1972 EEC-Swiss economic relations have been based on the Free Trade Area Agreement[57] and more than one hundred bilateral agreements of various relevance.[58] Sectoral EC-Swiss Agreements (SAs) were devised as substitutes for the EEA Agreement following the refusal by Swiss citizens in 1992 to join the EEA out of a fear that the Swiss legal system would be subordinate to the dynamic acquis communautaire.[59] In general, the SAs represent a form of *ad hoc* association[60] and integration into the EU on a higher scale than the EAs or the association with Mediterranean countries, but on a lesser scale than the EEA Agreement.[61] In 1999 the first bilateral sectoral agreements were signed between Switzerland on the one side and (then) EC and Member States on the other which facilitated the autonomous adaptation of the Swiss legal system with EU law.

In the meantime, more than twenty bilateral sectoral agreements have been concluded with Switzerland on the basis of Article 310 EC (now Article 217 TFEU). Quantity of bilateral sectoral agreements between the EU and Switzerland grows steadily every year. These agreements could be divided into so called "waves". In this book we focus on two first "waves" of EC-Switzerland sectoral agreements. The "first wave" of seven bilateral agreements was signed in 1999 and comprises : 1) the Agreement on Scientific and Technological Coopera-

---

57 Agreement of 22 July 1972 between the Swiss Confederation and the EEC, (O.J. 1972, L 300/189).
58 For instance: the Agreement on Mutual Cooperation in Custom Matters of 9 June 1997 (O.J. 1997, L 169/77); the Transit Agreement of 2 May 1992 (O.J. 1992, L 373/6); Framework Agreement on Scientific and Technical Cooperation (O.J. 1985, L 313/6).
59 For the comprehensive account of the EU-Swiss relations history see L. Goetschel, "Switzerland and European Integration: Change through Distance", 8 EFARev. 313-330 (2003). Also see M. Vahl and N. Grolimund, *Integration without Membership. Switzerland's Bilateral Agreements with the European Union* (Brussels, Centre for European Policy Studies 2006). For the most recent account of the EU-Swiss relations see R. Schwok, *Switzerland-European Union. An Impossible Membership?*, (P.I.E. Peter Lang Publisher 2009).
60 S. Breitenmoser insists that the EC-Swiss SAs belong to EC association agreements in the sense of Article 310 EC. He argues that the EC-Swiss SAs occupy a layer between EC cooperation and integration agreements, and even go further than some conventional EC association agreements (for instance with Turkey). See S. Breitenmoser, "Sectoral Agreements between the EC and Switzerland: Contents and Context", 40 CMLRev. 1137-1186 (2003).
61 *Supra note* 22 (Levrat, Schwok), at 337.

tion;[62] 2) the Agreement on Specific Aspects of Government Procurement;[63] 3) the Agreement on Mutual Recognition in relation to Conformity Assessment;[64] 4) the Agreement on Trade in Agricultural Products;[65] 5) the Agreement on Air Transport;[66] 6) the Agreement on the Carriage of Goods and Passengers by Rail and Road;[67] 7) the Agreement on the Free Movement of Persons.[68] On October 2004 Switzerland signed the "second wave" of bilateral agreements with the (then) EC: on processed agricultural products;[69] on the environment;[70] on statis-

---

62   O.J. 2002, L 114/468. The Agreement enables EU and Swiss research entities and scientists to participate in each other's scientific programmes and projects. January 16th 2004 the EU and Switzerland signed a research agreement which enables Swiss participation as an "associated country" in the 6th EU Framework Programme for Research and Technological Development 2003-2006.

63   O.J. 2002, L 114/430. The Agreement requires that Swiss authorities at the district and municipal levels apply EC rules to government procurement. This envisages the harmonisation of Swiss law on procurement to EC and WTO standards which enables Swiss economic operators to participate in public tenders within the EC territory.

64   O.J. 2002, L 114/369. The Agreement foresees the mutual recognition of conformity assessments for industrial products originating in the Contracting Parties. Both Parties recognise reports, certificates, and authorisations of the results of tests of conformity to standards for most industrial products. This agreement is based largely on a model agreement proposed by the EU and already in force in other third states (Canada, New Zealand, and USA). EU and Swiss technical requirements are recognised as equivalent and give equal access to the market of the other party.

65   O.J. 2002, L 114/132. The Agreement facilitates EC-Swiss trade through the regime of mutual recognition of legislation in agricultural products, plant protection, animal feed, seeds and organic farming, as well as veterinary rules with the purpose of facilitating trade in live animals and animal products.

66   O.J. 2002, L 114/73. The Agreement expands EC regulation of air transport to the Swiss territory by providing for the application of the non-discrimination principle by both Parties. The Commission has the competence to monitor compliance by the Parties in competition issues, while the ECJ interprets any implementation and application decisions by EU institutions. In return, Switzerland was given observer Status in several key Committees assisting the Commission in defining the evolution of European air transport policy. This agreement creates a totally unified legal regime for air transport, based on the strict reciprocity between rights and obligations conferred within the EU and Switzerland.

67   O.J. 2002, L 114/91. The Agreement encourages Parties to promote the rail and road mobility of nationals (freedom of transit) and the environmental protection of their own territory, the introduction in Switzerland of new road-charging road systems, and the reciprocal liberalisation of bilateral and transit road transport operations.

68   O.J. 2002, L 114/6. The Agreement foresees the gradual opening of the free movement of EU and Swiss nationals supplemented by the mutual recognition of their qualifications and social security schemes. Furthermore, it guarantees them the same living, employment and working conditions. From 2004, Swiss citizens will enjoy the full freedom of movement within the EU.

69   Agreement between the European Community and the Swiss Confederation amending the Agreement between the European Economic Community and the Swiss Confederation of 22 July 1972 as regards the provisions applicable to processed agricultural products. The Agreement aims at updating the Protocol No 2 of the bilateral Free Trade Agreement in

tics;[71] on the fight against fraud;[72] on the double taxation of retired EU civil servant pensions;[73] on the taxation of savings;[74] on the extension of Schengen and the Dublin Conventions' acquis to Switzerland;[75] on research;[76] on the media[77].

accordance with the results of the Uruguay Round and at adapting its product coverage. It also improves reciprocal market access for processed agricultural products (O.J. 2005, L 23/19).

70 Agreement between the European Community and the Swiss Confederation concerning the participation of Switzerland in the European Environment Agency and the European Environment Information and Observation Network (O.J. 2006, L 90/37). This Agreement grants to Switzerland conditions for participation in the activity of of the European Environment Agency and will comply with the obligations of the Agency Regulation by establishing the appropriate infrastructure for providing uniform environmental data and information on the state of the environment in its territory.

71 Agreement between the European Community and the Swiss Confederation on cooperation in the field of statistics (O.J. 2006, L 90). With this Agreement, Switzerland will be participating in many aspects of the EC Statistical Programme (attendance at certain meetings, publication of data on Switzerland in EU publications, etc.). Moreover, Switzerland will participate in the European Statistical System and adopt a large proportion of the statistical *acquis*.

72 According to this Agreement both sides will grant each other judicial co-operation and administrative assistance on fraud and all other illegal activities, including customs and indirect tax offences in connection with the trade of goods and services. Co-operation against money laundering will be improved considerably, covering in particular also serious cases of fraud and smuggling (O.J. 2009, L 046).

73 In force since 2005. Not reported in O.J. yet. For the text see "systematic collection of Swiss federal Law" (Recueil systématique) (RO 2005 2187; FF 2004 5593).

74 Agreement between the European Community and the Swiss Confederation providing for measures equivalent to those laid down in Council Directive 2003/48/EC on taxation of savings income in the form of interest payments (O.J. 2004, L 385/30). By means of this agreement the Swiss side undertakes to apply, as from 1 July 2005, measures equivalent to those laid down in the EU's Savings Tax Directive. The equivalent measures include a withholding tax on savings-interests paid to residents of EU Member States; a mechanism that allows revenue sharing between Switzerland and the Member State of residence of the recipient of the interest; voluntary disclosure of information regarding interest payments if the taxpayer so agrees; and the exchange of information on request in cases of tax fraud or the like.

75 Agreement between the European Union, European Community and the Swiss Confederation on the Swiss Confederation's association with the implementation, application and development of the Schengen acquis (O.J. 2008 L 53/52). Agreement between the European Community and the Swiss Confederation concerning the criteria and mechanisms for establishing the state responsible for examining a request for asylum lodged in a Member State or in Switzerland (O.J. 2008 L 53/5). The Agreement provides that Switzerland will be involved in all discussions taking place in the Council as far as the further development of the Schengen acquis is concerned.

76 Agreement on scientific and technological cooperation between the European Community and the European Atomic Energy Community and the Swiss Confederation (O.J. 2007 L 189).

77 Agreement between the European Community and the Swiss Confederation in the audiovisual field, establishing the terms and conditions for the participation of the Swiss Con-

Difficult and interrupted negotiations between the EU and Switzerland have resulted in the rejection of some important elements of the acquis communautaire initially to be imposed by Switzerland. For instance, despite its inclusion into the Schengen area, Switzerland is permitted to keep confidential information related to tax evasion on clients of Swiss banks.

The "first wave" of seven SAs are distinguished by a so-called "guillotine clause", which means that all agreements come in one package. In other words, these seven SAs come into force together and are all terminated if just one of them is terminated or not renewed by either Party. This formula was designed as a compromise to avoid a situation where Switzerland remained a party to SAs beneficial solely to her.[78] In addition, the "guillotine clause" formula displays the EU's interest in exporting the acquis as far as possible into the Swiss legal order.

The "guillotine clause" is not present in the "second wave" SAs which could be explained by two factors. The first factor is that the EU and Switzerland have acquired a different level of bilateral relations after the "first wave" of the SAs entered into force and started to function effectively. The second factor is that neither of the "second wave" SAs are of explicit benefit only for Switzerland. On the contrary, these agreements require considerable efforts on behalf of Switzerland not only to implement the relevant acquis communautarire into national legal system but also to ensure the application and implementation of the new acquis which can be issued after these agreements enter into force (SA on the extension of Schengen and the Dublin Conventions' acquis to Switzerland).

In general, the EC-Swiss SAs pursue an objective of liberalising mutual trade and policies within the SAs' subject areas, while providing privileged access to Swiss economic operators to the EU Internal Market.[79] One may argue that the EC-Swiss association and the EEA Agreement provide a unique opportunity for

---

federation in the Community programmes MEDIA Plus and MEDIA Training (O.J. 2006, L 90/23). The Agreement defines the conditions to be met by the Swiss broadcasting regulatory framework, as well as other relevant arrangements, that will have to be in force as of the moment the Agreement comes into force. Switzerland will conform to EU provisions, including controls by EU bodies.

78 Switzerland was eager to separate the SA on the free movement of persons from the other six agreements. It would have allowed Switzerland, in the case of a negative referendum on ratification of this agreement to continue to benefit from the legal regime of the other six agreements. However, these attempts did not succeed and the EU used all its political weight to "force" Switzerland to accept the "guillotine clause" formula (*supra note* 22 (Levrat, Schwok), at 347).

79 For instance, the SA on agriculture sets out the objective of the liberalisation of the agricultural market between the Parties "to strengthen free-trade relations between the Parties by improving the access of each to the market in agricultural products of the other" (Article 1 of the EC-Swiss SA on agriculture). The SA on free movement of persons is aimed at liberalising the access of nationals of the Parties to each other territory (Article 1 of the EC-Swiss SA on free movement of persons).

an associate country to benefit from major advantages of the EU Internal Market without formal EU membership.[80]

The implementation of the relevant acquis communautaire is an essential precondition for achieving the objectives of the SAs. Most of the "first wave" SAs Preambles explicitly hint that Switzerland can achieve objectives of the SAs through the effective application of the relevant acquis communautaire. For example, the Preamble of the SA on air transport unequivocally recognises that "it is appropriate to base rules on the legislation which is in force within the Community at the time of signature of this Agreement".[81] The Preamble of the SA on the free movement of persons endorses that the Parties are "resolved to bring about the free movement of persons between them on the basis of the rules applying in the European Community". The Preamble of the agreement on carriage of goods by rail and road acknowledges the need "to ensure consistency between Swiss transport policy and the general principles underlying the Community's transport policy, particularly in the context of the implementation of a coordinated legislative and regulatory framework". The objectives of the "first wave" of the EU-Swiss SAs have met a positive response in Switzerland. The Swiss government and the Parliament moved from the process of "autonomous adaptation" of national law to EU law to a legislative policy aiming specifically at euro-compatibility of Swiss legislation with the acquis communautaire within the areas of sectoral coopeartion.[82]

Objectives of the "second wave" SAs are more far reaching and vary from the need to "realise a gradual harmonization [in line with the relevant acquis] and ensure the coherent evolution of the legal framework [of Switzerland and the EU]" (SA on statistical cooperation) to the participation of Switzerland in the Schengen and Dublin/Eurodac acquis.

---

80   *Supra note* 22 (Levrat, Schwok), at 336.
81   Article 1 EC-Swiss SA on Air Transport. Furthermore, it states that rules for civil aviation contained the SAs shall not contradict rules contained in the EC Treaty and in particular the EC competences under Articles 81 and 82 EC (now Article 101 and 102 TFEU).
82   F. Maiani, "Legal Europeanization as Legal Transformation: Some Insights from Swiss "Outer Europe"", European University Institute (Max Weber Programme) Working Papers 2008/32. Article 14 of the Law on the Federal Parliament (Classified Compilation of Federal Law, 171.10) sets a general obligation of the Federal Government and Federal Parliament to access "euro-compatibility" of Swiss law to EU law.

2.2.2.2. The scope of the relevant acquis communautaire in the EC–Swiss SAs

Similarly to the EEA Agreement, the relevant "pre-signature" acquis communautaire must be applied by Switzerland. However, in contrast to the EEA Agreement, the acquis communautaire in the EC-Swiss SAs is "static". It means that neither of them foresees the adoption of the dynamic and homogeneous "post-signature" acquis communautaire. In other words, the EC-Swiss SAs envisage neither the timely implementation of the "post-signature" acquis communautaire into the Swiss legal order, nor the uniform interpretation of the adopted acquis communautaire. Contrary to the EEA principle of homogeneity (wherein the adoption of a relevant EU rule by the Council or the Commission commits the EEA Joint Committee to take decision on the appropriate amendment of the EEA Agreement "with a view to permitting a simultaneous application" of legislation in the EU and the EFTA Member States)[83] the EC-Swiss Joint Committees take a decision to amend the relevant "pre-signature" acquis communautaire by unanimous vote upon a respective political decision.[84] The same procedure relates to ECJ jurisprudence that "shall be brought to Switzerland's attention", but without the adequate information exchange procedure reminiscent of the EEA Agreement. Thus the EC-Swiss Joint Committee is in a position to solve the hard task of deciding which developments in the acquis communautaire are to be transposed into the Swiss legal system.[85]

The relevant "pre-signature" acquis communautaire is enshrined in Annexes and Appendices which form the integral part of the EC-Swiss SAs.[86] In accordance with these Annexes Switzerland must be treated as a Member State and must apply the relevant acquis communautaire "to which reference is made, as in force at the date of signature of the Agreement".[87] In some "second wave" SAs

---

83 Article 102(1) EEA Agreement.
84 For instance, Article 6 EC-Swiss SA on air transport and Article 14 EC-Swiss SA on free movement of persons.
85 *Supra note* 60, at 1164.
86 Article 15 EC-Swiss SA on Agriculture.
87 Article 1 of Annex 1 EC-Swiss SA on the free movement of persons states: "1) The parties agree, with regard to the coordination of social security schemes, to apply among themselves the Community acts to which reference is made, as in force at the date of signature of the Agreement and as amended by section A of this Annex, or rules equivalent to such acts; 2) The term "Member States" contained in the acts referred to in section A of this Annex shall be understood to include Switzerland in addition to the States covered by the relevant Community acts." Article 2 of the same Annex states: "1) For the purpose of applying the provisions of this Annex, the contracting parties shall take into consideration the Community acts referred to in or amended by section B of this Annex; 2) 1) For the purpose of applying the provisions of this Annex, the contracting parties shall take into consideration the Community acts referred to in or amended by section C of this Annex."

the need to apply the relevant "pre-signature" acquis communautaire flows from the participation of Switzerland in specific EU policies and institutions (European Environmental Agency, MEDIA Plus and MEDIA Training). For this purpose the SAs pursue the objective to ensure the compatibility of the relevant Swiss law with the sectoral acquis.[88] The Annexes to the EC-Swiss SAs amend the relevant acquis communautaire in force to include Switzerland and to extend the application of the relevant acquis communautaire to Swiss territory.[89]

In a similar manner to the EEA Agreement Annexes, SAs Annexes are constructed in such way as to display the hierarchy of EU acts to be applied by Switzerland.[90] The binding application of relevant pre-signature EU acts is emphasised by the phrase "acts referred to". Other sections of an Annex might refer to EU non-binding acts of which the Parties either "shall take due account" (decisions) or "shall take note" (recommendations, declarations, notifications). The scope of the "pre-signature" acquis communautaire is not limited by EU acts directly referred in the SAs and Annexes, but it does encompass any EC-Swiss SA provisions that are either equivalent to or resembles the relevant acquis communautaire.[91] For example, the SA on technical barriers obliges Switzerland to apply rules that are equivalent to EU legislation on the technical conditions governing road transport, and also rules equivalent to EU legislation on the technical controls for vehicles.[92]

The acquis communautaire in the EC-Swiss SAs is directly applicable in Switzerland.[93] This also relates to the direct effect of EC-Swiss SA provisions. According to rulings of the ECJ and Swiss courts, SA provisions are self-executing on the condition that they are sufficiently clear and precise to constitute a valid legal basis for a decision in individual cases. Conversely, SA provisions with indefinite and non-specific goals with substantial room for discretion or guiding principles may not be considered directly effective in the Swiss legal

---

88 For instance, Article 2 of the SA on media states that "Switzerland will implement the measures described in Annex II, with a view to completing its legislative framework so as to ensure the required level of compatibility with the *acquis communautaire*".
89 For instance the EC-Swiss SAs contain the following provision: "for the purposes of this Agreement, the Regulation shall be adapted as follows: (to include Switzerland)".
90 It relates to the EU-Swiss SA on Free Movement of Persons.
91 For instance Annex 1 EC-Swiss SA on the free movement of persons resembles the relevant (then) EC Treaty articles on the freedoms of the EU Internal Market. The same SA provides that the Parties "shall take all measures necessary to ensure that rights and obligations equivalent to those contained in the legal acts of the European Community to which reference is made are applied in relations between them".
92 Article 7 and 52(6) EC-Swiss SA on technical barriers. Furthermore, the annexes to this agreement frequently refer to equivalent EU legislation.
93 *Supra note* 60, at 1145-1146.

order.[94] As a result, one may argue over the hybrid character of the SAs as a part of both public international and supranational EU law which enables the direct applicability and direct effect of the acquis communautaire within a framework of an EU sectoral association agreement, but without explicit integration objectives.[95]

In general, the SAs do not envisage Switzerland's application of either "pre-signature" or "post-signature" ECJ case law. However, there are several exceptions to this observation in the "first wave" and "second wave" SAs. Two "first wave" SAs (on Free Movement of Persons and on Air Transport) consider the possibility of application by Switzerland of the "post-signature" ECJ case law. The former contains a soft obligation: "account shall be taken of the relevant case-law of the Court of Justice of the European Communities prior to the date of its signature".[96] The latter replicates almost identically Article 6 of the EEA Agreement, and obliges Switzerland to apply "pre-signature" ECJ case law and decisions of the Commission "insofar as they [SA provisions] are identical in substance to corresponding rules of the EC Treaty and to acts adopted in application of that Treaty".[97] In both cases relevant "post-signature" ECJ case-law is not applicable but is merely brought to Switzerland's attention for further political decision. At the request of either Contracting Party, the EC-Swiss Joint Committee determines the implications of "post-signature" ECJ case-law and takes the appropriate decision to ensure the proper functioning of the SA.[98] It is difficult to explain why the ECJ acquis concerns only these two SAs. It might indicate the particular importance of ECJ rulings and homogeneity for the effective application and functioning of the acquis communautaire in the areas of free movement of persons and air transport, since these areas are not fully harmonized on the EU level.

Some "second wave" SAs go even further. The SAs on statistical cooperation and on the media contain the list of the relevant EU acquis in the annexes to the agreement, which is binding for Switzerland. In case of the adoption of the new legislation by either of the Parties (in case of the SA on statistical cooperation only) the Joint Committee has the discretion to revise the list of the applicable acquis and/or to propose a revision of the provisions of the Agreement in order to incorporate any amendments to the relevant acquis communautaire. Two other "second wave" SAs (on the extension of Schengen and the Dublin Conventions' acquis to Switzerland) pursue the specific objective of ensuring the implementa-

---

94   *Ibid*, at 1145-1146.
95   *Ibid*, at 1153.
96   Article 16(2) EC-Swiss SA on the free movement of persons.
97   Article 1(2) EC-Swiss SA on Air Transport.
98   *Ibid*, Article 1(2).

tion, application and development of the EU sectoral acquis by Switzerland. The SAs on the extension of Schengen and the Dublin Conventions' acquis to Switzerland envisage higher degree of the adoption of the dynamic and homogeneous "post-signature" acquis communautaire by Switzerland then in other SAs. These agreements contain provisions which resemble the principle of homogeneity in the EEA Agreement. For instance, the SAs on the extension of Schengen/Dublin acquis to Switzerland provide for the possibility to export into the Swiss legal order not only the "pre-signature" acquis but also the "post-signature" acquis and case law of the ECJ. These SAs provide that common institutions established under the framework of the SAs (Mixed Committees) "shall keep under constant review developments in the case-law of the [ECJ], and in the case-law relating to such provisions of the competent Swiss courts".[99] The Parties to this agreement "shall ensure the prompt mutual transmission of the ECJ case law and case of Swiss national courts". The objective of the SAs on the extension of Schengen and the Dublin Conventions' acquis to Switzerland requires not only the actual implementation but also the simultaneous and harmonious application and interpretation of the Schengen/Dublin acquis by Swiss national courts. For this reason Switzerland undertook the commitment to report "on the way in which its administrative authorities and courts have applied and interpreted" the Schengen/Dublin acquis and the ECJ case law.[100] Systematic failure to ensure the timely implementation and harmonious interpretation of the Schengen/Dublin acquis by Swiss institutions and courts can lead to the eventual termination of the agreements.[101] These agreements illustrate the uncompromising position of the EU on the need to adopt and implement the dynamic "post-signature" EU sectoral acquis in full when a third country is willing to participate in a specific EU policy, which has achieved a high level of legal harmonisation. However, as Swiss legislative practice shows, the Swiss authorities tend to implement "post-signature acquis" on rather partial or selective basis, sometimes leaving outside important legal developments of the sectoral acquis.[102]

International law constitutes a considerable part of a whole acquis to be adopted by Switzerland.[103] The scope of international law within the SAs embraces major multinational trade agreements and international trade law principles. The WTO treaties and rules occupy a central part of the international law

---

99 Article 8 of the SA on the extension of Schengen acquis to Switzerland and Article 5 of the SA on the extension of Dublin acquis to Switzerland.
100 *Ibid*, Articles 9 and 6 respectively.
101 *Ibid*, Articles 10 and 7 respectively.
102 *Supra note* 82, at 8.
103 For instance, the EC-Swiss SA on technical barriers provides for the application of definitions laid down by ISO/IEC Guide 2 (1996 edition) and by European standard EN 45020 (1993 edition).

acquis to be implemented by Switzerland. In the first place it is justified by Swiss membership of the WTO. In the second place it is ensured by the objectives of liberalising trade and by establishing a mutual recognition regime between the Parties. For instance, the Preamble of the SA on agriculture encourages Parties to adhere to WTO standards with the purpose of the gradual elimination of trade barriers. Preambles of the SAs on scientific cooperation and public procurement contain no direct references to the acquis communautaire but explicitly refer to the relevant WTO rules and principles. Consequently, the principles of non-discrimination and reciprocity are considered essential for the association's ambitious objectives.[104] One may argue that these principles constitute unwritten essential elements because the SAs ensure their consistent application, even where either of the Parties introduces new legislation.[105] The scope of the principle of non-discrimination excludes any form of discrimination on the grounds of nationality, origin and competition.[106] Besides, it covers the transparency and effectiveness of certain procedures, as in the SA on public procurement.[107]

2.2.2.3. Concluding remarks

The EC-Swiss SAs are unique *ad hoc* association agreements aimed at the liberalisation of mutual trade and the subsequent establishment of the mutual recognition mechanism between the EU and its second-largest trading partner. Neither of the SAs targets political rapprochement with the EU, nor do they complete Switzerland's integration into the EU Internal Market as in the EEA Agreement or other association agreements. As a result, the scope of the acquis communautaire in the SAs reflects the limited but pragmatic objectives of EU-Swiss relations. Switzerland is bound by the relevant "pre-signature" acquis communautaire enshrined in the SAs provisions and Annexes. The applicability of international law is defined solely by international trade treaties and common principles of international trade, thereby emphasising the trade-focused nature of the EC-Swiss association. With the exception of those on Air Transport, the Free Movement of Persons and on the extension of the Schengen/Dublin acquis, the

---

104 Non-discriminatory access to each other's markets is one of the SA's major objectives . For instance, see Article 3 of the EC-Swiss SA.
105 Article 23 EC-Swiss SA on Air Transport.
106 For instance, Article 16 EC-Swiss SA on air transport, Article 2 EC-Swiss SA on the free movement of persons.
107 Articles 4(1)(d) and 5(1) EC-Swiss SA on public procurement. Article 6 EC-Swiss SA on public procurement and Annex X clarify the scope of the principle of non-discrimination with regard to public procurement.

SAs do not envisage the application of "post-signature" dynamic acquis (including the ECJ case law). In contrast to the EEA Agreement, the EU-Swiss common institutions (Joint/Mixed Committees) exercise an exceptionally significant influence in shaping the "post-signature" acquis communautaire. They have sole responsibility for reviewing and adopting the "post-signature" acquis communautaire, including its latest interpretation by the ECJ. It provides us with a certain expectation that the scope of the acquis communautaire in EC-Swiss SAs will gradually expand depending on a favourable political environment and subsequent political will within the EU-Swiss common institutions. The entrance into force of the two SAs on the extension of the Schengen/Dublin acquis to Switzerland will give the common institutions a considerable power to ensure the implementation and application of the dynamic Schengen/Dublin acquis similar to power of the common institutions in the EEA Agreement and the EU-Turkey Customs Union.

2.2.3. Europe Agreements (EAs)

2.2.3.1. Objectives of the EAs

The EAs are association agreements concluded between the EC, its Member States on one side and the Central and Eastern European countries (CEE countries) on the other in accordance with Article 310 EC (now Article 217 TFEU).[108] The objectives of the EAs set up "an appropriate framework for the political dialogue, allowing the development of close political relations between the Parties; to develop a free trade area… as well as to provide an appropriate framework for the…. gradual integration into the Community".[109] The EAs are not in force any more since all CEE countries have smoothly acceded into the EU through two accession "waves". Poland, Hungary, Czech Republic, Slovenia, Slovakia, Latvia, Estonia and Lithuania have joined the EU on May 1st 2004 through the "first wave" of accession.[110] The "second wave" of accession of Bulgaria and Romania

---

108 The EAs concluded with the following CEE countries: Poland (O.J. 1993 L 348/2, in force since 01 February 1994), Hungary (O.J. 1993 L 347/2, in force since 01 February 1994), the Czech Republic (O.J. 1994 L 360/2, in force since 1 February 1995), the Slovak Republic (O.J. 1994 L 359/2, in force since 01 February 1995), Romania (O.J. 1994 L 357/2, in force since 01 February 1995), Bulgaria (O.J. 1994 L 358/3, in force since 01 February 1995), Lithuania (O.J. 1998 L 51/3, in force since 01 January 1998), Latvia (O.J. 1998 L 26/3, in force since 01 January 1998), Estonia (O.J. 1998 L 68/3, in force since 01 January 1998), Slovenia (O.J. 1999 L 51/3, in force since 01 February 1999).
109 Article 1(2) of the EC-Estonia EA.
110 Act on the conditions of accession of the Czech Republic, the Republic of Estonia, the Republic of Cyprus, the Republic of Latvia, the Republic of Lithuania, the Republic of

took place on 01 January 2007.[111] Hitherto, the EAs constitute an important experience of the EU external policy, which is worth of our attention. The EAs represent an example of unique dynamic contractual framework between the EU and a group of ten formerly socialist countries, which resulted in adoption by the latter of European democratic and market economy standards with eventual membership in the EU. Consequently, either the whole framework of the EAs or its selected elements could be applied by the EU in the course of possible enlargement projects in the future.

From the outset, the EAs were seen as an alternative to full EU membership.[112] However, it has changed at the European Summit in Copenhagen in 1993 and adoption of the Copenhagen Criteria. Henceforth, the EAs were considered as full fledged contractual instruments to bring the CEE countries into the EU. The establishment of a free trade area between the EC and CEE countries constituted a priority objective of the EAs. In reality, the EAs have acted as an accession "waiting room" without any commitments on the part of the EU.[113] The EAs envisaged the possibility of EU full membership "bearing in mind that the final objective of [a CEE country] is to become a member of the Community" and the association, in the view of the Parties, will help to achieve this objective.[114] However, the EAs never provided for express legal pledges on the issue of EU membership, aside from the establishment of a free trade area. Indeed, shortly after signing the first EAs, the 1993 Copenhagen Summit opened the doors to EU membership for CEE nations. Thereafter, the objectives of the EAs have been given a much broader interpretation. The "pre-accession process" implied the adoption by CEE countries of the whole acquis communautaire, in order that they might qualify for EU membership.[115] The EAs still remain an illustrative example of one of the first substantive efforts in EU external policy to export the comprehensive scope of the acquis communautaire into the legal systems of

Hungary, the Republic of Malta, the Republic of Poland, the Republic of Slovenia and the Slovak Republic to the European Union (O.J. 2003, L 236).
111 Act on the conditions of accession of the Republic of Bulgaria and Romania to the European Union (O.J. 2005, L 157).
112 K. Inglis, "The Europe Agreements compared in the light of their pre-accession reorientation", 37 CMLRev. 1173-1210 (2000), at 1173 and M. Maresceau and E. Montaguti "The Relations between the European Union and central and eastern Europe: a legal appraisal", 32 CMLRev. 1327-1367 (1995), at 1328. Also see Van Elsuwege P., *From Soviet Republics to EU Member States. A Legal and Political Assessment of the Baltic States' Accession to the European Union* (Leiden: Martinus Nijhoff, 2008).
113 Commission Communication to the Council COM(90) 278 final of 27 August 1990.
114 For instance, the Preamble to the EC-Hungary EA.
115 See J. Laffrangue, R. M. D'Sa "Domestic implementation of EU Regulations in Estonia: a flawed methodology or necessary transposition?", 27 ELRev. 91-99 (2002), at 95 and K. Inglis, "The Europe Agreements compared in the light of their pre-accession reorientation", 37 CML Rev. 1173-1210 (2000), at. 1173.

neighbour countries within the framework of an association agreement. This chapter scrutinises the scope of the acquis communautaire in the "pre-Copenhagen" EAs. The scope of the acquis communautaire in the "post-Copenhagen" EAs must be understood broader. In other words, the content of the "post-Copenhagen" EAs did not change, but their objectives did, thereby changing and enhancing the scope of the relevant acquis to be adopted by the CEE countries.

2.2.3.2. The scope of the relevant acquis communautaire in the EAs

The preamble of the EAs referred to the existence of "traditional links between the Community, its Member States and [the CEE country] and the common values that they share". The EAs were one among first EU external agreements with a reference to shared/common values. Neither the EAs nor the EU institutions were explicit in what is covered by the phrase "common values". One may argue that this notion could be of either a political or legal nature, or indeed both. In practice, EAs nations' judiciaries have applied this notion in the course of the interpretation of national law in accordance with EU legal rules before their accession to the EU. For instance, back in 1996 the Czech Constitutional Court in the *Skoda Auto* case[116] emphasised the existence of general principles of law common to all EU Member States, which form "common European values". In accordance with the Constitutional Court judgment, these principles must be applied by Czech law enforcement authorities in order to follow the "European legal culture and European constitutional principles".[117]

The EAs (apart from the Polish and Hungarian) emphasised the importance of the essential elements of the agreements. Though the EAs did not clarify the meaning of the essential elements, their legal nature is derived from the 1969 Vienna Convention on Treaties, which states that "[a] material breach of a treaty, for the purposes of this article, consists in:... (b) the violation of a provision essential to the accomplishment of the object or purpose of the treaty".[118] The essential element clause allows the EU to suspend the agreement if any of the essential elements of the Association Agreement (notably respect for human rights and democracy) is breached. Respect for democratic principles and human rights and adherence to the principles of a market economy formed a foundation of the

---

116 *Scoda Auto,* Collection of decisions of the Czech Constitutional Court, (1997) vol. 8, p. 149.
117 Z. Kühn, "Application of European law in Central European candidate countries", 28 ELRev. 551-560 (2003), at 555.
118 Article 60(3)(b) 1969 Vienna Convention on Treaties.

"essential elements" concept within the EAs.[119] Consequently, the EAs' essential elements covered universal political and economic liberties, such as the rule of law and human rights, including the rights of minorities, a multiparty system with free and democratic elections, and liberalisation aimed at establishing a market economy.[120] The normative base for the EAs' essential elements laid down in multilateral international and regional instruments such as the European Convention on Human Rights, the European Energy Charter Treaty, as well as the Ministerial Declaration of the Lucerne Conference of 30 April 1993. EU institutions closely monitored the EA nations' policies through the prism of the fulfillment of essential elements, thereby displaying a consistent policy of political and democratic conditionality.[121]

The liberalisation of mutual trade was one of the major objectives of all Parties to the EAs. Therefore, the scope of the acquis communautaire to be implemented by the CEE countries was focused mainly on sectors related to free trade: trade barriers, agriculture, fisheries, services, capital, freedom of establishment, and standards. To achieve these objectives, the EAs imposed international law on EAs countries that comprises multilateral international trade agreements and international trade principles. The application of the WTO rules was important for the entire trade liberalisation process. The EAs explicitly stated that issues of tariffs reduction, combined nomenclature, anti-dumping, and freedom of payment must be based on the application of relevant WTO rules and principles.[122] CEE countries' national laws on the award of public contracts are based on the principle of non-discrimination and reciprocity regime in accordance with the General Agreement on Trade and Tariffs (GATT).[123]

In the field of protection of intellectual, industrial and commercial property rights, EA countries were expected to provide a level of protection similar to that already existing in the EC, including effective means of enforcing such rights.

---

119 In general, the EAs provisions on essential elements refer to the Helsinki Final Act (Universal Declaration of Human Rights – Slovenia EAs) and in the Charter of Paris for a New Europe, as well as the principles of market economy, market economy as reflected in the Document of the CSCE Bonn Conference on Economic Cooperation. For instance, Article 7(2) of the EC-Slovak EA. Notably, Article 7(2) of the EC-Romanian EA adds "the principles of market economy and the support by the Community through this Agreement are essential to the present association".
120 See the EAs Preambles.
121 F. Schimmelfennig, S. Engert, H. Knobel, "Cost, Commitment and Compliance: The Impact of EU Democratic Conditionality on Latvia, Slovakia and Turkey", 41 JCMS 495–518 (2003).
122 Article 8(1), 28 EC-Estonia EA, Article 64(2) EC-Estonia EA.
123 Article 67 EC-Estonia EA. Therein, Estonian companies were allowed access to contract award procedures in the EC pursuant to EC procurement rules under a treatment no less favourable than that accorded to EC companies.

Consequently, CEE countries undertook a commitment to accede to multilateral conventions on intellectual, industrial and commercial property rights referred to in the relevant Annexes to the EAs.[124] In addition to multilateral international treaties, CEE countries have pledged to implement soft international norms in various sectors of cooperation between the Parties: UN guidelines on consumer protection; international rules on standardisation;[125] FATF (Financial Action Task Force) standards to combat money laundering.[126] Some EAs referred to international law treaties specific to a particular CEE country. For instance, the Preamble of the Slovenia EA referred to the Osimo Agreements,[127] which encompass a framework treaty (Peace Treaty) and several annexes (agreement on economic co-operation with the elements on construction of roads, co-operation between the ports in the North Adriatic Sea and protection of the maritime environment).

The principle of non-discrimination played a pivotal role in the overall EAs liberalisation process. The EAs explicitly referred to this principle with regard to: fiscal discrimination;[128] the application of safeguard measures;[129] conditions of marketing and procurement of goods;[130] restrictions in trade of goods;[131] treatment of workers based on nationality and as regards working conditions, remuneration or dismissal compared with its own nationals;[132] the operation of companies;[133] free supply of services in international maritime transport;[134] the

---

124 Article 66 EC-Estonia EA.
125 Article 86(2) EC-Estonia EA and Article 96(2) EC-Estonia EA.
126 Article 89 (2) EC-Estonia EA. The Financial Action Task Force (FATF) is an intergovernmental body whose purpose is the development and promotion of policies, at both national and international levels, to combat money laundering and terrorist financing. The Task Force is therefore a "policy-making body" which works to generate the necessary political will to bring about national legislative and regulatory reforms in these areas. The FATF monitors members' progress in implementing necessary measures, reviews money laundering and terrorist financing techniques and counter-measures, and promotes the adoption and implementation of appropriate measures globally. In performing these activities, the FATF collaborates with other international bodies involved in combating money laundering and the financing of terrorism. There are 33 FATF Member States. See website <http://www.fatf-gafi.org>, last visited 18 January 2011.
127 These are agreements signed by the Italian Republic and former Socialistic Federal Republic of Yugoslavia in Osimo on 10 November 1975 in Italy, and to which the Republic of Slovenia succeeded after the dissolution of Socialistic Federal Republic of Yugoslavia.
128 For example, Article 26 EC-Estonia EA.
129 For example, Article 30 EC-Estonia EA.
130 For example, Article 32 EC-Estonia EA.
131 For example, Article 34 EC-Estonia EA.
132 For example, Article 36 EC-Estonia EA.
133 For example, Article 46 EC-Estonia EA.
134 For example, Article 53 EC-Estonia EA.

award of public contracts;[135] access to courts and administrative organs.[136] The EAs did not specify whether the principle of non-discrimination should be applied either in accordance with WTO rules or EC law. However, in practice the ECJ had supported this approach and considered provisions of the EAs on non-discrimination on the grounds of nationality, working conditions, remuneration or dismissal as directly effective and precluding both direct and indirect discrimination measures on behalf of the Member States in line with its previous case law.[137]

Fair competition and the abolition of discriminative state aid were considered of prime importance for the liberalisation of trade between the Parties. Therefore, the EAs chapters on competition and state aids referred to relevant WTO and acquis communautaire criteria to be applied by the CEE nations. For instance, the EAs provided that any uncompetitive practices of the Parties must be assessed on the basis of criteria arising from the application of the rules of Articles 85, 86 and 92 EC (now Articles 105, 106 and 112 TFEU).[138] Practices in the fields of agriculture and fisheries could have been assessed according to the criteria established on the basis of Articles 42 and 43 EC (now Articles 48 and 49 TFEU) and, in particular, of those established in Council Regulation No 26/62.[139] In these cases, the CEE countries were expected to apply both the "pre-signature" and "post-signature" acquis communautaire on a voluntary basis. However, the application of the "post-signature" acquis communautaire within these criteria went further than in the EEA Agreement and the EU-Swiss SAs. The Implementing Rules to the EAs clarified that the compatibility of aid awards and programmes in the CEE countries should be made "on the basis of the criteria arising from the application of the rules of Article 87 EC Treaty [now Article 107 TFEU], including the present and future secondary legislation, frameworks, guidelines and other relevant administrative acts in force in the Community, as well as the case law of the CIF [now the General Court] and the ECJ".[140] This means that the EAs ensured the application of the whole "post-signature" acquis communautaire within

---

135 For example, Article 67 EC-Estonia EA.
136 For example, Article 118 EC-Estonia EA.
137 C-257/99 *The Queen v Secretary of State for the Home Department, ex parte: Barkoci and Malik* [2001] ECR I-6557. C-63/99 *The Queen v. Secretary of State for the Home Department, ex parte: Gloszczuk* [2001] ECR I-6369. C-235/99 *The Queen v. Secretary of State for the Home Department, ex parte: Kondova* [2001] ECR I-6427. C-268/99 *Jany and Others v. Staatssecretaris van Justitie* [2001] ECR I-8615. C-162/00 *Land Nordrhein-Westfalen v. Pokrzeptowicz-Meyer* [2002] ECR I-1049. See case note by C. Hillion in 40 CMLRev. 465–491, 2003.
138 For example, Article 62(2) EC-Hungary EA.
139 Article 63(5) EC-Estonia EA.
140 Article 2(1) of the Implementing Rules to the EAs.

the legal orders of the CEE countries, without applying the lengthy homogeneity procedure used in the EEA Agreement.

Two questions arised when these criteria are applied. Firstly, did these criteria impose hard or soft commitments on the CEE countries? Secondly, was the scope of these criteria identical to the relevant acquis communautaire? With regard to the latter, we argue that references to EC primary and secondary law in the EAs did not presume an identical application within the CEE countries' legal orders. This is justified by the nature of the EAs objectives against the objectives of the founding EC treaties. Some commentators indicated the different context in which the fundamental acquis communautaire operates within the EAs.[141] For example, M. Cremona argued that "compatibility with the common market" and the "common interest" reflected in Article 87 EC (now Article 107 TFEU) should be perceived differently in the context of the EAs and SAAs objectives. She therefore believed that associate states' National Authorities had to develop their own interpretations of existing EC rules to take account of their own specific needs at a time of major economic and industrial reform.[142] However, one may argue that immature at that time legal systems of certain CEE nations were not able to undertake an authoritative interpretation of the acquis communautaire against national legislative priorities, owing to a lack of a common European legal heritage. It could have taken considerable time for CEE countries to absorb common European legal traditions through the judicial activism of national courts. Thus, as practice showed, while maintaining the refusal of the binding force of the acquis communautaire, most of the CEE national judiciaries consistently ensured the widest possible interpretation of national legislation in accordance with the dynamic acquis communautaire. For instance, the Hungarian Constitutional Court in the *European Agreement Judgment* (1998) identified the scope of Article 62(2) of the Hungary EA as similar to the relevant acquis communautaire, covering not only primary and secondary EC legislation, but latest ECJ jurisprudence.[143]

References to the EC primary and secondary law in the EAs did not automatically apply directly within the CEE countries' legal orders. The direct applicability and direct effect of EA provisions depended on the national constitutional arrangements of the CEE countries. Most of them share a monist system of inter-

---

141 M. Cremona, "State Aids Control: Substance and Procedure in the Europe Agreements and the Stabilisation and Association Agreements", 9 ELJ 265-287 (2003).
142 *Ibid*, at 272.
143 Decision 30/1998 (VI.25) AB of the Hungarian Constitutional Court. Therein, the Hungarian Constitution Court stated that "the content totality of Community competition law, including the developments of jurisprudence and the rules of the block exemption regulations under Article 85 EC [now Article 105 TFEU] as well as the experience gained in their application".

national law application in their national legal orders. The only CEE country with a dualist system is Hungary. The Hungarian Constitutional Court explicitly refused to consider that provisions of EC primary and secondary legislation enshrined in the agreement had any direct effect.[144] The Hungarian Constitutional Court suggested that the direct effect of the EC competition acquis (now Articles 101 and 102 TFEU) through Article 62(2) of the Hungarian EA is unconstitutional. This is because the EA implementing rules on the respective provisions could have conferred on Hungarian authorities the obligation to apply a future acquis communautaire, which undermines Hungarian sovereignty.[145] There was no consensus on the direct effect of the EAs within EA countries, which share the monist system of application of international law within their legal orders. Only the provisions of the Czech EA were recognised by the Czech courts as having direct effect.[146] These were self-executing provisions of the Czech EA,[147] which referred to Articles 85, 86, and 92 EC (now Articles 105, 106 and 112 TFEU). The remaining EA countries' judicial authorities pursued a more cautious approach in recognising the direct effect of the EAs provisions within their legal orders. In general, the EA countries' judicial bodies avoided ruling on the compatibility of conflicting national laws with EA provisions. Instead, they referred such cases to a national Constitutional Court[148] which preferred regarding conflicting EA provisions as a mere "strong persuasive source of law".[149]

Nonetheless, even rejecting the direct effect of the acquis communautaire within the EAs, the Polish, Czech and Hungarian Constitutional Courts emphasised the need to ensure consistent compatibility in the interpretation of domestic

---

144 Decision 30/1998 (VI.25.) AB of the Hungarian Constitutional Court.
145 Section V of the Decision 30/1998 (VI.25.) AB of the Hungarian Constitutional Court.
146 Judgment of the Czech High Court in the Olomouc case (2A6/96) and Judgment of the Czech Constitution Court in the Olomouc case (III.US 31/97-35).
147 Article 64 EC-Czech EA.
148 For instance, the Slovak Constitution, as amended by the constitutional law of 2001, states that "international treaties on human rights and basic freedoms, international treaties, which can be applied without a statute, and international treaties, which are based on rights or duties of natural or legal persons, if ratified and published in the manner prescribed by law, shall have priority over national statutes". However, in reality, ordinary Slovak judges do not have the power to set aside domestic law in conflict with international law (conflicting EA provisions), and must refer such cases to the Slovak Constitutional Court (*supra note* 117, at 557). A substantive overview of application of international law within legal orders of the EAs countries may be found in Chapter 2 "International Agreements in the legal orders of the candidate countries", in A. Ott / K. Inglis (eds.) Handbook on European Enlargement: a Commentary on the Enlargement Process, (The Hague, T.M.C. Asser Press 2002), 209-348.
149 Kühn argues that the use of EU law by CEE countries' constitutional courts is a special type of application of comparative law in the course of interpretation of domestic law (*supra note* 117, at 551).

laws in accordance with the relevant acquis communautaire by the national judiciary.[150] For instance, the Polish Constitutional Tribunal stated the following:

"Of course, EU law has no binding force in Poland. The Constitutional Tribunal wishes, however, to emphasize the provisions of Article 68 and Article 69 of the [Polish EA] ... Poland is thereby obliged to use 'its best endeavours to ensure that future legislation is compatible with Community legislations' ... The Constitutional Tribunal holds that the obligation to ensure compatibility of legislation (borne, above all, by the parliament and government) results also in the obligation to interpret the existing legislation in such a way as to ensure the greatest possible degree of such compatibility".[151]

Furthermore, the relevant acquis communautaire had to be taken into account and implemented by EAs national authorities in the course of law enforcement, owing to the specific integration-oriented objectives of the EAs.[152] As the Hungarian Constitution Court indicated in the *Europe Agreement Judgment* "the relevant Community law criteria, as soon as they appear in the decisions of the competition authority or the court of the Community or in the Community regulations, have to be taken into consideration and applied by the Hungarian competition law enforcement authority".[153]

---

150 See the comprehensive analysis of the so-called "European Agreement Judgment" by the Hungarian Constitutional Court in J. Volkai, "The application of the Europe Agreement and European Law in Hungary: the judgment of an activist constitutional court on activist notions", Harvard Jean Monnet Working Paper 8/99 (Harvard Law School, 2000) and J. Voklai, "Solutions to the Unconstituonality of the EC-Hungary Antitrust Cooperation Regime: Anti-Trust or Antitrust Cooperation?", CJEL 321-359 (2000). Also see A. Tatham, "Constitutional Judiciary in Central Europe and the Europe Agreement: Decision 30/1998 (VI.25) AB of the Hungarian Constitutional Court". 48(4) ICLQ 913-920 (1999). With regard to Czeck experience see article by Kühn, *supra note* 117, at 553. With regard to the Polish experience see W. Czaplinksi, "Harmonisation of laws in the European Community and approximation of Polish legislation to Community Law" 25 Polish Yearbook of International Law 45-55 (2001).
151 For instance, see Polish Decision K. 15/97, OTK [Orzecznictwo Trybunalu Konstytucyjnego, the collection of decisions of the Constitutional Tribunal], nr. 19/1997, at 380. For English translation of this case see 5 East European Case Reporter of Constitutional Law 271-284 (1998).
152 T. Toth "Competition Law in Hungary: Harmonisation towards EU Membership", 19(6) ECLR 358-369 (1998).
153 *Supra note* 150 (Voklai), at 325.

2.2.3.3. Concluding remarks

To conclude, on the one hand, the scope of the acquis communautaire in the EAs differed from the "accession acquis"[154] and must be seen within the specific objectives of the EAs. The objectives of trade liberalisation and possible integration into the EU have induced the CEE countries to embark upon the implementation of the acquis communautaire, which exceeds the scope of the acquis provided in the EEA Agreement and the EU-Swiss SAs. It comprised vague notions of common values and essential elements largely based on common/universal law principles and doctrines. The scope of international law sources had to be implemented by the CEE countries covered basic UN and Commission on Security and Cooperation in Europe (CSCE)[155] documents and international conventions in the areas of human rights, democratic freedoms and the protection of intellectual property rights. The process of trade liberalisation was based on the WTO acquis. The EAs contained references to criteria arising from the application of EC rules in areas of fair competition and state aid, as well as in internal market freedoms. References to these criteria were transferred into the CEE countries legal systems via the EAs implementing rules, which did not sometimes reflect the whole scope of the respective EC competition and state aid acquis.[156] However, the Polish, Czech and Hungarian judiciaries pioneered a consistent approach in ensuring the most favorable interpretation of national legislation and enforcement practices in accordance with the relevant EC law criteria, owing to the specific integration-oriented objectives of the EAs.

The favorable interpretation of the acquis communautaire by the EAs national courts may be explained by the *sui generic* nature of the EAs. Indeed, the EAs objectives have evolved from mere association agreements to one of the instruments of the "pre-accession" strategy. In this situation the major burden on applying and implementing the relevant acquis is laid on the CEE national courts. The "pre-accession" strategy played important role in elevating the role of the acquis communautaire within legal systems of the CEE countries. After the Copenhagen Summit in 1993 approximation commitments of the CEE countries were given a new dimension. It means that they became perceived by the EU and the CEE countries as a necessary pre condition to achieve objectives of the EAs.

154 For the comprehensive analysis of the scope of the accession acquis see section 1.5.2 above.
155 The Commission on Security and Cooperation in Europe, also known as the Helsinki Commission, is an independent U.S. Government agency created in 1976 to monitor and encourage compliance with the Helsinki Final Act and other OSCE commitments <http://www.csce.gov>, last visited 18 January 2011.
156 P. Schütterle, "State Aid Control- An Accession Criterion", 39 CMLRev. 577-590 (2002), at 579.

Accession Partnerships, NPAAs and regular Country Reports provided much needed institutional and legal guideline on the road to the EU. Despite the fact that the CEE countries' judiciaries have enjoyed significant freedoms in deciding to what extent their national legislation must reflect the relevant acquis communautaire[157] in many cases they preferred to "Europeanize" their national legal systems and to enrich their own legal traditions and culture. One of the consequences of this is the use of the teleological interpretation of EA national laws pursuant to the acquis communautaire by the CEE countries' judiciaries.[158]

2.2.4. Stabilisation and Association Agreements (SAAs)

2.2.4.1. SAAs objectives

EU relations towards the Western Balkan countries are governed by the Stabilisation and Association Process (SAP).[159] Its main objectives target the enhancement of the Western Balkan countries' progress in economic and political development; regional trade and cooperation; and cooperation in justice and home affairs.[160] The SAP supports the countries' development and preparations for future EU membership by combining three main instruments: 1) SAA; 2) autonomous trade measures and 3) substantial financial assistance. By taking part in the SAP, the Western Balkan countries have agreed to abide to EU conditionality in return for the remote objective of full EU membership.[161]

The SAAs were devised as "a new type of EA". They are association agreements concluded on the basis of Article 310 EC (now Article 217 TFEU).[162] Indeed, the SAAs resemble the EAs in their objectives, structure, institutional

---

157 *Supra note* 141, at 279. S. Blockmans, *Tough Love. The European Union's Relations with the Western Balkans* (The Hague, T.M.C. Asser Press 2007).
158 *Supra note* 117, at 582.
159 The following Western Balkan countries take part in the SAP: FYROM, Serbia and Montenegro, Bosnia and Herzegovina, Croatia, Albania.
160 The Third Annual European Commission's Report on the Stabilisation and Association process for South East Europe, COM(2004) 202/2 final.
161 Croatia, Montenegro and the FYROM have already filed their formal application for the EU membership and obtained the candidate country status.
162 At the moment of writing the SAAs have been concluded with the FYROM (O.J. 2004 L 084), Croatia (O.J. 2005 L 026), Albania (O.J. 2006 L 300), and Montenegro (O.J. 2010 L 108). The FYROM, Croatia, Albania and Montenegro SAAs entered into force on 03 May 2001, on 12 December 2001, 01 April 2009, and on 01 May 2010 respectively. The SAAs with Serbia and Bosnia and Herzegovina were signed and await ratification by all Member States in the nearest future. Until that, the relations between the EU and Serbia and Bosnia and Herzegovina are governed by Interim Agreements (Council Regulation 1616/2006 O.J. 2006 L 300).

framework and sectoral cooperation, but avoid any vagueness inherent to the EAs, *inter alia* with regard to the nature and priorities of the approximation process. Experts consider the SAAs an "appropriate alternative to the EAs" or a purpose-tailored association which offers the Western Balkan countries the tentative status of "potential candidate country".[163] Regardless of political objectives, the SAAs provide a solid foundation for the implementation of the comprehensive acquis communautaire by the Western Balkan countries. The Preambles of the SAA emphasise the commitment of the SAA countries "to approximate [their] legislation to that of the Community" which is one of the preconditions of their integration "into the political and economic mainstream of Europe" and the acquisition of the status of candidate for EU membership. The SAAs are more explicit than the EAs in clarifying the formal criteria for EU membership by stating that their future application for EU membership shall be considered in accordance with the requirements of the Article 49 TEU (Article 34 TEU amended by ToL), fulfillment of the Copenhagen criteria, and the "successful implementation of this Agreement, notably regarding regional cooperation". Remarkably, the requirements of regional cooperation and regional stability compound the key factors for further development and enhancement of the association. At the time of writing two Western Balkan countries (Croatia and FYROM) were granted the candidate countries status.

The SAAs envisage that the association with the EC should be achieved in ten years in the case of the FYROM and Albania, and in six years for Croatia.[164] The same periods of time are given to the Parties to "gradually establish a free trade area in accordance ...and in conformity with those of the GATT 1994 and the WTO rules",[165] and to approximate the SAAs countries' legislation to that of the EU.[166]

2.2.4.2. The scope of the acquis communautaire in the SAAs

In contrast to other EU association agreements, the political decision to conclude the SAA was based upon the presumption that a SAA country has already

---

163 D. Phinnemore, "Stabilisation and Association Agreements: Europe Agreements for the Western Balkans?", 8 EFARev 77-103 (2003), at 78 -80. M. Cremona advocates that the EAs and SAAs are "more than trade liberalisation but closer integration with the EC" in (*supra note* 141, at 266).
164 Articles 5 FYROM and Croatia SAA and Article 6 of the Albania SAA.
165 Article 15 FYROM and Croatia SAAs. Meantime, only Croatia (11/2000), Serbia and Montenegro (04/2003), Albania (09/2000) joined the WTO. Other Western Balkan countries have observer status to the WTO.
166 Article 1 FYROM and Croatia SAAs.

adopted a substantive acquis communautaire: respect for democratic principles, human rights, rule of law, protection of minorities, and the return of refugees.[167] Besides, the SAA countries are expected to adhere to additional political and legal commitments inherent to the Western Balkan region: to implement the Dayton Agreement; to cooperate with the International Criminal Tribunal for the former Yugoslavia (ICTY);[168] to ensure market economy reforms and regional co-operation. The SAAs are marked by a greater degree of EU conditionality than other EU association agreements. In contrast to the EEA Agreement and the EAs, the Western Balkan countries must demonstrate a substantive level of political and security regional stability and must be able to adapt a fundamental democratic acquis before opening formal association negotiations.[169] This approach is repeated in recent EU external policies (European Neighbourhood Policy).

The need to follow the "fundamental acquis" is strengthened by the SAA essential elements. The scope of the essential elements within the SAAs does not differ from similar EAs provisions. It covers the "democratic principles and human rights as proclaimed in the Universal Declaration of Human Rights and as defined in the Helsinki Final Act and the Charter of Paris for a New Europe, respect for international law principles and the rule of law as well as principles of market economy"[170] as reflected in documents of the CSCE.[171] However, there are some essential elements inherent solely to the SAAs. Since regional stability and cooperation count among the priority objectives of the SAAs, one may consider them an essential element of the association also. The SAAs oblige the Parties to conclude regional cooperation agreements with the SAP participants and potential candidates for EU membership.[172]

Preambles to the Former Yugoslav Republic of Macedonia (FYROM), Croatia and Albania SAAs contain frequent references to international law, which are characterised by a strong human rights and democratic dimension. The SAAs

---

167 This is based on the assumption that a SAA country has shown some success in adopting the EU common values which may become essential elements in the agreements and acquiring "the high level of political and economic development required to meet the increased reciprocal and mutual obligations of the relevant acquis" (COM 99 235 at para 3).
168 UN specialised court located in The Hague, The Netherlands <http://www.un.org/icty/>, last visited 18 January 2011.
169 Communication from the European Commission to the Council and the European Parliament "The Western Balkans and European Integration". COM (2003) 285 final.
170 Article 2 FYROM and Croatia SAAs. In addition to these elements of the "fundamental acquis" Article 2 Albania SAA refers to the ECHR.
171 The Commission on Security and Cooperation in Europe, also known as the Helsinki Commission, is an independent U.S. Government agency created in 1976 to encourage and monitor compliance with the Helsinki Final Act and other OSCE commitments <http://www.csce.gov>, last visited 18 January 2011.
172 Articles 13-14 FYROM and Croatia SAAs.

commit the Parties to implement "all principles and provisions" of: the UN Charter, OSCE documents "notably those of the Helsinki Final Act, the concluding documents of the Madrid and Vienna Conferences, the Charter of Paris for a New Europe, and of the Stability Pact for south-eastern Europe, as well as compliance with the obligations under the Dayton/Paris and Erdut agreements, so as to contribute to regional stability and co-operation among the countries of the region".[173] The liberalisation of trade and the establishment of a free trade area must be based on the "compliance with the rights and obligations arising out of the WTO"[174] and International Monetary Fund (IMF)[175] rules.[176] For instance, the SAAs provide that the antidumping and countervailing measures are applied in accordance with the relevant WTO acquis.[177] In the area of intellectual, industrial and commercial property rights, the FYROM and Croatia undertake to accede (within the five-year period in case of the FYROM, four-year period in case of Albania to the specified list of multilateral conventions.[178]

The application of the principle of non-discrimination ensures the gradual liberalisation of trade between the EU and the SAA countries. The SAAs explicitly refer to this principle in the areas of: fiscal discrimination;[179] the application of safeguard measures;[180] the procurement and marketing of goods;[181] the application of restrictions on free movement of goods;[182] with regard to working conditions, remuneration or dismissal;[183] the establishment of companies;[184] the supply

---

173 Albania SAA does not have any references to Dayton/Paris and Erdut agreements as well as the need to cooperate with the ICTY. However, it contains a separate chapter on cooperation on combating money laundering, terrorism financing, illicit drugs and cooperation in counter-terrorism.
174 For instance: GATT rules on dumping; rules on establishing a free trade area: as provided in the Croatia SAA Article 6 "The Agreement shall be fully compatible with the relevant WTO provisions, in particular Article XXIV of the GATT 1994 and Article V of the GATS".
175 The IMF is an international organization of 184 member countries. It was established to promote international monetary cooperation, exchange stability, and orderly exchange arrangements; to foster economic growth and high levels of employment; and to provide temporary financial assistance to countries to help ease balance of payments adjustment. See webpage <http://www.imf.org/>, last visited 18 January 2011.
176 Article 58 FYROM SAA.
177 Article 70(9) Croatia SAA.
178 Articles 71 FYROM and Croatia SAAs, Article 73 Albania SAA. The list of the conventions and treaties is in Annexes to these agreements.
179 Article 33 FYROM SAA, Article 34 Albania SAA.
180 Article 38 FYROM SAA.
181 Article 39 FYROM SAA, Article 40 Albania SAA.
182 Article 41 FYROM SAA, Article 42 Albania SAA.
183 Article 44 FYROM SAA, Article 46 Albania SAA.
184 Article 48 FYROM SAA, Article 50(2) Albania SAA.

of maritime transport services;[185] the award of public contracts;[186] education;[187] access to courts and administrative organs.[188]

The SAAs encourage Western Balkan countries to adopt EU sectoral acquis on competition and state aid.[189] Just like the EAs, the SAAs provisions replicate the relevant provisions of the (then) EC Treaty on fair competition and state aids (agreements, concerted practices; prohibition of dominant position; illegal state aids) and provide that "any practices contrary to this Article shall be assessed on the basis of criteria arising from the application of the rules of Articles 81, 82 and 87 of the EC Treaty [now Articles 101, 102 and 107 TFEU] and interpretative instruments adopted by the Community institutions".[190] Similarly to the EAs, this wording implies the application of the whole relevant EU sectoral acquis, including relevant soft law and the ECJ and General Court's case law. The SAAs encourage the export of a whole relevant acquis communautaire through soft references to the EU sectoral acquis, i.e. principles, standards and common systems. These references cover the broad range of EU policies: statistical cooperation;[191] banking, customs,[192] insurance and other financial services;[193] health and safety of workers;[194] social cooperation;[195] transport.[196] The SAAs reflect the dynamic evolution of the acquis communautaire through the inclusion of new titles in the audio-visual field, cross-border broadcasting, acquisition of intellectual property rights for programme and broadcast by satellite or cable, cooperation in electronic communications and associated services. The SAA provisions are striking for their emphasis on the full adoption of the sectoral acquis communautaire while saying very little on the appropriate procedures for its enforce-

---

185 Article 57(3)(c) FYROM SAA, Article 59(1) Albania SAA.
186 Article 72 FYROM SAA, Article 74 Albania SAA.
187 Article 100(2) Albania SAA.
188 Article 115 FYROM SAA, Article 123 Albania SAA.
189 Article 69 FYROM SAA, Article 70 Croatia SAA, Article 71 Albania SAA.
190 Article 70(2) Croatia SAA, Article 69(2) FYROM SAA.
191 Article 82 FYROM SAA and Article 83 Croatia SAA.
192 Article 89 Croatia SAA and Article 88 FYROM SAA.
193 Article 83 FYROM SAA and Article 84 Croatia SAA provide that "the cooperation shall focus on: the adoption of a common accounting system compatible with European standards".
194 Article 90(4) FYROM SAA and Article 91(4) Croatia SAA state that "the Parties shall develop cooperation between them with the aim of improving the level of protection of the health and safety of workers, taking as a reference the level of protection existing in the Community".
195 Article 91(4) Croatia SAA, Article 90(4) FYROM SAA provide that "the Parties shall develop cooperation between them with the aim of improving the level of protection of the health and safety of workers, taking as a reference the level of protection existing in the Community".
196 Article 98 FYROM SAA and Article 100 Croatia SAA call "to achieve operating standards comparable to those in the Community".

ment.[197] In this regard, the SAA provisions resemble the relevant EAs provisions. It is only in certain selected areas (state aids) that SAAs say more than EAs on enforcement measures (establishment of a state aid enforcement body).[198] Instead, the SAA envisage the conclusion of a separate agreement with the Commission on the modalities for the monitoring of the implementation of approximation of legislation and law enforcement actions undertaken by the Western Balkan countries.[199]

Furthermore, the SAAs envisage comprehensive approximation efforts on behalf of SAA countries in order to achieve the association's ambitious objectives.[200] In general, the approximation process comprises two stages. The first stage focuses on certain fundamental elements of the EU Internal Market acquis, as well as on other trade-related areas such as: competition law, intellectual property law, standards and certification law, public procurement law, financial services and data protection law. The list of these areas is not exhaustive and tends to expand in every successive SAA.[201] The legal approximation in most sectors of the EU Internal Market is due to be completed by the end of the transition period.

The two stage approach to the approximation of laws process is new to EU external agreements and can not be found elsewhere. Among all SAAs it is only the Albania SAA, which clarifies that the purpose of this division "is to make a thorough mid-term review of the implementation of this Agreement".[202] It means that the approximation of laws serves as key criteria for the successful implementation and enforcement of the SAAs by Western Balkan countries. Therefore, it indicates that the legal approximation is considered as an essential element of the SAAs and, therefore, gives it much higher value then in other EU external agreements. SAA Association Councils are given a power of "regularly

---

197 M. Cremona, "State Aids Control: Substance and Procedure in the Europe Agreements and the Stabilisation and Association Agreements", 9 ELJ 265-287 (2003), at 286.
198 Article 70(4) Croatia SAA.
199 For instance, Article 70(4) Albania SAA.
200 Articles 68 FYROM, 69 Croatia SAA, Article 70 Albania SAA. Provide that "the Parties recognise the importance of the approximation of the existing and future laws ....to those of the Community. The [SAA country] shall endeavour to ensure that its laws will be gradually make compatible with those of the Community."
201 At the time of writing Article 70(3) Albania SAA provided the most extensive list of the priority acquis among the SAAs "approximation shall focus on fundamental elements of the Internal Market acquis as well as on other important areas such as competition, intellectual, industrial and commercial property rights, public procurement, standards and certification, financial services, land and maritime transport – with special emphasis on safety and environmental standards as well as social aspects – company law, accounting, consumer protection, data protection, health and safety at work and equal opportunities. During the second stage, Albania shall focus on the remaining parts of the acquis".
202 Article 6 Albania SAA.

review the application of this Agreement and the accomplishment by [SAA country] of legal, administrative, institutional and economic reforms in the light of the Preamble and in accordance with the general principles laid down in this Agreement".[203] It means that the SAA Association Councils may issue binding decisions which specific proposals how to enhance the effectiveness of the legal approximation and what elements of the acquis should be considered as a priority of the approximation process in Western Balkan countries. Furthermore, the Albania SAA is distinguished by a considerable novelty never applied before in the EU external agreements. The approximation clause in the Albania SAA is underpinned by the somehow experimental conditionality clause which provides that the SAA Association Council "shall evaluate the progress made by Albania, and shall decide whether this progress has been sufficient for the passage into the second stage in order to achieve full Association".[204] In other words, the procedure of the intermediate monitoring of the approximation process implies that the EU wants to apply the conditionality clause within the approximation clause in the SAA with Albania. The SAA with Albania emphasises that the fulfillment of the second stage of the approximation process is equivalent to the achievement of the objective of association between the EU and Albania. At the same time, similar to the practice already employed by the EU throughout the accession process, the EU possesses a wide authority to monitor and, subsequently, to decide if a third country (Albania) has successfully fulfilled its approximation commitments before the EU. Undoubtedly, this novel provision could be applied in the next generation of the EU external agreements aimed at the closer integration and association of a third country with the EU, for instance, in the future agreements with the neighbouring countries.

Degree of the EU involvement into the approximation process highlights major similarities and differences between the SAAs and other EU external agreements (in particular the EAs). The EU was directly involved in shaping the approximation process in the CEE countries through the Accession Partnerships and NPAAs. In case of the SAAs the approximation process is formally based on joint ownership principle, which presumes consideration of an associate country priorities and objectives with regard to the approximation of laws. However, since 2003 the SAAs "approximation track" was *de facto* derailed to the EAs' track. It means that the EU prefers to apply familiar "pre-accession" experience with CEE countries with its monitoring and conditionality towards the Western Balkan. This process is governed by Accession Partnerships for the candidate

---

203 Article 5(2) Croatia SAA.
204 Article 6 Albania SAA.

countries Croatia and FYROM (from 2008)[205] and European Partnerships for other West Balkan countries, which nevertheless replicate the Accession Partnerships used towards the CEE countries.[206] For instance, the European Partnerships set an objective for Western Balkan countries to comply with the Copenhagen political, economic and legal criteria in order to acquire the full EU membership. The matrix of the European Partnerships resembles the Accession Partnership's frameworks.

In addition to approximation commitments, the SAAs provide for soft commitments on behalf of FYROM, Croatia and Albania to implement the relevant acquis communautaire. These relate to areas of: information society;[207] consumer protection;[208] the agriculture and agro-industrial sector;[209] the environment and nuclear safety;[210] the electronic communications infrastructure and associated services;[211] the information society;[212] transport[213] and other. In certain areas

---

205 Following the opening of accession negotiations with Croatia (on 3 October 2005), the Council adopted an Accession Partnership which updates the European Partnership of 13 September 2004. The advancement of the negotiations will be measured against the implementation of the Accession Partnership that will be regularly monitored by the Commission (Council Decision 2008/119/EC of 12 February 2008 on the principles, priorities and conditions contained in the Accession Partnership with Croatia (O.J. 2008 L 042/51), Council Decision 2008/212/EC of 18 February 2008 on the principles, priorities and conditions contained in the Accession Partnership with the former Yugoslav Republic of Macedonia (O.J. 2008 L 080/32)).

206 Council Regulation 533/2004 on the establishment of European partnerships in the framework of the stabilization and association process, (O.J. 2004 L 86/1). It was amended several times in order to make a distinction between European Partnerships and Accession Partnership.

207 Article 96 FYROM SAA, Article 97 Croatia SAA, Article 103 Albania SAA.

208 Article 74 Croatia SAA, Article 76 Albania SAA.Article 97 FYROM SAA state that "the Parties will cooperate in order to align the standards of consumer protection in .....on those of the Community.... To that end, and in view of their common interests, the Parties will encourage and ensure: the harmonisation of legislation and the alignment of consumer protection in ....on that in force in the Community; effective legal protection for consumers in order to improve the quality of consumer goods and maintain appropriate safety standards".

209 Article 100 FYROM SAA and Article 92 Croatia SAA provide that "cooperation in this field shall have as its aim...the gradual harmonisation of veterinary and phytosanitary legislation with Community standards". Article 103 Albania SAA provides that "Cooperation between the Parties shall focus on priority areas related to the Community acquis in the field of agriculture".

210 Article 103 FYROM SAA, Articles 102 and 103 Croatia SAA state that "cooperation could centre on the following priorities: continuous approximation of laws and regulations to Community standards". Article 108 Albania SAA provides that "Cooperation between the Parties shall focus on priority areas related to the Community acquis in the field of environment".

211 Article 98(1) Croatia SAA, Article 95 FYROM SAA.

[statistical cooperation] the SAAs envisage approximation to international standards (respect the fundamental principles of statistics issued by the UN) and some unspecified European regulations (stipulations of the European Statistical law) with the ultimate aim of issuing national laws pursuant to the acquis communautaire. To achieve that objective the Parties have undertaken a soft commitment [may cooperate] "to pursue harmonisation with international and European standards and classification in order to enable the national statistical system to adopt the Community acquis in statistics"[214] or as in case of the Albania SAA "to respect international and European obligations in the field of safety, security and environmental standards".[215] However, Albania is required to "harmonise its legislation concerning personal data protection with Community law and other European and international legislation on privacy".[216]

Similarly to other EU external agreements, the SAAs do not provide for the automatic direct effect of the relevant acquis communautaire in the national legal orders of the Western Balkan countries. The process of the acquis communautaire implementation should be done in accordance with national constitutional procedures. There is no evidence yet on the positions of Constitutional Courts of the Western Balkan countries regarding the full application and direct applicability of the acquis communautaire within their national jurisdictions. It is most likely that owing to the far-reaching integration objectives of the association, the Constitutional Courts of the Western Balkan countries might replicate the judgments of the Czech, Polish and Hungarian constitutional courts. In other words, Constitutional Courts of the Western Balkan countries could make the utmost effort to ensure the most favourable application and interpretation of the SAAs provisions within their legal orders, and consider the acquis communautaire within the SAAs as a "persuasive source of law" to be taken into account by national judiciaries.

---

212 Article 99 Croatia SAA, Article 96 FYROM SAA: provide that "The [SAA state] authorities will establish a plan for the adoption of Community legislation in the area of the Information Society".
213 Article 100 Croatia SAA, Article 98 FYROM SAA encourage the SAAs countries "to achieve operating standards comparable to those in the Community; develop a transport system compatible and aligned with the Community system; the adoption of coordinated transport policies that are compatible with those applied in the Community". Article 106 Albania SAA provides that "Cooperation between the Parties shall focus on priority areas related to the Community acquis in the field of transport".
214 Article 83 Croatia SAA and Article 82 FYROM SAA.
215 Article 59(2) Albania SAA.
216 Article 79 Albania SAA.

2.2.4.3. Concluding remarks

The attractive perspective of full EU membership has encouraged the Western Balkan countries to embark upon the challenging path of voluntary harmonisation to ensure as far as possible the implementation of the relevant acquis communautaire.[217] For this purpose the scope of the acquis communautaire within the SAAs is distinguished by elements which can not be found in other EC/EU association agreements. Firstly, under the pressure of the EU conditionality, the Western Balkan countries have been called to ensure regional stability and security within the region. In this regard, the SAA acquis refers to specific international law instruments, such as the Dayton/Paris and Erdrut agreements. Secondly, before the formal start of association negotiations, the Western Balkan countries are expected to implement the so-called "pre-negotiation" acquis that embraces the EU fundamental democratic and human rights acquis, including regional stability within the region. Thirdly, the SAAs ensure the gradual export of the acquis communautaire through the comprehensive approximation clauses and numerous non-binding references to sectoral acquis communautaire.

All Western Balkan countries have completed the negotiation process and signed the SAAs with the EU. In the opinion of the Commission, Serbia, Bosnia and Herzegovina have made considerable progress towards a closer relationship with the EU through the adoption of internal market and trade legislation in line with the EU acquis.[218] The Commission steers the process of acquis implementation by Western Balkan countries by means of European Partnerships (analogue of the Accession Partnership).[219] By identifying priority measures for the short and medium term, the European Partnerships provide Western Balkan countries with guidelines for their reforms and preparations for future EU membership.

---

217 Notably the Croatia SAA refer to the "Community acquis" (Article 69) instead of the "Community legislation" in the FYROM SAA (Article 68).

218 For example, Bosnia and Herzegovina 2009 Progress Report (COM(2009) 533), Serbia 2009 Progress Report (COM(2009) 533).

219 Objectives of the legal approximation in the Western Balkan countries which are not parties to the SAAs were specified in the European Partnerships which laid down the principles, priorities and conditions of the relations between the Western Balkan counties and the EU and *de facto* prepared these countries for the SAA negotiations (Council Decision of 30 January 2006 on the principles, priorities and conditions contained in the European Partnership with Serbia and Montenegro including Kosovo as defined by the United Nations Security Council Resolution 1244 of 10 June 1999 (O.J. 2006 L35/32), Council Decision of 22 January 2007 on the principles, priorities and conditions contained in the European Partnership with Montenegro (O.J. 2007 L20/16), Council Decision of 30 January 2006 on the principles, priorities and conditions contained in the European Partnership with Bosnia and Herzegovina (O.J. 2006 L35/19), Council Decision of 30 January 2006 on the principles, priorities and conditions contained in the European Partnership with Albania (O.J. 2006 L35/1).

The Western Balkan countries are strongly encouraged to develop plans for the implementation of the European Partnership priorities with a timetable, and to indicate where possible their allocation of human and financial resources required for reforms.

However, the success of the ambitious acquis communautaire export programme lies in the hands of the SAAs common institutions and national authorities. Indeed, the major workload of applying the relevant acquis communautaire is vested in the Association Councils and national authorities responsible for sectoral cooperation (the Croatian SAA explicitly provides the establishment of a Croatian national authority in state aid). Nevertheless, they must pursue a considerable degree of legislative and judicial activism to ensure the quick and swift implementation of the European legal heritage into the Western Balkan legal systems.[220]

---

[220] Croatia has been praised by the European Commission for its success in meeting the political and economic criteria of Copenhagen. As a result the European Commission has recommended opening accession negotiations with Croatia. Furthermore, the European Commission has emphasised that Croatia's further progress on the road to EU membership depends on the adoption and enforcement of the EU acquis. See Communication from the Commission "Opinion on Croatia's Application for Membership of the European Union" (COM (2004) 257 final) and Croatia Progress 2009 Report (COM (2009) 533).

2.2.5. EUROMED Association Agreements (EMAAs)

2.2.5.1. Introduction

So-called "EuroMed" association agreements are products of the Euro-Mediterranean Partnership agreed by the EU foreign ministers and ten Mediterranean partners[221] in Barcelona in November 1995. The ultimate objectives of the Euro-Mediterranean Partnership are enshrined in the Barcelona Declaration.[222] These objectives aim at the establishment of a zone of peace, prosperity and stability in the Mediterranean region without formal EU membership.[223] The ambitious goals of the Euro-Mediterranean Partnership are supplemented by the Barcelona Process, endorsed by the Common Strategy for the Mediterranean Region (adopted by the European Council in Santa Maria da Feira in June 2000). The Barcelona Declaration lays out objectives in three major areas: 1) the political and security; 2) the economic; 3) the social and cultural. Among the specific targets of the Barcelona Declaration are: a) the creation of a zone of peace and stability based on shared fundamental values, particularly the respect for human rights and democracy; b) the construction of a region of shared prosperity through the gradual establishment of a free trade area by the target date of 2010.[224] These far-reaching objectives circumscribe the tentative boundaries of the acquis communautaire to be implemented by the Mediterranean countries.

The Euro-Mediterranean Partnership is implemented bilaterally through the EMAAs negotiated between the EU ((then) EC) and its Member States and the ten Euro-Mediterranean countries on the basis of Article 310 EC (now Article 217 TFEU). The EMAAs aim to establish, over a transitional period, free trade in industrial goods and the progressive liberalisation of trade in the agricultural sector; liberalisation of trade in services; cooperation in political, economic, social and cultural matters, and justice and home affairs. Commentators consider the EMAAs "a half-way house between Lome and the EU, characterised by political dialogue, security ties, free trade and sectoral cooperation", with an expli-

---

221 Algeria, Egypt, Israel, Jordan, Lebanon, Morocco, Syria, Tunisia, Turkey, and the Palestinian Authority. Two initial participants of the Euro-Mediterranean Partnership (Cyprus and Malta) joined the EU in 2004.
222 Adopted at the Euro-Mediterranean Conference on 27-28 November 1995.
223 For a comprehensive account of the Barcelona Declaration see F. Hakura, "The Euro-Med Policy: The Implications of the Barcelona Declaration", 34 CMLRev. 337-366 (1997).
224 The Euro-Mediterranean Partnership is accompanied by substantial financial assistance from the EU (principally the MEDA programme) and by European Investment Bank loans. See P. Holden, "The European Community's MEDA Aid Programme: A Strategic Instrument of Civilian Power?", 8 EFARev. 347-363 (2003).

cit objective of opening EMAA countries' markets to intense European competition.[225]

Notwithstanding their common objectives, the EMAAs display explicit differentiation and conditionality of EU foreign policy. Each of the EMAAs shows specific EU policy approaches towards a particular Mediterranean country. Therefore, the scope of the acquis communautaire to be adopted by the EMAA countries is not uniform. The EMAAs may be arranged into several groups or "generations". The (then) EC has concluded "first-generation" association agreements with Turkey, Malta and Cyprus (which are not strictly EMAAs) with the purpose of establishing customs unions. In the end, only the EC-Turkey customs union has come into existence as a "consolation prize" for the delay of its membership perspectives. Customs unions with Malta and Cyprus (the customs union with Cyprus was partly achieved)[226] were never established, though these countries eventually became full Member States in 2004. Turkey is only one Mediterranean country with candidate country status whereas majority of the EMAA countries are associated countries without perspective of the full EU membership. Therefore, the EC-Turkey EMAA should be considered separately from other agreements due to considerable re-orientation of objectives of the former towards the EU membership. The EC-Israel EMAA occupies a special niche within the whole Euro-Mediterranean Partnership since it envisages the unprecedented mutual harmonisation of legislation in the course of the liberalisation of economic relations. The remaining EMAAs belong to the next group. Therein the acquis communautaire scope suits the comparatively limited objectives of Euro-Mediterranean Partnership which carefully avoids any perspective of EU membership. Therefore this section focuses on the EMAAs with Turkey, Israel, and Tunisia as the most typical examples of the abovementioned generations of EMAA.

In the unforeseeable future most of the EMAAs will be substituted by new enhanced neigbhourghood agreements to be emerged as a result of the Euro-Mediterranean countries' participation in the European Neighbourhood Policy (ENP). Nine Euro-Mediterranean countries[227] participate in the ENP since 2003.[228] The ENP pursues the objective to develop further regional integration within the region, building on the achievements of the Euro-Mediterranean part-

---

225 *Supra note* 223, at 352.
226 For detailed account of the EC-Cyprus trade relations see P. Koutrakos, "Legal Issues of EC-Cyprus Trade Relations", 52(2) ICLQ 489-498 (2003).
227 Algeria, Egypt, Israel, Jordan, Lebanon, Morocco, Syria, Tunisia and the Palestinian Authority.
228 Communication from the Commission to the Council and the European Parliament "Wider Europe – Neighbourhood: A New Framework for Relations with our Eastern and Southern Neighbours". (COM (2003) 104 final).

nership, notably in the area of democracy, security and trade. Most importantly, the ENP envisages more enhanced access of the Euro-Mediterranean countries to the EU Internal Market under condition that the neighbouring states pursue the voluntary adoption of the acquis communautaire without participating in EU decision-making and legislative procedures. The scope of the acquis communautaire to be adopted by the Euro-Mediterranean countries is specified in bilateral Action Plans.[229] As it follows from the Action Plans the tailor-made approach to different Euro-Mediterranean countries is maintained and is likely to be replicated in the future enhanced agreements. For the discussion on the possible scope of the future enhanced neighbourhood agreements see the final chapter of this book.

Since 2008 the Euro-Mediterranean Partnership and the Barcelona Process are being substituted by French inspired new external initiative of the EU – the Union for the Mediterranean.[230] This initiative embraces wider geographical area beyond the Mediterranean region. It covers not only 11 Mediterranean countries which participate in the ENP but also some Western Balkan countries (Albania, Bosnia & Herzegovinia, Croatia and Montenegro), 27 EU Member States and some other third countries (Mauritania, Monaco). The Union for Mediterranean is built on the Euro-Mediterranean Partnership and the Barcelona Process acquis and called to ensure deeper regional and sub-regional cooperation between the participants. It also offers some important structural innovations. In contrast to other EU regional initiatives (ENP) the Union for Mediterranean strengthens its effectiveness through introducing a single institutional framework (rotating co-presidency with one EU President and one president of a Mediterranean country; Joint Secretariat based in Barcelona). Furthermore, the Union for Mediterranean pursues very specific regional initiatives with global dimension, like de-pollution of the Mediterranean Sea; the establishment of maritime and land highways; civil protection initiatives to combat natural and man-made disasters; a Mediterranean solar energy plan; the inauguration of the Euro-Mediterranean University in Slovenia; and the Mediterranean Business Development Initiative focusing on micro, small and medium-sized enterprises. It is likely that to achieve so ambitious objectives the Union for Mediterranean will actively promote the adoption of relevant acquis communautaire by concerned countries through various soft law instruments and political actions.

---

229 At the time of writing action plans were issued for all the Euro-Mediterranean countries apart from Algeria, Libya and Syria, available at <http://ec.europa.eu/world/enp/documents_en.htm>, last visited 18 January 2011.
230 Joint Declaration of the Paris Summit for the Mediterranean in Paris on 13 July 2008, available at <http://ec.europa.eu/external_relations/euromed/index_en.htm>, last visited 18 January 2011.

2.2.5.2. EC-Turkey Association Agreement

2.2.5.2.1. Objectives of the Agreement

EU-Turkey political and economic relations are still based on the 1963 EEC-Turkey Association Agreement (the so-called "Ankara Agreement").[231] Its eventual objective is the establishment of a customs union which subsequently entails the adoption by Turkey of the EC/EU external trade acquis (the EC Common Customs Tariff and an "approximation to the other Community rules on external trade").[232] However since the granting to Turkey the candidate country status in 1999 and launch of the accession negotiations with the EU on 3 October 2005 the Ankara Agreement could be seen as a contractual foundation for the pre-accession process with regard to Turkey. This particular feature sharply distinguishes the Ankara Agreement from other EMAAs in the region. The Ankara agreement may be considered one of the first EEC association framework agreements manifestly targeted at the far-reaching export of the acquis communautaire into the Turkish legal system. Indeed, the Ankara Agreement imposes on Turkey hard and soft commitments for the application of the relevant EC internal market acquis,[233] with subsequent "recognition" and application of legal principles in EC competition, state aid and taxation.[234]

2.2.5.2.2. The scope of the acquis communautaire to be implemented by Turkey

The major objective of the Ankara Agreement – the establishment of a customs union – has been achieved through binding decisions of the EC-Turkey association institutions: *inter alia* Decision 1/95 the EC-Turkey Association Council;[235] Decision 1/96 of the EC-Turkey Customs Cooperation Committee;[236] Decision 2/97 of the EC-Turkey Association Council[237]. These decisions successfully fill

---

231 O.J. 1973 C 113/2.
232 Article 10 Ankara Agreement.
233 For example, see Articles 12, 13, 14 Ankara Agreement.
234 Article 16 of the Ankara Agreement provides: "The Contracting Parties recognise that the principles laid down in the provisions on competition, taxation and the approximation of laws contained in Title I of Part III ECT must be made applicable in their relations within the Association".
235 O.J. 1996 L 35/1.
236 "Decision 1/96 of the EC-Turkey Customs Cooperation Committee laying down detailed rules for the application of Decision 1/95" (O.J. 1996 L 200/14).
237 "Decision 2/97 of the EC-Turkey Association Council establishing the list of Community instruments relating to the removal of technical barriers to trade and the conditions and arrangements governing their implementation by Turkey" (O.J. 1997 L 191/1).

the gap left by the Ankara Agreement by identifying the precise scope of the relevant acquis communautaire to be implemented by Turkey in the course of establishing a customs union with the (then) EC.

In accordance with Decision 1/95 Turkey committed itself to adhere to the EC/EU Common Commercial Policy (CCP) and to apply the substantive EC/EU customs acquis.[238] Furthermore, Turkey committed to "align itself with the EC preferential customs regime"[239] and to apply "substantially the same commercial policy as the Community" in the textile sector, including the agreements or arrangements on trade in textiles and clothing.[240] However, the WTO Appellate Body ruled out the legitimacy of any new trade restrictions on behalf of Turkey as incompatible with the GATT. It judged in the *India Turkey textiles case* that the Turkish imposition of quantitative restrictions against the import of Indian textiles was not justified by derogations in Article XXIV GATT. As a result, Turkey was asked to revise its textile arrangements within the customs union in line with the WTO acquis.[241] Therefore, this decision by the WTO Appellate Body made impossible the full alignment of the Turkish custom policy with that of the EU.

Turkey is bound to implement the relevant acquis communautaire on the removal of technical barriers to trade and fair competition.[242] In the area of competition, Turkey ensures the application of the principles of relevant EC primary and secondary legislation, as well as the relevant ECJ/General Court ((then)CFI) case law.[243] In the area of state aid to the textiles and clothing sector, Turkey is bound to adapt even relevant soft law – EC frameworks and guidelines.[244] Turkish binding commitments are strengthened by specific deadlines. In most cases Turkey is expected to adapt its legislation to that of the EC before the entry into force of the customs union. In other cases, deadlines are limited by terms from two to five years.[245] In a similar manner to the EEA Agreement, Decision 2/97 exports the relevant acquis communautaire on the removal of technical barriers through the comprehensive Annex. Besides, Decision 2/97 ensures that rights and obligations imposed upon the EC Member States within the CCP are also conferred or imposed upon Turkey.[246]

---

238 Article 28 of the Decision 1/95.
239 Article 13 Decision 1/95.
240 Article 12 Decision 1/95.
241 Report of the WTO Appellate Body, Turkey – Restrictions on Imports of Textile and Clothing Products, AB – 1999-5, on 22 October 1999.
242 Article 39 Decision 1/95.
243 Article 39(2)(a) Decision 1/95.
244 Article 39(2)(c) Decision 1/95.
245 Article 39 Decision 1/95.
246 Article 7 Decision 2/97.

The scope of international law applicable to Turkey in the Decision 1/95 is circumscribed by fundamental multilateral treaties in the area of intellectual property.[247] It is emphasized that "the Customs Union can function properly only if equivalent levels of effective protection of intellectual property rights are provided in both constituent parts of the Customs Union". To achieve this objective, Turkey is committed to securing a level of protection of intellectual, industrial and commercial property rights equivalent to that already existing in the EC.[248]

Within the framework of Decision 1/95 Turkey pursues soft commitments in the application of the acquis communautaire by pledging to approximate its own legislation to that of the EC in certain areas: standardization, metrology and calibration, quality, accreditation, testing and certification,[249] and agricultural policy.[250]

The Ankara Agreement does not envisage a homogeneity procedure similar to the EEA Agreement. However, Decision 1/95 is explicit in persuading Turkey to follow the "post-customs union" ECJ/General Court ((then) CFI) case law. Therein, Turkey is obliged to interpret provisions of Decision 1/95 identical in substance to the corresponding provisions of the EC Treaty in conformity with the relevant ECJ/General Court ((then) CFI) case law,[251] and to ensure (by the end of the first year following the entry into force of the Customs Union) the application of principles contained in the EC primary and secondary legislation, as well as those developed by the ECJ/General Court ((then) CFI).[252] These provisions go far beyond similar provisions on the application of the ECJ rulings in the EEA Agreement and in the EC-Swiss SAs. On the one hand, this approach disproportionately extends EC judicial authority over the Turkish legal system without offering the Turkish side any real possibilities to be involved in the EU

---

247 Article 31 Decision 2/97. The list of binding international conventions is provided in Annex 8 of the Ankara Agreement
248 Article 2 Decision 1/95.
249 Article 8(4) Decision 1/95.
250 Article 25 Decision 1/95 states that "Turkey shall adjust its policy in such a way as to adopt the common agricultural policy measures required to establish freedom of movement of agricultural products".
251 Article 66 Decision 1/95 provides that "The provisions of this Decision, in so far as they are identical in substance to the corresponding provisions of the Treaty establishing the European Community shall be interpreted for the purposes of their implementation and application to products covered by the Customs Union, in conformity with the relevant decisions of the Court of Justice of the European Communities".
252 In accordance with Article 42 of Decision 1/95 Turkey is bound to apply "post-signature" ECJ case law: "Application of EC principles and case law follows from the commitment by Turkey to ensure that, by the end of the second year following the entry into force of this Decision, no discrimination regarding the conditions under which goods are procured and marketed exists between nationals of the Member States and of Turkey with regard to State monopolies of a commercial character".

decision-making process. On the other hand, from the accession perspective, it ensures the effective implementation of the EC judicial acquis into the Turkish legal system.

2.2.5.2.3. Concluding remarks

The example of Ankara Agreement represents a special case in EU external relations. This is one of few association agreements that have eventually achieved the objective of establishing a customs union between the (then) EC and an associate country. The customs union objective implied the necessity of the implementation of the relevant EC external trade acquis into the Turkish legal system. However, the Ankara Agreement does not contain specific provisions for the scope of the acquis communautaire to be adopted by Turkey. Instead, the major bulk of the acquis communautaire was exported into the Turkish legal system through binding decisions of EC-Turkey common institutions. These decisions ensured the adoption by Turkey of the relevant "pre-customs union" and "post-customs union" acquis, though without any possibility of participation in the EU decision-making processes.

However, due to the evolving and deepening nature of the EU-Turkey association the contemporary scope of the acquis communautaire relevant to Turkey is not limited by the trade-oriented objectives of the Ankara Agreement. Today it must be viewed in the light of the whole Euro-Mediterranean Partnership and recent Turkish "pre-accession" policy. At the Helsinki Summit in December 1999 the EU finally agreed to accept Turkey as a candidate country.[253] Shortly afterwards the Accession Partnership towards Turkey was launched in 2001[254] which was supported by a considerable EU financial assistance package. Only in the period 2007-2009 Turkey was granted nearly 1,6 billion Euros of EU assistance, half of which went to the implementation and enforcement of the relevant acquis communautaire in the Turkish legal system.[255] The Turkish NPAA was issued in 2001, thereby beginning the process of adopting the whole acquis communautaire as part of the "pre-accession" strategy. These global legal reforms implied the revision of foundations of the whole Turkish legal system in line with the "acquis criterion". Only in October 2001 34 constitutional amendments were im-

---

253 Turkey formally applied for EU membership in 1987.
254 G. Avci, "Putting the Turkish EU Candidacy into Context", 7 EFA Rev. 91-110 (2002).
255 See "European Commission completes multi-annual planning of financial assistance to the candidate and potential candidate countries", available at <http://europa.eu/rapid/pressReleasesAction.do?reference=IP/07/856>, last visited 18 January 2011. Also see D. Kanarek, "Turkey and the European Union: The Path to Accession", 9 CJEL 457-473 (2003).

plemented to speed up the Turkish pre-accession process. Henceforth, Turkey has embarked upon the challenging programme of voluntary harmonization of her national legislation to that of the EU. Two major constitutional reforms and about a dozen of legislative packages were adopted by the Turkish Parliament to align the Turkish legislation with the acquis communautaire[256] including codification of national legislation (Civil Code and Penal Code). Numerous other laws, regulations, decrees and circulars outlining the application of these reforms have been issued. Considerable legal reforms have taken place in the areas of fundamental democratic freedoms and the protection of human rights. Hitherto, Turkey has already acceded to major fundamental human rights multilateral conventions; international commercial treaties; international framework agreements in environment, education.[257] The European Commission Regular Reports praise Turkey's progress in liberalizing national economy and aligning the protection of fundamental freedoms and democracy to established European standards and the acquis communautaire. However, it states that some economic and human rights criteria have only been partially met and therefore require further advancement (women's rights, certificates' control, fight with corruption, investment services and securities markets, renewable energy, indirect taxation and other).[258] The alignment of national legislation to the acquis communautaire remains an attractive objective for other scenarios of the EU-Turkey relations then the accession into the EU (privileged partnership and gradual integration).[259]

2.2.5.3. EC-Israel EMAA

2.2.5.3.1. Objectives of the Agreement

The EC-Israel Association Agreement was signed in Brussels on 20 November 1995 and came into force on 1 June 2000[260] consequently replacing the 1975 EEC-Israel Cooperation Agreement. The EC-Israel Association Agreement was concluded on the basis of Article 310 EC (now Article 217 TFEU). The Pream-

---

256 E. Örücü, "Seven Packeges Towards Harmonisation with the European Union", 10(4) EPL 603-621 (2004).
257 E. Örücü, "Turkey Facing the European Union – Old and New Harmonies", 25(5) EL Rev. 523-537 (2000), at 531.
258 European Commission's 2008 Regular Report on Turkey's progress towards accession (SEC(2008) 2699), Council Decision 2008/157/EC of 18 February 2008 on the principles, priorities and conditions contained in the Accession Partnership with the Republic of Turkey (O.J. 2008 L 051/04).
259 C. Karakas, "Gradual Integration: an Attractive Alternative Integration Process for Turkey and the EU", 11 EFA Rev. 311-331 (2006).
260 O.J. 2000 L 147/1.

ble of the Agreement emphasises the existence of traditional links between the (then) EC and Israel and the common values which they share.[261] The association is aimed at supporting lasting relations between the EC and Israel, based on reciprocity, partnership and the "promotion of the further integration of Israel's economy into the European economy".

The Agreement pursues objectives mainly of an economic character: mutual and reciprocal liberalisation in trade in goods and services; reciprocal liberalisation of the right of establishment; progressive liberalisation of public procurement; free movement of capital; intensification of cooperation in science and technology "to promote the harmonious development of economic relations between the EC and Israel".[262] The possibility is not ruled out that the association might lead to "the maintenance or establishment" of customs unions, free trade areas or other arrangements for improving mutual trade.[263] Israel was invited to join the first wave of the EU Neighbourhood Policy, with the subsequent possibility of signing a new framework neighbourhood agreement. One may foresee that the future EU-Israel neighbourhood agreement will take into account the progress achieved in the adoption of the acquis communautaire within the EU-Israel EMAA.

2.2.5.3.2. The scope of the acquis communautaire in the EC-Israel Agreement

The EC-Israeli EMAA is characterised by distinctive means to export the acquis communautaire into the Israeli legal system. First, the Agreement prioritises the application of the relevant WTO acquis over the acquis communautaire. The Agreement explicitly provides that the functioning of the future EC-Israel free trade area should be based on the application of the relevant WTO rules.[264] Consequently, the EC-Israel EMAA contains almost no reference to the acquis communautaire. For instance, there is no reference to the relevant acquis communautaire in titles on capital movements, public procurement, competition or intellectual property. These titles refer to the respective WTO provisions only. The only attempt to impose the acquis communautaire may be deduced from the Agreement's provision on fair competition which replicates the wording of the

---

261 The Preamble of the EC-Israel Agreement provides: "Considering the importance of the existing traditional links between the Community, its Member States and Israel, and the common values that they share....the Community, its Member States, and Israel wish to...promote a further integration of Israel's economy into the European economy".
262 Article 1 EC-Israel Agreement.
263 Article 21 EC-Israel Agreement.
264 Title II on free movement of goods EC-Israel Agreement.

EC Treaty.[265] However, the Agreement clarifies that the relevant provisions of the GATT should be applied in the course of the implementation of the competition/state aid provisions. Second, the Agreement envisages the simultaneous application of EC and Israeli trade laws by the Parties. There is a reference to the application of the Combined Nomenclature and the Israeli customs tariff for the classification of goods in trade between the Parties. This means that relevant EC and Israeli rules may be simultaneously applied by EC Member States and Israel, which is a rare example of the application by the EC of national laws of an associated country.[266] The EU-Israel EMAA envisages the gradual approximation of Israeli laws to those of the EC through the unique approximation clause: "The Parties shall use their best endeavours to approximate their respective laws in order to facilitate the implementation of this Agreement".[267] In applying such a wording, the EC directly recognises the possibility of the mutual approximation of laws, thereby equating the Israeli legal system with that of the EC, and envisaging at least the possibility of exporting the Israeli legal heritage into the acquis communautaire. One can argue that this particularity of the EC-Israel approximation clause is of political nature in order to praise special status of the Israeli legal system among other EMAAs. It is hardly any positive experience of the EU institutions to import principles and elements of third countries' legal systems into the acquis communautaire. Furthermore, such policy could undermine the EU's role as a global rule maker and generator.

The EC-Israel Agreement imposes soft approximation commitments on the Parties to cooperate towards the harmonisation of their legislation and standards in areas of agriculture[268] and information and telecommunications[269] as well as the adoption of the considerable scope of the regulatory acquis communautaire.[270]

The Israeli participation in the ENP targets the objectives of deepening political dialogue and close involvement into key EU policies. The objective to export the acquis communautaire into legal system of Israel is pursued by soft means. The ENP does not envisage any commitments of Israel to implement relevant acquis communautaire but simply encourages Israel to do so. Instead, the EU-

---

265 Article 36(1) EC-Israel Agreement.
266 Article 6 EC-Israel Agreement.
267 Article 55 EC-Israel Agreement.
268 Article 46 EC-Israel Agreement.
269 Article 52 EC-Israel Agreement.
270 G. Harpaz, "Enhanced Relations between the European Union and the State of Israel under the European Neighbourhood Policy: some Legal and Economic Implications", 31(4) Legal Issues of Economic Integration 257-274 (2004). See also G. Harpaz, "When East meets West: Approximation of laws in the EU-Mediterranean context"43(1) CML Rev. 993-1022 (2006).

Israeli Action Plan states that the parties only "explore the possibility of approximation of economic legislation".

Regular monitoring on behalf of the EU on realization of the EU-Israeli Action Plan praises the Israeli active participation in the EU policies and programmes (for example, 7th Framework Programme for Research and Development). In particular the EU's monitoring revealed strengthened political dialogue between the EU and Israel carried by common institutions (Association Council and committees and other bodies) set up under the framework of the EU-Israeli EMAA. There is increased cooperation between the EU and Israel in field of justice, freedom and security. At the same time the EU's monitoring highlights some serious problems in fulfilling objectives of the EU-Israeli Action Plan. For instance, it concerned protection of the Israeli Arab minority, restrictions of movement in West Bank and Gaza Strip and other issues related to the Israeli-Palestinian conflict. While praising improved cooperation in approximating national laws to the "sectoral acquis" the EU institutions emphasized poor progress in aligning Israeli legislation with the "sectoral acquis" especially in fields of competition, intellectual property rights, company law. It can be acknowledged that Israel has very little incentive to accelerate own approximation efforts since the EU offers quite modest financial support to Israeli reforms directed at adoption of the "acquis-related activities" (14 million Euro under the 2007-2013 National Indicative Programme).[271]

2.2.5.3.3. Concluding remarks

The EC-Israel EMAA occupies a distinctive place within the EMAAs. Firstly, the Agreement envisages a remote but clear perspective of closer rapprochement between Israel and the EU. Secondly, the Agreement omits any reference to the acquis communautaire even in areas traditionally occupied by the acquis communautaire in EU external agreements (such as competition and public procurement). Conversely, the EC-Israel EMAA envisages the possibility of the application of Israeli customs laws by the EC, thereby confirming its "privileged" attitude towards Israel, and endorsing the possibility that the acquis communautaire might be enriched by from the Israeli legal system. The EC intentionally distinguishes Israel from the group of the EMAAs countries and acknowledges its advanced economic and political potential. Experts argue that the too broad framework for cooperation in the EC-Israel EMAA did not result in effective adoption and implementation of the regulatory acquis (standards, competition, procure-

---

271 Commission's Progress Report on Israel 'Implementation of the European Neighbourhood Policy in 2009' (SEC(2010) 207).

ment, trade in services). The liberalization of trade between the EU and Israel is not achieved yet. Therefore, high hopes are placed on the active participation of Israel in the ENP, effective implementation of the bilateral Action Plan and the subsequent negotiation of an enhanced neighbourhood agreement in the future. Commentators believe that the differentiation (tailor-made) principle which lies in the core of the ENP would help to "translate advanced technological and economic status [of Israel] into substantial economic advantages in the form of liberalized legal regimes".[272]

2.2.5.4. EC-Tunisia EMAA

2.2.5.4.1. Objectives of the EC-Tunisia EMAA

Tunisia was the first Mediterranean country (out of Algeria, Israel, Jordan, Lebanon, Morocco, Palestinian Authority) to sign the so-called "third-generation" Association Agreement with the EU in 1995.[273] The "third-generation" Association Agreements are aimed at the gradual liberalisation of the mutual trade in goods, services and capital, the promotion of trade and the expansion of harmonious economic and social relations between the Parties.[274] Ultimately the Parties agreed to set up a free trade area over a twelve-year transitional period in conformity with WTO rules.[275]

The "third-generation" EMAAs are built upon so-called "second-generation" EMAAs, cooperation agreements between the EC and certain Mediterranean countries (Egypt, Lebanon, Syria, Jordan, Algeria) concluded in late 1970s and were concluded on the basis of Article 310 EC (now Article 217 TFEU).[276] Today, most of the "second-generation" EMAAs countries have already signed or negotiated association agreements with the EU. These agreements belong to the so-called "third-generation" EMAAs.[277] The "second-generation" EMAAs promote overall cooperation with the EU, with a specific emphasis on improving mutual trade without envisaging the application of either an EU democrat-

---

272 G. Harpaz, "Mind The Gap: Narrowing the Legitimacy Gap in EU–Israeli Relations", 13(1) EFA Rev. 117-137 (2008).
273 O.J. 1998 L 097. The Agreement came into force on the 1st of March 1998.
274 Article 1 EC-Tunisia EMAA.
275 Article 6 EC-Tunisia EMAA.
276 EC-Jordan (O.J. 1978 L 268); EC-Lebanon (O.J. 1978 L 267); EC-Syria (O.J. 1978 L 269); EC-Egypt (O.J. 1978 L 266); EC-Algeria (O.J. 1978 L 263).
277 Negotiations with Egypt were concluded in June 1999 and the Agreement signed in June 2001. Negotiations with Algeria were concluded in December 2001, and those with Lebanon in January 2002.

ic/human rights or trade acquis. These agreements prioritise the application of the relevant WTO acquis over the acquis communautaire by either of the Parties.[278]

2.2.5.4.2. The scope of the acquis communautaire in the EC-Tunisia EMAA

The Preamble of the EC-Tunisia EMAA emphasises the existence of traditional links between the EC, its Member States and Tunisia, and the common values that they share. Reciprocity, partnership and co-development are considered the basis of lasting relations between the Parties. The "essential element" clause contains the recognised international democratic and human rights acquis. In contrast to similar clauses in the EAs and SAAs which list the basic international multilateral conventions, the EC-Tunisia "essential element" clause is rather vague. It refers to the recognised international democratic and human rights acquis without clarifying their precise scope.[279]

The objective of the establishment of a free trade area between the (then) EC and Tunisia entails the application of the relevant WTO acquis. The Combined Nomenclature of goods shall be applied in trade between the two Parties.[280] Liberalisation efforts in the areas of: free movement of goods;[281] the right of establishment and services;[282] and payments and movement of capital[283] all imply the application of the relevant WTO rules, thereby avoiding direct reference to the acquis communautaire. In a similar fashion to the EAs and SAAs, the EAs state that any uncompetitive practice by any Party must be assessed on the basis of criteria arising from the application of the rules of Articles 85, 86 and 92 EC (now Articles 105, 106 and 112 TFEU). Practices in agriculture and fisheries should be assessed according to the criteria established on the basis of Articles 42 and 43 EC (now Articles 48 and 49 TFEU) and, in particular, of those established in Council Regulation 26/62.[284] The practice of the Tunisian courts on the application of these criteria is not as extensive as in the EAs. However, one can hardly expect a favourable interpretation of these criteria by Tunisian courts, ow-

---

278 Article 33 EC-Egypt Cooperation Agreement.
279 Article 2 EC-Tunisia EMAA reads: "Relations between the Parties, as well as all the provisions of the Agreement itself, shall be based on respect for human rights and democratic principles which guide their domestic and international policies and constitute an essential element of the Agreement".
280 Article 30 EC-Tunisia EMAA.
281 Artile 6 EC-Tunisia EMAA.
282 Article 31 EC-Tunisia EMAA.
283 Article 35 EC-Tunisia EMAA.
284 Article 36(2) EC-Tunisia EMAA.

ing to the relatively moderate objectives of the EC-Tunisia EMAA, which do not envisage any possibility of full EU membership.[285]

2.2.5.4.3. Concluding remarks

On the whole, the EC-Tunisia EMAA exports a considerable scope of the relevant international and acquis communautaire into the Tunisian legal system. The WTO acquis is essential for achieving the major objective of the EC-Tunisia Agreement –the establishment of a free trade area. However, the EC-Tunisia EMAA provides all possible means to impose the acquis communautaire in order to instigate "voluntary harmonisation" efforts on behalf of Tunisia. The EC-Tunisia Agreement approximation clause imposes generalised and non-specific commitments as compared to EAs and SAAs, in order to approximate the Tunisian legislation to that of the EU within priority cooperation areas.[286] However, the "voluntary harmonisation" framework does offer very few incentives for the Tunisian government genuinely to adopt the relevant acquis communautaire. As a result, the success of this process relies too much on political will in Tunisia and subsequent injections of EU financial assistance.[287]

2.2.5.5. Conclusion

The scope of the acquis communautaire within the EMAAs is not uniform, but reflects specific objectives of the three "generations" of association agreements. The aim of establishing a customs union in the "first generation" Association Agreements entailed the adoption of the whole EC external trade acquis by Turkey, Cyprus and Malta. Decisions of the EC-Turkey association institutions have shaped and defined the scope of the relevant acquis to be applied by Turkey. In these cases, it covers the whole relevant acquis communautaire, including the dynamic ECJ/General Court ((then) CFI) case law. Granting the status of candidate country to Turkey in 1999 considerably accelerated Turkish approximation efforts towards adoption of the "accession acquis". However, till now, Ankara Agreement remains the major contractual base for the EU-Turkish relations.

---

285 Article 1(2) EC-Tunisia EMAA.
286 Article 52 EC Tunisia EMAA provides: "Cooperation shall be aimed at helping Tunisia to bring its legislation closer to that of the Community in the areas covered by this Agreement". In areas like public procurement the Parties only endeavour to meet their efforts at a reciprocal and gradual liberalisation (Article 41 of the EC-Tunisia EMAA).
287 P. Holden, "The European Community's MEDA Aid Programme: A Strategic Instrument of Civilian Power?", 8 EFA Rev. 347-363 (2003).

The EC-Israel Association Agreement occupies a distinct place among the EMAAs. It carefully avoids any reference to the acquis communautaire to be adopted by Israel. Instead, it prioritises the implementation of international law over the acquis communautaire with the subsequent aim of the equal standing of the EC and Israeli legal systems.

The second and third "generations" of the EMAAs secure minimum and practical objectives to open up EMAA markets to European companies and to establish a favourable trade regime between the EC and the Mediterranean countries. The EMAAs do not envisage full EU membership. Therefore, on the one hand, the EMAAs countries do not impose on the Mediterranean countries any "hard" obligation to align their legislation to that of the EC, but instead encourage EMAA countries to initiate "voluntary harmonisation" of their legal systems to that of the EU. On the other hand, the EMAAs favour the application of the WTO acquis and relevant international law rules and principles for the ultimate purpose of the association – a Mediterranean free trade area. The observance of human rights and political and economic freedoms forms the very basis of the "essential elements" of the EMAAs and underpin the whole association. Nevertheless, in contrast to the EEA Agreement and the SAAs, the modest objectives of the EMAAs do not specify the scope of the international human rights acquis, thereby leaving many gaps in their enforcement by either Party.[288]

The EMAAs have been given new impetus following the 2003 launch of the European Neighbourhood Policy (ENP)[289] and, as a supplementary initiative - Union for the Mediterranean in 2008.[290] The ENP sets up a "ring of neighbours" including the Southern Mediterranean countries (Algeria, Egypt, Israel, Jordan, Lebanon, Morocco, Syria, Tunisia and the Palestinian Authority). The ENP's objective is to open certain sectors of the EC internal market and to enhance political dialogue between the EU and neighbour countries in return for substantive political, economic, and legal reforms. These objectives may be met through the implementation of a set of priorities in tailor-made jointly-agreed Action Plans within key areas: political dialogue; economic reform; trade; cooperation within justice and home affairs. The Action Plans define the way ahead over the next three to five years. The next step could consist of offering a new privileged partnership in the form of European Neighbourhood Agreements (ENA) to replace

---

288 For instance, the EC-Tunisia EMAA reads that the Parties respect "principles of the United Nations Charter, particularly the observance of human rights and political and economic freedom, which form the very basis of the Association".

289 Communication from the Commission "Wider Europe— Neighbourhood: A New Framework for Relations with our Eastern and Southern Neighbours" (COM (2003) 104 final).

290 Communication from the Commission "Barcelona Process: Union for the Mediterranean" (COM(2008) 319 final).

the present generation of bilateral agreements when Action Plan priorities are met. Objectives of the ENP make us believe that future ENAs will be distinguished with even more degree of differentiation then the EMAAs and, therefore, will reflect different level of political, economic and legal advancement of every Euro-Mediterranean country, on the one hand, and, different EU policy towards them, on the other hand. If the EMAAs could be divided into three "generations" the future ENAs might possess even more individual specifics. For example, the future ENA between the EU and Morocco is likely to pursue one of the objectives to strengthen the Moroccan efforts to combat illegal immigration to the EU. The future ENA between the EU and the Palestine Autonomy is likely to enhance the Palestinian capacity to combat terrorism and illegal trade in arms. The future ENA between the EU and Israel will definitely prioritise the enhanced economic and trade cooperation between the parties.

Furthermore, the moderate objectives of the EMAAs could be detrimental for their direct applicability within the legal orders of Mediterranean countries (with the exemption of Turkey) which have embarked upon the full fledged "pre-accession" process. The ECJ has been generous in recognising the direct effect of the Ankara Agreement in the EC legal order, thereby encouraging adequate actions by the Turkish national courts.[291] In the case of the two subsequent generations of the EMAAs, one may hardly expect a similar response by either the ECJ or the EMAA national courts.

2.2.6. Partnership and Cooperation Agreements (PCAs)

2.2.6.1. Objectives of the PCAs

The original EC/USSR Trade Development and Cooperation Agreement (TDCA)[292] was superseded by new bilateral agreements with almost all the former Soviet republics shortly after the Presidents of Russia, Belarus and Ukraine signed an agreement establishing the Commonwealth of Independent States (CIS) and acknowledging the end of the Soviet Union.[293] Until now, the TDCA

---

291 Case 12/86 *Demirel v. Stadt Schwäbisch Gmünd* [1987] ECR 3719 and Case C-18/90 *Onem v. Kziber* [1991] ECR I-199.
292 Council Decision of 26 February 1990 on the conclusion by the European Economic Community of an Agreement between the European Economic Community and the European Atomic Energy Community and the Union of Soviet Socialist Republics on trade and commercial and economic cooperation (O.J. 1990, L 68/1).
293 The CIS itself was formally established on 21 December 1991 when Presidents of eleven former USSR republics signed the CIS Agreement in Alma-Ata (Kazakhstan).

continues to be the main tool for relations with Belarus and Turkmenistan.[294] Owing to the fact that the CIS was not given a legal personality, the EU decided to enter into bilateral agreements with all former Soviet republics, except the three Baltic republics. Latvia, Estonia and Lithuania were invited to sign free trade agreements and subsequently the EAs. As a consequence they joined the club of candidate countries for accession. Partnership and Cooperation Agreements (PCAs) with Newly Independent States (NIS) were signed in spring 1994 with the Russian Federation, Ukraine, Kazakhstan and the Kyrgyz Republic. Moldova signed the PCA in July 1994 and Belarus in the December of the same year. PCAs with Armenia, Azerbaijan, Georgia were signed in April 1996, and with Uzbekistan that June. The EU-Tajikistan PCA entered into force in 2010. Ten out of twelve PCAs are currently in force.[295] Certain political considerations inhibit the enactment of the PCAs with Belarus and Turkmenistan (signed in March 1998).[296]

The PCAs constitute a separate group of "partnership" agreements among "association", "cooperation", "stabilisation" and "development" agreements entered into by the EC.[297] As *"ad hoc* political creations"[298] it is rather puzzling to fit the

---

294 See M. Maresceau and E. Montaguti, "The relations between the European and Central and Eastern Europe: a legal appraisal", 32 CMLRev. 1327-1367 (1995). M. Mikiyevich, *Mizhnarodno-pravovi aspekty spivrobitnitstva Evropeyskogo Souzy z tretimy krainamy* (Lviv National University Press 2001). Neither the PCA with Belarus nor the Interim Agreement has yet come into force owing to the suspension of bilateral relations between the EU and Belarus. The EU has not recognised the Belarus Constitution of 1994 and the Presidential elections in 2010. The EU decided upon a number of political and economic sanctions against Belarus. The PCA with Turkmenistan was signed in 1998 and is under ratification by the Member States. The Interim Agreement is not yet operational.
295 EC-Russia PCA (OJ 1997 L 327), entered in force 01 December 1997; EC-Ukraine PCA (O.J. 1998, L 49), entered in force 01 March 1998; EC-Moldova PCA (O.J. 1998, L 181), entered in force 01 July 1999; EC-Armenia PCA (O.J. 1999, L 239), entered in force 01 July 1999; EC-Azerbaijan PCA (O.J. 1999, L. 246), entered in force 01 July 1999; EC-Georgia PCA (O.J. 1999, L 205), entered in force 01 July 1999; EC-Republic of Kazakhstan PCA (O.J. 1999, L 196), entered in force 01 July 1999; EC-Kyrgyz Republic PCA (O.J. 1999, L 196), entered in force 01 July 1999; EC-Uzbekistan PCA (O.J. 1999, L 229), entered in force 01 July 1999; EC-Republic of Belarus PCA (COM (95)137 final), signed in 1995, but in 1996 EU-Belarus relations were stalled following political setbacks; EC-Turkmenistan PCA (COM (97) 693 final); EU-Tajikistan PCA (O.J. 2009, L 350), entered in force 01 January 2010.
296 For a more comprehensive historical overview of the EU/USSR and NIS relations see M. Maresceau (ed) *Enlarging the European Union: Relations Between the EU and Eastern Europe* (Longman, London 1997) and C. Hillion, "Partnership and Cooperation Agreements between the European Union and the New Independent States of the Ex-Soviet Union", 3 EFA Rev. 399-420 (1998).
297 For a concise classification of the EU external agreements see D. McGoldrick, *International Relations Law of the European Union* (London, Longman 1997).

PCAs into the order of politicised EU external agreements.[299] However, the PCAs may be classified as "entry-level" agreements that do not envisage membership, but instead endorse potential interest in the further development mutual cooperation between Parties. The PCAs are mixed agreements based on Articles 133 and 308 EC (now Articles 207 and 352 TFEU). The EC/EU exclusive competence covers PCAs provisions on trade in goods and services, including the cross-border supply of services. The number of specific bilateral agreements is concluded on the basis of the EC/EU exclusive competence,[300] although the PCAs went beyond the EC framework and clarified the EU's cross-pillar dimension.[301]

Preambles of the PCAs intentionally omit any reference to "the process of European integration" or "the objective of membership in the EU", as these are provided in the EAs and SAAs.[302] Besides, the PCAs do not consider the establishment of a free trade area with the EC in the same way as the EMAAs. The PCAs are aimed solely at the development of close political relations; the promotion of trade, investment and harmonious economic relations between the Parties; the sustenance of cooperation and the support of efforts by any PCA nation to complete its transition to a market economy.[303] The PCAs' objectives merely pave the way for further political and economic cooperation between the Parties "to provide a basis for mutually advantageous economic cooperation; to promote trade and investment harmonious economic relations". The PCA objectives indirectly underline the transitional character of the agreements, which could eventually lead to a new and improved form of cooperation.[304] In this context, the third "generation" EMAAs objectives are more explicit. They promulgate the establishment of a free trade area and unequivocally state that the mutual liberalisation of trade and access to their respective markets is a major objective of the association.[305]

---

298 This expression is used by S. Peers in "EC Frameworks of International Relations: Co-operation, Partnership and Association" in A. Dashwood and C. Hillion (eds.), *The General Law of EC External Relations* (London, Sweet & Maxwell 2000), 161-176.
299 S. Peers insists that "The Community"s classification of agreements is governed by politics, not law". *Ibid,* at 175
300 For example, the EC-Russia Agreement on trade in textile products (O.J. 1998, L 222).
301 See C. Hillion, "Institutional Aspects of the Partnership Between the European Union and the Newly Independent States of the Former Soviet Union: Case Studies of Russia and Ukraine", 37 CML Rev. 1211-1235 (2000).
302 Preamble to the Hungary EA.
303 Article 1 EC-Ukraine PCA.
304 Muraviov V., *Pravovi zasady regulyvania ekonomichikh vidnosyn Evropeiskogo Souzy z tretimy krainamy (teoria I praktika),* (Kiev, Akadem Press 2002).
305 See the Preambles and Articles 6 EC-Israeli and EC-Tunisia EMAAs.

2.2.6.2. The scope of the acquis communautaire in the PCAs

The PCAs acknowledge the existence of historical links and common values shared by the Parties. Each PCA contains a clause of "essential elements" which respect democratic principles, human rights, and the principles of market economy. A violation of the mentioned principles implies a material breach of the agreement and allows the other Party to suspend unilaterally the implementation of the agreement.[306] The principle of free transit of goods constitutes an essential condition for attaining the objectives of the PCAs but its violation does not entail the suspension of the PCAs.[307] Unsurprisingly, the limits of the "essential elements" are not precisely defined in the PCAs, but they encompass international treaties and documents of general application, thereby leaving the EU wide scope for political maneuvering towards the NIS countries.[308]

The scope of international law to be applied by PCA countries covers a wide range of international documents in the relevant areas. The PCAs underline the Parties' "firm" commitment to the full implementation of all principles and provisions contained in the Final Document of the CSCE, the concluding documents of the Madrid and Vienna follow-up meetings, the document of the CSCE Bonn Conference on economic cooperation, the "Charter of Paris for a New Europe" and the CSCE Helsinki document 1992 "The Challenges of Change".[309]

Provisions of Russian and Ukrainian PCAs refer to the full scope of the Most Favoured Nation (MFN) treatment envisaged in Article 1 paragraph 1 of the GATT.[310] The Parties have committed themselves to allow the unrestricted transit of goods through their territories in accordance with GATT rules.[311]. The PCAs were the first international agreements to impose obligations on the PCA countries pursuant to GATT, thereby making possible their application without

---

306 See the joint declarations annexed to the EC-Russia and EC-Ukraine PCAs (articles 107 and 102 respectively).
307 For example see Article 11 EC-Ukraine PCA.
308 The PCAs' essential elements comprise "democratic principles and human rights as defined in particular in the Helsinki Final Act, and Charter of Paris for a New Europe and principles of market economy including those enunciated in the Documents of the CSCE Bonn Conference" (Article 2 EC-Ukraine PCA).
309 These two documents are explicitly mentioned in Article 21(2)(c) TEU.
310 Article 10(1) EC-Russia and EC-Ukraine PCAs. The remaining PCAs commit the Parties to MFN treatment in certain areas, such as: "custom duties and charges applied to imports and exports, rules of customs clearance, transit, warehouses and transhipment; taxes and other internal charges of any kind applied directly or indirectly to imported goods; methods of payment and the transfer of such payments; the rules relating to the sale, purchase, transport, distribution and use of goods on the domestic market" (Article 9(1) of the Azerbaijan PCA).
311 For example see Article 10 EC-Azerbaijan PCA.

formal WTO membership.[312] Furthermore, GATT wording is used in the PCAs' fiscal discrimination, safeguard and exemption clauses. Anti-dumping and anti-subsidy rules must also accord with GATT provisions. The prohibition of imports, exports or goods in transit is subject to derogations similar to those listed in Article 30 EC (now Article 36 TFEU).[313] Since WTO accession is an objective of the PCAs, the application of the WTO acquis may be seen as a preparatory step on the road to WTO accession by the PCA countries.

The Russian, Ukrainian and Moldavian PCAs provide a framework for cooperation in competition matters, although they hardly commit either Party to undertake any specific actions. The Parties have agreed "to work to remedy or remove" restrictions on competition and to enforce competition laws to combat such restrictions.[314] There is no reference that such laws should be identical to EC law, but EC competition rules are mentioned among the priorities of the approximation process in the PCA countries.[315] In contrast, the SAAs and EAs replicate rules on incompatible practices banned in Articles 81, 82 and 87 EC (now Articles 101, 102 and 107 TFEU), thereby arguably entailing their direct effect within the EC legal order. The direct effect on national legal orders depends on their constitutional law.[316]

Competition provisions as well as provisions on state monopolies and state aid are enshrined in the "European" Russian, Ukrainian and Moldavian PCAs, and are omitted in the Asian and Caucasus PCAs. The last contain only a reference to

---

312 V. Muraviov, "Polozhenia Ugody pro partnerstvo ta spivrobitnitsvo, yaki reguluyt sferu pidpriemnitsva ta investitsiy (pitania implementasii)", 2 Ukrainskiy Pravoviy Chasopys 31-35 (1998). O. Malskiy, "Poniatie statusa strany s rynochnoy ekonomikoy v mezhdunarodnom torgovom prave: vygody i nedostatki dlia Ukrainy" №25 (391), Yuridichna Praktika (2005). Meanwhile majority of the NIS countries are not Members of the WTO, with the exception of Armenia (acceded on 5 February 2003), Moldova (acceded on 26 July 2001), Georgia (acceded on 14 June 2000) and Kyrgyz Republic (acceded on 20 September 1998). Ukraine has completed the negotiation process and is due to join the WTO in 2008.
313 The PCAs permits prohibitions or restrictions on imports, exports or goods in transit on grounds of public morality, public policy or public security; the protection of health and life of humans, animals or plants; the protection of natural resources; the protections of national treasures of artistic, historic or archaeological value or the protection of intellectual, industrial and commercial property or rules relating to gold and silver. Such prohibitions should not constitute a means of arbitrary discrimination (For example, see Article 20 of the EC-Ukraine PCA).
314 For example see Article 53 EC-Russia PCA.
315 For example, see Article 51 EC-Ukraine PCA.
316 For example, see Article 69(1) and (2) EC-FYROM SAA. The wording of this agreement such as "the following are incompatible with the proper functioning of the Agreement" and "any practices of this agreement shall be assessed on the basis of criteria arising from the application of the rules of the EC Treaty" could prove even the direct effect of its provisions.

the possibility of examining the coordination of competition laws when trade is affected.[317] However, the Georgian PCA provides that Georgia may be provided with technical assistance in implementing EC competition and state anti-monopoly rules.[318]

The principle of non-discrimination plays an essential role in meeting the objectives of the partnership. It applies with regard to the non-discrimination treatment of the PCA and EU nationals,[319] of state monopolies of a commercial character.[320] The principle of non-discrimination applies with regard to: fiscal discrimination;[321] the application of safeguard measures;[322] the conditions of marketing and procurement of goods;[323] the treatment of workers based on nationality as regards working conditions, remuneration or dismissal and in comparison with its own nationals;[324] the establishment and operation of companies;[325] the free supply of services in international maritime transport;[326] and access to courts and administrative organs.[327]

All PCAs countries except Russia have made a commitment to provide, by the end of the fifth year after the entry into force of the Agreement, a level of protection and enforcement of intellectual, industrial and commercial property rights

---

317 For example, see Article 44(4) EC-Kyrgyz PCA.
318 Article 44 EC-Georgia PCA.
319 Article 23 EC-Russia PCA. Similar to the EAs and the SAAs nationals the PCAs and EU nationals enjoy right to non-discrimination based on nationality, as regards working conditions, remuneration or dismissal. However, the wording of the respective obligations varies from one PCA to the other, indicating the "asymmetrical" approach by the EU. The Russian PCA explicitly and unambiguously says that the Parties "shall ensure" right to non-discrimination. The Ukrainian, Moldavian, Kazakh PCAs contain a less explicit wording and provide that the Parties undertake "to endeavour to ensure" the nondiscrimination treatment of other Party nationals with respect to their labour conditions. The most asymmetrical obligations are contained in the Caucasus PCAs along with the remaining Asian PCAs. Therein, it is provided that the EU "shall endeavour to ensure" non-discrimination with regard to the labour conditions of respective PCA nationals, while the PCA countries "shall ensure" non-discriminative of EU nationals (For example, see Article 20 EC-Azerbaijan PCA).
320 For example, see Article 49(2.4) EC-Ukraine PCA. The respective declaration is effective from the third year after signing of the PCA in Russia and after the fourth year in Ukraine and Moldova. The Parties to the PCAs "declare their readiness" to ensure non-discrimination towards activities of each other nationals and companies.
321 For example, Article 52(7) EC-Russia PCA.
322 For example, Article 19 EC-Russia PCA.
323 For example, Article 53(2.4) EC-Russia PCA.
324 For example, Article 23 EC-Russia PCA.
325 For example, Article 29(3) EC-Russia PCA.
326 For example, Article 40(2) EC-Russia PCA.
327 For example, Article 98 EC-Russia PCA.

similar to those existing in the EC.[328] However, Russia did not go so this far, and only confirmed the importance of "[ensuring] the adequate and effective protection and enforcement of intellectual, industrial and commercial property rights". Furthermore, by the end of the fifth year after entry into force of the Agreement, all PCA countries are obliged to accede to the major multilateral conventions on intellectual, industrial and commercial property rights.[329] The EA and SAA commitments in the field of intellectual, industrial and commercial property are similar but contain a much stronger level of commitment. For example, the SAAs countries "shall take the necessary measures to guarantee" a level of protection similar to that existing in the EC after five years of entry into force of the Agreement, including the effective means of enforcing such rights.[330]

Recently, the ECJ recognised in the *Simutenkov* case that principle of non-discrimination set out in the Russian PCA is directly effective.[331] Furthermore, the ECJ clearly stated that limited objectives of the Russian PCA which do not provide for either association or further accession of Russia into the EU do not prevent "certain of its provisions from having direct effect".[332] Consequently, we argue that non-discrimination provisions in other PCAs must be considered as having direct effect in the EU legal order. Furthermore, we believe that PCA clauses which satisfy all the conditions of direct effect could be directly applied by NIS nationals in the EU. These are the PCA provisions concerning the right of entry of the "key personnel" and the right to sign a contract on the provision of services, as well as the MFN clause.[333] The issue of direct applicability of the

---

328 For example, see Article 50 EC-Ukraine PCA. Notably, the EC-Kyrgyz PCA gives the possibility for the EU-Kyrgyz Cooperation Council to extend this deadline "in light of particular circumstances" (Article 13(1) EC-Kyrgyz PCA).
329 All PCAs refer to such multilateral conventions, such as: the 1967 Paris Convention for the protection of industrial property; the 1967 Madrid Agreement concerning the international registration of marks; the 1977 Nice Agreement concerning the international classification of goods and services for the purposes of the registration of marks; the 1977 Budapest Treaty on the international recognition of the deposit of microorganisms; the 1970 Patent Cooperation Treaty; the 1989 Protocol relating to the Madrid Agreement concerning the international registration of marks (Article 54(2) of the EU-Russia PCA). However, the list of conventions is extended for some PCA countries.
330 For example see Article 71 EC-FYROM SAA.
331 Case C-265/03, *Simutenkov v. Ministerio de Educacion y Cultura, Real Federacion Espanola de Futbol* (Judgment of the ECJ of 12 April 2005). Case notes by K. Schuilenburg, "The ECJ Simutenkov Case: Is Same Level not Offside after All?" 13 Policy Papers on Transnational Economic Law (2005), available at <http://www2.jura.uni-halle.de/telc/
PolicyPaper13.pdf>, last visited 18 January 2011, see also case note by C. Hillion in 45 CML Rev. 815-833 (2008).
332 *Ibid* (Case C-265/03), at para 28.
333 R. Petrov, "Rights of third country/NIS nationals to pursue economic activity in the EC", 4(2) EFA Rev. 235-253 (1999).

PCAs within legal orders of the NIS countries depends on their constitutional arrangements. However, the NIS countries are reluctant to ensure the direct applicability of PCAs provisions by national courts. It happens because the NIS countries are eager to protect their vulnerable domestic industries (automobile; electronics; professional services) from the penetration of European competitors. For this purpose, the PCAs' countries frequently employ dubious safeguard schemes. One such scheme was witnessed in Ukraine, where the government gave substantive tax preferences to a Daewoo investor in a declining national car plant, with the express purpose of excluding European competitors.[334] However, as recent practice shows, Russian and Ukrainian courts more frequently refer to provisions of the PCA in order to protect rights of foreign investors and to ensure the application of international acquis in national legal systems.[335]

2.2.6.3. Concluding remarks

The PCAs may be seen as quite a successful formulation in EU external policy. They have served their purpose as a reliable legal instrument in sustaining long-term relations with PCA states. In the time being all PCAs are being prolonged for indefinite period of time due to their expiry in 2007-2009. The PCAs will gradually be substituted by a new generation of neighbourhood agreements which are envisaged by the ENP as a reward prize for the neighbouring countries. It is expected that these new agreements will be association agreements and foresee the enhanced political dialogue, free trade area and better access of the neighbouring countries' nationals to the EU Internal Market. In time of writing only Ukraine has entered and successfully pursued the negotiation process on the new neighbourhood agreement with the EU.[336]

The scope of the acquis within the PCAs is constructed in such a way as to bring PCA nations into the world market economy. It broadly covers international law acquis in the area of democratic freedoms and fundamental rights. Principles of liberal trade, reciprocity and fair competitiveness serve as cornerstones in fulfilling the objectives of the agreements. Application of the MFN treatment

---

334 C. Hillion "Trade dispute overshadows entry into force of EC agreement", 6 EU Focus (1998).
335 On the application of the PCA by Russian courts see P. Kalinichenko, "Primenenie Soglashenia o partnerstve i sotrudnichestve mezhdu RF i EC v rossiiskikh sudakh", 11 Zakon 225-234 (2007).
336 R. Petrov "Legal basis and scope of the new EU-Ukraine enhanced agreement. Is there any room for further speculation?", European University Institute Working Papers, 2008/17.

and the Generalised System of Preferences (GSP)[337] regime significantly liberalise the mutual trade in goods. Furthermore, companies within the PCA countries can rely on non-discriminatory treatment once they decide to establish themselves in the EU. The PCA countries are encouraged to approximate their laws to the EU, particularly in areas such as competition and the protection of intellectual property. The WTO rules have become applicable in trade relations between the Parties, despite the fact that most PCA nations have not yet acceded to the WTO. In the end, the PCAs should be understood as "entry-level" agreements with a great degree of variation, which establish objectives for the PCA countries while the EU is busy dealing with pursuing its expansion in Central and Eastern Europe.

The evolution of relations between EU and NIS countries implies the extension of the scope of the acquis communautaire to be adopted by PCA countries. This was a result of two additional EU external policy initiatives: 1) Common Strategies (CS);[338] and 2) ENP. The CSs were used during the "pre-Lisbon" period only. They clearly differentiated the EU's policy towards certain PCA countries in accordance with geopolitical and geographic factors, economic progress, and further engagement in cross-border cooperation. Besides, the CSs provided revisited and refined guidelines of mutual cooperation, including the approximation efforts between EU and NIS countries. The European Council has endorsed only three CSs with Russia[339] and Ukraine,[340] and Mediterranean,[341] which share

---

337 In 1968, the United Nations Conference on Trade and Development (UNCTAD) recommended the creation of a "Generalised System of Tariff Preferences" under which industrialised countries would grant trade preferences to all developing countries. This authorises developed countries to establish individual GSP schemes. The European Community was the first to implement a GSP scheme in 1971. More detailed information on the GSP see at <http://ec.europa.eu/trade/wider-agenda/development/generalised-system-of-preferences>, last visited 18 January 2011.
338 Articles 13, 14 and 15 TEU (repealed after the Treaty of Lisbon entered into force). European Council Common Strategy towards Russia (O.J. 1999 L157/1). European Council Common Strategy towards Ukraine (O.J. 1999 L331/1). For more information on the procedure of adoption of the CSs and the historical background see C. Hillion, "Institutional Aspects of the Partnership Between the European Union and the Newly Independent States of the Former Soviet Union: Case Studies of Russia and Ukraine", 37 CML Rev. 1211-1235 (2000). Pursuant to Article 13 TEU (repealed after the Treaty of Lisbon entered into force) the European Council was able to "decide on common strategies to be implemented by the Union in areas where the Member States have important interests in common". The CSs were implemented via the application of common actions and common positions.
339 The European Council meeting in Cologne in June 1999 adopted the CS towards Russia. See point 78, Presidency Conclusions, Cologne European Council (O.J. 1999 L 157/1). The CS towards Russia is terminated.
340 The CS towards Ukraine was adopted at the Helsinki European Council in December 1999. See point 56, Presidency Conclusions, Helsinki European Council (O.J. 1999 L

a common border with the EU. If the CS towards Russia focused mainly on consolidating democracy, the rule of law and public institutions, as well as strengthening stability and security in Europe, the CS towards Ukraine explicitly encourages the Ukrainian authorities to accelerate the approximation process, and also expands the scope of the priority areas of the acquis to be adopted by PCA countries to cover data protection and fiscal legislation.[342]

In 2003 the EC Commission initiated the "Wider Europe-Neighbourhood" policy towards third countries which share an immediate post-enlargement border with the EU.[343] The EC Commission offered a "privileged partnership" to the Western NIS countries, including: Russia, Ukraine, Belarus, and Moldova. Later, the ENP expanded further East to cover the whole Caucasian region (Georgia, Armenia and Azerbaijan). Following the Council's endorsement, the EC Commission issued the Strategy Paper "European Neighbourhood Policy" in 2004. In accordance with this Strategy Paper, the ENP envisages the access of neighbour countries to the EU Internal Market "without sharing common institutions". In other words, the ENP encourages neighbouring states to embark upon the voluntary adoption of the acquis communautaire without participating in EU decision-making and legislative procedures. Bilateral Action Plans and Association Agenda (applied only towards Ukraine since November 2009) clarify the precise scope of the acquis communautaire to be adopted by a neighbouring state.[344] For example, in the case of Ukraine, the eventual aims of the ENP are: 1) the establishment of a free trade area between the EC and Ukraine; 2) access to selected segments of the EU Internal Market and the EU "financial packages". The PCAs remain the basis for the ENP vis-à-vis the Western NIS countries. Eventually, the ENP includes the possibility of concluding the "Neighbourhood Agreement", though without any clear guidelines as for its legal basis and objectives.

The ENP Strategy Paper enhances the scope of the acquis communautaire to be adopted by Ukraine. First, the ENP elaborates on the concept of "shared values". It "promotes the commitment to shared values" on behalf of neighbouring states. The effective implementation of shared values is an essential element of

---

331/1). The CSs were adopted for duration of four years with the possibility of being prolonged, reviewed and if necessary adapted by the European Council.
341   CS of 19 June 2000 on the Mediterranean region (O.J. 2000 L 183/5).
342   Article 20 of the EU CS towards Ukraine.
343   Communication from the Commission to the Council and the European Parliament "Wider Europe – Neighbourhood: A New Framework for Relations with our Eastern and Southern Neighbours". (COM (2003) 104 final). For detailed academic overview of the ENP see S. Blockmans and A. Lazowski, (eds.) *The European Union and its neighbours* (The Hague, T.M.C. Asser Press 2006).
344   At the time of writing the Action Plans are issued with regard to the following NIS countries: Moldova, Armenia, Georgia, and Azerbaijan, available at <http://ec.europa.eu/world/enp/documents_en.htm>, last visited 18 January 2011.

the whole ENP. The concept of "shared values" calls for respect of human dignity, liberty, democracy, equality, the rule of law and respect for human rights. These values are to be laid down in the foundation of society which cherishes pluralism, tolerance, justice, solidarity and non-discrimination. In other words, the ENP's shared values strengthen the scope of core constitutional principles shared by the EU and its neighbours. The level of the EU's ambition in developing links with each partner through the ENP will depend on the extent to which shared values are effectively shared. The Action Plans towards the NIS countries contain specific priorities intended to strengthen the commitment to shared values and to adoption of the EU dynamic acquis.[345] The pace of the NIS countries reforms aimed at adoption of the EU acquis is being regularly monitored by the Commission which vigilantly scrutinizes the NIS countries' successes and failures and proposes specific measures for improvements.[346]

The acquis' export oriented nature of the ENP was endorsed by the newest EU external initiative "Eastern Partnership" (launched with the the framework of the ENP) which is directed at post-Soviet neighbouring countries (Ukraine, Belarus, Moldova, Armenia, Georgia, Azebaijan).[347] One of the objectives of the "Eastern Partnership" is to encourage voluntary legislative and regulatory approximation of the post-Soviet neighbouring countries to EU law in return for closer economic and political rapprochement of these countries with the EU.

Therefore the "post-PCAs" EU external policy instruments ensure that the scope of the acquis communautaire to be adopted by the NIS countries reflects the dynamic nature of EU external policy towards the neighbouring countries.

---

345 With regard to shared values these include strengthening democracy and the rule of law, the reform of the judiciary and the fight against corruption and organised crime; respect of human rights and fundamental freedoms, including freedom of media and expression, rights of minorities and children, gender equality, trade union rights and other core labour standards, and the fight against the practice of torture and the prevention of ill-treatment; support for the development of civil society; and co-operation with the International Criminal Court.
346 Country Progress reports are available at <http://ec.europa.eu/world/enp/documents_en.htm>, last visited 18 January 2011.
347 Communication from the Commission and the European Parliament to the Council "Eastern Partnership" (COM (2008) 823 final). Joint Declaration of the Prague Eastern Partnership Summit (Prague, 7 May 2009), 8435 (Presse 78). The Eastern Partnership covers Ukraine, Moldova, Belarus, Georgia, Armenia and Azerbaijan.

2.2.7. Cotonou Agreement

2.2.7.1. Objectives of the Cotonou Agreement

The Cotonou Agreement is a framework development partnership agreement concluded between the (then) EC and the Group of African, Caribbean and Pacific (ACP) countries[348] on the basis of Articles 179 and 310 EC (now Articles 209 and 217 TFEU) and now for a period of twenty years (signed on June 2000 and entered into force on 1 April 2003).[349] The Cotonou Agreement inherits the objectives and principles of all previous ACP framework development agreements from Yaounde to Lome IV. Parties to the Cotonou Agreement are committed to pool their efforts to meeting the aims of poverty eradication, sustainable development and the gradual integration of ACP countries into the world economy. Furthermore, the Cotonou Agreement enhances the prospects for economic cooperation between the EC and the ACP countries. It envisages the eventual conclusion of economic partnership agreements aimed at the gradual integration of the ACP countries into the world economy with the subsequent establishment of bilateral free trade areas. In general, the Cotonou Agreement sets a coherent agenda for relations between EU-ACP members, and provides the long-term legal framework of their partnership.[350] At the same time, the Cotonou Agreement emphasises the differentiation to be applied by the EU in the course of EU-ACP cooperation.[351]

The Cotonou Agreement is distinguished by a unique "revision clause" (Article 95) which foresees the review of the acquis to be adopted by the ACP countries every five years (with the exception of the economic and trade provisions, for which there is a special revision procedure). The first and second revisions took place in 2005 and in 2010 and resulted in considerable enhancement of the international law acquis to be adopted by the ACP countries.

The Cotonou Agreement safeguards the maintenance of the non-reciprocal preferential trade regime only until 2008.[352] By then, more balanced trade agreements should be negotiated with individual ACP countries or groups of

---

348 At the present moment in time there are 78 ACP nations-signatories to the Cotonou Agreement.
349 O.J. 2000 L 317/3. The duration of the Cotonou Agreement is from 1 March 2000 to 1 March 2020.
350 For a comprehensive account of the Cotonou Partnership see B. Martenczuk, "From Lome to Cotonou: The ACP-EC Partnership Agreement in a Legal Perspective", 5 EFA Rev. 461-487 (2000).
351 Article 2 of the Cotonou Agreement reads: "cooperation arrangements and priorities shall vary according to a partner's level of development, its needs, its performance and its long-term development strategy".
352 This is with the exception of South Africa.

ACP countries; ideally, these agreements should qualify as free trade arrangements within the meaning of Article XXIV(5) GATT, and subsequently, shall establish the timetable for the progressive removal of barriers to trade between the parties in accordance with the relevant WTO rules. It is anticipated that the framework of these new agreements (likely to be called "European Partnership Agreements" (EPA)) may take several options: 1) a singe EPA with all ACP countries as a block; 2) EPAs with individual ACP countries separately; 3) EPAs with ACP regional groupings.[353] In the meantime, the negotiation process on these agreements is underway since 2002. However, it is expected that future EPAs will be built on principles of differentiation and regionalization similar to what is to be applied in the future ENAs and with extensive approximation of laws clauses which are likely to commit the ACP countries to the implementation of the sectoral acquis communautaire and international acquis (primary the WTO acquis).

2.2.7.2. The scope of the acquis communautaire in the Cotonou Agreement

As the instrument of the EU development policy, the Cotonou acquis embraces objectives enshrined in Article 177(2) EC (now Article 208 TFEU and Article 21 TEU), namely: democracy; rule of law; respect of human rights and fundamental freedoms. Consequently, these elements constitute the essential elements of the Cotonou Agreement.[354] In contrast to other EU external agreements, the Cotonou Agreement regards the principle of good governance as a *"fundamental element"* of the partnership,[355] violation of which (corruption, serious cases of bribery) might lead to its termination. Measures aimed at peace-building and conflict prevention are considered "important elements" of the acquis in the Cotonou

---

353 M.G. Desta, "EC-ACP economic partnership agreements and WTO compatibility: an experiment in North-South interregional agreements?", 43(5) CML Rev. 1343-1379 (2006). On this issue also see G. Thallinger, "From Apology to Utopia: EU–ECP Economic Partnership Agreements Oscillating between WTO Conformity and Sustainability", 12(4) EFA Rev. 499-516 (2007).
354 Article 9 Cotonou Agreement.
355 P. Hilpold emphasises the vagueness of the "good governance" concept in the Cotonou Agreement. He refers to the notion of "good governance" in the Communication to the Council and the European Parliament of 1998 (COM (1998) 146 final). Therein "good governance" contains the following elements: equity and the primacy of law; the institutional capacity to manage the country's resources effectively; transparency; public participation in the decision-making processes concerning the management and allocation of resources. See P. Hilpold, "EU Development Cooperation at a Crossroad: The Cotonou Agreement of 23 June 2000 and the Principle of Good Governance", 7 EFA Rev. 53-72 (2002).

Agreement. The notions of "fundamental elements" and "important elements" are not specified, thereby leaving some space for *ad hoc* interpretation by either of the Parties to the Agreement.[356] Experts believe that the scope of the essential elements is not uniform for all ACP countries, but varies in accordance with their level of development, thereby reflecting the principle of differentiation.[357] In any case, adherence to the essential and fundamental elements is indispensable in order to maintain access to trade preferences by the ACP countries. The Cotonou Agreement contains a fully-worked procedure in case of the violation of essential elements which have been used. For instance, the EU terminated political and economic cooperation and financial assistance to Liberia in response to the violation of the essential elements.[358] At the same time, the principle of good governance may be considered of somewhat lesser value than the essential elements of the partnership, since its violation does not trigger similar sanctions on behalf of the EU.[359]

As in the Lome Agreement, the Cotonou Agreement contains numerous references to the relevant international law acquis in the field of fundamental democratic freedoms and human rights by providing an impressive outlook into major fundamental international and regional multilateral treaties in democratic freedoms and human rights.[360] Furthermore, the Cotonou Agreement sets develop-

---

356 Article 8(5) and 11 Cotonou Agreement.
357 K. Arts, "ACP-EU Relations in a New Era: The Cotonou Agreement", 40 CML Rev. 95-116 (2003).
358 "Decision concluding consultations with Liberia under Articles 96 and 97 of the ACP-EC Partnership Agreement" (O.J. 2002 L96/23-26).
359 Violations of good governance can be sanctioned only under specific conditions set out in Article 97 of the Cotonou Agreement. This is inherent in the designation of good governance as a "fundamental" rather an "essential" element, which excludes it from the field of application of Article 96 Cotonou Agreement. This interpretation is confirmed by Article 9(3) of the Cotonou Agreement according to which the parties agree "that only serious cases of corruption, including acts of bribery leading to such corruption, as defined in Article 97 of the Cotonou Agreement constitute a violation of the fundamental element....this provision, unlike Article 96 of the Cotonou Agreement, is not reciprocal in nature".
360 The Preamble of the Cotonou Agreement refers to: the principles of the UN Charter; the Universal Declaration of Human Rights; the conclusions of the 1993 Vienna Conference on Human Rights; the Covenants on Civil and Political Rights and on Economic, Social and Cultural Rights; the Convention on the Rights of the Child; the Convention on the Elimination of all forms of Discrimination against Women; the International Convention on the Elimination of all forms of Racial Discrimination; the 1949 Geneva Conventions and the other instruments of international humanitarian law; the 1954 Convention relating to the status of stateless persons; the 1951 Geneva Convention relating to the Status of Refugees and the 1967 New York Protocol relating to the Status of Refugees. Furthermore, the Cotonou Agreement refers to almost all regional Conventions on fundamental human rights that may be relevant to the ACP countries: the European Convention for the Protection of Human Rights and Fundamental Freedoms; the African Charter on Human

ment policy targets, echoing the targets of leading international agencies. For instance, the Parties agreed to set targets and principles agreed in UN Conferences, and fixed by the Organisation for Economic Cooperation and Development (OECD)[361] Development Assistance Committee, namely to reduce by one half the proportion of people living in extreme poverty by 2015. For this purpose, ACP countries are expected to respect basic labour rights, taking account of International Labour Organisation (ILO)[362] principles. The scope of the relevant international law acquis has considerably expanded as a result of the first five-year review of the Cotonou Agreement in 2005. Thereafter, the ACP countries agreed to implement international conventions and legislative instruments with purpose to: prevent mercenary activities; allow the ratification of the Rome Statute of the International Criminal Court; fight against terrorism; countering the proliferation of weapons of mass distraction.[363] Henceforth, the ACP countries adherence to countering the proliferation of weapons of mass distraction along with human rights, democratic freedoms and the rule of law constitute the essential elements of the Cotonou Agreement[364] and, therefore, a subject of the constant monitoring on behalf of the EU.

The progressive liberalisation of trade in goods and services in accordance with WTO principles is considered one of major priorities of the Cotonou Agreement and further bilateral ACP agreements. This objective should be undertaken in accordance with the provisions of GATT and General Agreement on Trade in Services (GATS), and particularly those relating to the participation of developing countries in liberalisation agreements.[365] It implies the asymmetric nature of commitments in relations between the Parties, owing to the fact that not all ACP countries have obtained formal WTO membership.

To secure "an investment-friendly climate", the Parties to the Agreement pursue the introduction and implementation of effective and sound competition pol-

---

and Peoples' Rights; the American Convention on Human Rights, including decisions of the Libreville and Santo Domingo declarations of the Heads of State and Government of the ACP countries at their Summits in 1997 and 1999.
361 The OECD groups 30 Member States sharing commitment to democratic government and the market economy. The OECD is best known for its publications and its statistics, as well as its works on economic and social issues <http://www.oecd.org>, last visited 18 January 2011.
362 The International Labour Organization is the UN specialised agency which seeks the promotion of social justice and internationally recognised human and labour rights. It was founded in 1919 and is the only surviving major creation of the Treaty of Versailles which brought the League of Nations into being and it became the first specialised agency of the UN in 1946 <http://www.ilo.org>, last visited 18 January 2011.
363 A. Hadfield, "Janus Advances? An Analysis of EC Development Policy and the 2005 Amended Cotonou Partnership Agreement", 12(1) EFA Rev. 39-66 (2007).
364 Articles 9 and 11(b)(1) Cotonou Agreement.
365 Article 41 Cotonou Agreement.

icies and rules. The Cotonou Agreement does not impose the relevant acquis communautaire in competition. However, the Cotonou Agreement provisions do mirror the compatible EC/EU competition acquis.[366] This means that ACP countries should prevent any agreements aimed at the distortion of fair competition, and prohibit any abuse of the dominant position in the common market between the Parties to the Agreement. Considering the low level of unification in international competition rules, it is most likely that the Parties to the Agreement would borrow the relevant EC criteria in the course of the application of these provisions.

The Parties to the Cotonou Agreement have agreed to cooperate more closely in the field of standardisation, certification and quality assurance, in order to remove unnecessary technical barriers and to reduce the differences between them. In this context, the Cotonou Agreement parties reaffirm their commitments under the Agreement on Technical Barriers to trade, annexed to the WTO Agreement (TBT Agreement). Cooperation in standardisation and certification between the EU and the ACP countries targets promotion of compatible systems between the Parties, as well as the greater use of international technical regulations, standards, and conformity assessment procedures, including sector specific measures, in accordance with the level of economic development of the ACP nations.

The Parties to the Cotonou Agreement recognise the need to ensure an adequate and effective level of protection for intellectual, industrial and commercial property rights, and other rights in line with international standards with a view to reducing distortions and obstacles to bilateral trade. For this purpose, ACP countries are expected to adhere to the WTO Agreement on trade-related aspects of intellectual property rights (TRIPS), as well as the Convention on Biological Diversity (CBD). Furthermore, the ACP countries are also to agree on the need to accede to all relevant international conventions on intellectual, industrial and commercial property as referred to in Part I of the TRIPS Agreement, in line with their level of development.

---

366 The Parties to the Cotonou Agreement have agreed to implement national or regional rules and policies including the control of and, under certain conditions, the prohibition of agreements between undertakings, decisions by associations of undertakings and concerted practices between undertakings, which have as their object or effect the prevention, restriction or distortion of competition. The Parties further agreed to prohibit the abuse by one or more undertakings of a dominant position in the EU Internal Market or in the territory of ACP States.

2.2.7.3. Concluding remarks

The aims of the Cotonou Agreement emphasise the need for ACP countries to implement the principles of EU development policy. Therefore, peace-building and conflict prevention are equally important for the partnership, as well as the observance of the essential, fundamental and important elements to the Cotonou Agreement. This Agreement does not provide any direct references to the relevant acquis communautaire. Instead, it relies heavily on the relevant international law acquis. Thus, it embraces almost all regional conventions on the protection of fundamental human rights. All efforts in the liberalization of trade and services should be made in accordance with the WTO, ILO, and basic intellectual property conventions. This approach displays the EU's intention to bring the ACP countries into the competitive world market economy, and to create a new market environment compatible, but not equivalent, to that in the EU.

2.2.8. Trade development and cooperation agreements (TDCAs)

2.2.8.1. Introduction

The EU and Member States have entered into TDCAs with countries from almost all continents. The TDCAs have proved to be successful tools for liberalising mutual trade, and encouraging third countries to integrate into the competitive environment of the world economy. In a similar fashion to the PCAs, these agreements are based on Articles 133 and 308 EC Treaty (now Articles 207 and 352 TFEU). However, the TDCAs are not identical to the PCAs. The TDCAs' major focus is economic cooperation and the liberalisation of trade in goods and services. Consequently, the TDCAs omit the cross-pillar dimension inherent to the PCAs. Besides, in contrast to the PCAs, the aims of the TDCAs consider the perspective of establishing bilateral free trade areas between EU and TDCAs countries. Therefore, in regard to the export of the acquis communautaire, the TDCAs must be seen in a different way to the PCAs. This paper focuses on three TDCAs from three different continents: Asia, Africa and Latin America. The TDCAs with South Africa, Korea, and Mexico display perfectly common elements of the TDCAs, as well as differentiation of EU foreign policy towards each Party. Furthermore, this title reviews the nature and objectives of the EC-MERCOSUR Interregional Framework Cooperation Agreement, which is a transitional agreement aimed at the establishment of an EC-MERCOSUR Interregional Association and a free trade area. The transitional character of this agreement gives us a chance to identify the priority areas of acquis adoption in EU external relations.

2.2.8.2. EC- South Africa TDCA

2.2.8.2.1. Objectives of the EC-South Africa TDCA

South Africa is party to several framework agreements with the (then) EC. The first agreement is the Cotonou Agreement, which South Africa signed as a "qualified member" without access to its financial instruments and preferential trade regime. The second agreement is the South Africa TDCA, signed shortly after South Africa abandoned its disreputable apartheid regime.[367] These agreements

---

367 EC-South Africa TDCA (O.J. 1999 L 311/3). The EC-South Africa TDCA entered into force on 1 May 2004 (Council Decision of 26 April 2004 concerning the conclusion of the Trade, Development and Cooperation Agreement between the EC and its Member States the Republic of South Africa (O.J. 2004 L 127/47).

complement each other. The latter enhances economic cooperation between the Parties while preserving the strong human rights and democratic freedom dimension of the former. The Preamble of the EC-South Africa TDCA emphasises "the importance of the existing links of friendship and cooperation between the Community, Member States and South Africa and the common values that the Parties share". In the democratic dimension, the EC-South Africa TDCA is aimed at the eradication of poverty, and at consolidating the foundations of a democratic society in which human rights and fundamental freedoms are respected. In the economic dimension, the EC-South Africa TDCA promotes the reciprocal liberalisation of the mutual trade in goods, services and capital, and encourages the smooth and gradual integration of South Africa into the world economy. Therefore, the economic and democratic/human rights dimensions of the EC-South Africa TDCA objectives determine the scope of the acquis communautaire to be implemented by South Africa.

The EC-South Africa relations received further reinvigoration with the Commission proposals to the Council and the European Parliament of 28 June 2006 to initiate a Strategic Partnership between the EU and South Africa. Objectives of the Strategic Partnership could be fulfilled through the implementation of a joint Action Plan which was signed on 14 May 2007.[368] The Strategic Partnership builds on and enhances the objectives of the EC-South Africa TDCA by engaging South Africa into: regional, African and international issues; enhancing existing sectoral cooperation; developing stronger and sustainable economic cooperation; and extending cooperation to trade-related areas and to the social, cultural and environmental fields. In particular, the EC-South Africa Joint Plan foresees the participation of South Africa in the international fight against terrorism, fight against drugs, money laundering and organised crime, adoption of the International Criminal Court Statute, non-proliferation of weapons of mass destruction and other international commitments, further trade liberalization and further alignment of the South African legislation to sectoral acquis communautaire (energy, transport, agriculture and sanitary and phyto-sanitary matters). To achieve these objectives the parties decided to launch negotiations on the EU-South Africa Economic Partnership Agreement, which will considerably enhance the level of relations in the EC-South Africa TDCA and will contribute to the achieving objectives of the Strategic Partnership.[369]

---

368 The Council of Ministers Press Release "The South Africa-European Union Strategic Partnership Joint Action Plan" 9650/07 (Presse 105).
369 The Council of Ministers Press Release "EU-South Africa Strategic Partnership, 10 October 2007 Joint Communiqué" 13825/07 (Presse 230).

2.2.8.2.2. The scope of the acquis communautaire within the EC-South Africa TDCA

"Respect for democratic principles and fundamental Human Rights as laid down in the Universal Declaration on Human Rights, as well as for the principles of the rule of law" form the essential elements of the Agreement.[370] The Parties also reaffirm their adherence to the application of the principle of good governance. The Preamble of the Agreement contains references to international law in the area of fundamental freedoms and human rights. Thus, the Parties confirm their commitment to apply values and principles set out in: the UN Charter, the Universal Declaration on Human Rights, the Cairo International Conference, the Copenhagen Summit, the Beijing Women World Conference, and ILO rules.

Cooperation between Parties and the further liberalisation of mutual trade are based on the application of the principle of non-discrimination within the areas of: customs duties of a fiscal nature;[371] internal fiscal measures;[372] trade in goods;[373] supply of services;[374] employment and occupation.[375] Furthermore, a separate article on non-discrimination prohibits any form of discrimination with regard to persons and companies in relations between the Parties.[376]

The EC and South Africa have agreed to establish a free trade area over a transition period of up to 12 years, in conformity with the WTO rules.[377] Therefore, the application of WTO rules is of particular importance in achieving the aims of the cooperation. The Agreement envisages the application of WTO rules with regard to the rules of origin of agricultural products,[378] anti-dumping or countervailing measures,[379] and the right of establishment and supply of services.[380] In the area of protection of intellectual, industrial and commercial property rules, the Parties are bound by the TRIPS and relevant international conventions.[381]

---

370 Article 2 EC-South Africa TDCA.
371 Article 8 EC-South Africa TDCA.
372 Article 21 EC-South Africa TDCA.
373 Article 27 EC-South Africa TDCA.
374 Article 30 EC-South Africa TDCA.
375 Article 86 EC-South Africa TDCA.
376 Article 100 EC-South Africa TDCA.
377 Article 15 EC-South Africa TDCA.
378 Article 13 EC-South Africa TDCA.
379 Article 23 EC-South Africa TDCA.
380 Article 29(1) EC-South Africa TDCA provides: "In recognition of the growing importance of services…the Parties underline the importance of strict observance of the GATS, in particular its principle on most favourable nation treatment, and including its applicable protocols with annexed commitments".
381 Article 46(6) EC-South Africa.

The Agreement does not refer to South Africa's application of the acquis communautaire. However, within specific sectors of cooperation South Africa is encouraged to follow the principles of the relevant acquis communautaire in the course of adopting new national legislation. For instance, in the area of competition, the EC-South Africa TDCA provides a three-year deadline for South Africa to adopt national competition legislation. The scope of the "competition" clause in the EC-South Africa TDCA mirrors Articles 81 and 82 EC (now Articles 101 and 102 TFEU). It ensures the prohibition of any form of abuse of market power and uncompetitive agreements, and concerns practices by companies of either Party. Despite omitting any direct references to the relevant acquis communautaire in the EC-South African TDCA, the South African legislature would have to follow the EC competition acquis to ensure some degree of compatibility of their competition legislation. This approach replicates the wording of provisions on competition in the Cotonou Agreement,[382] but differs from the respective provisions of the PCAs. For instance, the PCAs do not contain the "competition clause", and do not use the same legal terminology as the EC-South African TDCA.[383]

2.2.8.2.3. Concluding remarks

The scope of the acquis communautaire within the framework of the EC-South Africa TDCA is distinguished by strong democratic and human rights dimensions. The EC-South Africa TDCA aims to build a solid foundation for common values shared by Parties to the TDCA. Therefore, the essential elements clause within the EC-South Africa TDCA embraces major international democratic and human rights instruments. The aim of the gradual establishment of a free trade area justifies the application of the relevant WTO acquis, including the principle of non-discrimination. Although the EC-South Africa TDCA does not make any references to the acquis communautaire, the agreement ensures the application of the sectoral principles of the acquis communautaire (competition, state aid, procurement) within the South African legal order.

---

382 Article 45(2) Cotonou Agreement.
383 For instance, the "competition clause" in Article 49(2.1) EC-Ukraine PCA states that the Parties "ensure that they have and enforce laws addressing restrictions on competition by enterprises within their jurisdiction".

2.2.8.3. The EC - Korea Framework Agreement for Trade and Cooperation

2.2.8.3.1. Objectives of the EC-Korea Framework Agreement for Trade and Cooperation

The EC-Korea TDCA indicates the growing economic and political importance of South Korea in the Asian region. This is the only TDCA (apart from the EC-Macao TDCA) concluded by the (then) EC with a North-East Asian state. The decision to negotiate the framework TDCA by the EU was a response to improving democratic processes and economic recovery in South Korea. The EC-Korea TDCA was signed in October 1996 and entered into force on 1 April 2001.[384] In a similar fashion to other TDCAs, this agreement is based on Articles 133 and 308 EC Treaty (now Articles 207 and 352 TFEU). Hitherto, two sectoral agreements were concluded between the EC and South Korea.[385] The year 2010 was marked by an impressive breakthrough in the EU-South Korea relations. Two important agreements were signed that year: new Framework Agreement between the EU and Korea (signed on 10 May 2010); and Agreement of free trade area between the EU and Korea (signed on 06 October 2010).[386] These agreements will substitute the EC-Korea TDCA when they enter into force. Before that, the EC-Korea TDCA will remain a framework agreement governing bilateral relations in political and economic areas.

The EC-Korea TDCA reflects general EU policy objectives towards the whole Asian region. Asia is the EU's third largest trading partner and its fourth-largest regional investment destination. Therefore, the EC-Korea TDCA objectives emphasise the need to strengthen mutual trade and investment flows through the removal of non-tariff barriers to trade and investment, and the enhancement of the mutual business environment. At the same time, the EC-Korea TDCA, like other Asian TDCAs, contains a strong human-rights dimension to ensure the spread of democracy, good governance and the rule of law within the Asian region. Thus, the EC-Korea TDCA pursues a threefold objective: 1) the intensification of the political dialogue, and encouraging the inter-Korean reconciliation process; 2) enabling market access and the flow of investments into South Korea; 3) promoting democratic freedoms in South Korea. The EC-Korea TDCA attaches specific interest to scientific, technological and industrial cooperation

---

384 O.J. 2001 L 090.
385 The Agreement on co-operation and mutual administrative assistance in customs matters (O. J. 1997 L121). The Agreement on telecommunications procurement (O. J. 1997 L321) provides for the mutual opening of procurement by telecommunications operators.
386 Texts of the new agreements is available at <http://www.eeas.europa.eu/korea_south/index_en.htm>, last visited 18 January 2011.

due to the potential of the Parties in this area.[387] In the meantime the EU is seeking to upgrade its contractual relations with South Korea. For this purpose the negotiation process on ambitious and comprehensive free trade area between the EC and South Korea has started in May 2007 and update of the EC-Korea TDCA in June 2008.

2.2.8.3.2. The scope of the acquis communautaire in the EC-Korea TDCA

The EC-Korea TDCA contains a clause which is standard to all TDCAs, calling on the Parties to respect democratic principles and human rights as defined in the Universal Declaration on Human Rights.[388] The scope of international law applicable to Korea is focused primary on the relevant WTO acquis, with an emphasis on the application of the principle of non-discrimination.[389] The EC-Korea TDCA foresees the application of WTO rules to ensure the liberalisation of mutual markets: to ensure improved market access; to ensure the introduction of MFN to customs duties; to eliminate barriers to trade, including non-tariff barriers, in a transparent and non-discriminatory manner.[390] In the field of public procurement, the Parties adhere to the WTO Government Procurement Agreement and commit themselves to "ensure participation in procurement contracts on a non-discriminatory and reciprocal basis".[391] In agriculture, the Parties confirm their commitment to comply with the WTO Agreement on Sanitary and Phyto-sanitary Measures. The Parties show "full respect" to the WTO anti-dumping and anti-subsidy Agreements.[392] However, in the area of fair competition, the EC-Korea TDCA refers neither to the acquis communautaire nor to the international law acquis, but relies on the relevant national laws. Thus the Parties bear a soft commitment to foster fair competition "through fully enforcing their relevant laws and regulations".[393] The relevant EC competition criteria (covering EC primary and secondary competition laws) apply to Korea until the EC-Korea Joint Committee issues the implementing rules. Cooperation in the area of fair competition is focused on the shipbuilding industry.[394]

---

387 Article 2 EC-Korea TDCA.
388 Article 1 EC-Korea TDCA.
389 In particular with regard to nationals and company-providers of maritime services (Article 7(2)(b) of the EC-Korea TDCA) and procurement rules (Article 5(4) EC-Korea TDCA).
390 Article 5 EC-Korea TDCA.
391 Article 5(4) EC-Korea TDCA.
392 Article 11(2) EC-Korea TDCA.
393 Article 5(3) EC-Korea TDCA.
394 Article 8(1) EC-Korea TDCA.

A similar soft obligation is imposed on Korea in the area of intellectual property. Similarly to other EU external agreements, the EC-Korea TDCA provides that the adequate and effective protection of intellectual, industrial and commercial property rights, including the effective means of enforcing such rights, shall be based on the TRIPS and the obligations contained in the relevant multilateral conventions.[395] However, the EC-Korea TDCA gives a free hand to Korea to accede "as soon as practicable" to these conventions.[396]

The scope of international law applicable within the EC-Korea TDCA embraces fundamental multilateral conventions and acts. Regarding technical regulations, standards and conformity assessment, the Parties will promote the use of internationally-recognised standards and conformity assessment systems with the subsequent possibility of concluding mutual recognition agreements.[397] The Agreement calls for the establishment of suitable standards against money laundering, taking into consideration those adopted by international forums in this field, in particular the FATF. The non-discrimination of mutual trade in goods and services is ensured through the application of the relevant international law agreements, such as the OECD Agreement on Shipbuilding.[398] In the course of the harmonisation of legislation in this area, the Parties take into consideration recognised standards of international agencies.[399] The Agreement emphasises the need for an enhanced data protection regime between the Parties. For that purpose, they have committed themselves to a high level of protection to the processing of personal and other data in accordance with the standards adopted by the relevant international organisations and the EC. The precise list of the standards in data protection is provided in the Annex which forms an integral part of this Agreement.[400]

2.2.8.3.3. Concluding remarks

The Commission's Communication, "A new partnership with South East Asia",[401] provides for the enhancement of EU-East Asia relations in the nearest future. In this, the Commission foresees the signing of new bilateral agreements with the countries of the region's countries. These agreements will embrace the cross-pillar EU sources and relevant international law sources to be adopted by

---

395 Article 9 EC-Korea TDCA.
396 Article 9 EC-Korea TDCA.
397 Article 10(1) EC-Korea TDCA.
398 Article 8 EC-Korea TDCA.
399 Article 6(3) EC-Korea TDCA.
400 Article 51 EC-Korea TDCA.
401 COM (2003) 399/4.

the East Asian states. New bilateral agreements will encompass freedom, justice and security, in particular: issues of migration, trafficking in human beings, money laundering, piracy, organised crime, drugs, regional stability and the fight against terrorism. The essential element will be widened to cover the principle of good governance in addition to fundamental human rights principles. These new bilateral agreements will eventually lead to free trade area agreements based on the application of WTO rules.

The EC-Korea TDCA may be considered a transitional framework agreement aimed at the liberalisation of mutual market access within specific priority areas (the trade in goods, shipbuilding, maritime transport, agriculture and fisheries, intellectual and industrial property protection and standards). The transitional character of the agreement partly justifies the EU's reluctance to impose the relevant acquis communautaire on Korea. However, one may expect that a new free trade agreement between the EC and Korea would contain binding and soft commitments on Korea to implement the relevant acquis communautaire and to ensure its effective enforcement.

2.2.8.4. EC - Mexico Framework Agreement for Trade and Cooperation

2.2.8.4.1. Objectives of the EC-Mexico Framework Agreement for Trade and Cooperation

The EU-Mexico relations are based on the EC-Mexico Economic Partnership, Political Coordination and Cooperation Agreement known as a "Global Agreement", which was signed on 8 December 1997 in Brussels and entered into force on 1 October 2000.[402] The Global Agreement complements the existing sectoral agreements between the (then) EC and Mexico[403] and pursues three major objectives: political dialogue; the reinforcement of bilateral cooperation; and the liberalisation of trade and services between the Parties.

The Global Agreement sets out the target of establishing the EC-Mexico free trade area in goods and services with the subsequent opening of national procurement, capital and financial markets. Besides, it emphasises the adherence of the Parties to a regime of fair competition and to internationally-recognised stan-

---

402 O.J. 2000 L 276.
403 The EC-Mexico Agreement on mutual recognition and protection of designations for spirit drinks (O.J. 1997 L 152), the EC-Mexico Agreement on co-operation regarding the control of precursors and chemical substances frequently used in the illicit manufacture of narcotic drugs or psychotropic substances (O.J. 1997 L 077), the EC-Mexico Agreement on Scientific and Technological Cooperation (O.J. 2005 L 290).

dards of intellectual property rights.[404] In addition to its strong economic dimension, the Global Agreement is characterised by its democratic/human rights and political dimensions. The Preamble of the Global Agreement underlines the Parties' "full commitment" to democratic principles and fundamental human rights, to principles of international the rule of law and to good governance.[405] The enforcement of the rule of law in Mexico has become one of the top priorities of EU-Mexico relations. In accordance with the 2007-2013 Country Strategy Paper,[406] the EU designates a substantive financial assistance package (55 millions EURO) to ensure the rule of law in Mexico. Furthermore, Mexico is one of the priority countries in Latin America for the European Initiative on Democracy and Human Rights.[407] Various projects are supported under this initiative, including a project to strengthen human-rights Ombudsmen in Mexico, and to promote the protection of women's rights.

2.2.8.4.2. The scope of the acquis communautaire in the EC-Mexico Framework Agreement for Trade and Cooperation

The essential element clause calls on Parties to respect democratic principles and fundamental human rights as proclaimed by the Universal Declaration of Human Rights.[408] Within the objectives of economic and policy cooperation, the Global Agreement encourages Mexico to accede to the relevant international law multilateral conventions.[409] The principle of non-discrimination must be applied in order to ensure the liberalisation of mutual trade, to dismantle fiscal discrimination in respect of taxes imposed on goods,[410] and to eliminate discrimination in public

---

404 Article 12 of the EC-Mexico TDCA.
405 The Preamble to the Global Agreement refer to the Universal Declaration of Human Rights, the UN Charter; 1994 San Paulo EU Ministerial Declaration.
406 Available at <http://ec.europa.eu/external_relations/mexico/csp/2007_sp_en.pdf>, last visited 18 January 2011.
407 See the EU Annual Report on Human Rights 2005, available at <http://www.consilium.europa.eu/uedocs/cmsUpload/HR2005en.pdf>, last visited 18 January 2011.
408 Article 1 EC-Mexico TDCA reads: "Respect for democratic principles and fundamental human rights, proclaimed by the Universal Declaration of Human Rights, underpins the domestic and external policies of both Parties and constitutes an essential element of this Agreement".
409 For instance, the Article 28 of the Global Agreement emphasizes the need to combat the illegal production of drugs. For this purpose the Parties agreed to apply the Agreement on the Control of Drugs Precursors and Chemical Substances signed by the Parties on 13 December 1996, and in the 1988 UN Vienna Convention.
410 Article 5(d) EC-Mexico TDCA.

procurement, competition and other trade-related areas.[411] The Global Agreement call on Parties to pursue the mutual liberalisation of the trade in goods and services; capital movements; intellectual, industrial, and commercial rights in accordance with multilateral international law treaties, *inter alia* the WTO acquis.

The EC-Mexico free trade area arrangements are formalised in EC-Mexico Joint Council decisions (Decision 2/2000 for trade in goods, and Decision 2/2001 for trade in services).[412] The EC-Mexico Joint Council Decision 2/2000 covers: the reciprocal liberalisation of trade in goods in accordance with Article XXIV GATT; the opening of government procurement markets; the establishment of a cooperation regime in fair competition; the setting up of a consultation mechanism in respect of intellectual property matters; and the establishment of a dispute-settlement mechanism.[413] The EC-Mexico Joint Council Decision 2/2001 covers similar objectives with regard to the trade in services: the reciprocal liberalisation of the trade in services in accordance with Article V GATS; the progressive liberalisation of investments and related payments; the adequate protection of intellectual property rights "with the highest international standards"; and the establishment of a dispute-settlement mechanism.[414] These decisions impose on Mexico a comprehensive scope of the relevant WTO acquis and international law acquis. At the same time, they carefully avoid any reference to the relevant acquis communautaire. For instance, in government procurement Decision 2/2000 elaborates detailed procedural and material rules, instead of referring these issues to the relevant acquis communautaire. In competition law, the Global Agreement envisages only the temporary application of the EC competition acquis by Mexico until the subsequent decision of the EC-Mexico Joint Council.[415] The subsequent Decision 2/2000 does not envisage the application of the EC competition law acquis by Mexico. It merely promotes cooperation between Parties regarding the application of their national competition laws and the elimination of anticompetitive activities. In other words, Decision 2/2000 provides

---

411 Article 10 EC-Mexico TDCA.
412 The EU-Mexico Joint Council Decision 2/2000 establishing a EC-Mexico free trade area in goods (O.J. 2000 L 157) and the EU-Mexico Joint Council Decision 2/2001 establishing a free trade area in services (O.J. 2001 L 70).
413 Article 1 Decision 2/2000.
414 Article 1 Decision 2/2001.
415 Declaration by the Community relating to Article 11 EC-Mexico TDCA provides: "The Community declares that, until the adoption by the Joint Council of the implementing rules on fair competition referred to in Article 11(2) it shall assess any practice contrary to that Article on the basis of the criteria resulting from the rules contained in Articles 85, 86 and 92 of the Treaty establishing the European Community, and, for products covered by the Treaty establishing the European Coal and Steel Community, by those contained in Articles 65 and 66 of that Treaty and the Community rules on State aids, including secondary legislation".

only for cooperation in the application of respective EC and Mexican competition laws, but does not oblige Mexico to adopt the EC competition acquis.[416] With regard to public procurement, Decision 2/2000 does not provide for the application of the acquis communautaire either. Instead it refers to the relevant WTO and North American Free Trade Agreement (NAFTA) acquis. However, the title on public procurement reiterates all the basic material and procedural principles of public procurement adopted in the EC (non-discrimination and bid challenge).

2.2.8.4.3. Concluding remarks

The EC-Mexico TDCA goes further than most TDCAs. The aim of establishing a free trade area between the EC and Mexico obliges Mexico to adhere to the relevant WTO acquis. As a result, the EC-Mexico TDCA prioritises the application of the relevant international law over the acquis communautaire. For instance, Decisions 2/2000 and 2/2001 provide for some degree of homogeneity of Mexican legislation with the WTO acquis (the WTO Agreement on Public Procurement).

2.2.8.5. EC-MERCOSUR Interregional Framework Cooperation Agreement (IFA)

2.2.8.5.1. Objectives of the EC-MERCOSUR Interregional Framework Cooperation Agreement

Early EC-MERCOSUR relations were based on the Interinstitutional Agreement which ensured some degree of technical and institutional support for the emerging MERCOSUR[417] common market project. The enhanced Inter-Regional Framework Agreement for Cooperation between the EC and its Member States and MERCOSUR (IFA)[418] was signed on 15 December 1995 and entered into

---

416 This cooperation concerns the mutual notification on anticompetitive activities and enforcement activities. Furthermore, the Decision 2/2000 advances the exchange of information procedure wherein the Parties "to the extent practicable" share relevant case law and information related to the application of competition legislation.
417 MERCOSUR is the acronym for the "Mercado Común del Cono Sur".
418 The MERCOSUR is the regional integration agreement between Argentina, Brasil, Paraguay, and Uruguay. The Treaty of Asuncion, that established the MERCOSUR, was signed in 1991. In accordance with the Treaty of Ouro Preto of 1994 the MERCOSUR common market should be established by 2006.

force on 1 July 1999.[419] In general, the IFA sets the foundation for continuing dialogue and partnership, with the intention of establishing an interregional association and a free trade area between the EC and MERCOSUR countries.[420] The IFA a transitional framework agreement aimed at improving political and economic relations between the Parties on the way to an Interregional Association Agreement between the EU and MERCOSUR, which should include as wide as possible liberalization of trade in goods and services, free trade area and a strengthened political dialogue. The negotiations on the EU-MERCOSUR Interregional Association Agreement have been launched in 1999, thirteen negotiations rounds have been conducted so far. The Parties aim for a comprehensive association agreement beyond a free trade area in good and services agreement. In particular, the future EU-MERCOSUR Interregional Association Agreement will foresee an enhanced political dialogue (support of democracy, cooperation in the area of freedom, security and justice) and mutual liberalised market access (public procurement, competition, intellectual property rights, standards).[421]

Since then the EC has entered into sectoral and bilateral relations with certain MERCOSUR countries with the purpose of enhanced cooperation. Sectoral agreements have been concluded with Argentina in the areas of: sea fisheries; nuclear energy; science and technology. Bilateral EC-MERCOSUR Member State relations are governed by the Framework Trade and Economic Cooperation agreements with Brazil, Argentina, Paraguay, and Uruguay.[422]

The IFA is underpinned by political and economic objectives which set up the basic foundation for cooperation between the EC and MERCOSUR countries. The IFA openly encourages the gradual and reciprocal liberalisation of trade between the Parties in accordance with WTO rules.[423] Liberalisation efforts within the IFA are focused on: market access; the liberalisation of trade (tariff and non-

---

419 O.J. 1996 L069, O.J. 1999 L112.
420 Article 2 IFA. Hitherto twelve negotiation rounds have been conducted on the framework of the future association agreement. Issues of trade barriers, customs, and competition have been finalised. The negotiation process on market access in goods and services, government procurement and investment, wines and spirits, intellectual property rights, business facilitation is still underway.
421 EU-MERCOSUR Regional Strategy Paper 2007-2013, available at <http://ec.europa.eu/external_relations/mercosur/rsp/07_13_en.pdf>, last visited 18 January 2011.
422 EC-Brazil Framework Trade and Economic Cooperation Agreement (O.J. 1995 L 262), EC-Argentina Framework Trade and Economic Cooperation Agreement (O.J. 1990 L 295/66), EC-Paraguay Framework Trade and Economic Cooperation Agreement (O.J. 1991 C 309/6), EC-Uruguay Framework Trade and Economic Cooperation Agreement (O.J. 1992 L 94/2).
423 Article 4 IFA.

tariff barriers); fair competitive practices; and the application of safeguard measures in accordance with relevant international rules.[424]

Bilateral EC-MERCOSUR Member State agreements pursue less ambitious objectives than those of the IFA. These agreements ensure the application of the MFN treatment in trade in accordance with GATT and "work of international organisations";[425] the elimination of tariff and non-tariff barriers in trade; and the fair application of anti-dumping and countervailing investigations. The agreements do not envisage the approximation of laws, but underline that cooperation in trade should be undertaken in accordance with the Parties' national laws.[426] Consequently, bilateral EC-MERCOSUR Member State agreements do not consider the export of the acquis communautaire and relevant international law in the MERCOSUR legal systems.[427] However, this could take place in the case of the application of the "future development clause", which envisages the enhancement and widening of the scope of cooperation thereby leading to the establishment a free trade area between the EC and MERCOSUR.[428]

2.2.8.5.2. The scope of the acquis communautaire in the EC-MERCOSUR IFA

The IFA essential element clause replicates the general and vague formula applied in other EC trade development and cooperation agreements, and calls for the "respect for the democratic principles and fundamental human rights established by the Universal Declaration of Human Rights".[429]

The central objective of the Agreement is to ensure the mutual liberalisation of the trade in goods and services within specific areas such as the agriculture sector. The IFA avoids direct reference to the relevant acquis communautaire but instead encourages MERCOSUR countries to apply the relevant WTO acquis.[430] Therefore, MERCOSUR countries must ensure the compatibility of trade libera-

---

424 Article 5 IFA.
425 For example, Article 6 EC-Brazil Framework Agreement.
426 For example, Article 6 EC-Brazil Framework Agreement.
427 For example, Article 12(2) EC-Brazil Framework Agreement provides: "[the Parties] undertake to ensure, so far as their laws, regulations and policies allow, that suitable and effective protection is provided for intellectual property rights".
428 For example, Article 35 EC-Brazil Framework Agreement.
429 Article 1 IFA.
430 See Article 4 IFA states: "The Parties shall undertake to forge closer relations with the aim of encouraging the increase and diversification of trade, preparing for subsequent gradual and reciprocal liberalization of trade and promoting conditions which are conducive to the establishment of the Interregional Association, taking into account, in conformity with WTO rules, the sensitivity of certain goods." Also see Article 5(c) IFA.

lisation with GATT and WTO rules,[431] and must also to ensure "suitable and genuine protection in intellectual property rights" in line with the TRIPS.[432] Notably, the Agreement does not oblige MERCOSUR countries to implement the fundamental international conventions on the protection of intellectual property rights.

Legislative cooperation within the IFA envisages the soft approximation of the MERCOSUR members' legislation to relevant international law. For instance, the IFA states that "the Parties shall undertake to cooperate in promoting the approximation of quality standards for agri-food products and industrial goods and of certification, in conformity with international criteria".[433] The IFA assumes some gradual alignment of the TDCAs countries' customs legislation "to improve and consolidate the legal framework for trade relations between them".[434] In statistics the Parties "shall agree to align statistical methods with the aim of achieving mutual recognition".[435] Pursuing cooperation in business, the Parties promote compliance with competition rules and "foster the tailoring of those rules to the needs of the market".[436] Similar soft approximation commitments refer to the promotion of investment;[437] telecommunications and information technology;[438] and to environmental protection.[439]

The priority of the soft approximation of the MERCOSUR members' legislation to relevant international law is preserved in the course of the negotiation of the new EU-MERCOSUR Interregional Association Agreement. It is likely that provisions on legislative cooperation of this Agreement will not contain any direct references to the acquis communautaire but mention the need to align the MERCOSUR Member States' legislation to international acquis within relevant fields of cooperation (sanitary standards, environment, food security and other areas).

As a transitional framework agreement, the IFA ensures that the MERCOSUR countries implement relevant international economic legislation to promote the liberalisation of trade between the Parties whilst at the same time avoiding any direct reference to the acquis communautaire. However, the IFA contains carefully-worded soft-approximation commitments which foresee the alignment of the MERCOSUR countries' sectoral legislation to EC standards. This might in-

---

431 Article 5 IFA.
432 Article 9 IFA.
433 Article 6(1) IFA.
434 Article 7 IFA.
435 Article 8 IFA.
436 Article 11(2)(c) IFA.
437 Article 12 IFA.
438 Article 16 IFA.
439 Article 17 IFA.

dicate the willingness of the EU to encourage approximation efforts in the MERCOSUR countries in order to lay a basis for deepening mutual sectoral cooperation.

2.2.8.5.3. Concluding remarks

The TDCAs prioritise the export of relevant international law over the acquis communautaire. The reason for this could be the need to strengthen democratic and market economy foundations in newly-emerged democracies/Parties to the TDCAs. It means that the (then) EC preferred to pave the way for the imposition of the relevant acquis communautaire into the legal orders of third countries, by ensuring the application of fundamental international law standards. For instance, the TDCAs contain standard essential element clauses which refer to commonly-recognised international human rights standards as proclaimed in the United Nations Declaration of Human Rights. In addition, the essential elements clause of the EC-South Africa TDCA covers principles of rule of law and good governance. Since there is no definition of these principles in EC law, international law standards are applicable in these cases too.

The major objective of the TDCAs is to liberalise the trade in goods and services between the Parties in order to establish a free trade area. Therefore, the TDCAs consider the achievement of these objectives by ensuring the application of the relevant WTO rules. The Parties are committed to eliminate trade barriers and to establish transparent and non-discriminatory conditions in trade, in accordance with recognised WTO standards. In general, the TDCAs avoid imposing the acquis communautaire owing to the geographical, political, and economic remoteness of the parties from EU territory. However, in areas of specific importance to economic relations, some TDCAs may contain direct references to the relevant acquis. For example, the EC-Mexico TDCA envisaged the application of the EC competition acquis, and the EC-Korea TDCA provided for the application of the acquis in data protection. This indicates the desire of the EU to "export" its sectoral acquis into the legal systems of the MERCOSUR countries. This mainly concerns areas with particular importance for EU economic interests. As a result, the soft approximation of the MERCOSUR countries' legislation to that of the EU could pave the way for furthering sectoral cooperation with the EU.

2.3. Conclusion

This chapter pursued two tasks. Firstly, the scope of the external dimension of the acquis communautaire was analysed. In particular, we have focused on one aspect – the scope of the acquis communautaire in EU external agreements. Secondly, we have endeavoured to comprehend EU policy on the export of its acquis communautaire into the legal orders of third countries. For this purpose we scrutinized elements of the acquis communautaire in the major groups of EU external agreements. As a result of this study, it was suggested that the scope of the acquis communautaire is not uniform, but rather varies from one agreement to another in accordance with the objectives of EU external agreements.

Our study indicates that EU external agreements refer to the acquis communautaire in both extended and limited terms. In the former case, EU external agreements encompass vague legal categories such as "essential elements", "common/shared values", principles of international public law and international trade law, principle of non-discrimination, and European standards. None of these elements is precisely defined in EU external agreements, thereby providing a wide scope for interpretation by either Party. Nevertheless, these elements are considered important for the construction of a common legal environment between the Parties in the course of the enhancement of mutual relations. For instance, the ENP emphasises the significance of the "common/shared values" concept for the eventual upgrade of bilateral relations with each neighbour state. The Lisbon Treaty partly rectifies this puzzle by providing a set of the "Union's values" and principles applicable to both internal and external EU policies. However, the specific legal meaning of the "Union's values" remain far from clear. It could be expected that even after the Lisbon Treaty comes into force, EU institutions will retain the "final word" on identifying the scope of the "Union's values" applicable within EU external policy.[440] We have noticed that EU external agreements frequently refer to the "relevant" acquis, which usually means the EU sectoral legislation which is enshrined in the text of an agreement and/or in annexes of an EU external agreement. As it follows from our study, the "relevant acquis" is not a static concept but a dynamic legal category which changes its scope in accordance with the specific objectives of the EU external agreement. That is to say that the "relevant acquis" within the EC-Switzerland SAs differs from the "relevant acquis" within the EC-Mexico TDCA. This is because the EC-Switzerland SAs provide for the implementation of a sectoral acquis communautaire into the Swiss legal system, while the EC-Mexico TDCA

---

440 P. Leino, R. Petrov, "Between 'Common Values' and Competing Universals: The Promotion of the EU's Common Values through the European Neighbourhood Policy", 15(5) ELJ, 654-671 (2009).

establishes a free trade area between the EC and Mexico on the basis of the relevant WTO acquis. Furthermore, EU external agreements tend to reflect the evolution of the acquis communautaire within specific sectors of EC competence. For instance, the latest generation of association agreements with Western Balkan countries (SAAs) refers to the newly-occupied sectors of the acquis communautaire (audio-visual aspects, cross-border broadcasting, acquisition of intellectual property rights for programmes and broadcasts by satellite or cable, and co-operation in electronic communications and associated services).

It also can be argued that the concept of the "relevant acquis" does not coincide with the internal dimension of the acquis communautaire. Two points are relevant here. Firstly, none of the EU external agreements replicates the far-reaching objectives of the EU founding Treaties. Thus the "relevant acquis" in an EU external agreement should be applied in accordance with the objectives of these agreements. For instance, as decided by the ECJ, the "pre-signature" acquis communautaire within the EEA Agreement must be applied and implemented in accordance with the EAA Agreement objectives, which are different to the objectives of the EU founding Treaties. Secondly, the "relevant acquis" within the EU external agreement must be perceived as having a different legal nature from the acquis communautaire. The "relevant acquis" departs from the supranational nature of the acquis communautaire. It may be enforced only via national constitutional procedures as part of the international law applicable in that country. As a result, constitutional courts in third countries can exercise broad discretion in interpreting the relevant acquis within their legal orders.[441] Even in EEA Agreements, where the export of the relevant acquis is equipped by a sophisticated homogeneity procedure, it is left to the discretion of the national constitutions of EFTA Member States to implement in a homogeneous fashion certain elements of the "post-signature" EC "relevant acquis". This is because the homogeneity formula relies on the unpredicted political will of the EFTA Member States for the voluntary adaptation of the dynamic acquis communautaire into their legal orders. The objectives of EU external agreements and the latest trends of EU external policy towards certain third countries may influence the interpretation of third countries constitutional courts' regarding the relevant acquis within their national constitutional orders, as witnessed in the *Sveinbjörnsdottir* case judged by the EFTA Court, and in the *Scoda Auto* case judged by the Czech Constitutional Court.

---

441 The EFTA Court in *Sveinbjörnsdottir* case characterised the EEA Agreement as "an international treaty *sui generic* which contains a distinctive legal order of its own" (Case E-9/97, *Erla Maria Sveinbjörnsdottir v. the Government of Iceland*. Advisory Opinion of the EFTA Court of 10 December 1998, Report of the EFTA Court, at 97).

Furthermore, we have highlighted explicit links between the scope of the acquis communautaire to be imposed on a third country and factors such as EU external policy towards third countries and EU recognition of their legal systems. For instance, associate agreements with EFTA countries and with Switzerland contain neither essential elements clauses, nor any reference to the human rights or the fundamental freedoms acquis. In the case of Switzerland, the absence of these essential elements may be explained by the absence of a framework agreement between the EU and Switzerland. In the case of the EEA Agreement, this may be explained by an insufficient attitude on behalf of the (then) EC towards human rights and commitments to fundamental freedoms in the EU external agreements at time of signing. The EEA Agreement may have been conceived purely as an economic framework agreement aimed at bringing the EFTA countries closer to the EC Internal Market. The Israeli EMAA displays considerable recognition by the EU for the Israeli legal system, far beyond other EMAAs. For example, the approximation clause in the EC-Israel association agreement envisages the possibility of the mutual convergence of the Parties' legislation, while other EMAAs provide direct and indirect means for the acquis communautaire to be exported into the legal systems of Mediterranean countries.

These observations provide us with the conclusion that the EU pursues a consistent policy which targets the export of the acquis communautaire into the legal orders of third countries. It can be argued that the EU acts as an international harmonisation agency in order to achieve this ambitious objective. The EU eagerly encourages the expansion of the EU Internal Market acquis into the legal orders of third countries (especially the EU competition and state aids acquis). For this purpose, many EU external agreements contain direct and indirect references to the EU sectoral acquis, justifying it by the absence of relevant international rules and principles.[442] Many EU external agreements replicate in almost identical terms the relevant articles of the EU founding Treaties. This approach encourages third countries to import the acquis communautaire core principles voluntarily, even before the start of formal "pre-accession" negotiations. However, approximation commitments in EU external agreements refer not only to candidate countries, but also to third countries that either do not plan to join the EU, or who will not be given such an opportunity for some time. In the latter instance, EU external agreements target the promotion of the acquis communautaire at any cost, with the purpose of bringing third countries as close as possible to the EU legal environment. For instance, the EU applies the consistent policy

---

442 M. Cremona, "Multilateral and Bilateral Approaches to the Internationalisation of Competition Law: an EU Perspective" in Cremona, in: J. Fletcher / L. Mistelis (eds.), *Foundations and Perspectives of International Trade Law,* (London, Sweet and Maxwell 2001) 135-169.

towards third countries, which are willing to join one or several EU policies. In these cases third countries must adhere to the relevant acquis communautaire, and, consequently, to adopt not only the "pre-signature acquis" but also the "post-signature acquis" including the ECJ case law (EC-Swiss SAs on the extension of Schengen/Dublin acquis to Switzerland). Furthermore, EU external agreements with non-candidate countries frequently justify the need to follow soft-approximation commitments through the harmonisation of legislation at an international level. For instance, the EC-Swiss SAs states that the aligning of legislation contributes to the "harmonisation at an international level of the technical regulations, standards and principles governing implementation of conformity assessment procedures".[443]

In general, the export of the acquis communautaire takes place in an individual, tailor-made manner, taking into account various political, economic and legal aspects of EU external policy towards third countries. In some cases, the EU is ready to compromise the integrity of the acquis communautaire by allowing third countries to implement the relevant sectoral acquis in a "piece-by-piece" approach. For example, owing to a tough negotiation strategy, Switzerland was allowed to derogate from some important elements of the EU internal market acquis in the SA on taxation of savings income. In other cases, the EU strengthens its pressure on third countries to adopt the whole acquis communautaire, which in turn promulgates their will to upgrade the format of bilateral relations with the EU. For instance, the latest SAAs stipulate the adoption of the so-called "pre-negotiation" acquis by the Western Balkan countries.

We conclude this chapter with the suggestion that the concept of "acquis" in EU external agreements is being frequently and successfully applied as a sophisticated tool of EU external policy towards third countries.

---

443 For example, see the Preamble to the EC-Swiss SA on technical barriers.

Chapter 3. Substantive and Procedural Means of Exporting the Acquis Communautaire into the Legal Systems of Third Countries

3.1. Introduction

In the first chapter we analysed the concept of the "acquis communautaire" in its internal and external dimensions. In the second chapter we considered the issue of "what the EU wants to export into legal orders of third countries". Subsequently it is logical to clarify other issues which are essential for the academic exploration of the topic of our study.

Firstly, "how does the EU export its acquis?" For this purpose, in this chapter we shall focus our attention on selected substantive and procedural means by which the EU exports the acquis into the legal systems of third countries. The phrase "substantive means" refers to the fundamental ways in which the acquis communautaire is implemented into third country legal orders. In the course of our study we shall focus on the substantive means of exporting the fixed and dynamic acquis communautaire. "Procedural means" relates to specific technical/procedural tools which either directly or indirectly encourage the implementation of the acquis communautaire into third country legal orders. We shall equip our examination by the following procedural means: formal/informal involvement in the EU legislation procedure, the exchange of information and technical and financial assistance on behalf of the EU. A brief comparison is also made with the role of common institutions in the process of exporting the acquis communautaire into third country legal systems.

Secondly, "does the EU apply substantive and procedural means of exporting the acquis communautaire in line with the objectives of EU external agreements?" We argue that the substantive and procedural means of exporting the acquis communautaire is not uniformly applicable, but may be exercised taking into account specific objectives of EU external agreements. Also we shall argue that the composition and competence of common institutions are set up in such a way as to suit the objectives of EU external agreements.

Thirdly, "do the substantive and procedural means of exporting the acquis communautaire truly encourage third countries to europeanise their institutional and legal structures"? For this purpose we develop a case study wherein we endeavour to observe if specific objectives of EU external policies cause positive results in adoption of the acquis communautaire by judiciary in Ukraine. This country represents very good case for our study because it has been experiencing deep internal political and legal reforms under close monitoring on behalf of the

EU. At the same time the EU-Ukraine relations do not pursue an objective of Ukraine accession into the EU but aimed at close economic and political integration of Ukraine and the EU.

In general, our goal is not to provide an exhaustive analysis of the substantive and procedural means of exporting the acquis communautaire into third country legal systems, but to highlight the impact of the objectives of EU external agreements on the process of exporting the acquis communautaire and, therefore, to evaluate our findings of the previous chapters.

3.2. Substantive means of exporting the acquis communautaire into the legal systems of third countries

Below we examine and systemise the major substantive means of exporting the acquis communautaire into third country legal systems in EU external agreements. These means serve as the basic tools to ensure the implementation of the acquis communautaire into third country legal orders. For the purpose of our study we propose distinguishing two types of the acquis applicable within EU external agreements, namely fixed and dynamic. Consequently, the objectives of external agreements and the need to export either a fixed or dynamic acquis imply different substantive means of exporting the acquis communautaire.

3.2.1. Export of the fixed acquis into the legal systems of third countries

The export of the fixed or so-called "pre-signature" acquis into third country legal systems means that parties to external agreements agree to fix the scope of the acquis communautaire at the point of the formal signature of an agreement. However, the scope of the fixed acquis does not exclude its further revision in the course of the evolution and enhancement of bilateral relations between the EU and a third country. A political decision to set specific objectives in external agreements, or to exercise an evolutionary clause (the establishment of a customs union or free trade area or close sectoral economic cooperation), could force the parties to revise the entire scope of the relevant acquis.

The substantive means of exporting a fixed acquis are not common to all EU external agreements. In general, they are inherent to external agreements which aim to promote close economic or political relations between the EU and third countries, but which do not foresee the eventual integration of the latter into the EU. That is to say, the export of the fixed acquis serves to fit the specific objectives of EU external agreements (the establishment of a customs union, free trade area or mutual recognition regime), but not their dynamic objectives (association or full EU membership). As an example, the fixed "pre-signature" acquis is intrinsic to the EEA Agreement and the EC-Swiss SAs, which are not aimed at the full EU membership of a third country. On the other hand, EU external agreements targeted at either full or associate EU membership (SAAs, EAs) prioritise the export of a dynamic acquis into third country legal systems.

In general, the fixed acquis is embedded either in the main text or the annexes to the EU external agreements. Both constitute an integral part of third countries' legal orders, subject to respective national constitutional requirements. EU external agreements/annexes specify the scope of the acquis communautaire applicable to third countries (object, subject, exemptions) and indicate the hierarchy of the relevant acquis, thereby clarifying its binding force for a third country legal order. For instance, within the EEA Agreement the binding acquis is labelled "acts referred to". The relevant soft acquis (Commission Communications and Recommendations, Council Resolutions and Recommendations) is identified as "acts of which the Contracting Parties shall take note". However, one must always be aware that a reference to a specific EC/EU act in external agreements/annexes does not automatically imply the identical application of an EC/EU act within a third country legal order. As EU external agreements and EU institutions frequently reiterate, the relevant EC/EU act should be applicable in accordance with the objectives of the EU external agreement.[1]

The primacy of the fixed acquis communautaire within third country legal orders derives from their national constitutional arrangements.[2] The effective implementation and uniform interpretation of the relevant acquis within third country legal systems also depends on their national constitutional procedures. Furthermore, we argue that progress in bilateral relations with the EU directly influences third countries' attitude towards the implementation of the acquis. In other words, it could be argued that any decision to accomplish the effective implementation of the relevant acquis is both political and legal. For instance, the success of EEA integration, and the acknowledgment of the integrative nature of the acquis communautaire by the EFTA Member States, has overturned the initial sceptical forecasts regarding the effective implementation of the acquis into the legal orders of the EFTA Member States. Past and recent case law of the EFTA Court shows that it takes full account of both ECJ "pre-signature" and "post-signature" rulings.[3] Thus, the EFTA Court has voluntarily decided to keep pace

---

1   See EEA Agreement Protocol 1 "On horizontal adaptations" of the EEA Agreement. Case 270/80 *Polidor Ltd. v. Harlequin Record Shops* [1982] ECR 329.
2   For instance, see Articles 7 and 103 EEA Agreement. See Protocol 35 of the EEA Agreement.
3   Case E-9/97, *Erla Maria Sveinbjörnsdottir v. the Government of Iceland*, 1998 EFTA Court Report, 95. Case E-1/02, *EFTA Surveillance Authority v. Norway*, 2003 EFTA Court Report, 1. Case E-1/94 *Ravintoloitsijain Liiton Kustannus Oy Restamark*, 1994-

with the dynamic acquis communautaire for the purpose of ensuring the success of general EU-EFTA economic and political rapprochement.

3.2.2. Exporting the dynamic acquis communautaire into the legal systems of third countries

3.2.2.1. Introduction

The timely implementation of the fixed "pre-signature" acquis does not automatically imply the coherence of a third country's legal order with the dynamic acquis communautaire following the formal signature of an EU external agreement. A link between the "pre-signature" acquis and the dynamic acquis could eventually be lost if the former is not regularly amended and uniformly applied within third countries' legal orders. For this reason, EU external agreements refer to the substantive means of ensuring the uniform application and timely incorporation of the dynamic "post-signature" acquis. Analysis of EU external agreements allows us to consider the following means of exporting the dynamic acquis communautaire: 1) homogeneity; 2) binding and soft-harmonisation commitments; 3) approximation clauses; 5) a mutual recognition regime.

3.2.2.2. Homogeneity

The EEA Agreement is the only EU external agreement to employ so-called "homogeneity" as a means of ensuring the actual adaptation of the dynamic "post-signature" acquis communautaire into the legal orders of the EFTA Member States.[4] It should be clarified that the principle of homogeneity is not exclusive to the adaptation of the dynamic acquis. It is applicable in the course of the implementation of both fixed and dynamic acquis into EFTA Member States' legal orders. In the context of the latter, the principle of homogeneity means that as soon as a new relevant EU rule has been formally adopted by the Council or the Commission, the EEA Joint Committee must take a decision concerning the appropriate amendment of the EEA Agreement, "with a view to permitting a simultaneous application" of legislation in the EU and the EFTA countries.[5] The principle of homogeneity presumes the equality of the parties to this process, since

---

1995 EFTA Court Report, 15. Case E-1/99, *Storebrand Skadeforsikring AS v. Veronika Finanger*, 1999 EFTA Court Report, 119.
4   Chapter 2 Part VII EEA Agreement.
5   Article 102(1) EEA Agreement.

the incorporation of the relevant acquis cannot take place at all in the absence of an agreement between the EU on the one hand and the EFTA countries "speaking with one voice" on the other.[6] Overall, the application of homogeneity has proved to be a well-functioning mean of developing the legal systems of the EFTA countries and the EU in parallel.[7]

The concept of homogeneity is based on two elements: 1) the timely implementation of EU legislation into the EEA Agreement, "in order to guarantee the legal security and homogeneity of the EEA...as closely as possible to the adoption by the Community of the corresponding Community legislation",[8] and 2) the uniform interpretation of the adopted acquis and the EFTA rules.

Within the former context, the EEA Joint Committee takes sole responsibility for ensuring the timely implementation of the newly-adopted acquis within the legal orders of the EEA countries. If the EEA Joint Committee fails to amend the EEA Agreement annexes, then the EEA countries are not bound by the new relevant acquis. However, in such an instance, the provisional suspension of the relevant EEA Agreement annexes on behalf of the EU may be evoked.[9] Thereafter, it is the sole task of the EEA Joint Committee to find a mutually-acceptable solution, which terminates the suspension of the EEA Agreement annexes, under the threat of potential dispute with an EFTA Member State.[10] In practice, the EEA Joint Committee has never challenged the relevant dynamic acquis communautaire because of understanding that if an EFTA Member State wants to influence the process of the acquis adoption it must eventually join the EU.

Within the latter context, the EEA Joint Committee keeps the ECJ and the EFTA Court case law under constant review, in order to preserve the homogeneous interpretation of the EFTA Member States' legislation and the relevant dynamic acquis.[11] The constant review of ECJ and EFTA Court case law is underpinned by the system of information exchange, established under the EEA Agreement. The exchange of information concerns judgments made by the EFTA Court, the ECJ, the General Court (former CFI), as well as the EFTA Member States' courts of last instance.[12] In addition to the exchange of informa-

---

6   Article 93(2) EEA Agreement.
7   For procedural details of the homogeneity process see section 3.3. below.
8   Article 102(1) EEA Agreement.
9   Article 102(5) EEA Agreement provides that if the EEA Joint Committee does not take decision to amend the relevant EEA Agreement annexes in 6 months after the term in Article 102(4) EEA Agreement, they should be regarded as provisionally suspended.
10 Article 102(6) and Article 111(3) EEA Agreement.
11 In case of failure to preserve the homogeneous interpretation within two months following a difference in the case law of these two Courts, the procedure in Article 111 EEA Agreement applies.
12 The exchange of information within the EEA Agreement comprises the following stages: a) transmission to the Registrar of ECJ judgments of the mentioned courts on the inter-

tion, a court or a tribunal of an EFTA Member State may, if it deems necessary, ask the ECJ to rule on the interpretation of an EEA Agreement provision identical in substance to the acquis communautaire.[13] This means that the particular EFTA Member State's court or tribunal has the choice of applying either for a request for the exchange of information with the ECJ/General Court, or for a formal request for the ECJ to rule on the interpretation of the EEA Agreement provision for the purposes of homogeneity.

Furthermore, the EEA Joint Committee is charged with keeping under constant review the case law of the two courts in order to "preserve the homogeneous interpretation of the Agreement". It is important to note that decisions of the EEA Joint Committee are not to affect the case law of the ECJ, owing to "the autonomy of the EC legal order".[14] On the other hand, the ECJ's interpretation is binding for EFTA Member States, since the EEA Joint Committee, as a political organ, is ostensibly given the task of reconciling differences between the two judicial organs in favour of the former. Thus, under no circumstance may the decisions of the ECJ be overridden by an act of the EEA Joint Committee.

Hitherto, the homogeneity procedure within the EEA Agreement has proved to be steady and consistent. The EEA Annual Reports show that regular progress has been made by EEA members in implementing the dynamic acquis communautaire.[15] In the period of launch of the EEA (between 1994 and 1997) the EFTA Member States had adopted no less than 1697 new EC regulatory acts (including 1255 directives, of which more than 90 percent had already been transposed into the EFTA Member States' legal orders). The activism of the EFTA Court has

---

pretation and application of the EEA and the EC founding treaties, as well as the acts which concern provisions identical in substance to those in the EEA; b) the Registrar of the ECJ classifies these judgments, including as far as necessary the drawing up and publication of translations and abstracts; c) the Registrar of the ECJ issues communications of the relevant documents to the competent national authorities, which are to be designated by each Contracting Party (Article 106 of the EEA Agreement).

13 Protocol 34 to the EEA Agreement "On the possibility of courts and tribunals of EFTA states to request the Court of Justice of European Communities to decide on the interpretation of EEA rules corresponding to EC rules".

14 Opinion 1/92 [1992] ECR 2821, at 6(1)

15 In 2001 the EEA Joint Committee adopted 165 decisions incorporating 222 legal acts. In 2002 the EEA Joint Committee adopted 168 decisions incorporating 324 legal acts. In 2005 the EEA Joint Committee implemented 314 legal acts, 349 legal acts in 2006 and 469 acts in 2007-2008, 283 legal acts in 2009. For instance the 2002 EEA Joint Committee Annual Report indicates that the number of EU acts considered by EFTA was reduced by half, i.e. from 170 to 85. This is the result of the successful reinforcement of organisational procedures in order to speed up the processing of new acts. Besides, the EFTA Member States reduced their transposition deficits severely between 2001 and 2009, information available at <http://secretariat.efta.int/eea/eea-institutions/eea-joint-committee.aspx>, last visited 18 January 2011.

proved to be relatively modest in comparison to its EU counterpart, thereby providing evidence for the successful and smooth implementation of the dynamic acquis into the EFTA Member States' legal orders.[16] Besides, this could mean that EFTA Member States prefer to follow the interpretation of the relevant acquis by the ECJ, instead of referring identical requests for interpretation to the EFTA Court.

Other EU external agreements do not replicate the EEA homogeneity formula in full. This could be explained by the relatively high costs incurred by the permanently-expanding EU in implementing the homogeneity procedure. The EU has not been eager to apply the homogeneity formula in its relations with third countries on the eve of the unprecedented institutional and legislature reforms envisaged in the Lisbon Treaty. Instead, the EU has embarked upon a more cautious strategy. It simply employed specific elements of the homogeneity, which are in line with specific objectives of the relevant EU external agreements. In our opinion, EU external agreements, which envisage either close economic cooperation (EC-Turkey customs union), or close sectoral cooperation (EC-Swiss SAs), encourage the uniform interpretation of third countries' legal systems with the dynamic acquis communautaire. For example, the aim of establishing a customs union with the EC allows Turkey to ensure, on a unilateral basis, the timely implementation and uniform interpretation of the relevant dynamic acquis communautaire. Provisions of the Decision 1/95 which are identical in substance to the corresponding provisions of the (then) EC Treaty should be interpreted in conformity with the relevant ECJ case law to ensure the proper functioning of the EC-Turkey Customs Union.[17] Furthermore, Turkey must ensure that the principles of the EC Treaty are upheld, along with the principles contained in the secondary legislation and the case-law developed on this basis.[18] Besides, Turkey is committed to ensuring the compatibility of its laws with the relevant acquis communautaire by keeping pace with the relevant dynamic acquis.[19] In case of the adoption, abolition, or modification of new EC legislation on block exemption, aid in the textiles and clothing sector, or state aid to other sectors, Turkey

---

16   The EFTA Court issued 5 advisory opinions in 1997, 6 advisory opinions and 2 judgments in 1998, 2 judgments and 2 advisory opinions in 1999, 3 in 2000, 6 in 2001, 8 judgments in 2002, 6 judgments in 2005, 4 judgments in 2006, 11 judgments in 2007, 11 judgments in 2008, 9 judgments in 2009, and 8 judgments in 2010. The number of cases related to the EEA by the ECJ and the CFI is also low. See the EFTA Court web page <http:// http://www.eftacourt.int>, last visited 18 January 2011. J. Forman, "The EEA Agreement five years on: Dynamic homogeneity in practice and its implementation by the two EEA courts" 36 CML Rev. 751-781 (1999).
17   Article 66 Decision 1/95.
18   Article 41 Decision 1/95.
19   Article 39 Decision 1/95 (in areas of competition laws, state aid to the textile, clothing sector and other areas of trade cooperation).

must be informed by the (then) EC in due course, and is expected to align its legislation within one year "if necessary".[20]

On the other hand, the objective of bilateral sectoral cooperation between the EU and Switzerland (relating to the EC-Swiss SAs on the free movement of persons and air transport) could justify non-binding commitments on behalf of Switzerland regarding the uniform interpretation of the dynamic "post-signature" acquis communautaire within the Swiss legal system. For example, the EC-Swiss Joint Committees (set up under the framework of each EC-Swiss SA) have full discretion to "determine the implications" of the post-signature ECJ case law on the functioning of the EC-Swiss SAs.[21] In other words, Switzerland is not bound by the dynamic "post-signature" acquis communautaire (with partial exception of the Schengen/Dublin agreements which contain a soft obligation to ensure "as homogeneous as possible" interpretation of the acquis communautaire). The relevant acquis adopted after the date of signature of this Agreement is to be communicated to the EC-Swiss Joint Committees for its final political decision. Nevertheless, as commentators note, Swiss courts show impressive consistency in following "Euro-compatible" interpretation of national law in their decisions.[22]

Some elements of the EEA homogeneity formula could be found in the Treaty on the European Energy Community.[23] Objectives of close sectoral cooperation between the EU and third countries in field of energy imply some degree of ho-

---

20 *Ibid.* "If necessary" discretion relates to competition legislation only.
21 Article 16(2) of the EC-Swiss SA on the free movement of persons reads as following: "Case-law after that date shall be brought to Switzerland's attention. To ensure that the Agreement works properly, the Joint Committee shall, at the request of either Contracting Party, determine the implications of such case-law". Article 1(2) of the EC-Swiss SA on Air Transport provides that its provisions identical in substance to corresponding rules of the acquis "shall, in their implementation and application, be interpreted in conformity with the relevant rulings and decisions of the Court of Justice and the Commission ....given prior to the date of signature of this Agreement. The rulings and decisions given after the date of signature of this Agreement shall be communicated to Switzerland. At the request of one of the Contracting Parties, the implications of such latter rulings and decisions shall be determined by the Joint Committee in view of ensuring the proper functioning of this Agreement".
22 For more detail on application of the ECJ case law by Swiss courts see F. Maiani, "Legal Europeanization as Legal Transformation: Some Insights from Swiss "Outer Europe"", EUI Working Papers MWP 2008/32.
23 The European Energy Community is a community between the EU and the neighbouring countries (at the time of writing the following countries joined the European Energy Community: Albania, Bosnia and Herzehovina, Croatia, FYROM, Montenegro, Serbia, Moldova, Ukraine, and Kosovo). The Treaty on the European Energy Community (O.J. 2006 L 198) was signed in Athens on 25 October 2005 and entered in force on 01 July 2006. More information is available at <http://www.energy-community.org>, last visited 18 January 2011.

mogeneity of legislation of the latter with the relevant EU acquis. The European Energy Community extends the EU acquis in areas of energy, environment and competition to the countries some of which do not have even associate relationships with the EU. The homogeneity formula under the framework of the European Energy Community is distinguished by several features, which differentiate it from the homogeneity in the EEA Agreement and EC-Swiss SAs. The first feature is that the binding commitment of the European Energy Community's Member States outside the EU to implement the EU "energy acquis" (in fields of: electricity, gas, environment, competition, renewables, and energy efficiency) is substantially weakened by the necessity to take "into account both the institutional framework of this Treaty and the specific situation of each of the Contracting Parties".[24] The second feature is that the European Energy Community does not offer effective judicial support for homogenious interpretation of dynamic relevant EU "energy acquis" with the European Energy Community's acquis. The common institutions of the European Energy Community "shall interpret any term of other concept used in this Treaty that is derived from European Community law in conformity with the case law of the Court of Justice or the Court of First Instance of the European Communities".[25] However, unlike in the EFTA, the European Energy Community's institutional framework does not envisage the establishment of a permanent judicial organ with a competence to rule on interpretation of dynamic relevant EU acquis. It means that, if the European Energy Community's common institutions fail to offer timely and good quality interpretation of dynamic EU "energy acquis", this task will be incumbent upon the judiciaries of the European Energy Community's Member States outside the EU. These judiciaries will face the necessity to follow the evolution of the EU "energy acquis" and the ECJ case law in order to provide interpretation of relevant EU acquis in their legal systems, and, consequently, to study not only "presignature" relevant EU "energy acquis" and ECJ case law but also dynamic "after signature" EU "energy acquis" and ECJ case law.

To sum up, we emphasise that the principle of homogeneity has not become universally applicable in EU external agreements, owing to its complexity and the need for relatively close cooperation with third country legal systems. Instead, recent EU external policy has tended to apply selected elements of the homogeneity mechanism that suit specific objectives of its external agreements (access to mutual markets, mutual recognition, sectoral cooperation etc.).

---

24 Article 24 of the Treaty on Energy Community.
25 Article 94 of the Treaty on Energy Community.

3.2.2.3. Binding and soft-harmonisation commitments

The application of binding and soft-harmonisation commitments in EU external agreements is one of the frequently-used means of exporting the dynamic acquis into third country legal systems.[26] We propose distinguishing between binding and soft-harmonisation commitments in accordance with the criteria below. First, binding and soft harmonisation commitments are differentiated by the specific wording of an agreement's provisions. For instance, binding harmonisation commitments in the SAAs are emphasised by phrases such as "shall ensure", "shall take measures", "shall take the necessary measures", "undertake to authorise", and "the SAA Council may decide to oblige...". Soft harmonisation commitments are distinguished by non-binding terminology as well as by the wide discretion granted to third countries in the course of implementing the acquis communautaire. In general, soft harmonisation commitments are contained in phrases such as: "shall take the necessary measures in order to gradually achieve", "shall seek to promote the use of Community regulations", "will establish a plan", "will cooperate in order to align the standards of... on those of the Community", "cooperation ...shall have as its aim ...the gradual harmonisation..", "the Parties may cooperate", and "the cooperation shall focus".

Second, binding harmonisation commitments set a deadline for the implementation by third countries of the relevant acquis. For example, the EC-Swiss SA on technical barriers obliges Switzerland to "adopt, no later than six month after signature of this Agreement, arrangements that are equivalent to Community legislation on the technical conditions governing road transport". The Parties to the EC-FYROM SAA and the PCAs undertake a commitment to accede within five years to the specified list of multilateral conventions on intellectual, industrial and commercial property rights.[27] Turkey is expected to "incorporate into its internal legal order the Community instruments relating to the removal of technical barriers to trade" within five years from the date of entry into force of Decision 1/95.[28]

On the other hand, soft harmonisation commitments are worded to avoid any explicit deadlines for the implementation of the acquis communautaire. Instead,

---

26 V. Mouraviov, "Pytannia harmonisatsii vnutrishnogo prava neassociovannykh krain z pravom Evropeyskogo Souzy" 4 Pidpriemnitsvo, hospodarstvo ta pravo 91-94 (2003). For the comprehensive account of the concept "harmonisation" see L. Mistelis, "Is Harmonisation a Necessary Evil? The Future of Harmonisation and New Sources of International Trade Law" in Cremona/ J. Fletcher / L. Mistelis (eds.), *Foundations and Perspectives of International Trade Law*, (London, Sweet & Maxwell 2001), 3-27.
27 Articles 71 FYROM and Croatia SAAs. For the list of the conventions see Annex III EC-Ukraine PCA.
28 Article 8(1) Decision 1/95.

soft harmonisation commitments provide sufficient flexibility for a third country to achieve the objectives of the agreement. For instance, Decision 1/95 provides: "Turkey shall adjust its policy in such a way as to adopt the common agricultural policy measures required to establish freedom of movement of agricultural products".[29] Parties to the EC-Korea TDCA "shall examine" measures to harmonise health and plant-health, as well as environmental standards and rules with a view to facilitating trade. This should be achieved taking account of the legislation in force for both Parties, and in conformity with WTO rules.[30] The harmonisation process within the EU-Mexico TDCA is aimed at the mutual liberalisation of trade and the establishment of a favourable investment legal environment.[31]

Third, we argue that harmonisation commitments must be read in line with the objectives of EU external agreements. This especially relates to situations where the objectives of the external agreements evolve in accordance with the revision of EU policy towards third countries. For instance, the aim of "gradual integration into the Community" has from the outset presumed the eventual full compatibility of CEE countries' legislation with the selected areas of the acquis communautaire, which are of particular importance for the association, such as consumer protection,[32] standards and conformity assessment[33] and customs law.[34] In a short period of time, the nature of harmonisation commitments within the EAs has been revisited alongside the reconsideration of political relations between EU and EA members. This has changed following the EU's political decision to offer CEE countries candidate country status. Thereafter, the same wording of the approximation provisions in the EAs has been read in different ways according to the enhanced objectives of cooperation, *inter alia* eventual full EU membership. This means that, following the Copenhagen Summit, approximation provisions in the EAs have been given a new dimension. In particular, the CEE countries have committed themselves to the whole "accession acquis" to fulfil the requirements of EU membership.[35] One may argue that the political reconsideration of EA objectives has not altered the legal nature of the harmonisation/approximation commitments. Indeed, from the outset, the CEE countries have accepted the political commitment to adopt the "accession acquis". How-

---

29   Article 25 Decision 1/95.
30   Article 21(2) EC-Korea TDCA.
31   Article 15(b), (c) EC-Mexico TDCA.
32   For example, Article 94(1) EC-Estonia EA.
33   For example, Estonia was obliged to use and implement EC technical regulations and standards, as well as conformity assessment procedures within the areas of cooperation. In general, the CEE countries were expected to adhere to *de minimis* EC standards, but they were free to develop and implement higher standards if necessary in the course of adopting EC standards (Article 75 EC-Estonia EA).
34   For example, Article 92 EC-Hungary EA.
35   For the detailed analysis of the "accession acquis" see section 1.5.2. above.

ever, after some period of time, the parties have embarked upon specific legal commitments in order to meet the requirements for full EU membership. The EU has drafted the NPAAs and has carefully monitored their implementation with regard to each CEE candidate country. This means that the political decision to launch membership negotiations depends on the successful implementation of the NPAAs by CEE candidate countries.

The so-called "Ankara Agreement" is another example of the scope of the acquis being revised in accordance with the evolving objectives of EU external agreements. From the outset, the Ankara Agreement did not specify the nature of harmonisation commitments with regard to Turkey. However, at later stage, the specially-tailored principle of harmonisation[36] was introduced in Decision 1/95 with the aim of establishing an EC-Turkey customs union. In accordance with this principle, Turkey is committed to adopting the relevant fixed and dynamic acquis communautaire, and to reconsidering her own international trade commitments relevant to the functioning of the Customs Union.[37] The principle of harmonisation is formulated in Decision 1/95 which contains direct references to the relevant articles of the (then) EC Treaty, which consequently imply the application of (then) EC secondary legislation and the ECJ case law within the Turkish legal order.[38]

The EU external agreements that target neither full EU membership, nor common economic structures (customs union, free trade area) between the EU and third countries, do not impose binding harmonisation commitments. They are justified by very few binding commitments on behalf of the EU towards third countries. Simply speaking, these agreements could offer a third country very little in return for pursuing the binding harmonisation programme. In general, parties to these agreements are encouraged to pursue voluntary harmonisation procedures which could be rewarded by an enhancement in mutual relations (free

---

36 The principle of harmonisation reads as following: "In areas of direct relevance to the operations of the Customs Union, and without prejudice to the other obligations… Turkish legislation shall be harmonized as far as possible with Community legislation" (Article 54(1) Decision 1/95).

37 These are commercial policy and agreements with third countries with a commercial dimension for industrial products, legislation on the abolition of technical barriers to trade in industrial products, competition and industrial and intellectual property law and customs legislation. This list is not exclusive and may be extended by the EC-Turkey Association Council (Article 54 of Decision 1/95). Furthermore, the EC-Turkey Association Council may recommend that the Parties to take measures to approximate their laws in fields which are not covered by Decision 1/95, but which have a direct bearing on the functioning of the EC-Turkey Association.

38 For instance, Article 35 Decision 1/95 provides that "Any practices contrary to Articles 32, 33 and 34 shall be assessed on the basis of criteria arising from the application of the rules of Articles 85, 86 and 92 of the Treaty establishing the European Community [now Articles 105, 106 and 112 TFEU] and its secondary legislation".

trade area, mutual recognition agreement). For example, the objectives of the PCAs' and TDCAs regarding closer economic and political cooperation imply adequate non-binding harmonisation commitments. These agreements provide that the parties may cooperate on issues ranging from the promotion and protection of investments and developing conditions on open and competitive public procurement, to the facilitation of cultural cooperation. However, these non-binding harmonisation commitments may be enhanced by so-called "evolutionary clauses". The concept of the latter indicates the example of "conditional differentiation" in EU external policy.[39] In general, evolutionary clauses provide the non-binding possibility of further progress in relations between the EU and a third country in meeting the political and economic conditions set out in an agreement.[40] The EU has frequently inserted evolutionary clauses into agreements with third countries likely to promote further bilateral relations. This can be seen in earlier pre-European agreements with Baltic States and the SAAs.[41] With regard to the PCAs, the most significant evolutionary clause is enshrined in the Russian, Ukrainian and Moldavian agreements, but this is carefully omitted elsewhere. In these cases, an evolutionary clause refers to the possibility of entering into negotiations, with a view to establishing a free trade area between the parties upon the recommendation of a Cooperation Council. Such a recommendation may be issued on the condition of further advancement in economic reform and the development of particular titles of the Agreement, including the successful harmonisation of third countries' laws to those of the EU.[42] Subsequently, this could result in the conclusion of new "association", "free trade

---

39 For more about the types of differentiation in EU external policy including "conditional differentiation" see M. Cremona, "Flexible Models: External Policy and the European Economic Constitution", in G. de Búrca / J. Scott (eds.), *Constitutional Change in the EU From Uniformity to Flexibility?* (Oxford, Hart Publishing 2000), 60-61.

40 The "evolutionary clause" in the Russian, Ukrainian, Belarus and Moldavian PCAs explicitly envisages the start of negotiations on the establishment of a free-trade area following "advances in market-oriented economic reforms and the economic conditions". Distinctive from all the other PCAs, the preamble of the Russia PCA explicitly promulgates the objective "to create the necessary conditions for the future establishment of a free trade area between the Community and Russia" (Article 3 of the Russian PCA, Article 4 of the Ukraine PCA). For more elaborate analysis of evolutionary clauses see C. Hillion, "Approximation of laws in the context of EU-NIS partnership", in A. Nikodem (ed.), *Perspectives of the Legal Approximation Process in Central and Eastern Europe – Mutual Experiences*, (Budapest: Academy of European Law and Istvan Bibo College of Law, 2001), 86-98. C. Hillion, "Institutional Aspects of the Partnership Between the European Union and the Newly Independent States of the Former Soviet Union: Case Studies of Russia and Ukraine", 37 CML Rev. 1211-1235 (2000).

41 See Article 13 of the trade and economic cooperation agreements between the EC and Estonia, Latvia, Lithuania (O.J. 1992 L 403) and Article 5(3) EC-FYROM SAA.

42 For example, Article 4 EC-Ukraine PCA.

area" or "sectoral agreements" (the last referring to the enhanced cooperation in certain fields such as trade in goods or services). Therefore, evolutionary clauses indirectly encourage third countries to consider non-binding harmonisation commitments and to embark upon harmonisation reforms, in order to enhance bilateral relations with the EU and consequently to improve the format of relations between the parties.

Fourth, the effective enforcement of the harmonised legislation is an important pre-condition to the fulfilment of commitments by third countries. An overview of EU external agreements provides us with several important observations to prove this proposition.

The first observation is that EU external agreements regarding close economic cooperation or integration into the EU (EAs, SAAs, EC-Swiss SAs, or the EEA Agreement)[43] require the effective enforcement of EC/EU rules within the territory of a third country. For example, the SAAs urge the FYROM and Croatia to "take the necessary measures in order to guarantee no later than five years (three years in case of Croatia) after entry into force of this agreement a level of protection of intellectual, industrial and commercial property rights similar to that existing in the Community, including effective means of enforcing such rights".[44]

The second observation is that the soft harmonisation commitments in EU external agreements encourage third countries to harmonise their legal systems with either the acquis communautaire or international law standards. For example, the EC-Ukraine PCA calls on the parties to pursue the "gradual approximation of Ukrainian standards to Community technical regulations concerning industrial and agricultural food products".[45] The Cotonou Agreement promotes the voluntary application of international technical regulations, standards and conformity assessment procedures by the ACP countries.[46] Another way to promote the voluntary harmonisation of legislation is the acceptance by a third country of the level of legal regulation already existing in the EU.[47] This method of voluntary harmonisation can attain its objectives if it is underpinned by either enhancing the objectives of EU external agreements, or by laying out an efficient conditionality policy towards third countries. In the latter case, EU external agreements may link the progress of third country harmonisation to the further development and enhancement of mutual economic and political relations between the parties. For instance, Decision 1/95 envisages the possibility of reviewing and

---

43 Article 16(1) EC-Swiss SA on free movement of persons.
44 Articles 71(2) EC-FYROM and EC-Croatia SAAs.
45 Article 60 EC-Ukraine PCA.
46 Article 47 Cotonou Agreement.
47 Article 91(1) EC-Estonia EA.

consequently suspending the application of trade defense measures in the case of Turkey's progress in harmonising her legislation to that of the EU.[48]

To sum up, harmonisation commitments are an efficient way of exporting the acquis communautaire into third countries' legal systems. Of course, this is conditional upon the effective application of these commitments by third countries. Most of the EU external agreements envisage soft harmonisation commitments, thereby encouraging third countries to embark upon the voluntary harmonization of their legislation to that of the EU. Achieving the objectives of EU external agreements depends on the effective enforcement and implementation by third parties of the harmonisation commitments. Nonetheless, we believe that third countries possess some degree of discretion in enforcing soft harmonisation commitments in accordance with their own policy priorities and needs. In other words, third countries may pursue the enforcement of soft-harmonization commitments in parallel with developing bilateral political relations with the EU (such as the example of the PCAs countries).[49] "Conditionality clauses" may significantly elevate the effective enforcement of non-binding harmonisation commitments. In this case, the EU may enhance the format of its relations with certain third countries, and may subsequently reconsider the binding force of its harmonisation commitments. These processes have already taken place with regard to the CEE countries and selected EMAA countries.

3.2.2.4. Approximation clauses

So-called "approximation clauses" may be considered the most frequently applied means of exporting the acquis communautaire into the legal systems of third countries. Approximation clauses differ from harmonisation commitments in several aspects. Firstly, approximation clauses represent a distinct binding/non-binding legal provision in EU external agreements. Secondly, approximation clauses have more or less the similar structure and wording throughout EU external agreements. Thirdly, approximation clauses can be found under a separate title in EU external agreements, namely under the heading "approxima-

---

48　The EC-Turkey Association Council is authorised to monitor whether Turkey "has implemented competition, state aid control and other relevant parts of the acquis communautaire which are related to the internal market and ensured their effective enforcement, so providing a guarantee against unfair competition comparable to that existing inside the internal market" (Article 44 Decision 1/95).

49　R. Petrov, "Recent Developments in the Adaptation of Ukrainian Legislation to EU Law", 8(2) EFA Rev. 125-142 (2003).

tion of laws/legislative cooperation".[50] Fourthly, the general objective of an approximation clause is to encourage a signature to an EU external agreement to approximate its legislation to the acquis communautaire on a voluntary basis. In other words, contrary to harmonisation commitments, approximation clauses do not envisage the mutual convergence of the parties' legislation to an EU external agreement. Notably, the EC-Israel EMAA envisages the possibility of the mutual approximation of laws, thereby equating the Israeli legal system to that of the EC's, and also envisaging at least the possibility of exporting the Israeli legal heritage into the acquis.[51] However, this is rather an exception rather than a rule in EU external relations.

Below we shall examine the major features of approximation clauses which influence the export of the acquis into third country legal systems.

The first feature is the influence of EU external agreement objectives on the legal force of approximation clauses. We argue that the nature of approximation clauses is linked to the objectives of EU external agreements. In other words, the structure and wording of the approximation clauses mirror the objectives of the EU external agreements. For instance, the potential objective of the integration of the CEE countries into the EU was emphasised in the EAs approximation clause: "The Contracting Parties recognise that the major precondition[52] for [...] integration into the Community is the approximation of [...]" that country's [...] existing and future legislation to that of the Community". EU external agreements, against the perspective of either close economic integration of a third country with the EU (an EC-Turkey customs union), or eventual EU membership (SAAs, EAs), imply the binding nature of the approximation clause. This is emphasised by wording such as: "[the parties] shall act to ensure that future legislation is compatible with Community legislation as far as possible".[53] The example

---

50 For instance, these are: the EAs Title V "Payments, Capital, Competition and other economic provisions, Approximation of Laws"; the SAAs Title VI "Approximation of Laws and Law Enforcement".
51 The approximation clause in the EC-Israel EMAA reads: "The Parties shall use their best endeavours to approximate their respective laws in order to facilitate the implementation of this Agreement" (Article 55 EC – Israel EMAA). On indirect acknowledgment of this fact from the Commission side see A. Herdina, "Approximation of Laws in the Context of the European Neighbourhood Policy – a View from Brussels", IX(3) European Journal of Law Reform 501-504 (2007).
52 In some EAs this was an "important condition" (Article 68 EC-Estonia EA, Articles 69 EC-Latvia, EC-Lithuania, EC-Romania, EC-Bulgaria EAs).
53 See Article 67 EC-Hungary EA. Other EAs did not have binding approximation clauses. Article 68 of the Poland EA contained a slightly different wording: "Poland shall use its best endeavours to ensure that future legislation is compatible with Community legislation". The rest of the EAs (those with Bulgaria, Romania, Estonia, Latvia, Lithuania, the Czech Republic Slovak Republic, and Slovenia) envisaged soft approximation commitments: "shall endeavour to ensure that its legislation will be gradually made compatible

of the PCAs and the SAAs provides another perfect case for our study. These agreements contain identically-worded approximation clauses: "[the parties] shall endeavour to ensure that its legislation will be gradually made compatible with that of the Community".[54] However, the objectives of the SAAs and the PCAs are not identical. The Preambles to the SAAs emphasise the need "to approximate [the SAA country's] legislation to that of the Community" in order to integrate the SAAs countries "into the political and economic mainstream of Europe", and to obtain candidate country status. On other hand, the PCAs do not pursue the objective of eventual integration of NIS countries into the EU. The PCAs' objectives merely pave the way for further political and economic cooperation between the Parties: "to provide a basis for mutually advantageous economic... cooperation; to promote trade and investment harmonious economic relations".[55] Despite the almost identical wording and structure of the PCA approximation clauses, the notion of approximation within the PCAs is not uniform. This is because the PCA approximation clauses are linked to the objectives of every partnership agreement, which are differentiated by evolutionary clauses inserted into the agreements with Russia, Ukraine, Moldova and Belarus (known as "European" PCAs).

The second feature is the fact that changes in political relations between the EU and third countries might entail the political and legal reconsideration of approximation clauses in EU external agreements. In other words, identical approximation clauses within the group of the EU agreements with similar objectives might be revisited in accordance with the review of EU external policy towards a specific third country. In our opinion, the political and legal aspects of such revision are interconnected. Therefore, the state of political relations between the parties may indirectly influence approximation commitments in EU external agreements. This does not mean that the political environment alters the legal nature of approximation commitments. We argue that a change in political relations between the EU and third countries could entail either a positive or

---

with that of the Community". The difference in wording in the approximation clauses could have been designed to indicate a different external policy format of the EC towards the EA countries, which have become irrelevant following the Copenhagen Council. In any case it is perplexing to contemplate the legal meaning of the "best endeavours" commitment in the approximation clauses. From one point of view this might envisage the obligation to act, not the obligation of the result; therefore the EA countries made efforts towards the approximation of their laws, disregarding the end result. From another point of view, this committed the EA countries to incorporate the relevant acquis to the fullest extent as an important condition of attaining "gradual integration into the Community".

54 For example, Article 51(1) EC-Ukraine PCA, Article 68 EC-FYROM SAA and Article 69 EC-Croatia SAA.
55 Article 1 EC-Ukraine PCA.

negative reconsideration of soft-approximation commitments by third countries depending on the progress in bilateral relations. For example, the PCA "approximation clauses" are almost identical. Nevertheless, they must be read differently, according to whether they concern a so-called "European" PCA country (Russia, Ukraine, Belarus, Moldova), or a "non-European" PCA country. Even within the same group of "European" PCA countries, the role of the approximation varies. For instance, just two years after the PCAs entered into force, the European Council promulgated a "strategic partnership" solely towards two PCA countries, namely Russia and Ukraine.[56] Among all "European" PCA countries, only Ukraine has been repeatedly urged to accelerate its approximation process as a condition of further rapprochement with the EU.[57] On the other hand, the EU-Russia legislative cooperation lacks the intensity and momentum inherent to EU-Ukraine relations: it is more focused on developing cooperation in the field of the JHA and the CFSP pillars.[58] Therefore, in contrast to all PCA countries, the Ukrainian government was alone in initiating the voluntary harmonisation of its national legislation to that of the EU. In response to the positive and encouraging signals from the EU (CS towards Ukraine in 1999 and the EU-Ukraine Action Plan 2005), the appropriate legal and institutional frameworks were established in order to accelerate the harmonisation process in Ukraine.[59] Notably, all these legal and institutional reforms are based on, and targeted at, the implementation of the non-binding EU-Ukraine approximation clause. Thus, we argue that in case of "differentiating" and "deepening" relations with a PCA country, the EU tends to exceed the non-binding scope of the "approximation clause", and regard it as an intrinsic condition of the further activation of the "evolutionary clause" and its gradual engagement into the EU economic and political regime.

The third feature is that the political influence on approximation clauses may be exercised through various EU foreign policy instruments, such as European

---

56 European Council Common Strategy towards Russia (O.J. 1999 L157/1). European Council Common Strategy towards Ukraine (O.J. 1999 L331/1).

57 *Ibid*, at 20 and 52 The CS towards Ukraine prioritised the support for the democratic and economic transition in Ukraine, including the progressive approximation of Ukrainian legislation to EU laws.

58 In particular, the EU encourages Russian legal reforms to fight organised crime, corruption, money laundering, trafficking in drugs and human beings, and illegal immigration. Only recently, the approximation of Russian legislation to EU laws on competition, public procurement, customs, services and standardisation was considered a key issue in establishing the EU-Russia common European economic space. Road Maps on: Common Economic Space, Common Space for Freedom, Security and Justice; Common Space for External Security; Common Space on Research, Education and Culture, issued in Moscow on 10 May 2005, envisage mutual approximation of Russian legislation with that of the EU <http://ec.europa.eu/external_relations/russia/common_spaces/index_en.htm>, last visited 18 January 2011.

59 *Supra note* 49.

Council's decisions adopted under Title V of the TEU "The Union's External Action and Specific Provisions on a Common Foreign and Security Policy", the Commission's strategy papers and communications or EU *troika* summits. For instance, the importance of approximation for the success of the Euro-Mediterranean Partnership was endorsed in the European Commission's Communiqué "Wider Europe" and in the ENP Strategy Paper:[60] "[w]hile some Association Agreements with the EU still need to be ratified, the Mediterranean partners are already being encouraged to approximate their legislation to that of the Internal Market".[61] Furthermore, this Commission's Communiqué and the ENP Strategy Paper enhanceed the importance of the PCA approximation clause for the "European" NIS countries (the Communiqué terms them "Western Newly Independent States"). In return for aligning their legislation to the relevant acquis Russia, Ukraine, Moldova and Belarus have been offered access to the EU Internal Market freedoms in order to "come as close to the Union as it can be without being a member". The initiative calls for the establishment of common rules and standards, thereby encouraging PCA countries to accept the EU Internal Market acquis as a model for "undertaking institutional and economic reform". Acknowledging that the PCAs do not provide any deadlines for legislative or regulatory approximation, the Communiqué and the ENP Strategy Paper encourage the setting of a more substantive timetable for legislative approximation, based on the approximation programme within the Common European Economic Space initiative launched with Russia. Approximation in this context may go as far as engaging the PCA counterparts in selected EU programmes and activities (consumer protection, environment, standards, and research cooperation). Specific tasks to achieve these objectives are contained in the bilateral three-year Action Plans, proposed by the EU to each neighbour country.[62] For example, the EU-Ukraine Action Plan stated that the approximation of Ukrainian legislation to

---

60 Communication from the European Commission "European Neighbourhood Policy Strategy Paper" COM (2004) 373 final.
61 Communication from the Commission to the Council and the European Parliament "Wider Europe – Neighbourhood: A New Framework for Relations with our Eastern and Southern Neighbours". COM (2003) 104 final. The former EC Commission President Romano Prodi emphasised that "Europeans would like to see the values and principles on which our European home is built recognised throughout the Mediterranean, starting with human rights. For the Mediterranean countries, acceptance of these principles will greatly enhance the credibility of their political proposals. A keystone of the new neighbourhood policy will be the extension, as far as possible, of principles, rules, standards and sectoral cooperation to the Union's neighbours, which will enable us to develop a truly all-embracing special relationship" (Romano Prodi speech "Europe and the Mediterranean: time for action". UCL - Université Catholique de Louvain-la-Neuve, 26 November 2002").
62 In fact, within the PCA countries the EU has proposed Action Plans to all countries of the Eastern Partnership (Association Agenda for Ukraine) but not to Russia or Belarus.

that of the EU will build a "solid foundation" for further economic integration, including the EU-Ukraine Free Trade Area and WTO membership. The ultimate objective of the Action Plans is to pave the way for future enhanced bilateral agreements – European Neighbourhood Agreements which will be association agreements supported by comprehensive free trade areas between the EU and the neighbouring countries.

Furthermore, results of the EU *troika* summits (regular meetings between a head of a third country state and the EU *troika* (President of the Commission, Foreign Minister of an EU Member State holding the rotating presidency in the Council and High Representative of the EU for Foreign Affairs and Security Policy) could be considered an important incentive for elevating the significance of an approximation clause in EU external agreements. For example, regular EU-Ukraine *troika* summits consistently emphasise the need to approximate Ukrainian legislation to EU legal standards. They repeatedly stress that this must be regarded as one of the key elements of the intensified relationship between Ukraine and the EU. These summits reiterate that the approximation of Ukrainian legislation to EU norms and standards, as well as WTO rules, is the best way to improve the undergoing enlargement process in Central and Eastern Europe.

In conclusion, we argue that legal nature of approximation clauses is inextricably linked to the objectives and priorities of EU external policy towards third countries, as well as to their general relations with the EU. That is why approximation clauses in EU external agreements are not static. Indeed, any enhancement and change in bilateral relations between the EU and a third country could imply the revision of the political and legal effect of approximation commitments of a third country/party to an EU external agreement.

3.2.2.5. Mutual recognition agreements

The conclusion of mutual recognition agreements (MRAs) between the EC/EU and third countries serves as an alternative substantive method of exporting the acquis communautaire for third countries which would never embark upon the harmonisation of their legislation to that of the EU. Generally, MRAs are concluded with third countries with an advanced level of economic and political development, and which are unlikely to join the EU in the foreseeable future (USA, Canada, and Australia). The mutual recognition regime presumes the existence of mutually-recognised legal principles and standards between the parties. Mutual recognition agreements target the establishment of mutually-recognised regulatory and conformity assessment systems which are underpinned by the increase in confidence between mutual recognition agreement partners. To this end, the EC/EU mutual recognition agreements encourage third countries to use relevant international conformity assessment standards, guides and recommendations, as well as harmonised EC/EU and international conformity assessment procedures. In general, the mutual recognition regime focuses on specific areas that are important for ensuring the liberalisation of mutual trade between the EU and third countries. For example, these areas are: conformity assessment, standardisation, metrology, quality control, agricultural products and professional qualifications. The structure of an EC/EU mutual recognition agreement is not different from any other EU external agreement. In practice, EC/EU mutual recognition agreements comprise two parts: a Framework Agreement and Sectoral Annexes. The Framework Agreements establish the principles and procedures of mutual recognition. EC/EU mutual recognition agreements' sectoral annexes specify, among other elements, the scope of the relevant EC/EU or international law acquis to be applied between the parties to an agreement.

To the present date, the EC has entered into bilateral mutual recognition agreements with Australia,[63] New Zealand,[64] Canada,[65] the United States,[66] Israel,[67] Japan,[68] and Switzerland.[69] The following countries have also been listed by the EU as priorities for mutual recognition agreement partnership: Hong Kong, Singapore, Philippines, South Korea, China, South Africa, Malaysia, Indonesia, Thailand and Turkey. The EU undertakes negotiations on mutual recog-

---

63 Agreement on Mutual Recognition in Relation to Conformity Assessment, Certificates and Markings between the European Community and Australia (O.J. 1998 L 229/3; entered into force on January 1, 1999).
64 Agreement on Mutual Recognition in Relation to Conformity Assessment between the European Community and New Zealand (O.J. 1998 L 229/62; entered into force on January 1, 1999)
65 Agreement on Mutual Recognition between the European Community and Canada (O.J. 1998 L 280/3; entered into force on January 1, 1998).
66 Agreement on Mutual Recognition between the European Community and the United States of America (O.J. 1999 L 31/3; entered into force on December 1, 1998).
67 Agreement on Mutual Recognition of OECD Principles of Good Laboratory Practice (GLP) and Compliance Monitoring Programmes between the European Community and the State of Israel (O.J. 1999 L 263/10; entered into force on May 1, 2000). See also Agreed Minutes concerning this Agreement (O.J. 1999 L 263/7). The EC-Israel mutual recognition agreement differs from the others in that the Parties do not recognise conformity assessment results in accordance with each other's regulations and standards. Instead, the Parties have agreed to recognise the equivalence of each other's Goods Laboratory Practice compliance monitoring programmes, and in turn to accept studies and data produced by testing facilities participating in the Goods Laboratory Practice compliance programme of the other Party.
68 Agreement on Mutual Recognition between the European Community and Japan (O.J. 2001 L 284/3; entered into force on January 1, 2002).
69 Agreement between the European Community and the Swiss Confederation on mutual recognition in relation to conformity assessment (O.J. 2002 L 114/369; entered into force on June 1, 2002).

nition regimes with the Mediterranean countries within the framework of the ENP and the Union for the Mediterranean.[70]

The EU institutions have been clear on the focal importance of the MRAs for trade with important trading partners. For instance, the Commission has claimed on many occasions that the adoption of MRAs is one of the EU's strategies for pursuing its trade objectives in the areas of standards and conformity assessment.[71] As far as the EU and third countries are concerned, the utility of MRAs for opening up foreign markets is conditional on the full confidence in the other party's conformity assessment processes, i.e. comparable concepts of product testing and approval, and comparable or mutually acceptable systems of certification. MRAs do not require any "pre-emptive" harmonisation of the parties' technical standards. In general, the parties to MRAs are free to establish and to maintain own regulations and standards before and after the signing MRAs. Therefore, only a sufficiently high level of trade between the EU and a third country could justify the significant costs of setting up a mutual recognition agreement. Up until now, the EC has signed a moderate number of MRAs with third countries, all of whom it considers important trading partners with an advanced level of economic and political development. The EU foreign policy does not consider the conclusion of MRAs a part of its conditionality policy towards third countries. In other words, the EU launches mutual recognition agreement negotiations only on the proviso that a third country undertakes considerable economic, political and legal reforms. For example, some EU external agreements provide that at some stage, "when the circumstances are right", the parties may conclude agreements for the mutual recognition of certifications.[72] The EU conditionality goes further in EC-ACP legislative cooperation which cites mutual recognition agreements in sectors of mutual economic interest in successful ACP countries' liberalisation efforts.[73]

In the end, a mutual recognition regime may be considered one of the most sophisticated substantive means of the acquis export, since it requires a considerable degree of confidence on behalf of the EU in the legal system of a third country. However, it does not prevent the EU from associating the opening of negotiations on a mutual recognition regime with its conditionality policy towards third countries. In general, conditionality clauses in EU external agree-

---

70 For the comprehensive account of the EC MRAs see J. Clarke, "Mutual Recognition Agreements" International Trade Law & Regulation 31-36 (1996) and P. Beynon "Community Mutual Recognition Agreements, Technical Barriers to Trade and the WTO's Most Favoured Nation Principle", EL Rev. 231-249 (2003).
71 For example, see European Commission Communication "Community External Trade Policy in the Field of Standards and Conformity Assessment" COM (1996) 564 final.
72 For instance, see Article 40 of the EC-Ukraine PCA.
73 Article 47 of the Cotonou Agreement.

ments are constructed in such a way as to encourage the voluntary harmonisation of third country legal systems with that of the EU, in return for a vague prospective of a mutual recognition regime.

3.2.2.6. Regional integration initiatives

The EU pursues an active role as a promoter of regional integration worldwide. In most cases the EU does it in the course of its development cooperation policy (Article 208 TFEU). For this purpose the EU supports and promotes regional integration in major areas of the developing world and beyond. In the meantime, the EU has indicated its desire to provide technical and financial assistance as a part of its development cooperation policy to regional integration initiatives in: the Asian region (South Asia, North-East and South-East Asia, Australasia and Central Asia); the Latin American region (Mexico, Central America (Costa Rica, El Salvador, Guatemala, Honduras, Nicaragua and Panama), and the Caribbean (13 countries). Also the EU is supporting the regional integration within the existing regional integration initiatives: the Andean Community of Nations (CAN) (Colombia, Ecuador, Bolivia, Peru) and MERCOSUR (Argentina, Brazil, Uruguay, Paraguay and Venezuela) plus Chile). The Commission has issued several Region Strategy Papers which lay down foundations and guidelines for the developing countries in their regional integration efforts which could be financially supported by the EU. In particular, the Commission has issued Region Strategy Papers towards: Latin America (for the period 2007-2013);[74] Central America (for the period 2007-2013);[75] Asia (for the period 2007-2013);[76] with the CAN;[77] with Central Asia (for the period 2007-2013).[78]

In general, these Strategy Papers pursue the common objectives to strengthen democracy, political stability and to enhance regional dialogue and cooperation between the countries of the region. From own behalf the EU is willing to assist in reinforcing democracy, rule of law in the region and to improve effectiveness of law enforcement. For instance, under the framework of the EU-CAN coopera-

---

74 Available at <http://ec.europa.eu/external_relations/la/rsp/07_13_en.pdf>, last visited 18 January 2011.
75 Available at <http://ec.europa.eu/external_relations/ca/rsp/07_13_en.pdf>, last visited 18 January 2011.
76 Available at <http://ec.europa.eu/external_relations/asia/rsp/07_13_en.pdf>, last visited 18 January 2011.
77 Available at <http://ec.europa.eu/external_relations/andean/rsp/07_13_en.pdf>, last visited 18 January 2011.
78 Available at <http://ec.europa.eu/external_relations/central_asia/rsp/07_13_en.pdf>, last visited 18 January 2011.

tion the EU provides the technical assistance and institutional building assistance within specific CAN sectoral policies (environment, statistics, civil society, drugs prevention) supported by considerable package of financial assistance from the new "Development Cooperation & Economic Cooperation" Instrument (DCECI).[79] The EU-CAN Regional Strategy Paper does not envisage any direct means of exporting the acquis communautaire into the legal systems of the CAN countries. Instead, the EU encourages harmonisation of the CAN countries laws ("common standards") in specific sectors (statistics, competition, technical standards and mutual recognition) on regional level. For this purpose the EU designates a substantial part of the financial assistance addressed to the CAN countries. However, one may predict that indirectly this assistance will prioritise and encourage the adoption of the relevant EC acquis by the CAN countries through the promotion of "better models and procedures for drafting and sharing laws". In case the CAN countries have not yet adopted legislation in the most sensitive sectors of cooperation (competition law, public procurement, state aids, protection of intellectual property) they may be encouraged to export already existing and well functioning sectoral EU acquis.

The EU regional integration initiatives are not associated solely at the development policy but go beyond that. For example in 2005 the EU developed the "Northern Dimension" which promotes deeper regional cooperation between the EU, some of its Northern Member States (Nordic and Baltic countries), some countries of the EEA (Norway and Iceland) and Russia.[80] The Northern Dimension is realised and implemented within the framework of the EC-Russia PCA and the four Common Spaces project. The key priorities of the regional cooperation within the Northern Dimension are: 1) economy and business; 2) education, culture, scientific research and health; 3) cross-border cooperation and regional development; 4) justice and home affairs. One of the major objectives of the Northern Dimension is to assist and to encourage a comprehensive regulatory reform in Russia focusing particularly on approximation of technical regulations and standards from the EU. In particular, the EU encourages the Northern Dimension partners to harmonise environmental standards and other sectoral legislation within the four Common Spaces of cooperation between the EU and Russia for the purpose of better regulatory convergence, economic cooperation on issues of joint interest and a better integration of Russia in the world economy. Among priorities of the legal harmonization is competition law, financial servic-

---

79 Regulation 1905/2006 on the European Parliament and the Council of Ministers establishing a financial instrument for development cooperation (O.J. 2006 L378/41).
80 Available at <http://ec.europa.eu/delegations/russia/eu_russia/fields_cooperation/regional_issues/northern_dimension/index_en.htm>, last visited 18 January 2011.

es, transport and industry. In this regard the Commission strongly supports the activities of Baltic Sea Task Force to link its activities to strengthen regional multidisciplinary law enforcement cooperation in the Baltic Sea Region with the implementation of the EU-Russia Action Plan on Organized Crime and the EU-Russia Road Map for a Common Space of Freedom, Security and Justice. The Northern Dimension documents issued by the EU do not explicitly mention the need for Russia to adopt and implement the relevant EU acquis. However, the Commission acknowledges that one of the objectives of the Northern Dimension is to promote the regulatory approximation of technical regulations and standards in Russia in order to ensure better integration of Russia into international and EU economy.[81]

Another examples of the promotion of the EU acquis through the regional integration are the Black Sea Synergy Initiative and Eastern Partnership Initiative. The Black Sea Synergy was proposed by the Commission in 2007 after two major Black Sea area countries (Bulgaria and Romania) joined the EU.[82] The Black Sea Synergy Initiative is a supplementary tool to the ENP which covers most of the countries of the Black Sea region (apart from Turkey and Russia). The Black Sea Synergy Initiative focuses on cooperation sectors which reflect common priorities for the EU and the countries of the Black Sea region: 1) democracy, respect for human rights and good governance; 2) managing movement and improving security; 3) the "frozen" conflicts; 4) energy; 5) transport; 6) environment; 7) maritime policy; 8) fisheries; 9) trade; 10) research and educational networks; 11) science and technology; 12) employment and social affairs; 13) regional development. The Commission Communication on the Black Sea Synergy Initiative explicitly states that one of the main objectives of the regional cooperation is to "provide a clear, transparent and non discriminatory framework [in the countries of the Black Sea region], in line with EU acquis", and "progressive regulatory approximation of legislation and practices to the EU-related acquis continue to play an important role in regional trade-facilitation and integration". It means that the export of the EU acquis will be an important precondition for achieving objectives of the Black Sea Synergy Initiative. It is most likely that packages of technical and financial assistance to be available under the Black Sea Synergy Initiative will target the export the relevant EU acquis into legal systems of third countries.

The Eastern Partnership Initiative was initiated by two EU Member States (Poland and Sweden) and formally launched on 20th March 2009. This Initiative

---

81 2006 Annual Progress Report on the Implementation of the Northern Dimension Action Plan (SEC(2007) 791).
82 Communication from the Commission to the Council and the European Parliament "Black Sea Synergy – A New Regional Cooperation Initiative" (COM(2007) 160 final.

builds up on the ENP and proposes an enhanced version of strategic partnership between the EU and the neighbouring countries in the post-Soviet area (apart from Russia).[83] In return for the upgrade of contractual relations with the EU (association agreement), establishment of a comprehensive free trade area and visa facilitation regime with the EU the participating countries are expected to devote themselves to the adoption of European democratic values and voluntary implementation of the acquis communautaire under vigilant monitoring of the Commission.[84] In particular, the Eastern Partnership emphasizes that legislative and regulatory approximation "leading to convergence with EU laws and standards" is crucial "to those countries willing to make progress in coming closer to the EU".[85]

It can be concluded therefore that the EU does consider its support of regional integration initiatives as a good reason to promote either directly of indirectly the acquis communautaire abroad. The degree of the export of the EU acquis may depend on many circumstances like the existing level of cooperation and geographical remoteness of the regional integration entity. However, it is quite clear that the EU is interested to export its legal standards and principles to the closest neighbourhood (Northern Dimension, Black Sea Synergy Initiative and Eastern Partnership Initiative) in order to establish safer and predictable legal environment around European borders.

3.2.2.7. Concluding remarks

To conclude, we have set out a number of considerations which lead us to perception of the dynamic nature of harmonisation/approximation commitments within EU external agreements. The first consideration is that the latest EU external agreements prioritise the substantive means of exporting the dynamic acquis, over the export of a fixed acquis into third country legal systems. This is done to ensure some degree of homogeneity between the legal orders of third countries, and the constantly evolving acquis communautaire. For this purpose, the latest EU external agreements deliberately avoid specifying the applicable fixed acquis in the annexes, but encourage third countries to embark upon so-called "voluntary harmonisation", which proves to be the "cheapest", most effi-

---

83 The Eastern Partnership covers Ukraine, Moldova, Belarus, Georgia, Armenia and Azerbaijan. It does not exclude participation of other third countries in the Initiative's projects on case by case basis.
84 Communication from the Commission to the European Parliament and the Council "Eastern Partnership" (COM(2008) 823 final).
85 Joint Declaration of the Prague Eastern Partnership Summit (Prague, 7 May 2009), 8435 (Presse 78).

cient and less vulnerable way to safeguard externally the prerogatives and dynamic nature of the EU legal system. The second consideration is that harmonisation and approximation commitments in EU external agreements are not static or uniform. The objectives of EU external agreements and the status of political relations between the parties constantly evolve. Therefore, a particular political and legal environment in relations between the parties could help us understand the short-term and long-term perspectives in the effective enforcement of the harmonisation/approximation process within each EU external agreement. Especially it relates to the regional integration initiatives through which the EU is exporting the acquis communautaire abroad. The degree of the acquis export through regional integration projects depends on a political proximity and interest of the EU towards a specific region. Examples of the Northern Dimension and the Black Sea Synergy Initiative display that the EU is interested to promote own legal standards and principles into legal systems of the neighbour countries in order to create a friendly legal environment in countries which share the common border with the EU. In our opinion, the substantive means of exporting the acquis could be applied in line with the objectives of EU external agreements, and also in line with the general level of bilateral relations between the EU and a third country. On the one hand, the aims of establishing a customs union and providing access to the EU Internal Market entail binding commitments on third countries to implement the dynamic "post-signature" acquis. On the other hand, the aims of sectoral cooperation justify non-binding commitments on behalf of third countries to implement the dynamic "post-signature" acquis. The establishment of a mutual recognition regime between the parties constitutes one of the most advanced levels of bilateral relations, since this implies the highest degree of trust and reliance between the parties. This eventually allows the liberalisation of mutual trade, and dismantles obstacles in trade between the parties to an agreement.

3.3. Procedural means of exporting the acquis communautaire into the legal systems of third countries

In this title we examine the major procedural means by which the acquis communautaire is exported into the legal systems of third countries. Despite their secondary nature, the procedural means of exporting the acquis provide a strong case in proving our findings in this chapter. Similar to what has been argued above we suggest that the procedural means of the acquis export are not common to all EU external agreements, but rather they mirror specific objectives of the EU external agreements.

3.3.1. Formal/informal involvement of third countries
in the EU decision-making process

The most advanced and sophisticated procedural mechanism for the involvement of third countries in the EU decision-making process is elaborated in the EEA Agreement. The far-reaching objectives of the EEA Agreement, which ensure access of the EFTA Member States to the EU Internal Market, entail the comprehensive adoption by the latter of the relevant acquis. For this purpose, the procedure of "homogeneity" ensures the export of the "pre-signature" acquis and the timely implementation of the "post-signature" acquis into the legal systems of the EFTA countries.

The incorporation of the acquis communautaire within the EEA Agreement takes two procedural forms: "decision shaping" and "decision taking".[86] These procedural forms are exercised within a "twin-pillar" EEA structure, which comprises EU and EFTA institutions. This means that both decision-shaping and decision-taking within the EEA are conducted under close cooperation between EU and EFTA bodies. At the same time, neither the EFTA institutions nor the EEA Member States are involved in EU decision-making. In accordance with Article 99 (1) of the EEA Agreement, "decision-shaping" provides a forum for early consultations of the Commission with the EFTA countries' experts. The Commission "*shall informally* (emphasis added) seek advice from the EFTA experts in the same way as it seeks advice from the EC Member States for the elaboration of its proposals".[87] This means that the EFTA Member States' experts may access the Commission's committees for the purpose of taking part in drafting

---

86 These expressions were used by J. Forman (*supra note* 16, at 756). Therein he referred to the "decisions shaping", as it is termed, with regard to the adoption of the acquis at EU level and "decision taking" as regards the EEA Joint Committee decisions themselves.

87 Article 99(1) EEA Agreement.

the relevant EU legislation.[88] Participation in the committees ensures the efficient incorporation of new EU legislation. At the present moment in time, representatives of the EFTA Member States have access to some 360 committees, working groups, as well as to numerous scientific committees.[89] Then, the Commission transmits to these experts a copy of a drafted legislative proposal (not necessarily drafted in close cooperation with the experts) in the areas covered by the EEA Agreement. Thereafter, a preliminary exchange of views on the proposal takes place in the EEA Joint Committee "at the request of one of the Contracting Parties".[90] However, it is not clear if such an exchange of views may be influenced by possible negative feedback made by the EFTA experts.

In exchange for having to "accept" the dynamic acquis communautaire, EFTA countries have been given an opportunity to indirectly engage in the EU internal decision-making process, so that their views on EU legislative drafts may be made known to the EU institutions. So-called "EFTA Comments" are to be handed over to the Commission at Subcommittee level, after having been drafted in relevant working groups within the "continuous information and consultation process".[91] On the EFTA side, a mirroring structure operates under the Standing Committee, supported by some 50 experts and working groups which cover all aspects of EEA cooperation. Therefore, the EEA Agreement offers EFTA countries the opportunity to participate to a certain extent in EU decision-shaping, by means of early consultations in drafting EU legislative proposals. However, the EU is not bound by any serious commitments, apart from the direct request of EFTA Member States to provide its views on the EU legislative proposal. Furthermore, there is nothing in the EEA Agreement which obliges the EU institutions to take the views of the EFTA experts into consideration, since their involvement in the EU legislative procedure is excluded. The Commission merely represents the views and interests of the EFTA countries when necessary, and keeps them informed of the internal legislative progress. Cooperation between the Contracting Parties is based on the principle of "good faith" for the purpose of facilitating decision-taking in the EEA Joint Committee.[92]

The objective of the "decision-taking procedure" is to ensure the "legal security and the homogeneity of the EEA".[93] Within this procedure, the EEA Joint Committee takes decisions to ensure as closely as possible the simultaneous ap-

---

88 Articles 100, 101 EEA Agreement.
89 The EFTA countries experts are taking part in work of hundreds EU committees (EEA Joint Committee Annual Report 2009 <http://secretariat.efta.int/eea/eea-institutions/eea-joint-committee.aspx>, last visited 18 January 2011).
90 Articles 99(2) and 99(3) EEA Agreement.
91 Article 99 EEA Agreement.
92 Article 99(3) EEA Agreement.
93 Article 102(1) EEA Agreement.

plication of the "new" and "old" acquis communautaire within the annexes of the EEA Agreement.[94] For this purpose, the Commission is responsible for "early warnings" to EFTA countries, via the EEA Joint Committee, whenever the EU legislature adopts new legislation on an issue governed by the EEA Agreement. Thereafter, the EEA Joint Committee is expected to make every effort to ensure the amendment of a relevant EEA Agreement annex.[95] Where the EEA Joint Committee fails to amend the annex, it shall examine all further possibilities to maintain "the good functioning of the EEA".[96] However, the EEA Joint Committee cannot immediately ensure homogeneity as its decisions can only be binding on Contracting Parties after having been approved by their national parliaments or by referendum, depending on national procedure. Therefore, national constitutional requirements determine the date of entry into force of EEA Joint Committee decisions.[97]

None of the EU external agreements replicates the "depth" of the formal/informal involvement of third countries into the EU legislative process in the EEA Agreement. This is because the homogeneity procedure was a part of the political compromise reached exclusively between the EU and the EFTA signatories to the EEA Agreement. Instead, the latest EU external agreements envisage a degree of third-party involvement in the EU decision-making process, which is in line with the specific objectives of these agreements, and which is also in accordance with bilateral political arrangements between the EU and third countries. The aim of a customs union between the EU and a third country could entail a considerable degree of involvement by that third country's experts in the EU decision-making process. For instance, in accordance with Decision 1/95 Turkish experts should be informally consulted by the EU at the drafting stage of EU legislation, where this falls in an area of direct relevance to the operation of the EC-Turkey Customs Union. Moreover, the Commission is obliged to provide Turkey with copies of draft legislation submitted to the Council of Ministers, and furthermore to consult each other within the Customs Union Joint Committee.[98] In areas of direct relevance to the proper functioning of the Customs Union, the Commission must ensure that Turkish experts are involved "as far as possible" in the preparation of draft measures to be submitted to the Commission's committees. In this regard, when drafting legislative proposals, the Commission is ob-

---

94   Article 102(1) EEA Agreement.
95   Article 102(3) EEA Agreement. This procedure requires the unanimous agreement of all the EFTA Member States in order to make a decision.
96   Article 102(4) EEA Agreement.
97   In accordance with Article 103(2) EEA Agreement the Joint Committee decision is to be applied provisionally pending the fulfilment of constitutional requirements, unless a Contracting Party notifies that provisional application cannot take place.
98   Article 55(1) and (2) Decision 1/95.

liged to consult experts from Turkey on the same basis that it consults experts from the Member States: the Commission must also make its views known to the Council.[99] It must be noted that the Commission is not obliged to follow the advice of the Turkish experts. The experts may be involved in the work of a number of technical committees, which assist the Commission in the exercise of its executive powers, in areas of direct relevance to the functioning of the Customs Union.[100]

However, the Turkish side pays a substantial price for its informal involvement in EU decision-making. Harmonisation has significantly restricted Turkish legislative freedom in areas directly impinging on the functioning of the Customs Union. This means that, while drafting new legislation, Turkish legislators must take into account the consequences and impact on the Customs Union. For that purpose, Turkey informally seeks the views of the Commission on the proposed legislation in question.[101] The Customs Union Joint Committee is responsible for settling possible conflicts and disparities, and for preserving the consistency of the Turkish legal system with the EC-Turkey Customs Union legal framework.[102] We argue that Decision 1/95 employs methods of exporting the relevant acquis into the Turkish legal system, which are almost identical to the EEA Agreement procedures. This may be explained by the relative similarity in the objectives of both the EEA and Ankara Agreements. This procedural means ensures the informal involvement of Turkish experts in the process of drafting EU legislation, which is relevant to the EC-Turkey customs union. However, in return, the Turkish side enjoys some degree of national legislative freedom to ensure consistency in Turkish and EU legislation.

The EC-Swiss SAs implies the informal binding involvement of Swiss experts in the drafting of the dynamic acquis communautaire. Under the EEA Agreement, the Commission is obliged to consult the EFTA Member States' experts on the early stages of preparation of any new relevant EU law, however, in contrast, the EC-Swiss information exchange procedure means that Switzerland must be

---

99   Article 59 Decision 1/95.
100 Article 60 Decision 1/95.
101 Article 57 Decision 1/95.
102 The information exchange procedure allows Turkey with the opportunity to be informed about any legal acts or the ECJ case law that might affect Turkey's interests in issues covered by the application of Articles 85, 86 and 92 EC (Article 40 Decision 1/95). The Parties communicate to each other all amendments to their laws and cases "concerning restrictive practices by undertakings and other areas of direct relevance to the functioning of the Customs Union" (Article 39(3) Decision 1/95). The EC immediately informs Turkey via the Customs Union Joint Committee, which allows Turkey to adopt her legislation, which ensures the proper functioning of the Customs Union (Article 54 (2) Decision 1/95).

notified of the acquis once it already has been adopted.[103] During the preparatory drafting stage of the acquis, Swiss experts may be informed and consulted "as closely as possible" before and after the meetings of EU experts. It is only "at the request of one of the Contracting Parties [that] a preliminary exchange of views may take place in the Joint Committee".[104]

The remaining EU external agreements consider neither the formal nor the informal involvement of third countries in EU decision-making processes. Recent EU external agreements avoid references to such commitments. Instead, EU external agreements offer wider options for the mutual exchange of information, and technical/financial assistance, to encourage the export of the acquis into the legal orders of third countries (PCAs, SAAs, TDCAs). The EU external development agreements contain mere statements of intent for mutual legislative cooperation. For example, the Cotonou Agreement calls for "developing functioning links between ACP and European standardisation, conformity assessment and certification institutions", and to exchange information on their legislation,[105] experiences and policies.[106]

At this point, we note that the involvement of third countries in EC decision-making process within the EEA Agreement, EC-Swiss SAs, and the EC-Turkish customs union, is distinguished by hard commitments. In these, the EU "shall informally seek advice", "shall take a decision" and "shall informally consult Turkish experts". The nature of hard commitments in these agreements is justified by the specific "close economic integration" objectives of the agreements (access of the EFTA Member States into the EU Internal Market, establishment of the EC-Turkey customs union and close sectoral cooperation). On the other hand, EU external agreements which are not targeted at close economic integration do not envisage the involvement of third countries in EU decision-making processes. This discrepancy may be explained by the specific objectives and na-

---

103 Similarly to the EEA Agreement, the EC-Swiss SA on Free Movement of Persons envisages the exchange of information not only on developments in legal acts but also in the ECJ case law. Article 17 of the EC-Swiss SA on Free Movement of Persons provides: "1) As soon as one Contracting Party initiates the process of adopting a draft amendment to its domestic legislation, or as soon as there is a change in the case-law of authorities against whose decisions there is no judicial remedy under domestic law in a field governed by this Agreement, it shall inform the other ...Party through the Joint Committee. 2) The Joint Committee shall hold and exchange of views on the implications of such an amendment for the proper functioning of the Agreement".
104 Article 23 of the EC-Swiss SA on air transport provides: "As soon as new legislation is being drawn up by one of the Contracting Parties, it shall informally seek advice from experts of the other Contracting Party. During the period preceding the formal adoption of new legislation the Contracting Parties shall inform and consult each other as closely as possible".
105 Article 50(2) Cotonou Agreement.
106 Article 51 Cotonou Agreement.

ture of the EEA Agreement, EC-Swiss SAs and the EC-Turkish customs union. These agreements are similar in two dimensions. Firstly, they apply either some or all elements of the homogeneity procedure. Secondly, these agreements do not contain the objective of full EU membership. Therefore, the successful application of the homogeneity procedure requires some degree of encouragement on behalf of the EU towards the EFTA Member State, Turkey and Switzerland. We believe that a binding commitment on behalf of the EC, which ensures the informal involvement of the EFTA Member States, Turkey and Switzerland in the EU decision-making procedure, solves this dilemma and constitutes an appropriate reward for these countries for participating in the homogeneity procedure.

We conclude with two points. Firstly, the EU is reluctant to extend to the latest EU external agreements the involvement of third country experts, which we can witness in the EU decision-making procedure applied in the EEA Agreement and in the decisions taken by the EC-Turkey Association Council. The example of the EEA Agreement has probably proved costly and too advanced for the specific format of relations between the EU and a third country. This might indicate that the EU considers this procedural means suitable only for external agreements with a high level of mutual economic integration (customs union or access to mutual markets). Even the EU external agreements with the objective of eventual EU membership (SAAs, EAs) do not foresee the level of formal/informal involvement similar to they cited in economic integration agreements (EAA Agreement, EC-Turkey customs union). Secondly, the degree of involvement of third country experts in EU decision-making is linked to the nature of the harmonisation/approximation commitments, and to the entire objectives of the EU external agreements. If these agreements envisage binding harmonisation/approximation commitments, and if they pursue close economic integration (EEA Agreement, EC-Swiss SAs, Ankara Agreement), then some degree of formal/informal involvement is possible. On the other hand, EU external agreements which impose soft approximation/harmonization commitments, and which avoid the prospective of close economic integration (PCAs, EMAAs, TDCAs), do not consider the possibility of involvement in EU decision-making. In this regard, our study shows that the latest EU external agreements offer other options (informational assistance, technical and financial support) to third countries which have embarked upon the process of voluntary harmonisation, in order to fulfill soft approximation/harmonisation commitments. We consider these alternatives in detail below.

3.3.2. Exchange of information

The exchange of information is one of the most frequently applied procedural means of exporting the acquis communautaire into the legal systems of third countries. EU external agreements envisage various methods of information exchange. Similar to what has been argued above, we believe that the procedures of information exchange are directly linked to the aims of the EU external agreements. To prove our findings we shall consider the substance of the procedure of information exchange within selected groups of EU external agreements.

In the EEA Agreement, the EC-Turkey Customs Union and the EC-Swiss SAs, the exchange of information serves as a fundamental procedural tool, in order to achieve the uniform interpretation and timely implementation of the acquis communautaire in EU external agreements.

The procedure of information exchange underpins the whole mechanism of the homogeneous interpretation of the EFTA countries' legislation, as well as the "post-signature" acquis in the EEA Agreement.[107] For this purpose, the EEA Joint Committee keeps the ECJ and the EFTA Court case law under constant review.[108] Furthermore, a court or tribunal from an EFTA Member State, if it considers necessary, may ask the ECJ to rule on the interpretation of an EEA Agreement provision identical in substance to the acquis communautaire.[109] The ECJ has been protective regarding its own monopoly on the interpretation of the acquis, and the potential threat from the EEA Court, as envisaged in the first draft of the EEA Agreement.[110] These problems were subsequently rectified in the second version of the EEA Agreement. The "twin-pillar" structure set up in the second version of the EEA Agreement clearly distinguishes the EC from the EFTA Member States from an institutional point of view, and no longer affects

---

107 Recital 15 EEA Agreement and Article 105(1) EEA Agreement encourages the Parties "to arrive at as uniform an interpretation as possible of the provisions of the Agreement and those provisions of Community legislation which are substantially reproduced in the Agreement".
108 In case of failure to preserve the homogeneous interpretation within two months after a difference in the case law of these two Courts the procedure of dispute settlement in Article 111 EEA Agreement applies. It is important to note that the decisions of the EEA Joint Committee are not to affect the case of the ECJ, owing to "the autonomy of the EC legal order" expressed in the ECJ opinions 1/91 and 1/92. The ECJ interpretation is binding for the EFTA Member States since the EEA Joint Committee, as a political organ, is ostensibly given the task of reconciling differences between the two judicial organs in favour of the former. Thus, in no case may the decisions of the ECJ be overridden by an act of the EEA Joint Committee.
109 Article 107 EEA Agreement. See Protocol 34 "On the possibility of courts and tribunals of EFTA states to request the Court of Justice of European Communities to decide on the interpretation of EEA rules corresponding to EC rules".
110 Opinion 1/91 [1991] ECR 6079, at 30 - 46.

either the exercise of power by the EC and its institutions, or the interpretation of the acquis communautaire. Thus, the ECJ has acknowledged that within the "twin-pillar" approach the autonomy of the EC legal order is secure.[111]

In accordance with Article 106 of the EEA Agreement, the system of information exchange comprises the following stages: a) transmission to the Registrar of the ECJ judgments of the listed courts on the interpretation and application of the EEA and the EU founding Treaties, as well as the acts concerning provisions identical in substance to those in the EEA; b) the Registrar of the ECJ classifies these judgments, including as far as necessary the drawing up and publication of translations and abstracts; c) the Registrar of the ECJ issues the relevant documents to the competent national authorities, which are to be designated by each Contracting Party.

In the EC-Turkey Customs Union the procedure of information exchange is equivalent to that of the EU Member States.[112] This means that Turkey must submit information to the Commission in all cases where the Member States must do so. In return, the Commission is obliged to share its reports and assessments with Turkey.[113] The Parties are committed to publish all information related to the instruments employed.[114]

The procedure of information exchange within the EC-Swiss SAs does not equate to the consultation and information procedure set up within the EEA Agreement and the EC-Turkey customs union. Within the EC-Swiss SAs, the information exchange procedure of the newly adopted acquis communautaire must be formally notified to Switzerland and *vice versa* within eight days. However, the EC-Swiss Joint Committees has full discretion on deciding whether to implement the new acquis communautaire into the Swiss legal system.[115]

In the EAs and SAAs, the procedure of information exchange constitutes an intrinsic part of the technical assistance package on behalf of the EU. This tech-

---

111 Opinion 1/92 [1992] ECR 2821, at 18 - 35.
112 The Parties should cooperate in good faith during the information and consultation phase, with a view to facilitating, at the end of the process, the decision most appropriate for the proper functioning of the Customs Union (Article 55 Decision 1/95).
113 The distribution of information on behalf of Turkey to other EC Member States is achieved via the Commission. Only in urgent cases is the rapid transfer of information is envisaged (Annex I (5) to Decision 1/95).
114 See Annex I (6) to Decision 2/97.
115 Article 12 EC-Swiss SA on technical barriers presumes that the Parties pursue: "The Parties shall exchange all relevant information regarding implementation and application of the legislative, regulatory and administrative provisions listed in Annex 1."; (2) "Each Party shall inform the other Party of the changes it intends to make to the legislative, regulatory and administrative provisions relating to the subject matter of this Agreement and shall notify the other Party of the new provisions at least 60 days before their entry into force".

nical assistance package is aimed at assisting CEE and SAA countries in their approximation efforts, and drafting their national legislation in accordance with EU standards,[116] to meet the aims of eventual EU membership. Neither EAs nor SAAs envisage formal/informal involvement in EU decision-making procedures. Instead, the procedure of information exchange in the EAs and SAAs presumes the EU's informational assistance to the CEE and SAAs countries on the correct application and enforcement of the acquis communautaire and EU policies.[117] Besides, the procedure of information exchange also covers the public education dimension. For instance, the EAs and the SAAs are supplemented by the so-called "information and communication" procedure, which is aimed at providing the general public with basic information on the EU and on the EU policies and institutions through educational events, trainings and conferences.[118]

EU external agreements, which do not envisage the eventual integration of a third party into the EU do not provide a procedure of information exchange, but offer informational assistance within specific sectors of cooperation between the parties. For instance, the EC-South Africa TDCA envisages the mutual exchange of information procedures on customs,[119] investment opportunities,[120] postal co-operation and policy,[121] consumer policy,[122] cooperation on the recognition of degrees and diplomas[123] and health.[124] The PCAs refer to informational assistance on behalf of the EU on investment opportunities, mining, transfer of technologies, regional policies, employment, media and customs. Besides, Parties to the PCAs promote the exchange of information on standards, inspection and certification in the field of telecommunications and information technology.[125]

---

116 For example, see Article 86 EC-Estonia EA or Article 83 EC-Hungary EA.
117 This includes the application principles of the EU law; the functioning of EU policies; the exchange of information and experience; the exchange of information on dangerous products, methods of investigation, and know how; the exchange of information on laws, regulations and administrative practices.
118 Article 93 EC-Estonia EA provided: "specific circles in Estonia with more specialised information, including, where possible, access to Community databases". Article 82(3) Croatia SAA provides: "At the request of Croatian authorities, the Community may provide assistance designed to support the efforts of Croatia towards the gradual approximation of its policies towards those of the Economic and Monetary Union. Cooperation in this area will include informal exchange of information concerning the principles and the functioning of the Economic and Monetary Union and the European System of Central Banks". Furthermore, see Article 84 Croatia SAA on banking, insurance and other financial services.
119 Article 48 EC-South Africa TDCA.
120 Article 52 EC-South Africa TDCA.
121 Article 56 EC-South Africa TDCA.
122 Article 64 EC-South Africa TDCA.
123 Article 89(3) EC-South Africa TDCA.
124 Article 92(3) EC-South Africa TDCA.
125 For example, Articles 54(1), 57(2), 63(3), 70(2), 71(2), 74, 76(2) EC-Ukraine PCA.

Information assistance in EU external agreements on cooperation and development (EC-MERCOSUR IFA, the Cotonou Agreement) focuses at sharing EU legislation, experiences and information on the functioning of EU policies. In specific areas, the exchange of information contributes to the drafting and implementation of national legislation by third country/parties to these agreements. In this form, the informational assistance is supported by the following measures: the development of new training techniques and the coordination of activities in the relevant international organisations, and the exchange of officials and senior personnel and technical assistance.[126] However, the scope of legal cooperation within EU agreements on cooperation and development is not static, and may expand as to enhance the levels of cooperation by means of additional bilateral agreements on specific sectors or activities.[127]

We conclude that the procedure of information exchange is applied in line with the objectives of the EU external agreements. The above analysis shows that the EU external agreements, which aim at the establishment of a customs union, close sectoral cooperation and access to markets between the EC/EU and a third country (EEA Agreement, EC-Swiss SAs, Ankara Agreement), all envisage a binding procedure of information exchange, which is in turn underpinned by the informal involvement of third country experts in the EU decision-making process. On the other hand, EC/EU association, development, and partnership agreements (PCAs, EAs, SAAs, MERCOSUR and others) refer to a non-binding "information assistance" procedure which does not commit but gives an opportunity for a party to the agreement to be informed and consulted on new EU legislation. In practice, information assistance within EU association, sectoral cooperation, development and partnership agreements have become a one-sided process with a strong educational dimension, where a third country acts as a mere recipient of what the EU institutions select to offer. The information assistance procedure aims to support the so-called "voluntary harmonisation", by supplying information on the acquis communautaire without any binding commitments on behalf of the EU. In our opinion, these dimensions clearly illustrate that the EU carefully tailors the format and objectives of the procedure of information exchange to specific objectives of its EU external agreements.

---

126 Article 7(2) EC-MERCOSUR IFA.
127 *Ibid*, Article 23.

3.3.3. Technical, administrative, and financial assistance on behalf of the EU to third countries

3.3.3.1. Introduction

The export of the acquis communautaire into the legal orders of third countries is supported by technical and financial assistance packages on behalf of the EU. The EU provides technical and financial aid through different legal instruments. Some of them are thematic, such as the European Initiative for Democracy and Human Rights (EIDHR), Instrument for Pre-Accession Assistance (IPA). Most of them are geographical, such as the European Development Funds (which are, for instance, applied to the ACP countries), or purposefully tailored technical and financial assistance programmes (European Neighbourhood Policy Instrument (ENPI)). In the last case, the objectives and scope of the EU technical and financial assistance packages may have common elements, but they differ in substantive issues, in line with the objectives of either EU external agreements or the status of political and economic relations between the EU and a third country. Technical assistance is provided under the auspices of EU-funded assistance programmes, encompassing a variety of activities, ranging from investment in infrastructure to assistance in legal drafting and education.[128] In general, EU technical and financial assistance targets the creation of good governance in third countries. However, there is a serious criticism of shortcomings on transparency and bureaucratisation within the technical assistance itself, in particular in the tendering procedures. Some projects are ineffective, since they have not been adapted to local needs and specifics, and consultants are not sufficiently qualified. As some commentators correctly note, this situation hampers the promotion of EU values to the wider world.[129] Below, we examine the main types of EU technical and financial assistance programmes, and focus on their contribution to the export of the acquis communautaire into the legal systems of third countries.

---

128 In general, EU technical assistance covers the following activities: the exchange of experts, the exchange of experience and know-how, the provision of early information especially on relevant legislation, the organisation of seminars, training activities, aid for the translation of EU legislation in the relevant sectors, assistance in drafting national legislation in accordance with the acquis communautaire, and the modernisation and restructuring of specific sectors (agriculture, agro-industrial) in consistency with the EU rules and standards.

129 K. N. Metcalf, "Influence through Assistance – the EU assistance programmes", 9(3) EPL 425-442 (2003).

3.3.3.2. Reforms of the EU technical, administrative and financial assistance to third countries (ENPI and DCECI)

The EU has been going through considerable reforms to make its technical and financial assistance to third countries more effective in the near future (2007-2013).[130] Acknowledging that the efficient management of more than 30 legal instruments of technical and financial assistance has become increasingly difficult, the Commission has suggested a drastic simplification of these instruments, in order to facilitate the coherence and consistency of EU external activity. In particular, the Commission explicitly recognised that objectives of EU external agreements and EU external policy towards third countries should determine all forms of EU foreign assistance. In particular, the Commission stated that EU resources must be allocated according to expected and measured performances of third countries and better dialogue and coordination between donors and institutions, as well as with third countries, must be ensured.

Furthermore, the Commission has proposed significant structural reforms in the course of providing geographical-oriented programmes of technical and financial assistance. In particular, these proposals are concerned with the introduction of three new instruments of financial and technical assistance. Since 2007 the Pre-Accession Instrument (IPA) supersedes other geographically oriented EU funded programmes of technical assistance directed towards countries willing to join the EU (PHARE,[131] CARDS,[132] and pre-accession assistance to Turkey). Assistance provided under the IPA focuses on institution building, cross-border cooperation and regional development. Notably, assistance offered by the EU will reflect the status of a third country as either a recognised candidate country, or a potential candidate country.[133]

---

130 Communication from the Commission to the Council and the European Parliament "Building our common Future Policy challenges and Budgetary means of the Enlarged Union 2007-2013" (COM (2004) 101 final/2). Communication from the Commission to the Council and the European Parliament on Financial Perspectives 2007 - 2013 (COM (2004) 487 final).
131 Originally created in 1989 to assist Poland and Hungary, the PHARE programme covered 10 former candidate countries which are now new Member States (the Czech Republic, Estonia, Hungary, Latvia, Lithuania, Poland, Slovakia, Slovenia, Bulgaria and Romania). The PHARE's legal base was Council Regulation 3906/89 on economic aid to the Republic of Hungary and the Polish People's Republic (O.J. 1989 L 375).
132 Supported the participation of Western Balkan nations (Albania, Bosnia and Herzegovina, Croatia, Serbia, Montenegro and the Former Yugoslav Republic of Macedonia) in the Stabilisation and Association Process (Council Regulation 2666/2000 (O.J. 2000 L038) on assistance for Albania, Bosnia and Herzegovina, Croatia, the Federal Republic of Yugoslavia and the Former Yugoslav Republic of Macedonia).
133 Regulation 1085/2006 establishing an instrument for Pre-Accession Assistance (IPA) (O.J. 2006 L 210/49).

In 2003 the Commission proposed introducing the European Neighbourhood and Partnership Instrument (ENPI) – a new package of technical and financial assistance for the participant states of EU Neighbourhood Policy.[134] Assistance aimed at the implementation of the acquis communautaire into legal systems of neighbourhood countries is one of major objectives of the ENPI, and of the Wider Europe Communication.[135] The ENPI develops a single approach to cooperation across the EU external borders, based on pre-existing MEDA,[136] TACIS,[137] and INTERREG[138] programmes. The ENPI assumes the funds of the mentioned programmes. In general, it pursues the following objectives: sustainable economic and social development in border areas, addressing common challenges in the areas of environment, public health and the prevention of and fight against organised crime, ensuring efficient and secure borders with neighbouring countries, and promoting local "people-to-people" type actions. In 2006 the EU institutions issued and adopted a single Regulation 1638/2006 which governs the ENPI to fund activities both inside and outside the EU, based on a single budget line.[139] According to this Regulation the ENPI is a "policy-driven" programme of

---

134 Communication from the Commission "Paving the way for a New Neighbourhood Instrument" (COM (2003) 393 final).
135 Communication from the Commission "Wider Europe-Neighbourhood: A New Framework for Relations with our Eastern and Southern Neighbours" (COM (2003) 104 final).
136 Council Regulation 1488/96 on financial and technical measures to accompany (MEDA) the reform of economic and social structures in the framework of the Euro Mediterranean partnership (O.J. 1998 L 189) (known as MEDA I). It was amended by Council Regulation 2698/2000 of 27 November 2000 amending Regulation 1488/96 on financial and technical measures to accompany (MEDA) the reform of economic and social structures in the framework of the Euro Mediterranean partnership (O.J. 2000 L 311/1) (known as MEDA II).
137 Launched by the EC in 1991, the TACIS Programme provided grant-financed technical assistance to 12 NIS countries (Armenia, Azerbaijan, Belarus, Georgia, Kazakhstan, Kyrgyzstan, Moldova, Russia, Tajikistan, Turkmenistan, Ukraine and Uzbekistan). Mongolia was also covered by the TACIS programme from 1991 to 2003, but is now covered by the so called "ALA programme" (Council Regulation 443/92 O.J. 1992 L52/1 on financial assistance and technical assistance to, and economic cooperation with, the developing countries in Asia and Latin America). Council Regulation 99/2000 (O.J. 2000 L 012) concerning the provision of assistance to the partner States in Eastern Europe and Central Asia. Regulation 99/2000 has expired on 31 December 2006.
138 The INTERREG Community Initiative is a financial instrument within the framework of the European Union's Structural Funds. It supports cross-border and international cooperation among the EU Member States and neighbouring countries. Although INTERREG programmes involve neighbouring countries directly, Structural Funds can only be used inside the Union. INTERREG programmes at the European Union's external border therefore require a source of finance for activities taking place within the neighbouring country (Council Regulation 1260/1999 laying down general provisions on the Structural Funds O.J. 2000 L161 and the INTERREG III Guidelines O.J. 2000 C 143).
139 The European Parliament and the Council Regulation laying down general provisions establishing a European Neighbourhood and Partnership Instrument (O.J. 2006 L 310/1).

technical and financial assistance, and will operate on an identical footing on both sides of the EU's external borders. In other words, it is logically linked to, and coherent with, various external policy agendas and process, and would take account of the different regional priorities already developed with EU external policy. The ENPI's priorities should take account of individually-tailored bilateral Neighbourhood Agreements and Action Plans. Through the Regulation 1638/2000 does not explicitly mention the need for the countries-beneficiaries to adopt and implement the acquis communautaire this flows from quite broad objectives and scope of the assistance envisaged by the ENPI. For instance, the ENPI's objectives explicitly target the support of the countries-beneficiaries (the ENP countries and Russia) in their reforms to conduct political, economic and social reforms in line with European common values and aims of the ENP Action Plans. Importantly, the ENPI envisages technical and financial assistance to the countries-beneficiaries' efforts to pursue legislative and regulatory approximation, promoting the rule of law and good governance, promoting and protecting human rights and fundamental freedoms and other objectives. However, if the country-beneficiary fails to observe democratic and market economy principles the EU shall suspend the provision of assistance upon the results of the monitoring procedure envisaged in the Regulation 1638/2000.

Assistance under the framework of the ENPI is based on the principle of conditionality. Therefore, at least in theory, the EU assistance could be terminated if a recipient's policy infringes basic principles of the ENPI (principles of good neighbourness, values of liberty and democracy, human rights and rule of law). However, for example, the EU never applied any substantive sanctions towards Russia even during the conflict in South Ossetia in 2008 and in the Second Russia-Ukraine gas war in 2008-2009. Some commentators argue that it is quite hypothetical to believe that the EU Member States could ever reach a majority vote to apply Article 28 of the ENPI Regulation to suspend the EC assistance to Russia. It is unlikely to happen in the foreseeable future since "[the ENPI] has the potential of undermining the claims to partnership and joint ownership of EU-Russia relations".[140]

The "Development Cooperation & Economic Cooperation" Instrument (DCECI) supports developing countries in their efforts to integrate their markets into the world economy.[141] All third countries not covered by either the IPA or the ENPI will be eligible for DCECI assistance. This assistance will contribute to the objectives of EU development policy, such as the reinforcement of various

---

140 More on this subject see S. Blockmans "EU-Russia Relations Through the Prism of the European Neighbourhood and Partnership Instrument" 13 EFA Rev. 167-187 (2008).
141 Regulation 1905/2006 on the European Parliament and the Council of Ministers establishing a financial instrument for development cooperation (O.J. 2006 L 378/41).

social services, contribution to the core infrastructure required to sustain economic and social development, sustainable rural development and food security, the promotion of the rules of global trade and the principles of market economy; this will combined with the recognition of democratic values, good governance and human rights principles.

The three latest instruments of EU financial and technical assistance analysed above do not have thematic priorities, but cover all policy areas. It is hoped that this approach will help ensure that external aspects of EU internal policies are properly covered and effectively supported. In order to ensure the effective functioning of these new instruments, management will be shared between the internal policy and external Directorates of the Commission.

3.3.3.3. Technical, administrative and financial assistance within EU sectoral agreements

Not all EU external agreements are equipped with technical and financial assistance programmes like ENPI and IPA. EU external agreements that do not pursue close integration instead target technical/financial assistance in order to support sectoral cooperation between the parties. For example, the EU grants technical assistance to South Africa for the preparation of laws and the establishment of domestic offices and agencies involved in the protection and enforcement of intellectual property in accordance with basic international standards.[142] EC-Mexico legal cooperation envisages technical assistance on behalf of the EU in the field of customs law.[143]

Assistance in drafting national legislation in accordance with EU rules and standards is an important component of the EU technical assistance package. In general, the EU is eager to provide expertise and assistance in drafting the national legislation of third countries in accordance with international and EU standards. EU external agreements, which do not contain an approximation clause, refer to EU assistance on drafting national legislation in accordance with EU rules and standards. For example, in order to ensure the efficient enforcement of competition rules by both private and state enterprises, the Parties to the Cotonou Agreement are committed to cooperate on the drafting of an appropriate legal

---

142 Article 46 EC-South Africa TDCA.
143 Article 19(2) EC-Mexico TDCA. This covers the following activities: the exchange of information, the development of new training techniques and coordination of activities which should be undertaken within the international organisations specialising in this field, the exchanges of officials and senior personnel (Regulation 443/92 O.J. 1992 L 52/1 on financial and technical assistance to, and economic cooperation with, the developing countries in Asia and Latin America).

framework and its administrative enforcement. Furthermore, in the field of protection of intellectual property rights, Parties to the Cotonou Agreement cooperate on the preparation of laws and regulations for the protection and enforcement of intellectual property rights, as well as the establishment and reinforcement of domestic and regional offices and other agencies. This includes support for regional intellectual property organisations involved in enforcement and protection, including the training of personnel.

3.3.3.4. Concluding remarks

In summary, it can, therefore, be said that the procedural and substantive means of exporting the acquis communautaire into the legal systems of third countries are characterised by almost identical criteria. They are guided by the principle of conditionality towards third countries.[144] Similar to substantive means, procedural means are designed to suit the specific objectives of EU external agreements. On the one hand, EU external agreements which target close economic and political integration (EEA Agreement, EAs, SAAs, the Ankara Agreement) mirror the enhanced procedural means of exporting the acquis communautaire (homogeneity, formal/informal involvement into the EU decision making process, technical and financial assistance). On the other hand, EU external agreements which aim at moderate cooperation (PCAs, TDCAs) envisage less advanced procedural means of exporting the acquis communautaire (informational assistance, technical assistance aimed at specific sectors of cooperation). Programmes of technical and financial assistance on behalf of the EU (IPA, ENPI) promote and support the adoption and implementation by third countries of the international acquis and relevant acquis communautaire. As a rule, these programmes contain conditionality clauses, which make the provision of the technical and financial assistance to the countries-beneficiaries conditional on the effective adoption and implementation of the acquis communautaire by them.

Furthermore, our analysis reflects the EU's reluctance to allow any form of formal/informal involvement by third countries in its decision-making process. Instead, EU external agreements safeguard the institutional and legal autonomy of the parties by putting more emphasis on the informal exchange of information and the provision of financial and technical assistance to third countries all with the purpose of supporting their voluntary harmonisation of their law. As a result,

---

144 EU technical and financial assistance was terminated with regard to Belarus and some ACP countries as a result of the violation of human rights and fundamental freedoms. The EU uses trade preferences in its trading relations with third countries if the latter apply ILO standards on child labour and the freedom of association.

the EU maintains a "free hand" to steer the process of exporting the acquis communautaire by encouraging third countries to expedite the harmonisation of their law, and at the same time enhancing the format of their political relations with the EU.

3.4. Institutions set up within EU external agreements

3.4.1. Introduction

In this chapter we have embarked upon a study of the substantive and procedural means by which the acquis communautaire may be exported into third country legal systems. For this purpose, we analysed the relevant provisions of EU external agreements, which has helped us understand whether the substantive and procedural means influence the whole process of exporting the acquis. We believe that the common institutions established under EU external agreements also merit consideration, and should also therefore be scrutinised. We have argued that their competence and composition belong to the subject area of our study, since they form an intrinsic part of the whole process of exporting the acquis communautaire. Below we consider the impact of common institutions in detail.

3.4.2. The impact of common institutions set up under EU external agreements on the export of the acquis into the legal orders of third countries

The apex of the institutional pyramid within EU external agreements is usually occupied by the Council, which may be named either the Association Council or the Partnership and Cooperation Council, or more simply the Cooperation Council, or the Joint Council, depending on the particular external agreement. These Councils are common institutions made up of representatives of the Council of Ministers and of the European Commission on the one side, and of senior representatives of the government of a third country on the other. The work of the Councils is aimed at implementing the agreement and resolving potential disputes. The legal force of the decisions issued by the Councils varies from case to case. In general, Councils created under the EU external agreements targeted at closer economic and political integration have the authority to issue binding decisions and recommendations (EEAs Councils, SAAs Councils, EAs Councils and association agreements Councils).[145] Furthermore, the Councils may exam-

---

145 For example, Articles 39(2), 39(3), 106(2) EC-Polish EA.

ine the way in which any Party applies the external agreement.[146] As a result, following such an examination, the Association Council may decide to upgrade cooperation between the parties to the status of a free trade area or a customs union.[147] On the other hand, Councils instituted under agreements aimed at mere cooperation and partnership are denied the right to issue binding decisions (PCA Councils or the MERCOSUR IFA Council), and therefore cannot directly influence the pace at which the acquis is exported into national legal systems.[148]

The Councils are assisted by Joint Committees, which comprise representatives of the Council and the Commission on one side, and representatives of the third country government on the other (the Committee of Ambassadors in the Cotonou Agreement). The Joint Committees derive their powers from the Councils. However, the Joint Committees are not authorised to issue binding decisions or recommendations. Their main competence is to assist the Councils in ensuring the uniform application of the agreement. The objectives of EU external agreements may imply the creation of additional subcommittees within the institutional framework of each agreement. For example, the EEA Joint Committee has the competence to establish subcommittees or working groups to achieve the aims of the agreement.[149] Subcommittees work on the preparation and drafting of decisions to be adopted by the EEA Joint Committee. In general, the EEA Agreement sets up the following types of sub-committees and working groups: working groups of experts (to provide informal advice on the EC/EU acts drafts),[150] management committees (assistance in the exercise of executive powers),[151] programme committees and committees relevant for the good functioning of the agreement (sectoral cooperation),[152] and statistics committees (management and development of actions in field of statistics).[153] Commentators consider these committees an opportunity to influence the EU's internal decision-making process by participating in networking and coalition-building.[154] Some agreements may establish specialised Committees to enhance cooperation within the specific policy area. For instance, the EC-Israeli and EC-Tunisia EMAAs provide the establishment of Customs Cooperation Committees.

---

146 For example, Article 6(2) EC-Polish EA.
147 For example, Article 7(1) EC-Polish EA.
148 *Supra note* 49.
149 Article 94(3) EEA Agreement. For academic account of the EEA institutions see C. Reymond, 'Institutions, decision-making procedure and settlement of disputes in the European Economic Area', 30 CML Rev. 449-462 (1993) p. 449.
150 Article 99(1) EEA Agreement.
151 Article 100 EEA Agreement.
152 Articles 81(b) and 101(1) EEA Agreement.
153 Article 76 EEA Agreement.
154 A. Evans, *The Integration of the European Community and Third States in Europe: a Legal Analysis*, (Oxford, Clarendon Press 1996), at 337-339.

EU external agreements which focus on enhancing a political dialogue with third countries (EEA, EAs, SAAs, PCAs, the Cotonou Agreement) designate Parliamentary Committees or Joint Parliament Assemblies to ensure cooperation between those parties' parliaments/legislative bodies. The Parliamentary Committees are not empowered to produce any binding documents, but to issue resolutions and recommendations to the Council. They serve to ensure the control of democracy with regard to the implementation and application of the external agreement. Furthermore, Parliamentary Committees may express their views on the implementation and adherence of third countries to the EU's democratic values and principles.

EU external agreements do not set up common courts within the institutional frameworks of external agreements. The ECJ has appeared reluctant to acknowledge the existence of a competitor which could indirectly influence its autonomous jurisdiction.[155] The ECJ held in its opinion on the first version of the EEA Agreement that the establishment of the EEA Court might undermine the autonomy of the EC legal order, and was, therefore, incompatible with the EC Treaty. This was because the EEA Court was entrusted with the competence of issuing final decisions on the interpretation of the rules of that agreement, in substance identical to those of EC/EU law, and could, therefore, potentially rule on the distribution of powers between the EC/EU and EU Member States.[156] The ECJ emphasised that the EU institutions should not be bound by a particular interpretation of EU law made by the EEA Court. The ECJ justified its position by two arguments. Firstly, the EU external agreement must make it possible to prevent any undermining of the objective enshrined in Article 220 EC (now Article 19(1) TEU), that EC (now EU) law should be interpreted uniformly. Secondly, it is an exclusive function of the ECJ to review the legality of the activities of the EU institutions.[157] The ECJ hinted that risks to the foundations of the EU legal order may be reduced if the Parties to the EU external agreement are members of a single organization, which has its own judicial body and surveillance authority, both separate from the EU institutions. The second version of the EEA Agreement encompassed these suggestions by establishing the EFTA Court, which has jurisdiction only over EFTA Member States. As a result, the ECJ stated in the ruling on the second version of the EEA Agreement, that an EU external agreement may be regarded as compatible with (then) EC Treaty only if it does not alter the essential character of the powers conferred on the EU institutions by the EC Treaty.[158] In particular, the ECJ confirmed that EFTA Court judgments could

---

155 Opinion 1/91 [1991] ECR 6079 and Opinion 1/92 [1992] ECR 2821.
156 Opinion 1/91[1991] ECR 6079, at 30-46.
157 *Ibid,* at 41-46.
158 Opinion 1/92 [1992] ECR 2821, at 32-41.

in no circumstances affect the case law of the ECJ.[159] The institutional structures within more recent external agreements, which replicate the objectives of the EEA Agreement, are constructed in such a way as to avoid any of the discrepancies considered above. For instance, the Agreement on the European Common Aviation Area (ECAA) is based on the "one-pillar" institutional structure.[160] This means that this agreement does not create common institutional structures between the EU and third countries, but instead extends the powers of EU institutions towards third parties to the ECAA. The ECAA secures the independence of the EU institutions (in particular, the judicial independence of the ECJ) in three ways. Firstly, the ECAA Agreement allows third country national courts to refer questions to the ECJ for preliminary ruling. In the ruling on the ECAA Agreement, the ECJ judged that the "single-pillar structure must also be regarded a guarantee that the essential character of the powers of the EC institutions will remain unchanged".[161] Secondly, the ECAA Agreement extends the powers of the Commission, making it responsible for ensuring that the ECAA competition rules are complied with throughout that area. Thirdly, the ECAA Agreement makes the ECJ responsible for ruling on all questions concerning the legality of decisions taken by EC institutions under this Agreement. Thus, the ECJ's exclusive task of reviewing the legality of acts of the EU institutions, whether the latter are acting under the EU founding Treaties or under another international instrument, conferred on it by *inter alia* Articles 263 EC and 267 TFEU, is not called into question.

In general, Joint Committees are authorised to settle disputes which concern interpretation/application, and to ensure the harmonised/uniform interpretation of their respective EU external agreements with the acquis communautaire.[162] Besides, disputes may be settled by independent arbitration bodies set up equally by the parties to a dispute and the Council. The ECJ makes preliminary rulings on the interpretation of EU external agreements, and on their direct applicability and effect within the EU legal order. The ECJ rules on the interpretation of acts of common institutions within EU external agreements.[163] One must acknowledge the significant contribution of the ECJ as an agency for integration. Throughout its case law, the ECJ has consistently ensured the extension of the acquis com-

---

159 *Ibid*, at 18-35.
160 Opinion 1/00 [2002] ECR I-3493.
161 *Ibid.*
162 Articles 105 and 111(1) EEA Agreement.
163 Case C-192/89 *Sevince v. Staatssecretaris van Justitie* [1990] ECR 3461/3501 and Case C-355/93 *Hayriye Eroglu v. Land Baden-Württemberg* [1994] ECR I-5117.

munautaire into third country legal systems, and promoted the direct applicability and direct effect of EU external agreements within the EU.[164]

EU external agreements without far-reaching objectives of integration, or without enhanced political dialogue, do not envisage institutional frameworks equivalent to other agreements. Instead, their institutional frameworks are justified by the specific objectives of agreements, and are tailored to suit national constitutional requirements and other important factors, such as national public opinion. For instance, the EC-Swiss SAs establish the Joint Committees, which are responsible for the management and proper application of the agreement, and for solving disputes between the Parties "to ensure the satisfactory application of the legislative, regulatory and administrative provisions".[165] Therein, the Joint Committee mirrors the competence and composition of the Council in other EU external agreements. However, the Joint Committee does not have the authority to issue binding decisions, but may produce suggestions and recommendations for the agreement's parties.[166] Each of the EC-Swiss SAs provide for the creation of a mixed Committee guaranteeing the coherent application of the agreements. In our opinion, the EC-Swiss SAs institutional framework is designed for practical reasons to provide a simple and well-functioning mechanism for sectoral cooperation, without interfering with specific Swiss constitutional issues, or opposing public opinion on the issue of Swiss integration into the EU. Indeed, Swiss constitutional law is not yet clear on the issue of the primacy of international law within the Swiss legal order. Despite acknowledging this principle in the Swiss Constitution,[167] the Swiss Federal Tribunal has not yet confirmed the principle of the supremacy of international law over national law (except in its commitment to human rights). Therefore, the supremacy of rights guaranteed by the EC-Swiss SAs within the Swiss legal system, and their legal effect, is still open for further legal consideration. Besides, the authority of the EC-Swiss SAs common institutions to issue non-binding decisions is designed specifically with Swiss public opinion in mind. One must always remember that the Swiss population refused to endorse ratification of the EEA Agreement in 1992. Therefore, the institutional structure within the EC-Swiss SAs provides Swiss authorities with consid-

---

164 C-257/99 *The Queen v Secretary of State for the Home Department, ex parte: Barkoci and Malik* [2001] ECR I-6557. C-63/99 *The Queen v. Secretary of State for the Home Department, ex parte: Gloszczuk* [2001] ECR I-6369. C-235/99 *The Queen v. Secretary of State for the Home Department, ex parte: Kondova* [2001] ECR I-6427. C-268/99 *Jany and Others v. Staatssecretaris van Justitie* [2001] ECR I-8615. C-162/00 *Land Nordrhein-Westfalen v. Pokrzeptowicz-Meyer* [2002] ECR I-1049. See case note by C. Hillion in 40 CML Rev. 465–491 (2003).
165 Article 9(1) of the EC-Swiss SA on technical barriers.
166 The EC-Swiss Joint Committee can issue decisions to remedy the situation.
167 Article 5(4) Swiss Federal Constitution.

erable discretion in guaranteeing the uniform interpretation and proper implementation of the SAs.

The EU has launched the negotiation process on new enhanced agreements with the neighbouring countries which will substitute expired and outdated PCAs and EMAAs. At the time of writing the Commission is negotiating a new enhanced agreement with Ukraine. The future EU-Ukraine agreement will be the first association agreement among a new generation of external agreements to be negotiated by the EU and third countries under the framework of the ENP. Consequently, it will, to a certain extent, serve as a template and a point of reference for other future enhanced agreements to be concluded between the EU and other neighbouring countries which participate in the ENP. It is expected that future EU-Ukraine enhanced agreement will be distinguished by an enhanced institutional framework with the right to issue binding decisions at the level of Association Council and the possibility of the informal participation of experts from both parties in taking decisions related to the operation of the agreement and free trade area in particular.[168] The revision of the institutional framework in the enhanced agreement with Ukraine could imply significant impact on the legal system of Ukraine. It will be one of the first cases in which the decisions of common institutions set up under the framework of an international agreement could be directly effective in the legal system of Ukraine. In accordance with the Ukrainian Constitution decisions of the Association Council may have priority over Ukrainian primary and secondary laws, which implies a significant impact of these decisions on the legal system of Ukraine, especially in the fields of protection of foreign investors, non-discrimination, and the application of market economy principles. It could be argued that binding character of decisions of the Association Council will accelerate the Ukrainian legislature and judiciary to apply and implement selected elements of the acquis communautaire in order to achieve objectives of the new enhanced agreement. In a long term perspective greater role in dispute solving and competence of the common institutions in the future EU-Ukraine enhanced agreement to issue binding decisions may push Ukraine and other neighbouring countries to better sharing European and international common democratic values and to preserve integrity of the acquis communautaire in its external dimension.

---

168 Joint Declaration on the EU-Ukraine Associate Agreement, available at <http://www.delukr.ec.europa.eu/press_releases.html?id=48778>, last access 18 January 2011.

3.4.3. Concluding remarks

At a very basic level, we noted the impact of the objectives of EU external agreements on the competence and composition of common institutions set up within these agreements. Several observations may be advanced. Firstly, the structure and competence of common institutions set up under EU external agreements are linked to the objectives of those agreements. As our study indicates, EU external agreements which target closer economic and political cooperation between the EC/EU and third countries (the EEA Agreement, the EAs, the SAAs, the PCAs) envisage comprehensive institutional frameworks, which comprise at least two or three common institutions. In general, these institutions are authorised to issue binding decisions, thereby possessing a variety of means to ensure the export of the acquis communautaire into third country legal systems. On the other hand, EU external agreements aimed at economic or sectoral cooperation (EC-Swiss SAs, TCDAs) are characterised by less-sophisticated one-pillar institutional frameworks, which issue non-binding decisions. In these cases, third countries are expected to embark upon a process of voluntary harmonisation. Besides, national constitutional arrangements and public opinion within third countries may justify specific institutional frameworks between the parties. For example, the "one-pillar" institutional structure within the EC-Swiss SAs, with the authority to issue non-binding decisions, is designed to respond to two challenges. The first challenge is to push negative Swiss public opinion towards closer integration with the EU. The second challenge is to avoid problems associated with enforcing the decisions of common institutions within the Swiss legal order.

The second observation is that common institutions within EU external agreements do not replicate the EU institutional framework. In contrast to EU supranational institutions, common institutions set up within EU external agreements are of an inter-governmental nature. This means that their decisions are not always directly applicable within third country legal orders, but rely explicitly on the arrangements of their national constitutions. Therefore, institutions common to EU external agreement possess restricted means of ensuring the export of the acquis communautaire. The explicit integration objectives of the external agreements, and the significant progress in bilateral relations, provide considerable impetus for third countries to adopt the acquis communautaire. On the other hand, the restricted objectives of EU external agreements will hardly encourage third countries to fulfil their soft harmonisation commitments, especially the costly undertaking of voluntary harmonisation. It has become the established EU position that only EU Member States can "exert an effective influence on the life of the Community".[169] This means that, in the aftermath of the EEA Agreement experience, EU external agreements exclude any possibility of endangering the prerogatives and autonomy of the EU institutions by common institutions with these agreements. Therefore, common institutions within external agreements serve as a bridge for the acquis transition into third country legal orders, but can hardly ensure the same degree of reciprocity between the acquis communautaire and the legal heritage of third countries.

The third observation to be made is that common institutions set up within EU external agreements significantly contribute to the implementation of common European democratic and institutional values by third countries. Common institutions serve as a "waiting room" for third countries in bringing European "common values" closer to the political and legal orders of those nations. That is to say, third countries learn the basics of the European decision-making, parliamentary business, conflict solving and decision-enforcement techniques within the Councils and the Parliamentary Committees. Besides, certain EU external agreements (EAs, SAAs) encourage third countries to replicate within their national executives European-type monitoring institutions on state aid and competition.[170] Third countries where there is an absence of similar institutions within their national system, could decide to mirror EU monitoring agencies, and to endow them with powers similar in scope to those of the EU.[171]

---

169 Opinion on Problems Raised by Applications for Membership from the United Kingdom, Ireland, Denmark and Norway (Bull. EC. Supp. 4/68, 9). See also Council Resolution on relations between the EC and the EFTA states, (O.J. 1990 C15/336, at 8 and 9).
170 For instance, Article 70(4) EC-Croatia SAA.
171 M. Cremona, "State Aids Control: Substance and Procedure in the Europe Agreements and the Stabilisation and Association Agreements", 9 ELJ 265-287 (2003).

3.5. Adoption of the acquis communautaire by judiciary in Ukraine. Case study

This case study endeavours to examine the effectiveness of substantive and procedural means of exporting the acquis communautaire into legal system of Ukraine.

For this purpose we shall not deal with the multi-dimensional and complex phenomenon of the acquis communautaire export in its whole scope, but endeavour to clarify only one aspect of it which is the adoption of the acquis communautaire by judiciaries in third countries. We believe it is essential to ensure the success of acquis communautaire export mainly because neither the acquis communautaire nor European common values can be promoted abroad without their effective application by judiciaries in the recipient countries. It should be admitted that study of the application of the acquis communautaire by judiciaries in third countries is an ambitious and complex task. It warrants a sophisticated interdisciplinary approach in order to embrace not only legal but also socio-legal, historical and cultural aspects of this phenomenon. Otherwise it is very difficult to explain and comprehend why judiciaries in third countries could be inclined to align their legal practices with best European standards. However, this case study does not dire to acquire so ambitious objective. Instead it focuses only on one narrow aspect of the adoption of the acquis communautaire by judiciaries, which is application of the acquis communautaire by third countries' judges in their decisions.

Furthermore, the scope of the case study is confined to Ukraine. This country is an immediate geographical neighbour of the EU and takes an active part in the ENP, and aspires to enhance its contractual relations with the EU with a clear view to EU membership.[172] The EU expresses its well-justified interest in accelerating the Europeanization of the administrative and judicial institutions in Ukraine, owing to its strategic geographical position, and the importance of expanding the EU Internal Market. Therefore, the example of Ukraine can be a good case for studying if EU external policies have produced any impact on the Europeanization of the legal systems of third countries.

---

172 R. Petrov, "Legal and Political Expectations of Neighbouring Countries from the European Neighborhood Policy" in The European Neighbouhood Policy: A Framework for Modernisation? (eds: M. Cremona and G. Meloni), EUI Law Working Paper, 2007/21, 7-22.

3.5.1. The European Neighbourhood Policy and its impact on the adoption of the acquis communautaire by the judiciary in Ukraine

The ENP was devised as a framework policy to export democracy, stability and security to the EU's neighbours, in order to create a circle of friends around the EU's borders involving countries which can not join the EU in the near future.[173] Within this triangle the promotion of stability targets democratization, good governance and the stability of institutions in the neighbouring countries. One of the basic means to achieve these objectives is to ensure the effective functioning of the judiciary as a prerequisite of the correct and efficient application of the rule of law.[174] Judiciary reforms should be of prime importance for the neighbouring countries, which hope to join the EU in the long-term future. The so-called "fourth accession criteria", adopted at the Madrid European Council in December 1995, emphasizes that candidate countries must set up the institutional capacity of their administrative and judicial institutions to apply and implement the acquis communautaire. At the same time, the ENP does not hide the fact that judicial reform in the neighbouring countries could be of pragmatic benefit for the EU, since "strengthening of the functioning of the judicial system will also contribute to a better investment climate" for potential EU investors.[175] Therefore, the reform of the judiciary in third countries in line with European standards possesses a considerable ideological and practical importance for engaged third countries, and the entire EU. Specific steps to reform the judiciaries in neighbouring countries are identified in the bilateral Action Plans (AP), concluded with almost all countries participating in the ENP, and Association Agendas (AA) (at the time of writing signed only with Ukraine).[176] For example, the EU-Ukraine AA targets the objective:

"to consolidate democratic reforms notably reform of the judiciary, respect for the rule of law and human rights, transparency and democratic accountability, the fight against corruption as well as increasing citizens' participation in public decision-making in Ukraine.... continuing reform of the judiciary and of the court system so as to further strengthen the independence, impartiality, and professionalism of the judiciary and courts, notably by enhancing the training of judges, court officials and prosecutors as well as support staff and law enforce-

---

173 M. Cremona, C. Hillion, "L'Union Fait la Force? Potential and Limitations of the European Neighbourhood Policy as an Integrated EU Foreign and Security Policy", EUI LAW Working Paper, 2006/36.
174 For instance, Recommendation No. 1/2005 of the EU-Ukraine Partnership and Cooperation Council of 21/02/2005 on the implementation of the EU/Ukraine Action Plan.
175 *Ibid.*
176 Information is available at <http://ec.europa.eu/world/enp/documents_en.htm>, last access 18 January 2011.

ment agencies staff; effective implementation and enforcement of the civil, criminal and administrative codes and their corresponding procedural codes, based on European standards".[177]

Further means to strengthen the independence and effectiveness of the Ukrainian judiciary are envisaged in the bilateral EU-Ukraine Justice and Home Affairs Action Plan.[178]

Hitherto, the EU has influenced the Ukrainian judiciary in two ways. Firstly, the EU regularly monitors and encourages judiciary reform in Ukraine by soft law instruments borrowed from the EU accession process (AP, AA, country reports). Results of the monitoring display the EU's growing concern with the independence, impartiality and efficiency of the Ukrainian judiciary and law enforcement bodies. The EU continuously emphasises the existence of "high-level" corruption, including so-called "political corruption" within the Ukrainian judiciary and believes that the improvement of the business and investment climate in Ukraine is linked to the aim to set up a "transparent and predictable legal and administrative framework as well as an independent judiciary".[179]

Secondly, the EU offers considerable financial and technical assistance for the reform of the Ukrainian judiciary in line with EU best standards through the ENPI.[180] In the period 2007-2010 Ukraine expected to obtain 494 million Euro for the implementation of the EU-Ukraine AA, including the strengthening of the independence and effectiveness of the Ukrainian judiciary.[181] The EU funds projects to enhance the capacities of the Ukrainian judiciary and law enforcement bodies in international cooperation in criminal matters. The EU persistently encourages Ukraine to intensify cooperation with other European organisations (the CoE, Organisation for Security and Cooperation in Europe (OSCE)) and other

---

177 *Ibid.*
178 For example, EU Action Plan on Justice and Home Affairs in Ukraine (O.J. 2001 C 77/01).
179 For example, Joint Evaluation Report of EU-Ukraine Action Plan, March 2008, available at <http://ec.europa.eu/external_relations/ukraine/docs/ukraine_eu_joint_evaluation_2008_en.pdf>, last access 18 January 2011.
180 Regulation 1638/2006 of the European Parliament and the Council of 24 October 2006 laying down general provisions establishing a European Neighbourhood and Partnership Instrument. (O.J. 2006 L310/1). Article 2.2.(d) of the Regulation that assistance can be offered with objective "promoting the rule of law and good governance, including strengthening the effectiveness of public administration and the impartiality and effectiveness of the judiciary, and supporting the fight against corruption and fraud".
181 Available at <http://ec.europa.eu/world/enp/funding_en.htm>, last access 18 January 2011.

international institutions in combating corruption (for instance, joining the Council of Europe's Group of States against Corruption (GRECO)).[182]

The EU's attempts to reform the Ukrainian judiciary have achieved some degree of success.[183] The recent Ukrainian court system provides better transparency and information support (the creation of an electronic database of all national court decisions, establishing administrative courts). The Ukrainian law enforcement institutions and judiciary have embarked upon an active cooperation with EU agencies such as FRONTEX and EuroJust.[184] However, these changes have not helped to change the reputation of the Ukrainian judiciary as one of the most corrupted institutions in the country. EU experts warn that the Ukrainian judiciary has to solve serious problems in the quality and substance of the legal training of its judges, as well as their regular professional training and funding. As a result, judicial decisions in Ukraine do not always comply with democracy and rule of law standards, and are often based on arbitrariness.[185]

3.5.2. Adoption of the acquis communautaire by the Ukrainian judiciary

The legal system of Soviet Ukraine did not differ from that of the Union of Soviet Socialist Republics (USSR). Soviet Ukraine's legal doctrine unquestionably shared the Soviet concept of the relationship of international law to municipal law.[186]

---

182 Communication from the Commission to the Council and the European Parliament "On Strengthening the European Neighbourhood Policy. ENP Progress Report. Ukraine", COM (2006) 726 final. The EU stated that "progress [in Ukraine] is being hindered by endemic corruption, which is the main challenge to the development and economic growth of Ukraine, and by the lack of a truly independent judiciary". Communication from the Commission to the Council and the European Parliament "On Strengthening the European Neighbourhood Policy in 2007. ENP Progress Report. Ukraine", COM (2008) 164.
183 Available at <http://ec.europa.eu/world/enp/pdf/action_plans/ukraine_enp_ap_jls-rev_en.pdf>, last access 18 January 2011.
184 For instance, on 12 June 2007 the EU and Ukraine have signed a working agreement with FRONTEX (the European Border Exchange Agency) which allows better exchange of information and cooperation with courts in the EU.
185 See "The Rule of Law in Ukraine, Report by Sir Brian Neill and Sir Henry Brooke (The Slynn Foundation) from December 2008, available at <http://www.britishukrainiansociety.org/en/index2.php?option=com_content&do_pdf=1&id=171>, last access 18 January 2011. In particular, the Report puts forward the idea that arbitrary judicial decisions by Ukrainian judges are explained by luck of guidelines from higher courts and preference to apply procedural law over substantive law in their judgments.
186 For instance, see works of the former Soviet/Ukrainian judge of the International Court of Justice V. Koretskiy, Izbrannie trydy, (Kiev, Naukova Dumka (ed. Denisov V.) 1989).

The reform of the Ukrainian legal system started shortly after independence in 1991. As a priority, Ukraine set as its political objectives integration into international political and economic structures and, consequently, membership of the CoE and the EU. Once the CoE set the criteria for membership, the first attempts were made to ensure the conformity of legislation in the spheres of democracy, rule of law, and human rights. As a consequence, Ukrainian criminal, penal and social legislation underwent substantial changes, such as the abolition of the death penalty, and the adoption of new criminal, criminal procedural, and civil procedural codes. These reforms marked the first steps in the reception of European legal standards into the developing Ukrainian legal system.

Yet the Ukrainian judiciary is being criticized for its reluctant application and implementation of international agreements into its own legal system.[187] Ukrainian courts refer mainly to international agreements which are duly signed and ratified by the Ukrainian Parliament (Verkhovna Rada), and are self-executive within the Ukrainian legal system. Even in these cases, the correct application of international agreements is not guaranteed, since one of the most important impediments for the application of international law by the Ukrainian judiciary is the correct understanding of these international conventions by national judges. International and European organizations realize this problem, and target their assistance to eliminate the incorrect application of international law by Ukrainian judges. In the end, this has led to the rise of judicial activism among Ukrainian judges in the "post-Orange Revolution" era, such as in the *Yuschchenko* case, where the Ukrainian Supreme Court established its informal case law,[188] and

---

After gaining independence in 1991, and the adoption of the Constitution of Ukraine in 1996, Ukrainian courts acquired more flexibility in applying international law in their decisions. Article 9 of the Ukrainian Constitution of 1996 provides that: "International treaties that are in force, agreed to be binding by the Verkhovna Rada [Ukrainian Parliament] of Ukraine, are part of the national legislation of Ukraine. The conclusion of international treaties that contravene the Constitution of Ukraine is possible only after introducing relevant amendments to the Constitution of Ukraine".

187 This happens mainly owing to: 1) the belief that international case law is not relevant to civil law systems; 2) luck of translation of case law of international and European courts into Ukrainian to help judges to adapt their decisions to best European standards. Furthermore, the Verkhovna Rada of Ukraine is not always expedient in solving conflicts between ratified international agreements and national legislation. See D. Wilkinson, "Interpreting Ukrainian legislation in light of international law and jurisprudence", available at <http://www.library.ukma.kiev.ua/e-lib/NZ/NZV22_2003_suspil/11_vilkinson_d.pdf>, last visited 18 January 2011. Also see G. Burd, "High Commercial Court tramples international agreements", available at <http://www.kyivpost.com/opinion/op_ed/28483>, last visited 18 January 2011.

188 N. Prescott, "Orange Revolution in Red, White, and Blue: U.S. Impact on the 2004 Ukrainian Election", 16 Duke J. of Comp. & Int. Law 219-248 (2006).

opened a door for Ukrainian courts to apply judgments of other international tribunals and courts.

The Constitutional Court of Ukraine is one of the biggest recipients of international and European technical and expert assistance.[189] Subsequently, it has proved to be an undisputed leader among other Ukrainian courts in referring to international law and universally-recognized principles in its own decisions. In most cases, these references relate the protection of constitutional rights and freedoms: freedom of association, right to participate in public management, right to vote and to be elected, right to a fair trial, and others. The Constitutional Court of Ukraine justifies references to international legal documents by the fact that Ukrainian citizens, foreigners and stateless persons have a right to refer to international means of protection of their rights, in cases where they are not adequately protected by the judiciary in Ukraine. In majority of judgments the Constitutional Court of Ukraine tried its best to interpret the provisions of the Ukrainian Constitution in line with best international and European legal standards.[190] However, there is still no uniformity among Ukrainian constitutional judges on boundaries of applying international law and ECHR law in their decisions. Some judges believe that Ukrainian courts should apply European Court of Human Rights (ECtHR) case law in line with characteristics of national legal system in order to preserve national constitutional values.[191] Other judges are in favour of more frequent references to international law, and to ECHR and EU law, in order to guarantee more effective protection of the constitutional freedoms of Ukrainian nationals. Furthermore, some judges of the Constitutional Court advocate the necessity to apply in their decisions more elements of the acquis communautaire owing to Ukraine's pro-European policies and its aspirations for EU membership.[192] In the end, it cannot be ruled out that, in the near future, Ukrainian constitutional judges might change their preferences in line with

---

189 Judges of the Constitutional Court of Ukraine are regular visitors to international tribunals, European constitutional courts, participants to international and European professional and academic events. The Constitutional Court of Ukraine pursues active cooperation with the CoE, EU, Venice Commission and other international institutions. More information is available at <http://www.ccu.gov.ua/en/index>, last visited 18 January 2011.

190 M. Selivon, "Harmonistsia natsionalnogo zakonodavstva z normami mizhnarodnogo prava i yogo vykorystannia Konstitutsiynym Sudom Ukraini", 3 Vystnyk Konstitutsiynogo Sydy Ukrainy 36-51 (2003).

191 Decision of the Constitutional Court of Ukraine from 2001 (*bank savings* case) No 23/2001. See V. Temchenko, "Vydnosyny mizh praktikoy ECtHR i jurisprudentsii Konstitutsiynogo Sydy Ukrainy", 4 Vystnyk Konstitutsiynogo Sydy Ukrainy 91-99 (2007). On the same problem encountered in the after accession period by constitutional courts in Central and Eastern Europe see A. Albi, "Ironies in Human Rights Protection in the EU: Pre-Accession Conditionality and Post-Accession Conundrums" 15(1) ELJ 46-69 (2009).

192 V. Kampo, "Konstitutsionalisatsiya zovnishnoi politiki Ukraini: Eurointegratsionnie aspecty", 6 Vystnyk Konstitutsiynogo Sudu Ukrainy 50-61 (2007).

the depth and nature of political relations between Ukraine and international, European organizations (the EU in particular).

In most decisions taken by the Constitutional Court of Ukraine EU law is applied as a persuasive source of reference. For instance in the course of comparative analysis the Constitutional Court referred to EC Regulation 2004/2003,[193] along with international conventions, ECHR law, and ECtHR case law in its ruling on constitutionality of Ukrainian law entitled "On political parties in Ukraine".[194] Furthermore, the Constitution Court of Ukraine referred to EC Council Directive 2000/78[195] in its ruling on constitutionality of Ukrainian laws "On public service", "Diplomatic service", and "Local self governmental service" (case on the maximum retirement age for civil servants).[196] It is remarkable that in both cases the Constitutional Court did not provide any reasoning as to why it decided to refer to these particular sources of the acquis communautaire.

The Ukrainian decision to embark on a new political course, aimed at rapprochement with the EU, was proclaimed in 1994 with the signing of the PCA with (then) the EC and its Member States. By signing and subsequently ratifying the PCA, Ukraine accepted its soft commitment to *"endeavour to ensure* [emphasis added] that its legislation be gradually made compatible with that of the Community". In response to the ambiguous "approximation clause" in the PCA, Ukraine designed the notion of the "adaptation" of national law to EU legislation. For the time being, this notion is unique to Ukraine since, at least, it satisfies the PCA's soft approximation commitment, and at most, ensures that the EU pays attention to Ukraine's European aspirations. Furthermore, the adaptation of Ukrainian laws to EU legislation offers some hope that the EU might offer a new model of mutual relations which could potentially integrate Ukraine with an enlarged Europe.[197] In fact, soft approximation commitments in the EU-Ukraine PCA are of considerable legal value for the Ukrainian judiciary. This can be explained by external and internal factors. Externally, the Ukrainian judiciary acknowledges Ukraine's active engagement into the ENP and Eastern Partnership,[198] which both require Ukraine to harmonise its legislation in line with EU

---

193 Regulation 2004/2003 of the European Parliament and the Council of November 4 2003 "On the regulations governing political parties at European level and the rules regarding their funding" (O.J. L 297).
194 Decision of the Constitutional Court of Ukraine from June 12 2007, No. 2/2007.
195 EC Council Directive 2000/78 of 27 November 2000 establishing a general framework for equal treatment in employment and occupation (O.J. 2000 L 303/16).
196 Decision of the Constitutional Court of Ukraine from 16 October 2007, No. 8/2007.
197 *Supra note* 49.
198 This Initiative was proposed by Poland and Sweden in 2008 as complimentary to the ENP with objective to enhance political, economic and legal integration of Eastern neighbouring countries (Ukraine, Belarus, Moldova, Georgia, Armenia and Azerbaijan). The Eastern Partnership Programme was formally launched on 20 March 2009. Informa-

law. Internally, the Ukrainian judiciary takes into account national legislation on the step by step approximation of national legislation to the acquis communautaire. For instance, the law of Ukraine "On the All State Programme on the adaptation of Ukrainian legislation to EU laws",[199] envisages the export of the whole "accession acquis" into Ukraine's legal system, since the objective of this law is the "alignment of the Ukrainian legislation with the acquis communautaire, taking into consideration criteria specified by the EU towards countries willing to join the EU". In other words, Ukraine agreed to implement the "accession acquis" on a voluntary basis, without any perspective of full EU membership. It should be noted that the EU never indicated that voluntary harmonization would lead to the immediate recognition of Ukraine's hopes to join the EU. Nevertheless, in many official documents and public statements the Ukrainian government considers the voluntary harmonization of national legislation to EU law and gradual adoption of the acquis communautaire as a key factor to accelerate the Ukraine's integration into the EU.

Consequently, in light of these external and internal factors, the EU-Ukraine PCA is perceived by some national judges as not only a binding international document, but as something more. In case of conflict of PCA provisions with national law, Ukrainian courts recognize the priority and direct effect of the latter. For example, in the *Ryvne Customs Office v. Demyanyk* case,[200] the High Commercial Court of Ukraine recognised the direct effect and supremacy of Article 15 of PCA over conflicting national legislation regarding the regime of national treatment of European companies in Ukraine. Beyond that, some Ukrainian courts justify their references to EU law by the "soft" approximation clauses in Article 51 of the EU-Ukraine PCA. For instance, in the *Chernomortechflot v. Odessa Tax Office* case,[201] the High Commercial Court of Ukraine referred to the freedom of transit provided in the PCA, and to the "approximation clause" of the EU-Ukraine PCA (Article 51), as a justification for following the EU's definition of an "international transport corridor". The importance of Ukraine's soft approximation commitments and their far-reaching consequences for the legal system of Ukraine was emphasized by the District Administrative Court of Kiev in

tion is available at <http://ec.europa.eu/external_relations/eastern/index_en.htm>, last access 18 January 2011.
199 Law of the Verkhovna Rada of Ukraine "About the All State Programme of adaptation of Ukrainian legislation to that of the EU", 18 March 2004, No. 1629-IV.
200 Judgment of February 2 2005 No. 12/267. Also case *Closed Stock Company "Chumak" v. Kherson Custom Office* on March 25 2005 No. 7/299 by High Commercial Court of Ukraine. Also case *"Odek" LTD v. Ryvne Custom Office* on February 22 2005 No. 18/303.
201 Judgment on June 22 2004, No. 28/296-03-6901.

the *Person v. State Agency in nationalities and religions* case.[202] Therein, the Kiev District Administrative Court referred to the Ukrainian law "All State Programme on the adaptation of Ukrainian legislation to EU law", and stated that the aim of adapting Ukrainian legislation requires the alignment of Ukrainian legislation to the acquis communautaire, which covers EU law and the ECJ case law. For this purpose, the judgment of the Kiev District Administrative Court among other relevant sources of law mentions Directive 2004/83,[203] which is "frequently applied by the European Court on Human Rights" as a relevant guideline for the court.

The newly-born Ukrainian administrative judiciary, resulted after the active technical and expert support of international and European organizations (CoE, OSCE, EU),[204] proved to be another champion of the application of EU law in Ukrainian courts. The idea behind the administrative court reform in Ukraine to was to enhance the accountability of governmental bodies in line with best European principles, as was done in Central and Eastern European countries, which established administrative judiciary in order to qualify for EU membership.[205] It inspired Ukrainian administrative courts to import the general principles of EU law and to find inspiration from ECJ and ECtHR case law in cases related to state liability before individuals. In general Ukrainian administrative courts justify the application of ECJ case law by the need to follow ECtHR case law. For example, in the *Tsesarenko v. Representative office of the Pension Fund in Shevchenko district of Kiev* case,[206] the Administrative Court of the Kiev District stated that the principle of rule of law must be applied in line with ECtHR case law.[207] The Administrative Court of the Kiev District stated that the implementation of the best European standards of human rights protection in Ukraine will decrease the number of claims by Ukrainian nationals to the ECtHR against Ukraine.

In cases related to state liability before the individual, Ukrainian administrative courts have developed a previously unknown for the Ukrainian legal system

---

202 Judgment on May 22 2008, No. 4/48 and Judgment on October 13 2008 No. 4/375.
203 Directive 2004/83 of April 29 2004 "On minimum standards for the qualification and status of third country nationals or stateless persons as refugees or a persons who otherwise need international protection and the content of the protection granted" (O.J. 2004 L 304).
204 Only the OSCE conducted about 25 workshops for about 600 judges of administrative courts in Ukraine for the period of 2005-2008, funded exchange visits and trainings, available at <http://www.osce.org/item/35850.html>, last visited 18 January 2011.
205 F. Emmert, "Administrative and Court Reform in Central and Eastern Europe", 9(3) ELJ 288-315 (2003).
206 Judgment on November 18 2008, No. 9/556.
207 Law of Ukraine "About application of decision of the European Court of Human Rights", adopted on February 23 2006, No. 3477-IV.

concept of legal certainty. For example, in the *Person v. Kiev City centre for social assistance* case,[208] the Administrative Court of the Kiev District imported the principle of legal certainty from ECJ case law. Therein the Administrative Court of the Kiev District provided that rights of the disabled to claim social and financial assistance from the state flow from the principle of legal certainty. It means that a state cannot justify its failure to guarantee constitutional rights by absence of specific national law. For this purpose the Administrative Court of the Kiev District referred to the ECJ judgment in *van Duyn v. the Home Office* case,[209] wherein it is specified that nationals may rely on the state's obligations, even in cases when these obligations are provided in law without direct effect. Furthermore, Ukrainian courts developed the principle of legitimate expectations in the case of *Person v. Darnitsa District of Kiev Center for social assistance*,[210] concerning the rights to benefits of those who took part in the operation during Chernobyl disaster. The Kiev District Administrative Court provided that the principle of the state responsibility's to offer compensation to those involved in the Chernobyl catastrophe comes from *van Duyn v. Home Office* case. In particular, the Administrative Court of the Kiev District argued that if the state formally acknowledged its commitment to grant compensation to those involved in Chernobyl disaster, it cannot refer to its own failure to fulfil its commitments in order to avoid responsibility, and it would also harm the legitimate expectations of Ukrainian nationals.

3.5.3. Concluding remarks

As a logical conclusion, it can be argued that adoption of the acquis communautaire may be associated with the concepts of "integration without membership", and "transformation",[211] which implies that third countries can eventually join a legal space linked to the EU beyond EU borders.[212] The case Ukraine provides us a good illustration of the EU's considerable impact on the reforming legal systems in neighbouring countries in line with EU standards. The EU manages to achieve this objective by various substantive and procedural means. In the former case, soft approximation clauses in the EU-Ukraine PCA offered consider-

---

208 Judgment on November 25 2008, No. 2/416, Judgment on November 24 2008, No. 5/503. Judgment on December 1 2008, No. 5/451, Judgment on November 10 2008, No. 5/435.
209 Case 41/74, van Duyn v. Home Office, ECR 1974 1337.
210 Judgment on June 26 2008, No. 4/337.
211 For instance, F. Maini, "Legal Europeanisation as Legal Transformation: Some insights from Swiss 'outer Europe'", EUI Working Paper MWP 2008/32, at 16-17.
212 A. Lazowski, "Enhanced Multilateralism and Enhanced Bilateralism: Integration without Membership in the European Union", 45(6) CML Rev. 1433-1458 (2008).

able impetus towards the initial Europeanization of national judiciaries. Ukraine has managed to exercise an impressive advancement in distancing itself from introverted outdated legal traditions of the Soviet past. The example of Ukraine shows that national judiciary recognises the significant role of the PCA in its legal order, and apply the PCA as binding self-executing international agreement. Despite the fact that the approximation clause in the EU-Ukraine PCA does not have any binding legal force the Ukrainian judiciary displayed sometimes astonishing favourability in using this approximation clause as a source of "pro European" inspiration in their judgments. It could be explained by advanced level of the EU-Ukraine relations and Ukraine's active participation in the EU led external policies towards its close neighbourhood (ENP) and regional initiatives (Black Sea Synergy, Eastern Partnership).

The EU applies specific procedural means to export the acquis communautaire in line with different policy objectives in its relations with Ukraine, in order to reform its judiciary. The impact of the EU's political influence and its soft power is more evident. Since Ukraine is the key addressee of the ENP, the EU is straightforward in emphasizing combating the insufficient level of judicial protection and access to justice in Ukraine. The EU uses various soft law tools (action plans, association agendas, country reports) to screen the pace of judicial reform in Ukraine. Furthermore, judiciary reform is one of the priorities of EU financial and technical support for Ukraine. As a direct consequence of the EU's financial and technical assistance, some Ukrainian judges have become inclined to mention in their judgments not only to ECJ judgments, but also certain principles of EU law. As a result, the principle of legal certainty is widely applied by administrative courts in Ukraine. The Constitutional Court of Ukraine refers to EU law in its own decisions in interpreting the Ukrainian Constitution. It creates a solid fundamental for gradual aligning of the Ukrainian legal system with the acquis acommunautaire.

3.6. Conclusion

The process of exporting the acquis communautaire should be seen as an indispensable part of the "dynamic experiment in which new methods of integration, multi-level and multi-centred governance and new constitutionalism are being worked on and bargained, and are evolving".[213] Indeed, the adoption of the acquis communautaire encourages third countries to revisit the compatibility of their national rules and standards to those of the EU, in order to share European "common values" in the course of adopting the acquis. Furthermore, the export of the acquis communautaire contributes to the establishment of a friendly legal environment between the EU and third countries, therefore encouraging the flow of investment and the liberalisation of markets.

The initial purpose of this chapter was to scrutinise means of exporting the acquis into the legal systems of third countries. In particular, we analysed whether the objectives of EU external agreements have an effect on this process. We attempted to answer two major research questions. Firstly, how does the EU export its acquis? For this purpose, we concentrated in the third chapter on selected substantive and procedural means of exporting the acquis into the legal systems of third countries. We argued that the former referred to the fundamental ways of implementing the acquis communautaire into third country legal orders. The latter related to specific technical/procedural tools, which either directly or indirectly, encourage the implementation of the acquis communautaire into third country legal orders. The second question we tackled is: does the EU apply substantive and procedural means to export the acquis communautaire in line with the objectives of the EU external agreements? In the course of our study, we argued that the substantive and procedural means of exporting the acquis communautaire are not uniformly applicable, but are rather exercised in accordance with the specific objectives of EU external agreements. Indeed, our study shows that the objectives of the EU agreements unquestionably constitute a driving force behind understanding the role and mechanism of the substantive and procedural means of exporting the acquis. Among all these, homogeneity remains the most advanced tool for exporting the acquis communautaire. Nevertheless, the most recent EU external agreements do not replicate the entire homogeneity procedure found in earlier agreements. Instead, they apply selected elements of the homogeneity procedure in order to achieve the specific objectives of the EU external agreements. On the one hand, objectives to bring about closer economic and political cooperation (customs union, free trade area, mutual recognition regime) imply that third countries will accept binding substantive and procedural means

---

213 M. Cremona, "The Union as a Global Actor: Roles, Models and Identity", 41 CMLRev. 553-573. (2004).

to implement the acquis communautaire into their own legal system. On the other hand, the objectives of EU partnership, cooperation and development agreements envisage less ambitious substantive and procedural means (non-binding harmonisation/approximation of laws commitments, supported by technical and educational assistance on behalf of the EU; they also do not envisage the involvement of a third country in EU decision-making procedures). In the former case, the EU expects candidate countries to import the fixed and dynamic acquis communautaire as widely and as soon as possible, whereas the latter EU external agreements encourage third countries to embark upon a process of voluntary harmonisation through the gradual adoption of the relevant acquis.[214]

Our study also can display that the level of institutional integration reflects the objectives of EU external agreements. In particular, we argue that the composition and competence of common institutions are set up in such a way as to suit the objectives of the EU external agreements. This means that the EU external agreements which pursue closer economic and political cooperation with third countries (EAs, SAAs, PCAs) institute the Councils, Committees, and Parliamentary Committees. On the other hand, external agreements which do not contain any far-reaching integration objectives usually establish a simple one-pillar institutional framework (Joint Committees). Common institutions within EU external agreements significantly contribute to the implementation of European common values envisaged in the Lisbon Treaty such as transparency and accountability, democracy and judicial control.

In the end of our study we approached a question if the substantive and procedural means of exporting the acquis communautaire truly encourage third countries to europeanise their institutional and legal structures? For this purpose we considered if different objectives of EU external policies may cause different results in adoption of the acquis communautaire by third countries. We focused on Ukraine and observed that enhanced level of bilateral political and economic cooperation with the EU imply that Ukrainian judges in domestic courts and Constitutional Court are wholeheartedly positive in applying elements of the acquis communautaire as a source of inspiration in their decisions.

In conclusion to this chapter, it is also important to emphasise several important observations. The first is that almost all EU external agreements prioritise the substantive and procedural means, which ensure the adoption of the dynamic acquis (homogeneity, binding/soft harmonisation, approximation clauses, and mutual recognition). This shows that the EU is eager to ensure that third coun-

---

214 A. Evans, The Integration of the European Community and Third States in Europe: a Legal Analysis, (Clarendon Press Oxford 1996), 381-383. In general A. Evans is critical regarding the nature of voluntary harmonisation within the EAs. In his opinion, voluntary harmonisation is ill-adapted to structural economic problems faced by these countries.

tries keep track of, and quickly implement, the latest developments in the EU legal order.

Another observation is that the substantive and procedural means of exporting the acquis communautaire are supported by strong conditionality requirements. The further enhancement of bilateral relations between the EU and a third country, in particular the opening of negotiations on a mutual recognition regime, depends on the success of approximation efforts.

These observations highlight our initial suggestion that the EU considers the export of the acquis communautaire an intrinsic part of its foreign policy towards third countries. Indeed, the substantive and procedural means of exporting the acquis communautaire into EU external agreements inspire third countries to adopt as much as possible of the dynamic acquis in order to create a comparable and friendly legal environment beyond existing and potential EU boundaries.

3.7. Overall conclusion

Carried to its logical conclusion, our study confirms our initial proposition that the EU is active in pursuing the policy of "exporting" the acquis communautaire into the legal orders of third countries. That is to say that the enhancement of political and economic relations between the EU and a third country (offering a candidate state status, establishing a customs union, providing access to the EU Internal Market freedoms) could encourage the party to an agreement to embark upon the voluntary harmonisation of its legislation to that of the EU. Therefore, we insist on considering the acquis communautaire within EC/EU external agreements as a dynamic category, which directly depends not only on the explicit objectives of these agreements, but also on the wider framework of relations between the parties and the general political climate of bilateral relations.

Subsequently, we argue that the acquis communautaire should be regarded as a sophisticated tool of EU external policy. Recognising the established role of the EU as a "rule generator", we acknowledge that the vague concept of the "acquis communautaire" serves as an appropriate "wrapping" for the export of EU-generated rules abroad. Similar to a missionary, the acquis communautaire gradually establishes a friendly legal environment beyond EU borders through the export of its values, principles, and legal heritage abroad. In many cases, the EU does not worry about the non-binding nature of the approximation commitments. Reluctance and caution of third countries to adopt the acquis communautaire could be appeased by carefully-orchestrated EU external policy and the use of conditionality, which does not depend on the existence of binding harmonisation/approximation commitments.

These thoughts carry us to the conclusion that the omission of a precise definition of the concept of "acquis communautaire" in the Lisbon Treaty is not fortuitous, but intentional. In other words, despite being a guardian of constitutional values, these documents do not anchor the acquis communautaire to a shore of fixed and coherent legal definitions. Instead, the Lisbon Treaty paves the way for the continuation of the open-ended application of this category by the EU institutions, despite its being designed to simplify the EU legal order. We believe that this juncture explicitly supports our position that the past, recent, and future application of the acquis communautaire within the realm of EU external action is subordinated to tailor-made objectives and *de facto* relations with third countries. This view perfectly echoes the aphorism by the XIX century Russian satirist Kozma Putkov: "First buy a painting, and then look for a frame". Indeed, the acquis communautaire serves as a frame to support and to "embellish" EU external policy towards a third country. In return, one must be able to view the entire intricate picture of the EU relations with third countries, in order to evaluate the suitability and to recognise the scope of the acquis communautaire within a particular EC/EU external agreement.

Bibliography

Albi A., "Ironies in Human Rights Protection in the EU: Pre-Accession Conditionality and Post-Accession Conundrums", 15(1) ELJ 46-69 (2009)

Arnull A./ Dashwood A./ Ross M./ Wyatt D., *European Union Law* (4th Ed. London, Sweet & Maxwell 2000)

Arts K., "ACP-EU Relations in a New Era: The Cotonou Agreement", 40 CML Rev. 95-116 (2003)

Auzolai L., "The *Acquis* of the European Union and International Organisations", 11(2) ELJ 196-231 (2005)

Avci G., "Putting the Turkish EU Candidacy into Context", 7 EFA Rev. 91-110 (2002)

Baudenbacher C., Tresselt P., Orlygsson T., eds., *The EFTA Court. Ten Years on* (Oxford, Hart Publishing 2005)

Bell M., *Anti-discrimination law and the European Union* (Oxford University Press, 2002)

Berghe F. van den, "The EU and Issues of Human Rights Protection: Same Solutions to More Acute Problems?", 16 ELJ 112-157 (2010).

Beynon P., "Community Mutual Recognition Agreements, Technical Barriers to Trade and the WTO's Most Favoured Nation Principle", EL Rev. 231-249 (2003)

Blockmans S., *Tough Love. The European Union's Relations with the Western Balkans* (The Hague, T.M.C. Asser Press 2007)

Blockmans S. and Lazowski A., (eds.) *The European Union and its neighbours* (The Hague, T.M.C. Asser Press 2006)

Blockmans S. "EU-Russia Relations Through the Prism of the European Neighbourhood and Partnership Instrument", 13 EFA Rev. 167-187 (2008)

Breitenmoser S., "Sectoral Agreements between the EC and Switzerland: Contents and Context", 40 CML Rev. 1137-1186 (2003)

Bruzelius K., "The Impact of EU Values on Third Countries' National Legal Orders: EU Law as a Point of Reference in the Norwegian Legal System", in (F. Maiani, R. Petrov, E. Mouliarova, (eds.) *European Integration without EU Membership: Models, Experiences, Perspectives*, European University Institute (Max Weber Programme) Working Papers, 2009/10

Charlesworth A./ Cullen H., *European Community Law*, (London, Pitman Publishing 1994)

Czaplinksi W., "Harmonisation of laws in the European Community and approximation of Polish legislation to Community Law", 25 Polish Yearbook of International Law 45-55 (2001)

Clarke J., "Mutual Recognition Agreements" International Trade Law & Regulation 31-36 (1996)

Cremona M. "The "Dynamic and Homogenous" EEA: Byzantine Structures and Variable Geometry", 19 EL Rev. 508-526 (1994)

Cremona M., "The European Union as an International Actor: Issues of Flexibility and Linkage", 3 EFA Rev. 67-94 (1998)

Cremona M., "Flexible Models: External Policy and the European Economic Constitution", in G. de Búrca / J. Scott (eds.), *Constitutional Change in the EU From Uniformity to Flexibility?* (Oxford, Hart Publishing 2000), 60-61

Cremona M., "Multilateral and Bilateral Approaches to the Internationalisation of Competition Law: an EU Perspective" in Cremona/ J. Fletcher / L. Mistelis (eds.), *Foundations and Perspectives of International Trade Law*, (London, Sweet and Maxwell 2001) 135-169

Report by Prof. Marise Cremona M. "Regional Integration and the Rule of Law: Some Issues and Options" at the Conference on Regional Integration and Trade in the Development Agenda on 31 May – 1 June 2001, the Brookings Institution, Washington DC

Cremona M., "State Aids Control: Substance and Procedure in the Europe Agreements and the Stabilisation and Association Agreements", 9 ELJ 265-287 (2003)

Cremona M., "The Draft Constitutional Treaty: External Relations and External Action", 40 CML Rev. 1347-1366 (2003)

Cremona M., "The Union as a Global Actor: Roles, Models and Identity", 41 CML Rev. 553-573. (2004)

Cremona M., Hillion C., "L'Union Fait la Force? Potential and Limitations of the European Neighbourhood Policy as an Integrated EU Foreign and Security Policy", EUI LAW Working Paper, 2006/36

Davies G., "Subsidiarity: the Wrong Idea, In the Wrong Place, at the Wrong Time", 43 CML Rev. 63-84 (2006)

Delcourt C., "The *Acquis Communautaire:* Has the Concept Had Its Day?", 38 CML Rev. 829-870 (2001)

Dawes A., and Kunoy B., "Plate tectonics in Luxembourg: The *ménage à trois* between EC law, international law and the European Convention on Human Rights following the UN sanctions cases" 46 CML Rev. 73–104 (2009)

Denza E., *The Intergovernmental Pillars of the European Union* (Oxford University Press 2002)

Desta M.G., "EC-ACP economic partnership agreements and WTO compatibility: an experiment in North-South interregional agreements?", 43(5) CML Rev. 1343-1379 (2006).

Douglas-Scott S., "a Tale of Two Courts: Luxembourg, Strasbourg and the Growing European Human Rights *Acquis*", 43 CML Rev. 629-665 (2006)

Emmert F., "Administrative and Court Reform in Central and Eastern Europe", 9(3) ELJ 288-315 (2003)

Emiliou N., *The Principle of Proportionality in European Law* (The Hague, Kluwer, 1996)

Evans A. *The Integration of the European Community and Third States in Europe: a Legal Analysis*, (Oxford, Clarendon Press 1996)

Evans A., "Voluntary Harmonization in Integration between the European Community and Eastern Europe", 22 EL Rev. 201-220 (1997)

Eyjolfsson M., Case note on E-9/97, *Erla Maria Sveinbjörnsdottir v. the Government of Iceland*. Advisory Opinion of the EFTA Court of 10 December 1998, 37 CML Rev. 191-211 (2000)

Fischer P., Case note on T-115/94, *Opel Austria GmbH v. Council*, [1997], 35 CML Rev. 765-781 (1998)

Fitzmaurice G., "The General Principles of International Law", 92 Collected Courses of the Hague Academy of International Law 7 (1957)

Fredriksen H., "The EFTA Court 15 Years On", 59 ICLQ 731-760 (2010)

Forman J., "The EEA Agreement five years on: Dynamic homogeneity in practice and its implementation by the two EEA courts", 36 CML Rev. 751-781 (1999)

Gialdino C., "Some reflections on the acquis communautaire", 32 CML Rev. 1089-1121 (1995)

Goetschel L., "Switzerland and European Integration: Change through Distance", 8 EFA Rev. 313-330 (2003)

Graver H. P., "Mission Impossible: Supranationality and National Legal Autonomy in the EEA Agreement", 7 EFA Rev. 73-90 (2002)

Grundmann S., "The Optional European Code on the Basis of the *Acquis Communautaire*- Starting Point and Trends", 10(6) ELJ 698-711 (2004)

Hadfield A., "Janus Advances? An Analysis of EC Development Policy and the 2005 Amended Cotonou Partnership Agreement", 12(1) EFA Rev. 39-66 (2007)

Hakura F., "The Euro-Med Policy: The Implications of the Barcelona Declaration", 34 CML Rev. 337-366 (1997)

Harbo T.I.. "The EEA and Norway: A Case of Constitutional Pluralism", in (F. Maiani, R. Petrov, E. Mouliarova) (eds.) *European Integration without EU Membership: Models, Experiences, Perspectives*, European University Institute (Max Weber Programme) Working Papers, 2009/10

Hartley T. C. *The Foundations of European Community Law* (6th Ed. Oxford University Press 2007)

Harpaz G., "Enhanced Relations between the European Union and the State of Israel under the European Neighbourhood Policy: some Legal and Economic Implications", 31(4) LIEI 257-274 (2004)

Harpaz G., "When East meets West: Approximation of laws in the EU-Mediterranean context", 43(1) CML Rev. 993-1022 (2006)

Harpaz G., "Normative Power Europe and the Problem of a Legitimacy Deficit: an Israeli Perspective", 12(1) EFA Rev 89-109 (2007)

Harpaz G., "Mind The Gap: Narrowing the Legitimacy Gap in EU–Israeli Relations", 13(1) EFA Rev 117-137 (2008)

Herdina A., "Approximation of Laws in the Context of the European Neighbourhood Policy – a View from Brussels", IX(3) European Journal of Law Reform 501-504 (2007)

Hillion C., "Partnership and Cooperation Agreements between the European Union and the New Independent States of the Ex-Soviet Union", 3 EFA Rev. 399-420 (1998)

Hillion C. "Trade dispute overshadows entry into force of EC agreement", 6 EU Focus (1998)

Hillion C., "Institutional Aspects of the Partnership Between the European Union and the Newly Independent States of the Former Soviet Union: Case Studies of Russia and Ukraine", 37 CMLRev. 1211-1235 (2000)

Hillion C., "Approximation of laws in the context of EU-NIS partnership", in A. Nikodem (ed.), *Perspectives of the Legal Approximation Process in Central and Eastern Europe – Mutual Experiences*, (Budapest, Academy of European Law and Istvan Bibo College of Law 2001), 86-98

Hillion C., "The European Union is Dead. Long Live the European Union...A Commentary on the Treaty of Accession 2003", 29(5) EL Rev. 583-612 (2004)

Hillion C., Case note on C-257/99 *The Queen v Secretary of State for the Home Department, ex parte: Barkoci and Malik*; C-63/99 *The Queen v. Secretary of State for the Home Department, ex parte: Gloszczuk* [2001]; C-235/99 *The Queen v. Secretary of State for the Home Department, ex parte: Kondova* [2001]; C-268/99 *Jany and Others v. Staatssecretaris van Justitie* [2001]; C-162/00 *Land Nordrhein-Westfalen v. Pokrzeptowicz-Meyer* [2002], 40 CML Rev. 465–491 (2003)

Hillion C., "Mapping-Out the New Contractual Relations between the European Union and Its Neighbours: Learning from the EU–Ukraine "Enhanced Agreement"", 12(2) EFA Rev. 169-182 (2007)

Hillion C. Case note on C-265/03, *Simutenkov v. Ministerio de Educacion y Cultura, Real Federacion Espanola de Futbol* [2005] ECR I-2579, 45 CML Rev. 815-833 (2008)

Hilpold P., "EU Development Cooperation at a Crossroad: The Cotonou Agreement of 23 June 2000 and the Principle of Good Governance", 7 EFA Rev. 53-72 (2002)

Holden P., "The European Community's MEDA Aid Programme: A Strategic Instrument of Civilian Power?", 8 EFA Rev. 347-363 (2003)

Inglis K., "The Europe Agreements compared in the light of their pre-accession reorientation", 37 CML Rev. 1173-1210 (2000)

Inglis K., "The Accession Treaty and its Transitional Arrangements: A Twilight Zone for the New Member States", in C. Hillion (Ed.), *EU Enlargement: a legal appraisal* (Oxford, Hart Publishing 2004)

Inglis K., "The Union's Fifth Accession Treaty: New Means to make Enlargement Possible", 41 CML Rev. 937-973 (2004)

Inglis K., 'EU Enlargement: Membership Conditions applied to Future and Potential Member States', in S. Blockmans and A. Lazowski, eds., *The European Union and its Neighbours: a Legal Appraisal of the EU's Policies of Stabilisation, Partnership and Integration* (The Hague, T.M.C. Asser Press 2006)

Inglis K., "Case C–413/04, *European Parliament v. Council*, Judgment of the Court of Justice (Grand Chamber) of 28 November 2006; Case C–414/04, *European Parliament v. Council*, Judgment of the Court of Justice (Grand Chamber) of 28 November 2006. Case C–273/04, *Republic of Poland v. Council*, Judgment of the Court of Justice (Grand Chamber) of 23 October 2007", 46 CML Rev. 641-663 (2009)

Isiksel N., "Fundamental rights in the EU after *Kadi and Al Barakaat*", 16 ELJ 551-577 (2010)

Jacobs F., "The Evolution of the European Legal Order", 41 CML Rev. 303-316 (2004)

Jansen N., Zimmerman R., "Restating the Acquis Communautaire? A Critical Examination of the 'Principles of the Existing EC Contract Law'", 71(4) ML Rev. 505-534 (2008)

Kampo V., "Konstitutsionalisatsiya zovnishnoi politiki Ukraini: Eurointegratsionnie aspecty", 6 Vystnyk Konstitutsiynogo Sydy Ukrainy 50-61 (2007)

Kanarek D., "Turkey and the European Union: The Path to Accession", 9 CJEL 457-473 (2003)

Karakas C., "Gradual Integration: an Attractive Alternative Integration Process for Turkey and the EU", 11 EFA Rev. 311-331 (2006)

Kochenov D., *EU Enlargement and the Failure of Conditionality: Pre-Accession Conditionality in the Fields of Democracy and the Rule of Law* (The Hague, Kluwer Law International, 2008)

Kochenov D., "Substantive and Procedural Issues in the Application of European Law in the Overseas Possessions of European Union Member States", 17(2) Michigan State Journal of International Law 195-288 (2008-2009)

Koretskiy V., *Izbrannie trydy*, (Kiev, Naukova Dumka (ed. Denisov V.) 1989)

Koutrakos P., "Legal Issues of EC-Cyprus Trade Relations", 52(2) ICLQ 489-498 (2003)

Koutrakos P., *EU International Relations Law* (Oxford, Hart Publishing 2006)

Krenzler H. G. / Everson M., Preparing for the acquis communautaire. Report of the Working Group on the Eastward Enlargement of the European Union, October 1998 (European University Institute, RSC Policy Paper № 98/6)

Kühn Z., "Application of European law in Central European candidate countries", 28 EL Rev. 551-560 (2003)

Laffrangue J., D'Sa R. M., "Domestic implementation of EU Regulations in Estonia: a flawed methodology or necessary transposition?", 27 EL Rev. 91-99 (2002)

Lasok K. *Law & Institutions of the European Union* (7th Ed. London, Butterworths 2001)

Lavranos N., Joint Cases C-402/05P, *Ahmed Ali Yusuf and Al Barakaat International Foundation v. Council and Commission*; Case C-415/05, *Yassin Abdullah Kadi v. Council and Commission*, 36(2) LIEI 157-183 (2009)

Lavranos N., "Protecting European Law from International Law" 15 EFA Rev. 265-282 (2010)

Lazowski A., "And then They were Twenty-Seven...a Legal Appraisal of the Sixth Accession Treaty", 44 CML Rev. 401-430 (2007)

Lazowski A., "Enhanced Multilateralism and Enhanced Integration without Membership in the European Union", 45 CML Rev. 1433-1458 (2008)

Leino P., Petrov R., "Between 'Common Values' and Competing Universals: The Promotion of the EU's Common Values through the European Neighbourhood Policy", 15(5) ELJ, 654-671 (2009)

Lenaerts K., "The Rule of Law and the Coherence of the Judicial System of the European Union", 44 CML Rev. 1625-1659 (2007)

Lenaerts K., "In the Union We Trust": Trust-Enhancing Principles of Community Law", 41 CML Rev. 317-343 (2004)

Levrat N., Schwok R., "Switzerland's Relations with the EU after the Adoption of the Seven Bilateral Agreements", 6 EFA Rev. 335-354 (2001)

Lyndahl H., "Acquiring a Community: The *Acquis* and the Institution of European Legal Order", 9 ELJ 433-450 (2003)

Macleod I./ Hendry I./ Hyett S., *The External Relations of the European Communities* (Oxford, Clarendon Press 1996)

Maduro M., "Reforming The Market or the State? Article 30 and the European Constitution: Economic Freedom and Political Rights", 3(1) ELJ 55-82 (1997)

Maiani F., "Legal Europeanization as Legal Transformation: Some Insights from Swiss "Outer Europe"", EUI Working Papers MWP 2008/32

Maiskiy O., "Poniatie statusa strany s rynochnoy ekonomikoy v mezhdunarodnom torgovom prave: vygody i nedostatki dlia Ukrainy", 25 (391), Yuridichna Praktika (2005)

Maresceau M., Montaguti E., "The Relations between the European Union and Central and Eastern Europe: a Legal Appraisal", 32 CML Rev. 1327-1367 (1995)

Maresceau M. (ed) *Enlarging the European Union: Relations Between the EU and Eastern Europe* (London, Longman 1997)

Martenczuk B., "From Lome to Cotonou: The ACP-EC Partnership Agreement in a Legal Perspective", 5 EFA Rev. 461-487 (2000)

McGoldrick D., *International Relations Law of the European Union* (London, Longman 1997)

Metcalf K. N., "Influence through Assistance – the EU assistance programmes", 9(3) EPL 425-442 (2003).

Mikiyevich M., Mizhnarodno-pravovi aspekty spivrobitnitstva Evropeyskogo Souzy z tretimy krainamy (Lviv National University 2001)

Mistelis L., "Is Harmonisation a Necessary Evil? The Future of Harmonisation and New Sources of International Trade Law" in Cremona/ J. Fletcher / L. Mistelis (eds.), *Foundations and Perspectives of International Trade Law*, (London, Sweet & Maxwell 2001) 3-27

Mortelmans K., "Community Law: More than a Functional Area of Law, Less than a Legal System", 1 LIEI 23-48 (1996)

Muraviov V., "Polozhenia Ugody pro partnerstvo ta spivrobitnitsvo, yaki reguluyt sferu pidpriemnitsva ta investitsiy (pitania implementasii)", 2 Ukrainskiy Pravoviy Chasopys 31-35 (1998)

Muraviov V., "Pytannia harmonisatsii vnutrishnogo prava neassociovannykh krain z pravom Evropeyskogo Souzy" 4 Pidpriemnitsvo, hospodarstvo ta pravo 91-94 (2003)

Muraviov V., *Pravovi zasady regulyvania ekonomichikh vidnosyn Evropeiskogo Souzy z tretimy krainamy (teoria I praktika)*, (Kiev, Akadem Press 2002)

Muraviov V., "The Acquis Communautaire as a Basis for the Community Legal Order", 4(2) Miskolc Journal of International Law 38-45 (2007)

Müller-Graff P.-C., "The Legal Framework for the Enlargement of the Internal Market to Central and Eastern Europe", 6 MJICL 2 (1999)

Nazard J., "Soviet Yearbook on International Law 1987" 84(1) The American Journal of International Law, 303-305 (1990)

Neframi E., "The Duty of Loyalty: Rethinking its Scope through its Application in the Field of EU External Relations", 47 CML Rev. 323–359 (2010)

Nicolaides P., "Preparing for Accession to the European Union: How to Establish Capacity for Effective and Credible Application of EU Rules" in M. Cremona, ed., *The Enlargement of the European Union*, (Oxford University Press 2003)

Nicolaides P. / Boean S. R. / Bellon F. / Pezaros P., A Guide to the Enlargement of the European Union (ii). A Review of the Process, Negotiations, Policy Reforms and Enforcement Capacity, (Maastricht, European Institute of Public Administration 1999)

Oliver P., Roth W.-H., "The Internal Market and the Four Freedoms", 41 CML Rev. 407-441 (2004)

Örücü E., "Turkey Facing the European Union – Old and New Harmonies", 25(5) EL Rev. 523-537 (2000)

Örücü E., "Seven Packages Towards Harmonisation with the European Union", 10(4) EPL 603-621 (2004)

Ott A./ Inglis K. (eds.) *Handbook on European Enlargement: a Commentary on the Enlargement Process*, (The Hague, T.M.C. Asser Press 2002)

Phinnemore D., "Stabilisation and Association Agreements: Europe Agreements for the Western Balkans?", 8 EFA Rev. 77-103 (2003)

Peers S. in "EC Frameworks of International Relations: Co-operation, Partnership and Association" in A. Dashwood and C. Hillion (eds.), *The General Law of EC External Relations* (London: Sweet & Maxwell, 2000), pp. 161-176

Pescatore P., "Aspects judiciaries de l'acquis communautaire", RTDE 617-651 (1981)

Pescatore P., "The Doctrine of "Direct Effect": An Infant Disease of Community Law", 8 EL Rev. 135-155 (1983)

Petrov R., "Rights of third country/NIS nationals to pursue economic activity in the EC", 4(2) EFA Rev. 235-253 (1999)

Petrov R., 'The Partnership and Cooperation Agreements with the Newly Independent States' in A. Ott & K. Inglis (eds.), *European Enlargement Handbook* (The Hague, T.M.C. Asser Press 2002), pp. 175-194

Petrov R., "Recent developments in the adaptation of Ukrainian legislation to EU law", 8(5) EFA Rev. 125-141 (2003)

Petrov R., "Past and Future Action on Approximation of Ukrainian Legislation to that of the EU", 1 Sussex European Institute Seminar Papers Series 58 – 66 (2006)

Petrov R., "The dynamic nature of the acquis communautaire in EU external relations", 8(2) European Review of Public Law 741-771 (2006)

Petrov R., "Legal and Political Expectations of Neighboring Countries from the European Neighborhood Policy" in The European Neighbouhood Policy: A Framework for Modernisation? (eds: M. Cremona and G. Meloni), EUI Law Working Paper, 2007/21, 7-22

Petrov R., "Exporting the acquis communautaire into the legal systems of third countries", 13(1) EFA Rev. 33-52 (2008)

Petrov R., "Legal basis and scope of the new EU-Ukraine enhanced agreement. Is there any room for further speculation?" European University Institute Working Papers, 2008/17

Reymond C., "Institutions, decision-making procedure and settlement of disputes in the European Economic Area", 30 CML Rev. 449-462 (1993)

Prechal S., "Free Movement and Procedural Requirements: Proportionality Reconsidered", 35(3) LIEI 201-216 (2008)

Prescott N., "Orange Revolution in Red, White, and Blue: U.S. Impact on the 2004 Ukrainian Election", 16 Duke J. of Comp. & Int. Law 219-248 (2006)

Shaw J., "Constitutional Settlements and the Citizen After Amsterdam," in K. Neunreither / A. Wiener (eds), *Institutional Dynamics and Prospects for Democracy* (Oxford University Press 1999)

Schimmelfennig F., Engert S., Knobel H., "Cost, Commitment and Compliance: The Impact of EU Democratic Conditionality on Latvia, Slovakia and Turkey", 41 JCMS 495–518 (2003)

Schwok R., *Switzerland-European Union. An Impossible Membership?*, (P.I.E. Peter Lang Publisher 2009)

Schütterle P., "State Aid Control- An Accession Criterion", 39 CML Rev. 577-590 (2002)

Schuilenburg K., "The ECJ Simutenkov Case: Is Same Level not Offside after All?" 13 Policy Papers on Transnational Economic Law (2005) available at <http://www2.jura.uni-halle.de/telc/PolicyPaper13.pdf>, last visited 18 December 2010

Selivon M., "Harmonistsia natsionalnogo zakonodavstva z normami mizhnarodnogo prava i yogo vykorystannia Konstitutsiynym Sudom Ukraini", 3 Vystnyk Konstitutsiynogo Sydy Ukrainy 36-51 (2003)

Senden L., *Soft Law in European Community Law* (Oxford, Hart Publishing 2004)

Thallinger G., "From Apology to Utopia: EU–ECP Economic Partnership Agreements Oscillating between WTO Conformity and Sustainability", 12(4) EFA Rev. 499-516 (2007)

Tatham, A., "Constitutional Judiciary in Central Europe and the Europe Agreement: Decision 30/1998 (VI.25) AB of the Hungarian Constitutional Court". 48(4) ICLQ 913-920 (1999).

Temchenko V., "Vydnosyny mizh praktikoy ECtHR i jurisprudentsii Konstitutsiynogo Sydy Ukrainy", 4 Vystnyk Konstitutsiynogo Sydy Ukrainy 91-99 (2007)

Temple Lang J., "The duties of cooperation of national authorities and courts under Article 10 EC: Two more reflections", 26 EL Rev. 84-93 (2001)

Toth A., *Oxford Encyclopedia of European Community Law*, (Oxford: Clarendon Press 1990)

Toth T., "Competition Law in Hungary: Harmonisation towards EU Membership", 19(6) ECLR 358-369 (1998)

Tridimas T. *General Principles of EU Law,* (2d Ed. Oxford University Press 2007)

Usher J. *General Principles of EC Law* (London and New York, Longman 1998)

Vahl M., and Grolimund N., Integration without Membership. Switzerland's Bilateral Agreements with the European Union (Brussels, Centre for European Policy Studies 2006)

Van Elsuwege P., *From Soviet Republics to EU Member States. A Legal and Political Assessment of the Baltic States' Accession to the European Union* (Leiden: Martinus Nijhoff, 2008)

Van Vooren B., "A case-study of "soft law" in EU external relations: the European Neighbourhood Policy" 34 ELRev 696-719 (2009)

Volkai J., "The application of the Europe Agreement and European Law in Hungary: the judgment of an activist constitutional court on activist notions", Harvard Jean Monnet Working Paper 8/99 (Harvard Law School, 2000)

Voklai J., "Solutions to the Unconstituonality of the EC-Hungary Antitrust Cooperation Regime: Anti-Trust or Antitrust Cooperation?", CJEL 321-359 (2000)

Von Bogdandy A., "The Legal Case for Unity: The European Union as a Single Organisation with a Single Legal System" 36 CML Rev. 887-910 (1999)

Weatherill S., "Safequarding the *Acquis Communautaire*", in T. Heukels / N. Blokker/M. Brus (eds), *The European Union after Amsterdam,* (The Hague/London/Boston, Kluwer Law International 1998) 153-178

Wiener A., "The Embedded Acquis Communautaire: Transmission Belt and Prism of New Governance", 3 ELJ 294-315 (1998)

Wiener A., *European Citizenship Practice: Building Institutions of a Non-State* (Westview Press 1998)

Weiler J.H.H., "The Constitution of Europe "Do the new clothes have an emperor?" and other essays on European integration" (Cambridge University Press 1999)

Wellens K. C. / Borchardt G. M., "Soft Law in European Community Law", 14 EL Rev. 267-321 (1989)

Wyatt D., "New Legal Order or Old?", 7 EL Rev. 147-148 (1982)

Xanthaki H., "Trasposition of EC Law for EU Approximation and Accession: The Task of National Authorities", VII European Journal of Law Reform 89-110 (2005)

Xanthaki H., "Legislation transplants in legislation: defusing the trap", 57 ICLQ 659-673 (2008)

Zabludovsky J., "The Mexico-EU Free Trade Agreement: A Strategic Instrument to Position Mexico as the Transatlantic Hub for Trade and Investment", 6 EFA Rev. 147-154 (2001)

Table of Cases

European Court of Justice and Court of First Instance (now General Court)

Case 6/54 *Netherlands v High Authority* [1954-6] ECR 103
Case 13/61 *De Geus v Bosch* [1962] ECR 45
Case 26/62 *Van Gend en Loos v Nederlandse Administratie der Belastingen* [1963], CMLR 105
Case 32/62 *Alvis v Council* [1963] ECR 49
Joint Cases 90 and 91/63 *Commission v Luxemburg and Belgium* [1964] ECR 625
Case 108/63 *Merlini v High Authority* [1965] ECR 1
Case 6/64 *Costa v ENEL* [1964] ECR 585
Joint Cases 18 and 35 /65 *Gutmann v EAEC Commission* [1966] ECR 103
Joint Cases 63 to 69/72 *Werhahn and others v Council and Commission* [1973] ECR 1229
Case 5/67 *Beus v Hauptzollamt München* [1968] ECR 83
Case 27/67 *Fink-Frucht v HZA München-Landsbergerstrasse* [1968] ECR 223
Case 29/69 *Stauder v Ulm* [1969] ECR 419
Case 9/70 *Grad v Finganzamt Traunstein* [1970] ECR 825
Case 11/70 *Internationale Handelsgesellschaft v Einfuhr-und Vorratsstelle Getreide* [1970] ECR 1125
Case 32/71 *Sabbatini v European Parliament* [1972] ECR 345
Case 21-4/72 *International Fruit Co NV v Produktaschap voor Groenten en Fruit (№ 3)* [1972] ECR 1219
Case 4/73 *Nold v Commission* [1974] ECR 491
Case 10/73 *Rewe Central v Hauptozollant Kehl* [1973] ECR 1175
Case 167/73 *Commission v France* [1974] ECR 359
Case 181/73 *Haegeman v Belgium* [1974] ECR 449
Case 185/73, *Hauptzollamt Bielefeld v König* [1974] ECR 607
Case 17/74 *Transocean Marine Paint Association* [1974] ECR 1064
Case 41/74 *van Duyn v Home Office* [1974] ECR 1337
Case 2/75 *EVGF v Mackprang* [1975] ECR 607
Case 38/75 *Douaneagent der NV Nederlandse Spoorwegen v Inspecteur der Invoerrechten en Accijzen* [1975] ECR 1439
Case 43/75 *Defrenne v Sabena* [1976] ECR 455
Case 55/75 *Balkan v HZA Berlin-Packhof* [1976] ECR 11
Case 59/75 *Pubblico Ministero v Flavia Manghera and others* [1976] ECR 91
Opinion 1/76 [1977] ECR 741
Joint Cases 117/76 and 16/77 *Ruckdeschel v HZA Hamburg-St Annen* [1977] ECR 1753
Joint Cases 80 and 81/77 *Commissionnaires Rèunis et Ramel* [1978] ECR 927

Case 106/77 *Amministrazione delle Finanze dello Stato v Simmental* [1978] ECR 629
Case 142/77 *Statenskontrol v Larsen* [1978] ECR 1543
Case 99/78 *Weingut Gustav Decker KG v Hauptozollamt Landau* [1979] ECR 101
Case 230/78 *Eridania v Minister for Agriculture and Foresty* [1979] ECR 2749
Case 44/79 *Hauer v Land RheinlandPfalz* [1979] ECR 3727
Case 102/79 *Commission v Belgium* [1980] ECR 1473
Case 136/79 *National Panasonic v Commission* [1980] ECR 2033
Case 155/79 *AM & S Europe v Commission* [1982] ECR 1575
Case 812/79 *Attorney-General v Burgoa* [1980] ECR 2961
Case 270/80 *Polidor Ltd. V Harlequin Record Shops* [1982] ECR 329
Case 104/81 *Hauptzollamt Mainz v C.A. Kupferberg* [1982] ECR 3641
Case 230/81 *Luxemburg v Parliament* [1983] ECR 255
Case 266/81 *SIOT v Ministero delle Finanze* [1983] ECR 731
Joint Cases 286/82 and 26/83 *Luisi and Carbone* [1984] ECR 377
Case 14/83 *Von Colson v Land Nordrhein – Westfalen* [1984] ECR 1891
Case 63/83 *R v Kirk* [1984] ECR 2689
Case 117/83 *Karl Könecke GmbH v Bundesanstalt für landwirtschaftliche Marktordung* [1984] ECR 3291
Case 293/83 *Cravier v City of Liège* [1985] ECR 593
Case 294/83 *"les Verts" v European Parliament* [1986] ECR 1339
Case 44/84 *Hurd v Jones* [1986] 46 CMLR 2, 42
Case 67/84 *Sideradria v Commission* [1985] ECR 3983
Case C-152/84 *Marshall v Sauthampton and South West Hampshire Area Health Authority* [1986] ECR 723
Case 222/84 *Johnston v Chief Constable of the RUC* [1986] ECR 1651
Case 236/84 *Malt v HZA Düsseldorf* [1986] ECR 1923
Joined Cases 194/85 and 241/85 *Commission v Greece* [988] ECR 1037
Case 12/86 *Demirel v Stadt Schwäbisch Güdn* [1987] ECR 3719
Case 34/86 *Council v European Parliament* [1986] ECR 2155
Case 222/86 *UNECTEF v Heylens* [1987] ECR 4097
Case 316/86 *Firma P. Krücken* [1988] ECR 2213
Joint Cases 46/87 and 227/88 *Hoechst v Commission* [1989] ECR 2859
Case 70/87 *Fediol v Commission* [1989] ECR 1781
Case C-85/87 *Dow Benelux v Commission* [1989] ECR 3137
Case 186/87 *Cowan v Trésor public* [1989] ECR 195
Case C-265/87 *Schräder v Hauptzollamt Gronau* [1989] ECR 2237
Case C-374/87 *Orkem v Commission* [1989] ECR 3283
Case 5/88 *Hubert Wachauf v Federal Republic of Germany* [1989] ECR 2609
Case 2/88 *J.J. Zwartveld and Others* [1990] ECR 3365
Case C-331/88 *R v Minister of Agriculture, Fisheries and Food and the Secretary of State for Health, ex p. Fedesa* [1990] ECR I-4023
Case C-37/89 *Weiser v Caisse Nationale des Barreaux Français* [1990] ECR I-2395

Case C-44/89 *Gorg von Deetzen v Hauptzollamt Oldenburg (II)* [1991] ECR I-5119

Case C-69/89 *Nakajima v Council* [1991] ECR I-2069

Case C-106/89 *Mareleasing SA v La Comercial Internacional de Alimentacion SA* [1992] 1 CMLR 305

Case C-174/89 *Hoche v Bundesanstalt für landwirtschaftliche Marktordnung* [1990] ECR I-2681

Case C-192/89 *Sevince v Staatssecretaris van Justitie* [1990] ECR 3461/3501

Case C-213/89 *R v Secretary of State for Transport, ex parte Factortame* [1990] ECR I-2433

Case 309/89 *Codorniu v Council* [1994] ECR I-1853

Jointed Cases C-6 and C-9/90 *Francovich and Bonifaci v Italy* [1991] ECR I-5357

Case C-18/90 *Onem v Kziber* [1991] ECR I-199

Case C-286/90 *Anklegemindigheden v Poulsen and Diva Navigation* [1992] ECR I-6019

Opinion 1/91 on the first draft of the EEA Agreement [1991] ECR I-6079

Jointed Cases C-31-44/91 *SpA Alois Lageder and others* [1993] ECR I-1761

Case C-146/91 *Zuckerfabrik Schöppenstedt* [1994] ECR I-4199

Case C-188/91 *Deutsche Shell v Hauptzollamt Hamburg-Hamburg* [1993] ECR I-363

Opinion 1/92 on the second draft of the EEA Agreement [1992] ECR 2821

Case C-135/92 *Fiscano v Commission* [1994] ECR I-2885

Case C-353/92 *Creece v Council* [1994] ECR I-3411

Joint Cases C-46/93 and C-48/93 *Brasserie du Pecheur v Germany and The Queen v Secretary of State for Transport, ex-p Factorame* [1996] ECR I-1029

Case C-47/93 *Commission v Belgium* [1994] I-ECR 1593

Case C-63/93 *Duff and Others v Minister for Agriculture and Food, Ireland, and the Attorney-General* [1996] ECR I-569

Case C-65/93 *Parliament v Council* [1995] ECR I-643

Case C-143/93 *Gebroeders van Es Douane Agenten BV v Inspecteur der Invoerrechten en Accijnzen* [1996] ECR I-431

Case C-280/93 *Germany v Council* [1994] ECR I-4973

Case C-355/93 *Hayriye Eroglu v Land Baden-Württemberg* [1994] ECR I-5117

Opinion 2/94 [1994] ECR I-1759

Case C-13/94 *P v S and Cornwall County Council* [1996] ECR I-2143

Case C-38/94 *The Queen v Minister of Agriculture, Fisheries and Food, ex parte Country Land-owners Association* [1995] ECR I-3875

Jointed Cases C-178, C-179, C-188 to C-190/94 *Dillenkofer and Others v Federal Republic of Germany* [1996] ECR I-4845

Case C-61/94 *Commission v Germany* [1996] ECR I-3969

Case T-115/94 *Opel Austria GmbH v Council,* [1997] ECR II-39

Case C-268/94 *Portugal v Council* [1996] ECR

Case C-70/95 *Sodemare v Regione Lombardia,* [1997] ECR I-3395

Case C-84/95 *Bosphorus Hava Yollari Tourism ve Ticaret AS v Minister for Transport and the Attorney General* [1996] ECR I-3953

Case C-185/95 *Baustahlgewebe GmbH v Commission* [1998] ECR I-8417

Case C-409/95 *Marshall v Land Nordrhein Westfalen* [1997] ECR I-6363

265

Case C-162/96 *Racken v Hauptzollampt Mainz* [1998] ECR I-3641
Case C-233/96 *Kingdom v Denmark v Commission* [1998] ECR I-5769
Case C-375/96 *Galileo Zaninotto v Ispettorato Centrale* [1998] ECR I-6629
Jointed Cases C-36-37/97 *Hilmar Kellinghusen v Amt für Land-und Wasserwirtschaft Kiel and Ernst-Detlef Ketelsen v Amt für Land-und Wasserwirtschaft Husum* [1998] ECR I-6337
Case C-257/99 *The Queen v Secretary of State for the Home Department, ex parte: Barkoci and Malik* [2001] ECR I-6557
Case C-63/99 The *Queen v Secretary of State for the Home Department, ex parte: Gloszczuk* [2001] ECR I-6369
Case C-235/99 *The Queen v Secretary of State for the Home Department, ex parte: Kondova* [2001] ECR I-6427
Case C-268/99 *Jany and Others v Staatssecretaris van Justitie* [2001] ECR I-8615
Opinion 1/00 on Common European Aviation Area [2002] ECR I-3493
C-162/00 *Land Nordrhein-Westfalen v Pokrzeptowicz-Meyer* [2002] ECR I-1049
Case C-13/00 *Commission v Ireland* [2002] ECR I-2943
Case C-239/03 *Commission v France* [2004] ECR I-9325
Joined Cases C-354/03, C-355/03, and C-484/03 *"Optigen Ltd."* [2006] ECR 483
Case C-265/03 *Simutenkov v Ministerio de Educacion y Cultura, Real Federacion Espanola de Futbol* [2005] ECR I-02579
Case C-384/04 *"Federation of Technological Industries"* [2006] ECR 4191
Joint Cases C-402/05 and C-415/05 *Ahmed Ali Yusuf and Al Barakaat International Foundation v Council and Commission; Yassin Abdullah Kadi v Council and Commission* [2008] ECR I-6351.

European Free Trade Area Court

Case E-1/94 *Ravintoloitsijain Liiton Kustannus Oy Restamark v Helsingin piiritullikamari*, 1994-1995 EFTA Court Report, 15
Case E-6/96 *Tore Wilhelmsen AS v Oslo kommune*, 1997 EFTA Court Report, 53
Case E-2/97 *Mag Instrument Inc. v California Trading Company (Maglite)* (Judgment of the EFTA Court of 3d December 1997)
Case E-7/97 *EFTA Surveillance Authority v Norway*, 1998 EFTA Court Report, 62
Case E-8/97 *TV 1000 Sverige AB v The Norwegian Government*, 1998 EFTA Court Report, 68
Case E-9/97 *Erla Maria Sveinbjörnsdottir v the Government of Iceland* (Judgment of the EFTA of 10th December 1998)
Case E-10/97 *EFTA Surveillance Authority v Norway*, 1998 EFTA Court Report, 134
Case E-3/98 *Herbert Rainford-Towning*, 1998 EFTA Court Report, 205
Case E-5/98 *Fagtún ehf v Byggingarnefnd Borgarholtsskóla, íslenska ríkinu, Reykjavíkur og Mosfellsbær*, 1999 EFTA Court Report, 51
Case E-1/99 *Storebrand Skadeforsikring AS v Veronika Finanger*, 1999 EFTA Court Report, 119
Case E–2/99 *EFTA Surveillance Authority v Norway*, 2000-2001 EFTA Court Report, 1

Case E-1/00 *State Debt Management Agency v Íslandsbanki-FBA*, 2000-2001 EFTA Court Report, 8

Case E-1/01 *Hörður Einarsson v The Icelandic State*, 2002 EFTA Court Report, 1

Case E-4/01 *Karl K. Karlsson v The Icelandic State*, 2002 EFTA Court Report, 240

Case E-1/02 *EFTA Surveillance Authority v Kingdom of Norway*, 2003 EFTA Court Report, 1

Case E-2/02 *Technologien Bau- und Wirtschaftsberatung GmbH and Bellona Foundation v EFTA Surveillance Authority*, 2003 EFTA Court Report, 52

Case E-1/03 *EFTA Surveillance Authority v Iceland*, 2003 EFTA Court Report, 143

Case E-2/03 *Ákæruvaldið (The Public Prosecutor) v Ásgeir Logi Ásgeirsson, Axel Pétur Ásgeirsson and Helgi Már Reynisson*, 2003 EFTA Court Report, 185

Case E-1/04 *Fokus Bank ASA*, 2004 EFTA Court Report, 11

Joined Cases E-5/04, E-6/04 and E-7/04 *Fesil and Finnfjord and Others v EFTA Surveillance Authority*, 2005 EFTA Court Report, 117

Case E-8/04 *EFTA Surveillance Authority v the Principality of Liechtenstein*, 2005 EFTA Court Report, 46

Case E-2/05 *EFTA Surveillance Authority v Iceland*, 2005 EFTA Court Report, 202

Case E-3/05 *EFTA Surveillance Authority v The Kingdom of Norway* (Judgment of 3 May 2006)

ECtHR, Constitutional and High Courts of Central and Eastern European countries

Case *Hornsby v Greece* [19 March 1997], ECtHR Reports, 1997-II

Judgment of Czech Constitutional Court on *Scoda Auto* (Collection of decisions of the Czech Constitutional Court, vol. 8, p. 149).1997

Judgment of the Czech High Court in the *Olomouc* case (2A6/96)

Judgment of the Czech Constitution Court in the *Olomouc* case (III.US 31/97-35).

Decision of the Hungarian Constitutional Court 30/1998 (VI.25.)

Decision of the Polish Constitutional Court 15/97 OTK [*Orzecznictwo Trybunalu Konstytucyjnego, the collection of decisions of the Constitutional Tribunal*], nr. 19/1997

Judgment of the Constitutional Court of Ukraine on constitutionality of the International Criminal Court Statute, № 3-в/2001, 11 July 2001 (case №1-35/2001).

Decision 30/1998 (VI.25) AB of the Hungarian Constitutional Court

Judgment on 22 June 2004, No. 28/296-03-6901 of the High Commercial Court of Ukraine

Case *Closed Stock Company "Chumak" v Kherson Custom Office* on March 25 2005 No. 7/299 by High Commercial Court of Ukraine

Case *"Odek" LTD v Ryvne Custom Office* on February 22 2005 No. 18/303 by High Commercial Court of Ukraine

Judgment of the Constitutional Court of Ukraine, June 12 2007, No. 2/2007

Judgment of the Constitutional Court of Ukraine on the retirement age of civil servants, № 8/2007, 16 October 2007 (case №8/2007)

Judgment of the Constitutional Court of Ukraine on establishment of political parties, № 2/2007, 12 June 2007 (case №2/2007)

Judgment of the Kiev District Administrative Court, 22 May 2008, No. 4/48 and Judgment on 13 October 2008 No. 4/375

Judgment of the Kiev District Administrative Court, 26 June 2008, No. 4/337

Judgment of the Kiev District Administrative Court, 10 November 10 2008, No. 5/435

Judgment of the Kiev District Administrative Court, 24 November 24 2008, No. 5/503

Judgment of the Kiev District Administrative Court, 25 November 25 2008, No. 2/416

Judgment of the Kiev District Administrative Court, 1 December 1 2008, No. 5/451

Table of Laws

EU legislation

Treaty on the European Union (O.J. 2010 C 83/13)
Treaty on the Functioning of the European Union(O.J. 2010 C 83/47)
Treaty of Lisbon (O.J. 2007 C 306/50)
Treaty establishing the European Community (O.J. 2006 C 321/1)
Draft EU Constitutional Treaty (O.J. 2004 C 310)
Charter of Fundamental Rights of the EU (O.J. 2000, C 364/1)
The Treaty establishing the Constitution for Europe (O.J. 2004 C 310)
Final Act concerning the conditions of accession to the EU by Austria, Finland, and Sweden (O.J. 1994, C 241/22)
Final Act to the Treaty of Accession to the EU by the Czech Republic, the Republic of Estonia, the Republic of Cyprus, the Republic of Latvia, the Republic of Lithuania, the Republic of Hungary, the Republic of Malta, the Republic of Poland, the Republic of Slovenia and the Slovak Republicand other related documents (O.J. 2003 L 236)

EU external agreements

Agreement between the Swiss Confederation and the EEC (O.J. 1972, L 300/189)
EEC-Turkey Association Agreement (O.J. 1973 C 113/2)
EEC-Jordan Euro-Mediterranean Association Agreement (O.J. 1978 L 268)
EEC-Lebanon Euro-Mediterranean Association Agreement (O.J. 1978 L 267)
EEC-Syria Euro-Mediterranean Association Agreement (O.J. 1978 L 269)
EEC-Egypt Euro-Mediterranean Association Agreement (O.J. 1978 L 266)
EEC-Algeria Euro-Mediterranean Association Agreement (O.J. 1978 L 263)
EEC-Switzerland Framework Agreement on Scientific and Technical Cooperation (O.J. 1985, L 313/6)
EEC-Argentina Framework Agreement (O.J. 1990 L 295/66)
EEC-Paraguay Framework Agreement (O.J. 1991 C 309/6)
EEC-Uruguay Framework Agreement (O.J. 1992 L 94/2).
EEC-Switzerland Transit Agreement of 2 May 1992 (O.J. 1992, L 373/6)
EC-Poland Association Agreement (O.J. 1993 L 348/2)
EC-Hungary Association Agreement (O.J. 1993 L 347/2)
European Economic Area Agreement (O.J. 1994, L 1/3)
EC-Czech Republic Association Agreement (O.J. 1994 L 360/2)
EC-Slovak Republic Association Agreement (O.J. 1994 L 359/2)
EC-Romania Association Agreement (O.J. 1994 L 357/2)

EC-Bulgaria Association Agreement (O.J. 1994 L 358/3)
EC-Republic of Belarus Partnership and Cooperation Agreement (COM (95)137 final)
EC-Brazil Framework Agreement (O.J. 1995 L 262)
EC-Turkmenistan Partnership and Cooperation Agreement (COM (97) 0693 final)
EC-Mexico Agreement on co-operation regarding the control of precursors and chemical substances frequently used in the illicit manufacture of narcotic drugs or psychotropic substances (O.J. 1997 L 077)
EC-Mexico Agreement on mutual recognition and protection of designations for spirit drinks (O.J. 1997 L 152)
EC-Switzerland Agreement on Mutual Cooperation in Custom Matters of 9 June 1997 (O.J. 1997, L 169/77)
EC-Russia Partnership and Cooperation Agreement (OJ 1997 L 327)
EC-South Korea Agreement on co-operation and mutual administrative assistance in customs matters (O. J. 1997 L 121)
EC-South Korea Agreement on telecommunications procurement (O. J. 1997 L 321)
EC-Tunisia Euro-Mediterranean Association Agreement (O.J. 1998 L 097)
EC-Lithuania Association Agreement (O.J. 1998 L 51/3)
EC-Latvia Association Agreement (O.J. 1998 L 26/3)
EC-Estonia Association Agreement (O.J. 1998 L 68/3)
EC-Ukraine Partnership and Cooperation Agreement (O.J. 1998, L 49)
EC-Moldova Partnership and Cooperation Agreement (O.J. 1998, L 181)
Agreement on Mutual Recognition in Relation to Conformity Assessment, Certificates and Markings between the European Community and Australia (O.J. 1998 L229/3)
Agreement on Mutual Recognition in Relation to Conformity Assessment between the European Community and New Zealand (O.J. 1998 L 229/62)
Agreement on Mutual Recognition between the European Community and Canada (O.J. 1998 L 280/3)
Agreement on Mutual Recognition between the European Community and the United States of America (O.J. 1999 L 31/3)
Agreement on Mutual Recognition of OECD Principles of Good Laboratory Practice (GLP) and Compliance Monitoring Programmes between the European Community and the State of Israel (O.J. 1999 L 263/10)
EC-Armenia Partnership and Cooperation Agreement (O.J. 1999, L 239)
EC-Azerbaijan Partnership and Cooperation Agreement (O.J. 1999, L 246)
EC- Georgia Partnership and Cooperation Agreement (O.J. 1999, L 205)
EC-Republic of Kazakhstan Partnership and Cooperation Agreement (O.J. 1999, L 196)
EC-Kyrgyz Republic Partnership and Cooperation Agreement (O.J. 1999, L 196)
EC-Uzbekistan Partnership and Cooperation Agreement (O.J. 1999, L 229)
EC-South Africa Trade, Development and Cooperation Agreement (O.J. 1999 L 311/3)
Inter-Regional Framework Agreement for Cooperation between the EC and its Member States and MERCOSUR (O.J. 1999 L 112)
Association Agreement with Slovenia (O.J. 1999 L 51/3)
EC-Mexico Trade, Development and Cooperation Agreement (O.J. 2000 L 276)
Cotonou Agreement (O.J. 2000 L 317/3)

EC-Israel Association Agreement O.J. 2000 L 147/1).

EC-South Korea Trade, Development and Cooperation Agreement (O.J. 2001 L 090)

Agreement on Mutual Recognition between the European Community and Japan (O.J. 2001 L 284/3)

Agreement between the European Community and the Swiss Confederation on mutual recognition in relation to conformity assessment (O.J. 2002 L 114/369)

EC-Switzerland Agreement on Scientific and Technological Cooperation (O.J. 2002, L 114/468)

EC-Switzerland Agreement on Specific Aspects of Government Procurement (O.J. 2002, L 114/430)

EC-Switzerland Agreement on Mutual Recognition in relation to Conformity Assessment (O.J. 2002, L 114/369)

EC-Switzerland Agreement on Trade in Agricultural Products (O.J. 2002, L 114/132)

EC-Switzerland Agreement on Air Transport (O.J. 2002, L 114/73)

EC-Switzerland Agreement on the Carriage of Goods and Passengers by Rail and Road (O.J. 2002, L 114/91)

EC-Switzerland Agreement on the Free Movement of Persons (O.J. 2002, L 114/6)

EC-FYROM Stabilisation and Association Agreement (O.J. 2004 L 084)

EC-Mexico Agreement on Scientific and Technological Cooperation (O.J. 2005 L 290).

Agreement between the European Community and the Swiss Confederation amending the Agreement between the European Economic Community and the Swiss Confederation of 22 July 1972 as regards the provisions applicable to processed agricultural products (O.J. 2005, L 23/19)

EC-Croatia Stabilisation and Association Agreement (O.J. 2005 L 026/48)

Agreement between the European Community and the Swiss Confederation concerning the participation of Switzerland in the European Environment Agency and the European Environment Information and Observation Network (O.J. 2006, L 90/37)

Agreement between the European Community and the Swiss Confederation on cooperation in the field of statistics (O.J. 2006, L 090)

Treaty on the European Energy Community (O.J. 2006 L 198)

EC-Albania Stabilisation and Association Agreement (O.J. 2006 L 300)

Agreement between the European Community and the Swiss Confederation providing for measures equivalent to those laid down in Council Directive 2003/48/EC on taxation of savings income in the form of interest payments (O.J. 2004, L 385/30)

Agreement on scientific and technological cooperation between the European Community and the European Atomic Energy Community, of the one part, and the Swiss Confederation (O.J. 2007 L 189)

Agreement between the European Community and the Swiss Confederation in the audiovisual field, establishing the terms and conditions for the participation of the Swiss Confederation in the Community programmes MEDIA Plus and MEDIA Training (O.J. 2006, L 90/23)

Agreement between the European Union, European Community and the Swiss Confederation on the Swiss Confederation's association with the implementation, application and development of the Schengen acquis (O.J. 2008 L 53/52)

Agreement between the European Community and the Swiss Confederation concerning the criteria and mechanisms for establishing the state responsible for examining a request for asylum lodged in a Member State or in Switzerland (O.J. 2008 L 53/5)

EC-Tajikistan Partnership and Cooperation Agreement (O.J. 2009 L 350)

EC-Montenegro Stabilisation and Association Agreement (O.J. 2010 L 108)

International Treaties

Rome Convention on the Law Applicable to Contractual Obligations of 19 June 1980 (O.J. 1980, L 266/1).

Brussels Convention on Jurisdiction and Enforcement of Judgments in Civil and Commercial Matters of 27 September 1968, (O.J. 1972, L 299/32)

EU secondary legislation and "soft law"

Advisory Opinion of the Commission to the Council of 1 October 1969 concerning the accession requests of the UK, Denmark, Ireland and Norway (Bull EC, Suppl. 9/10-1969)

Council Regulation 3906/89 on economic aid to the Republic of Hungary and the Polish People's Republic (O.J. 1989 L 375)

Council Resolution on relations between the EC and the EFTA states (O.J. 1990 C 15/336)

Council Decision of 26 February 1990 on the conclusion by the European Economic Community of an Agreement between the European Economic Community and the European Atomic Energy Community and the Union of Soviet Socialist Republics on trade and commercial and economic cooperation (O.J. 1990, L 68/1).

Council Regulation 443/92 on financial assistance and technical assistance to, and economic cooperation with, the developing countries in Asia and Latin America (O.J. 1992 L 52/1)

Resolution on the environmental aspects of the enlargement of the Community to include Sweden, Austria, Finland and Norway, adopted by the European Parliament on 18 January 1994 (O.J. 1994 C 44/49)

Joint Declaration on the ownership of fishing vessels (concerning Norway) (O.J. 1994 C 241/387)

Decision 7/94 of the EEA Joint Committee of 21 March 1994 to amend Protocol 47 and certain Annexes to the EEA Agreement (O.J. 1994 L 160/1)

White Paper "Preparation of the associated countries of Central and Eastern Europe for integration into the internal market of the Union" (COM (95) 163)

Presidency Conclusions of the European Council of Madrid of December 1995 (EU Bull., 12-1995)

Commission Communication "Community External Trade Policy in the Field of Standards and Conformity Assessment" (COM (1996) 564 final)

Council Regulation EC/1488/96 on financial and technical measures to accompany (MEDA) the the reform of economic and social structures in the framework of the Euro Mediterranean partnership (O.J. 1998 L 189)

Decision 1/95 of the EC-Turkey of the EC-Turkey Association Council of 22 December 1995 on implementing the final phase of the Customs Union (O.J. 1996 L 35/1)

Decision 1/96 of the EC-Turkey Customs Cooperation Committee laying down detailed rules for the application of Decision 1/95" (O.J. 1996 L 200/14)

Agenda 2000 (EU Bull. Suppl. 5/97)

Presidency Conclusions of the European Council of Luxembourg of December 1997 (EU Bull., 12-1997)

Decision 2/97 of the EC-Turkey Association Council establishing the list of Community instruments relating to the removal of technical barriers to trade and the conditions and arrangements governing their implementation by Turkey" (O.J. 1997 L 191/1)

Council and Commission Decision of 26 January 1998 on the conclusion of the PCA between the EC and their Member States and Ukraine (O.J. 1998 L 49)

Council Regulation 622/98 on assistance to the applicant States in the framework of the pre-accession strategy, and in particular on the establishment of Accession Partnerships (O.J. 1998 L 85)

Commission Communication of 12 March 1998 on Democratisation, the rule of law, respect for human rights and good governance: the challenges of the partnership between the European Union and the ACP (COM (1998) 146)

Council Decision of 19 March 1998 on the sharing of the costs of preparing film masters for the uniform format for residence permits (O.J. L 099)

Regular report of the Commission on progress towards accession by Poland (COM (1998) 712 final of 17 Dec 1998)

Presidency Conclusions of the European Council of Helsinki of December 1999 (EU Bull., 12-1999)

European Council Common Strategy towards Russia (O.J. 1999 L 157/1)

European Council Common Strategy towards Ukraine (O.J. 1999 L 331/1)

Presidency Conclusions, Cologne European Council (O.J. 1999 L 157/1)

Common Position of 27 May 1999 adopted by the Council on the basis of Article 34 of the Treaty on European Union, on negotiations relating to the Draft Convention on Cyber Crime held in the Council of Europe (O.J. 1999 L 142)

Council Regulation 1260/1999 laying down general provisions on the Structural Funds (O.J. 2000 L 161)

EC-Mexico Joint Council Decision 2/2000 for trade in goods (O.J. 2000 L 157)

EC-Mexico Joint Council Decision 2/2001 for trade in services (O.J. 2001 L 70)

EC Council Directive 78/2000 of 27 November 2000 establishing a general framework for equal treatment in employment and occupation (O.J. 2000 L 303/16)

Council Regulation 99/2000 concerning the provision of assistance to the partner States in Eastern Europe and Central Asia (O.J. 2000 L 012)

Council Regulation 2666/2000 on assistance for Albania, Bosnia and Herzegovina, Croatia, the Federal Republic of Yugoslavia and the Former Yugoslav Republic of Macedonia (O.J. 2000 L 038)

Council Regulation 99/2000 on TACIS (O.J. 2000 L 012)

Common Strategy of the EU on the Mediterranean Region (O.J. 2000 L 183)

Council Common Position on the application of specific measures to combat terrorism (O.J. 2001 L 344)

"Towards the Enlarged Union" Strategy Paper and Report of the Commission on the progress towards accession by each of the candidate countries (COM (2002) 700 final)

Council Joint Action on the European Union's contribution to combating the destabilising accumulation and spread of small arms and light weapons and repealing Joint Action (O.J. 2002 L 191)

Council Framework Decision on joint investigation teams (O.J. 2002 L 162)

Commission's 2002 Regular Report on Bulgaria's Porgress towards accession (COM (2002) 700 final)

Commission Communication "Updating and simplifying the Community acquis" (COM(2003) 71 final)

Communication from the Commission "Wider Europe-Neighbourhood: A New Framework for Relations with our Eastern and Southern Neighbours" (COM (2003) 104 final

Communication from the Commission "Paving the way for a New Neighbourhood Instrument" (COM(2003) 393 final)

Communication from the Commission "European Neighbourhood Policy Strategy Paper" COM(2004) 373 final

European Commission Opinion of 19 February 2003 on the applications for accession to the EU by the Czech Republic, the Republic of Estonia, the Republic of Cyprus, the Republic of Latvia, the Republic of Lithuania, the Republic of Hungary, the Republic of Malta, the Republic of Poland, the Republic of Slovenia and the Slovak Republicand other related documents (O.J. 2003 L 236)

Communication from the European Commission to the Council and European Parliament "The Western Balkans and European Integration" (COM (2003) 285 final)

Council Directive 83/2004 of April 29 2004 "On minimum standards for the qualification and status of third country nationals or stateless persons as refugees or a persons who otherwise need international protection and the content of the protection granted" (O.J. 2004 L 304)

Council Regulation 533/2004 on the establishment of European partnerships in the framework of the stabilization and association process, (O.J. 2004 L 86/1)

Council Regulation 2004/2003 of the European Parliament and the Council of November 4 2003 "On the regulations governing political parties at European level and the rules regarding their funding" (O.J. L 297)

The Third Annual European Commission's Report on the Stabilisation and Association process for South East Europe (COM(2004) 202/2 final)

Council Decision on the principles, priorities and conditions contained in the European Partnership with Croatia (COM(2004) 275 final)

Communication from the Commission "Opinion on Croatia's Application for Membership of the European Union" (COM(2004) 257 final)

Commission's 2004 Regular Report on Turkey's progress towards accession (SEC(2004) 1201)

The Third Annual European Commission's Report on the Stabilisation and Association process for South East Europe (COM(2004) 202/2 final)

Communication from the European Commission "European Neighbourhood Policy Strategy Paper" COM(2004) 373 final)

Council Decision of 25 October 2004 on the signing and on the provisional application of certain provisions of the Agreement between the European Union, the European Community and the Swiss Confederation concerning the Swiss Confederation's association with the implementation, application and development of the Schengen acquis (O.J. 2004 L 368/26 and O.J. 2004 L 370/78)

Communication from the Commission to the Council and the European Parliament "Building our common Future Policy challenges and Budgetary means of the Enlarged Union 2007-2013" (COM(2004) 101 final/2)

Communication from the Commission to the Council and the European Parliament on Financial Perspectives 2007 - 2013 (COM(2004) 487 final)

Council Decision of 30 January 2006 on the principles, priorities and conditions contained in the European Partnership with Serbia and Montenegro including Kosovo as defined by the United Nations Security Council Resolution 1244 of 10 June 1999 (O.J. 2006 L 35/32)

Council Decision of 30 January 2006 on the principles, priorities and conditions contained in the European Partnership with Bosnia and Herzegovina (O.J. 2006 L 35/19)

Council Decision of 30 January 2006 on the principles, priorities and conditions contained in the European Partnership with Albania (O.J. 2006 L 35/1)

European Parliament and the Council Regulation 1638/2006 laying down general provisions establishing a European Neighbourhood and Partnership Instrument (O.J. 2006 L 310/1)

Commission Working Document accompanying the Communication from the Commission to the Council and the European Parliament "On Strengthening the European Neighbourhood Policy" Progress Report on Ukraine (COM(2006) 726 final)

"Green Paper on Review of the Consumer Acquis" (COM (2006) 744 final)

Council Regulation 1085/2006 establishing an instrument for Pre-Accession Assistance (IPA) (O.J. 2006 L 210/49)

Regulation 1905/2006 of the European Parliament and the Council of Ministers establishing a financial instrument for development cooperation (O.J. 2006 L 378/41)

Communication from the Commission to the Council and the European Parliament "Black Sea Synergy – A New Regional Cooperation Initiative" (COM(2007) 160 final

2006 Annual Progress Report on the Implementation of the Northern Dimension Action Plan (SEC(2007) 791)

Council Decision of 22 January 2007 on the principles, priorities and conditions contained in the European Partnership with Montenegro (O.J. 2007 L 20/16)

Council Decision 2008/119/EC of 12 February 2008 on the principles, priorities and conditions contained in the Accession Partnership with Croatia (O.J. 2008 L 042/51)

Council Decision 2008/212/EC of 18 February 2008 on the principles, priorities and conditions contained in the Accession Partnership with the former Yugoslav Republic of Macedonia (O.J. 2008 L 080/32)

Council Decision 2008/157/EC of 18 February 2008 on the principles, priorities and conditions contained in the Accession Partnership with the Republic of Turkey (O.J. 2008 L 051/04)

Communication from the Commission "Enlargement Strategy and Main Challenges 2008-2009" (COM (2008) 674 final)

Communication from the Commission "Barcelona Process: Union for the Mediterranean" (COM(2008) 319 final)

Communication from the Commission and the European Parliament to the Council "Eastern Partnership" (COM (2008) 823 final)

Commission's Regular Report 2008 on Turkey's progress towards accession (SEC(2008) 2699)

Communication from the Commission "Enlargement Strategy and Main Challenges 2008-2009" (COM (2008) 674 final)

Communication from the European Commission "Enlargement Strategy and Main Challenges 2009-2010" (COM (2009) 533)

Ukrainian legislation

Law issued by the Verkhovna Rada of Ukraine "On ratification of the Partnership and Cooperation Agreement between the European Communities and their Member States and Ukraine", № 237/94-ВР

Law of the Verkhovna Rada of Ukraine "About the All State Programme of adaptation of Ukrainian legislation to that of the EU", 18 March 2004, No. 1629-IV

Law of the Verkhovna Rada of Ukraine "About application of decision of the European Court of Human Rights", adopted on February 23 2006, No. 3477-IV

Annex I

Scope of the Acquis Communautaire in EU External Agreements

	EEA Agreement	Europe Agreements	EC-Swiss SAs	SAAs	PCAs	Cotonou Agreement
Pre-negotiation acquis	NA	NA	NA	- High level of political respect for democratic principles, human rights, rule of law, protection of minorities, and return of refugees	NA	NA
Common values	- Preamble refers to long standing common values and European identity; - peace, de-	- Preamble refers to common values that [Parties] share; - pluralist democracy based on the rule of law, human rights, including the rights of	NA	- Preamble refers to values that [Parties] share; - civil society and democratisation, institution building and public administration re-	- Preamble refers to common values that [Parties] share; -political and economic freedoms which constitute the very basis of the partnership;	- Reference to Article 177(2) EC (now Art. 208 TFEU) "developing and consolidating democracy and the rule of

277

mocracy, and human rights	persons belonging to minorities, and fundamental freedoms; - a multiparty system involving free and democratic elections; - principles of a market economy and social justice		form, enhanced trade and economic cooperation, the strengthening of national and regional security, as well as increased cooperation in justice and home affairs; political and economic freedoms as the very basis of this Agreement; - respect human rights and the rule of law, including the rights of persons belonging to national minorities; - democratic principles through free and fair elections and a multiparty system; - principles of free market economy	- commitment of the Parties to promote international peace and security as well as the peaceful settlement of disputes; - paramount importance of the rule of law and respect of human rights, particularly those of minorities; - the establishment of multiparty system with free and democratic elections; - economic liberalisation aimed at setting up a market economy	law, and to that of respecting human rights and fundamental freedoms"; - Preamble refers to political environment guaranteeing peace, security and stability, respect for human rights, democratic principles and the rule of law; - principle of good governance is part and parcel of long term development; acknowledging that responsibility for establishing such an environment rests primarily with the countries concerned.
Essential ele-	NA	- respect for democ-	NA	- respect for democ-	- respect for democ-	- respect for hu-

ments of the agreement		ratic principles and human rights, established by the Helsinki Final Act (reference to the Universal Declaration of Human Rights in the Slovenia EA) and in the Charter of Paris for a New Europe; - respect for principles of market economy, as reflected in the Document of the CSCE Bonn Conference on Economic Cooperation (not Poland and Hungary EAs)	ratic and human rights principles as proclaimed in the Universal Declaration of Human Rights and as defined in the Helsinki Final Act and the Charter of Paris for a New Europe; - respect for international law principles and the rule of law as well as principles of market economy as reflected in the Document of the CSCE Bonn Conference on Economic Cooperation	ratic and human rights principles; - adherence to principles of market economy as defined in the Helsinki Final Act and the Charter of Paris for a New Europe including enunciated in the CSCE Bonn Conference	man rights, democratic principles; - adherence to the rule of law and good governance; - measures aimed at peace-building and conflict prevention
International law acquis	NA	- the Helsinki Final Act; - the concluding documents of the Madrid, Vienna and Co-	NA	- Principles and provisions contained in the Final Document of the Conference on Security and Cooperation	- the UN Charter; - the OSCE documents notably those of the Helsinki Final Act, the concluding documents	- the UN Charter; - the Universal Declaration of Human Rights; - conclusions of

penhagen meetings; - the Charter of Paris for a New Europe; - conclusions of the CSCE's Bonn Conference; - the CSCE Helsinki document 1992 ; - European Convention on Human Rights; - the European Energy Charter Treaty; - the Ministerial Declaration of the Lucerne Conference of 30 April 1993; - the WTO agreements; - basic international IP conventions; - Osimo Agreement in the EC-Slovenia EA	of the Madrid and Vienna Conferences, the Charter of Paris for a New Europe, and of the Stability Pact for south-eastern Europe'; - compliance with the obligations under the Dayton/Paris and Erdut Agreements; - the WTO agreements; - IMF legal acts	in Europe (CSCE); - the concluding documents of the Madrid and Vienna follow-up meetings; - documents of the CSCE Bonn Conference on economic cooperation, the 'Charter of Paris for a New Europe' and the CSCE Helsinki document 1992 'The Challenges of Change'; - the WTO rules on trade (free transit; fiscal discrimination, safeguard and exemption clause, anti-dumping, anti-subsidy); - basic international IP conventions; - European Energy Charter and the Decla-	the 1993 Vienna Conference on Human Rights; -the Covenants on Civil and Political Rights and on Economic, Social and Cultural Rights; - the Convention on the Rights of the Child; - the Convention on the Elimination of all forms of Discrimination against Women; - the International Convention on the Elimination of all forms of Racial Discrimination; - the 1949 Geneva Conventions on of international hu-

ration of the 1993 Lucerne Conference	manitarian law; - the 1954 Convention relating to the status of stateless persons; - the 1951 Geneva Convention relating to the Status of Refugees and the 1967 New York Protocol relating to the Status of Refugees; - the Cotonou Agreement refers to almost all regional Conventions on fundamental human rights that could be relevant to the ACP countries: the European Convention for the Protection of Human

Rights and Fundamental Freedoms, the African Charter on Human and Peoples' Rights and the American Convention on Human Rights. principles agreed in United Nations Conferences and set by the OECD Development Assistance Committee. Libreville and Santo Domingo declarations of the Heads of State and Government of the ACP countries at their Summits in 1997 and 1999; - ILO principles; - the WTO agree-

			ments; - Convention on Biological Diversity; - basic IP conventions and treaties	No discrimination in trade in goods and employment
Principle of non-discrimination	No discrimination on grounds of nationality, trade in goods; marketing and procurement; transport; state aids; equal pay for men and women	No discrimination on grounds of nationality, trade in goods; marketing and procurement; transport; state aids; equal pay; operation of companies; fiscal discipline; application of safeguard measures; free supply of services in international maritime transport; award of public contracts; access to courts and administrative organs	Prohibition of discrimination within areas of sectoral cooperation	No discrimination on grounds of nationality, trade in goods; marketing and procurement; transport; state aids; equal pay; operation of companies; fiscal discipline; application of safeguard measures; free supply of services in international maritime transport; award of public contracts; equal access to courts and administrative organs	No discrimination on grounds of nationality, trade in goods; marketing and procurement; transport; state aids; equal pay; operation of companies; fiscal discipline; application of safeguard measures; free supply of services in international maritime transport; award of public contracts; equal access to courts and administrative organs
ECJ case law	Provisions of the EEA	NA	- the SA on free movement of	NA	NA

		persons provides that 'account shall be taken of the relevant ECJ's case law prior the date of the [agreement's] signature'; - the SA on participation in the Schengen/Dublin acquis states that the Mixed Committee shall keep under constant review developments in the "post-signature" case law of the ECJ; - Provisions of the SA on air transport which are identical in	
	Agreement which are identical in substance to EC rules must be interpreted in conformity with relevant "pre-signature" ECJ rulings		

			substance to EC rules must be interpreted in conformity with relevant "pre-signature" ECJ rulings			
Relevant sectoral EC/EU acquis	- Binding references to *EC internal market acquis* (free movement of goods, services, people and capital; competition and state aids; procurement; product liability; energy; social security; transport); - Binding and soft references	- Soft references to EC acquis on free trade, agriculture; fisheries; services, capital, freedom of establishment, standards; - Binding and soft references to criteria arising from specific articles of the EC Treaty including present and future secondary legislation, frameworks, guidelines and other relevant administrative acts in force in the EC	Binding references to the relevant EC sectoral acquis in the text of the agreements and in the annexes	- Soft references to the EC acquis on free trade, statistical cooperation, banking, financial services, health and safety of workers, social cooperation, transport; - Soft references to the EC acquis in audio-visual field, cross-border broadcasting, acquisition of IP rights for programme and broadcast by satellite or cable, cooperation in electronic communications and associ-	- Soft references to selected EC provisions (prohibition of imports, exports or goods in transit is subject to derogations similar that listed in Article 30 EC (now Art. 36 TFEU)); - The Parties agreed 'to work to remedy or remove' restrictions on competition and to enforce competition laws to combat such restrictions references though without any references to the rele-	Provisions of the Cotonou Agreement on competition mirror relevant EC acquis

to *EC flanking policies acquis* (research and technological development; education; social policy; training, and youth; SME; tourism; audio visual services and access to justice); - Binding and soft references to *horizontal provisions relevant to the EC four freedoms* (social security, including health and safety at work, labour law and equal	ated services; - Binding and soft references to criteria arising from specific articles of the EC Treaty including present and future secondary legislation, frameworks, guidelines and other relevant administrative acts in force in the EC
	vant EC acquis; - requirement to acquire the level of IP protection equivalent to what is in the EC

	EC- South Africa TDCA	EC- South Korea TDCA	EC- Mexico TDCA	EC-MERCOUSUR IFA	EC-Cyprus EMAA
	treatment of men and women; consumer protection; environment; statistics, and company law)				
Pre-negotiation acquis	NA	NA	NA	NA	NA
Common values	- Preamble refers to 'common values that the Parties share', -rule of law, human rights	- No reference to common values; - the agreement is based on principles of free trade and market economy	- No reference to common values; - references to common cultural heritage and the strong historical, political and	NA	NA

	and democracy, principles of international trade.	economic ties which unite the Parties		
Essential elements	- Respect for democratic principles and fundamental Human Rights as laid down in the Universal Declaration on Human Rights; - principles of the rule of law; - principle of good governance	Respect for democratic principles and human rights as defined in the Universal Declaration on Human Rights	- Respect for democratic principles and fundamental human rights, proclaimed by the Universal Declaration of Human Rights; - Preamble refers to the principles of the rule of law and good governance, as set out in the Rio Group/European Union Ministerial Declaration adopted in Sio Paulo in 1994); principles of	- Respect for the democratic principles and fundamental of human rights established by the Universal Declaration of Human Rights; - Adherence to the content and principles of the Charter of the United Nations and to democratic values, the rule of law and promoting and respecting human rights	NA

			market economy.		
International acquis	- the UN Charter, Universal Declaration on Human Rights; - principles of international trade and the need to apply them in transparent and non-discriminatory manner; - the WTO agreements; - documents of the Cairo International Conference, Copenhagen Summit, Beijing Women World Confer-	- the WTO agreements; - basic intellectual property (IP) international conventions; - internationally recognised standards on conformity assessment and data protection; - FATF documents in area of fight against money laundering; - OECD Shipbuilding Agreement	- Universal Declaration of Human Rights; - United Nations Charter, the principles of the rule of law and good government, as set out in the Rio Group/European Union Ministerial Declaration adopted in Sio Paulo in 1994; - Agreement on the Control of Drugs Precursors and Chemical Substances signed by the Parties on 13 December 1996; - the WTO	- the WTO agreements; - basic IP international conventions	- the GATT (dumping; subsidies)

	ence; - the ILO rules and standards; - basic IP international conventions	agreements related to liberalization of trade in goods and services; - the NAFTA agreements related to competition; - basic IP international conventions		- no internal fiscal discrimination; - non-discriminatory in goods and services
Principle of non-discrimination	- Prohibition of discrimination of nationals and firms; -non-discriminative application of custom duties of fiscal nature; - non-discriminatory application of	- Prohibition of discrimination of nationals and companies providing maritime transport services; - non-discriminatory application of public procurement rules (in accordance with WTO Government Procurement Agreement)	- non-discriminatory in goods; - no fiscal discrimination in respect of taxes imposed on goods, - fair competition, and public procurement rules and other trade related ar-	- non-discriminatory trade in goods and services; - fair competition, and public procurement rules and other trade related areas including IP	

290

	internal fiscal duties; - no discrimination in trade in goods and services; - non-discriminatory access to employment and occupation		eas including IP		
ECJ case law	NA	NA	NA	NA	NA
Relevant EC acquis	Provisions on competition mirror relevant EC acquis	Annex to the agreement contains the EC acquis on data protection. South Korea is bound to adhere to the EC acquis on data protection	Temporary application of the EC competition acquis criteria until adoption of the relevant decision by the Joint Committee	NA apart from soft approximation clause	Soft references to the EC customs acquis, EC competition acquis, EC agriculture acquis

Annex II

Export of the Acquis Communautaire in EU External Agreements

Agreement	Objective	Approximation clause	Substantive means of the acquis communautaire export	Procedural means of the acquis communautaire export	Legal force of the approximation clause	Interpretation of the agreement in accordance with the ECJ case law	Common institutions
EEA Agreement	- The creation of EC-EEA common rules and their effective enforcement; - a continuous and balanced strengthening of trade and economic relations between the Contracting Parties with equal	The principle of "homogeneity" provides: "In order to guarantee the legal security and the homogeneity of the EEA, the EEA Joint Committee shall take a decision concerning an amendment of	- Timely incorporation of the dynamic EC acquis into the EEA Agreement; - uniform interpretation of adopted EC acquis and EFTA rules	- Informal involvement of the EFTA Member States' experts into the EC legal drafting procedures; - the EEA Joint Committee takes a decision concerning the amendment of the EEA Agree-	- Binding and soft harmonisation commitments	- Provisions of the EEA Agreement that are identical in substance to corresponding EC rules must be interpreted in conformity with the relevant rulings of the "pre-signature" ECJ case law;	- EEA Council (takes political decisions leading to amendment of the agreement); - EEA Joint Committee (takes binding decisions); - EEA Joint Parliamentary Committee (non-binding reports

293

conditions of competition, and the respect of the same rules" with a view of creating a homogeneous EEA; - the equality of treatment of EC/EFTA undertakings and persons on the respective markets; - extension of the EC internal market four freedoms to the EFTA Member States; - fair competition; sectoral cooperation between the EC	an Annex to this Agreement as closely as possible to the adoption by the Community of the corresponding new Community legislation with a view to permitting a simultaneous application of the latter as well as of the amendments of the Annexes to the Agreement. To this end, the Community shall, whenever adopting a legislative act on an issue which is	- provisions of the EEA Agreement that are identical in substance to corresponding EC rules must be interpreted 'as uniform as possible' with relevant rulings of the "after signature" ECJ case law
	ment annexes as closely as possible to the corresponding dynamic EU acquis as to ensure the simultaneous application of new and old EEA annexes legislation; - constant review by the EEA Joint Committee of the ECJ and EFTA courts case law	and resolutions); - EEA Consultative Committee (non-binding reports and resolutions); - EFTA Surveillance Authority (binding decisions); -EFTA Court is competent to consider: 1) actions concerning the EFTA Member States surveillance procedure; (b) appeals concerning decisions in the field of competition taken by the EFTA Surveillance Authority; (c) the settlement

	and the EFTA Member States	governed by this Agreement, as soon as possible inform the other Contracting Parties in the EEA Joint Committee"					of disputes between two or more EFTA States
EC-Swiss SAs	- Liberalisation of mutual trade and relations within the SAs subject areas (free movement of persons; air transport; research; agriculture; overland transport; technical barriers; public procurement); - improvement of reciprocal,	- The SA on technical barriers bounds Switzerland 'to *adopt*, no later than six month after signature of this Agreement, arrangements that are equivalent to Community legislation on the technical conditions governing road transport';	- The possibility to conclude mutual recognition agreements subject to effective application of the relevant EC *acquis* in the Annexes to the SAs (seeds, certificates; professional qualifications); - binding and soft approximation clauses; - references to international and	- Joint Committee adopts decisions revising the annexes to incorporate and amend the relevant EC/EU *acquis* contained therein (the SA on the cooperation in the field of statistics); - informal involvement of Swiss experts into the drafting	- Binding and soft approximation commitments	- The SAs on free movement of persons envisages that: "insofar the application of this Agreement involves concepts of Community law, account shall be taken of the relevant case-law of the [ECJ] prior to the date of its signature. Case-	- Joint Committees or Mixed Committees (in case of the SA on the participation in the Schengen/Dublin acquis) have been set up with each SA (issue non-binding recommendations and binding decisions)

		law after that date shall be brought to Switzerland's attention"; - the SA on the participation in the Schengen/Dublin acquis provides that "the Mixed Committee shall keep under constant review developments in the case-law of the ECJ, and in the case-law relating to such provisions of the competent Swiss courts"
transparent and non-discriminatory access to mutual markets; -the SA on air transport bounds Switzerland to respect and adopt EC acquis in order to achieve the objectives of the agreement; -the SA on technical barriers targets setting up the regime of mutual recognition; - gradual harmonisation of the Swiss law with the relevant EC acquis	- the SA on agriculture contains the soft approximation clause "the Parties *shall endeavour to approximate* their laws on the marketing of seeds of the species' that are covered by the legislation listed in the relevant Appendixes"; - the SAs on statistical cooperation and on the participation in the Schengen/Dublin acquis envisage the application of the procedure	European standards; - references to the relevant EC/EU acquis in the annexes to the agreements; - the SA on free movement of persons envisages application of the "prior-signature" and "after-signature" ECJ case law by Switzerland: "insofar the application of this Agreement involves concepts of Community law, account shall be taken of the relevant case-law of the [ECJ] prior to the date of its signature. Case-law after that date shall be brought to Switzer-
		of the dynamic EC acquis; - informal advice from experts of the Parties when drafting new legislation in the field of mutual cooperation; - at the preparatory drafting stage Swiss experts are allowed to be informed and consulted 'as closely as possible' before and after the meetings of EU experts; - the exchange of information procedure presumes the formal notification of the newly adopted

("second generation" SAs); - participation of Swtzerland in the EU Schengen/Dublin acquis	similar to the homogeneity procedure in the EEA Agreement; - the SA on the media provides "Switzerland will implement the measures described in Annex II, with a view to completing its legislative framework so as to ensure the required level compatibility with the *acquis communautaire*"; - the SA on the participation in the Schengen/Dublin ac-	land's attention"	EC acquis to Switzerland and *vice versa* within 8 days

SAAs	- Enhanced political dialogue; -full and accelerated integration of the SAAs countries into the EU; -establishment of a free trade area and its transition into a market economy within the SAA countries; - approximation of the SAA countries legislation	- The EC-FYROM SAA approximation clause provides that the Parties "shall endeavour to ensure that its laws will be gradually make compatible with those of the Community"; - the EC-Croatia and the EC-Albania SAAs approximation clause provides	- Binding approximation clause; - soft harmonisation commitments; - binding commitment to implement basic international IP conventions; - setting up common systems compatible with European standards (audit system; operating standards; transport; energy); - promotion of usage of the EC standards	- Informal exchange of information concerning the functioning of the EC policies and institutions; - technical and financial assistance (IPA technical/financial assistance package) in the course of adopting the relevant EC acquis (providing services of ex-	Binding and non-binding approximation commitments	NA	- SAA Council (issues binding decisions and non-binding, recommendations); - SAA Committee (could be delegated by the SAA Council to issue binding decisions); - SAA Parliamentary Committee; - SAA Transport Committee is set up under the EC-FYROM Trans-

			port Agreement
lation to that of the EC that is the precondition of acquisition of the candidate country status	that Croatia and Albania "shall endeavour to ensure that its existing laws and future legislation will be gradually make compatible with the Community acquis"; - the EC-Albania SAA emphasises that "Albania shall ensure that existing and future legislation shall be properly implemented and enforced"; - approximation clauses envisage two stages of the approximation process (1st –	dards, tests and conformity assessment procedures in the SAA countries; -the EC sectoral acquis not as an objective but as a model or equivalent for the approximation process in the SAA countries	perts; organising information and training activities; modernisation and restructuring of specific sectors in consistence with EC rules and standards); - assistance in drafting national legislation in accordance with international and European standards; - "information and communication" procedure, which is aimed at the provision of general public with basic information about the

EAs	- Enhanced political dialogue; - close political relations; - expansion of trade and the harmonious	- EA's approximation clauses provided: "The Contracting Parties recognise that the major precondition for adoption of the internal market acquis and the acquis in other priority areas; 2d – other related areas) with the purpose to monitor the implementation and enforcement of the relevant EC acquis by the SAA countries by the end of each stage of the approximation process	- Binding and soft approximation clauses; - perspective to conclude mutual recognition agreements;	- Informal exchange of information concerning the functioning of the EC policies and institutions and priorities EU, functioning of the EC policies and institutions through educational events, trainings, and conferences	Binding and non-binding approximation commitments	NA	- Association Council (binding decisions; non-binding recommendations); - Association Committee (as-

economic relations; - gradual integration into the EC; - establishment of a free trade area	[...] integration into the Community is the approximation of [...] that country's [...] existing and future legislation to that of the Community"; - Polish and Hungarian EAs envisaged binding approximation clause: "[the Parties] shall act to ensure that future legislation is compatible with Community legislation as far as possible"; - other EAs contained soft approximation	- references to the EC acquis criteria (competition and state aids); -soft harmonization commitments; - promotion of the EC rules and standards; - improving national legislation taking as a reference the acquis communautaire.	ity sectors of co-operation; - technical and financial assistance (PHARE) in the course of adopting the relevant EC acquis (providing services of experts; organising information and training activities; translation assistance; modernisation and restructuring of specific sectors (agriculture, agro-industrial) in consistence with the EC rules and standards); - provision of early information	sists Council, delegated powers); - Association Parliamentary Committee (non-binding recommendations to the Association Council)

| | | clause: "[the Parties] shall endeavour to ensure that its legislation will be gradually made compatible with that of the Community" | and technical info especially on relevant legislation; - assistance in drafting national legislation in accordance with international and European standards; -"information and communication" procedure, which is aimed at the provision of general public with basic information about the EU, functioning of the EC policies and institutions through educational events, trainings, and |

			conferences		
Decision 1/95 of the EC-Turkey Association Council	- Establishment of the EC-Turkey customs union; - aligning the Turkish customs legislation to that of the EC	Decision 1/95 sets up the principle of harmonisation: "in areas of direct relevance to the operations of the Customs Union Turkish legislation shall be harmonized as far as possible with Community legislation"	- Binding harmonization commitments (specific deadlines for incorporation); - soft harmonizaton commitments (compatibility of Turkish laws with relevant dynamic EC acquis); - binding commitments to implement basic international IP conventions; - references to the relevant EC legal criteria in areas of competition and customs; - establishment of the mutual recognition regime for assessing industrial	- Informal exchange of information on drafting and adopting new laws by the EC and Turkey; - possibility to review and to suspend by either of the Parties the application of trade defense measures based on the evaluation of the progress of harmonization of legislation	Binding and soft harmonisation commitments	Provisions of the Decision, which are identical in substance to the corresponding provisions of the EC acquis, should be interpreted in conformity with the relevant ECJ case law	Association Council (binding decisions and non-binding recommendations)

Decision 2/97 of the EC-Turkey Association Council	Incorporation and implementation of the EC customs acquis (removal of technical barriers to trade) into Turkish legal order in light of the Decision 1/95 objectives	Incorporation of the relevant EC acquis takes place on the same foundations as the incorporation of the EC acquis by the Member States	products in conformity with the EC acquis - Binding adoption of the relevant EC acquis in sectors of mutual trade	- Formal and binding exchange of information and notification procedures between Turkey and the EC; - Commission is bound to share its reports and assessments with Turkey	Binding harmonisation commitments	Provisions of the Decision, which are identical in substance to the corresponding provisions of the EC acquis, should be interpreted in conformity with the relevant ECJ case law	Association Council (binding decisions and non-binding recommendations)
EC – Israel Association Agreement	- Support of lasting relations, based on reciprocity and partnership and promotion of further integra-	Approximation clause provides that "the Parties shall use their best endeavours to approximate their respective	- Soft references to the WTO rules on trade, competition, public procurement, and IP; - soft harmonisation in areas of agricul-	- Exchange of information, experiences and know-how; - exchange of information and where appropri-	Binding and soft harmonisation commitments	NA	- Association Council (binding decisions and soft recommendations); - Association Committee (bind-

304

	tion of Israel's economy into the European economy; - liberalisation of trade in goods and services, public procurement, rights of establishment, free movement of capital, intensification of sectoral cooperation; - improvement of cross border trade through establishment of customs unions, free trade areas or other arrangements	laws in order to facilitate the implementation of this Agreement"	ture, information and telecommunications; - mutual recognition procedure is envisaged in the area of standards to "reduce differences in standardisation and conformity assessment"	ate joint activities on drafting and implementation of national legislation; - joint training activities; - technical assistance (ENPI financial package)		ing decisions and soft recommendations)
EC-Tunisia Association	- Gradual liberalisation of trade	Approximation clause provides	- Binding harmonisation commitments	- Exchange of information on re-	Binding and soft harmoni-	NA	- Association Council (binding

| Agreement | in goods, services and capital; - promotion of trade and the expansion of harmonious economic and social relations between the Parties; - gradual establishment of a free trade area over a transitional period lasting a maximum of 12 years | that "Cooperation shall be aimed at helping Tunisia to bring its legislation closer to that of the Community in the areas covered by this Agreement" | in areas of competition and state aids; - soft harmonisation commitments in area of technical rules and standardisation, metrology, quality control and conformity assessment; - liberalisation of trade in goods and services, payments and movement of capital, establishment and services in accordance with the WTO rules; - perspective to conclude mutual recognition agreements on certifications "when the circumstances are right" | quest by either of the Parties; - technical assistance (ENPI financial package) to support legal drafting, joint training activities in Tunisia | sation commitments | | decisions and non-binding recommendations); - Association Committee (binding decisions and soft recommendations) |

| PCAs | - Close political relations; - promotion of trade, investment and harmonious economic relations between the Parties; - mutually advantageous cooperation and support of a PCA country efforts to complete its transition into a market economy | The PCA approximation clause provides that the Parties "endeavor to ensure' the gradual compatibility of its legislation to EC laws within priority areas" | - Binding harmonisation commitments to adopt the WTO acquis, CSCE rules, and basic IP conventions; - soft harmonisation commitments with specific sectors of cooperation; - perspective to conclude sectoral bilateral agreements aimed at the establishment of a free trade area with the EC | - Exchange of information on request in relevant sectors of cooperation (state aids and competition, customs); - technical assistance (ENPI financial package): the exchange of experts; provision of early information on relevant legislation; organization of seminars; training activities; aid for translation of EC legislation within relevant sectors of cooperation; - assistance on correct application of customs | Binding and soft harmonisation commitments | NA | - Cooperation Council (non-binding recommendations); - Cooperation Committee (non-binding recommendations); - Parliamentary Cooperation Committee (issues non-binding recommendations to the Cooperation Council) |

Cotonou Agreement	- Eradication of poverty; - sustainable development and gradual integration of the ACP countries into the world economy; - conclusion of economic partnership agreements of a more reciprocal nature and strong geographical differentiation between the ACP countries	NA -the ACP countries adhere to the recognized international law acquis (UN documents, international and regional human rights conventions, acts and principles of international organizations (CSCE, ILO, WTO))	- Binding harmonisation to principles and rules which govern international trade (references to the WTO agreements, fundamental IP conventions); - soft harmonisation commitments; - perspective to conclude mutual recognition agreements with the EC; - promotion of compatible systems between the Parties that could be acquired by the application of international technical legislation (protocol on mutual assistance in customs matters) - Cooperation in legal drafting and effective administrative enforcement; - exchange of information on legislation, experiences and policies within selected sectors of cooperation	NA Binding and soft harmonisation commitments	- The Council of Ministers (binding decisions; non-binding frame resolutions, recommendations, opinions); - The Committee of Ambassadors (non-binding acts aimed at the implementation of the agreement); The Joint Parliamentary Assembly (non-binding resolutions, recommendations); - Joint ACP-EC Ministerial Trade Committee (non-

	regulations, standards and conformity assessment procedures						binding recommendations); - ACP-EC Development Finance Cooperation Committee (non-binding guidelines); - Cooperation Council (binding decisions in all areas of cooperation)
EC – South Africa TDCA	- Reciprocal liberalisation of mutual trade in goods, services and capital; - encouragment of smooth and gradual integration of South Africa into the world economy	NA	- Binding harmonisation to the WTO rules on customs, competition, services, IP, - soft harmonisation to the UN, ILO standards; - perspective to conclude mutual recognition agreements with the EC	- Exchange of information in sectors of cooperation (competition, state aids, customs, investments); - technical assistance on: training activities within competition law and policy, standardisation and certification; telecom services standards; postal services; data	Binding and soft harmonisation commitments	NA	- Cooperation Council (binding decisions in all areas of cooperation)

			protection, and IP; - assistance on legal drafting; establishment of domestic offices and agencies involved in protection and effective enforcement of these rules		
EC – Korea Association Agreement	- Development of economic relations to facilitate the flow of mutual trade and investment; - sectoral cooperation (scientific, technological, and industrial cooperation); - liberalization	NA The Agreement contains the Title on legal co-operation	- Binding harmonization commitments to adopt the WTO acquis, fundamental IP conventions; - soft harmonization commitments (technical regulations, standards, conformity assessment, agriculture), seeking the compatibility of sectoral - Exchange of information and experts and encouraging cooperation between consumer bodies of both Parties; - organisation of training schemes and provision of technical assistance; - perspective	Binding and soft harmonisation commitments	NA	Joint Committee (exchanges opinions; make suggestions and recommendations)

310

	of trade and establishment of the improved market access between the Parties		legislation between the Parties; - perspective to conclude mutual recognition agreements with the EC; - promotion and adoption of international harmonized standards		
EC – Mexico Association Agreement	Lliberalization of trade in goods and services in accordance with international trade rules, especially the WTO acquis	NA	- Binding harmonisation commitments to adopt the WTO acquis; - soft harmonisation commitments (references to the EC competition acquis); - liberalisation of trade and establishment of favourable investment environment between the Parties;	- Exchange of information on policies, treatment, experience and experts within areas of sectoral cooperation; - exchanges of officials and senior personnel; - EC technical assistance to Mexico in the following areas: tele-	Binding and soft harmonisation commitments	NA	Joint Council (binding decisions; non-binding recommendations); Joint Committee (delegated powers to issue decisions)

			com, transport, consumer protection data protection		- Cooperation Council (issues non-binding recommendations and proposals); - Joint Committee (assists to the Cooperation Council, makes proposals to the Cooperation Council); - Joint Subcommittee on trade
MERCO SUR IFA	- Basis for future interregional association arrangements; - increasing and diversifying mutual trade; - gradual and reciprocal liberalisation of trade in accordance with WTO rules and	NA The Agreement contains the Title on legislative cooperation	- Binding harmonisation commitments to adhere to the WTO acquis; - soft harmonisation commitments to adopt international law standards within areas of sectoral cooperation	- Exchange of information on policies, know-how, legislation; - perspective to conclude mutual recognition agreements and bilateral agreements on protection of investments and prevention of double	Binding and soft harmonisation commitments	NA

					(makes proposals on liberalisation of trade)
			taxation with the EC; - legislative co-operation covers: development of new training techniques and coordination of activities in the relevant international organizations; exchanges of officials and senior personnel; technical assistance	
mutual market access					